# A Hundred Different Lives

"And each half-lives a hundred different lives."

Matthew Arnold did not have actors especially in mind when he wrote that line in *The Scholar Gypsy*. Still, it does express the disjointed course of an acting career. So I lift the poet's words from context and let them stand as the title of my book.

R.M.

# A Hundred Different Lives

an autobiography by

## RAYMOND MASSEY

Foreword by Christopher Plummer
Illustrated throughout with photographs

LITTLE, BROWN AND COMPANY · BOSTON · TORONTO

Quotations from OUR TOWN
(published by Harper & Row, New York, N.Y.;
© 1938, renewed 1966, by Thornton N. Wilder) are
printed by special permission of the Union Trust
Company, New Haven, Conn., Executor and Trustee
under the last will and testament of
Thornton N. Wilder.

The excerpts on pages 413, 414, and 416 are from
Tennessee Williams' THE NIGHT OF THE IGUANA,
copyright © 1961 by Two Rivers Enterprises, Inc.,
reprinted by permission of New Directions
and International Creative Management.

The author thanks the several ladies
who so patiently deciphered
his untidy handwriting and typed for him.

MV
PRINTED IN THE UNITED STATES OF AMERICA

I am grateful to Lily Poritz Miller whose
gentle but firm editorial guidance has been of
the greatest help to me.

Everyone mentioned in this book is a real and
not a fictitious person. All names are correct
except for one which I have changed lest
embarrassment be caused for well-
intentioned remarks.

Some of this book is in dialogue form.
Nothing between quote marks has been
wholly invented but the words cannot be
expected to be exact since I have never kept a
diary. The dialogues are as true to character
and purport as my memory can bring them.

*Also by Raymond Massey*
When I Was Young

*To Dorothy*
*again and always*

# FOREWORD

I suppose I must have been ten when I first set eyes on Cardinal Richelieu. His flowing robes, like the wings of the giant ichthyornis, cast a shadow which seemed to envelop the earth. When he moved it was with an awesome speed—a speed swifter than light, darker than devils. Black cavernous eyes pierced through to my soul and melted my limbs to a jelly. Above all, it was his countenance that chilled me with horror, for in the most oppressive degree it symbolized the very expression of autocracy, greed, lust and power. Here, indeed, was the Arch Demon who had professed such intimacy with God!

For some sinister reason our school had chosen to show *Under the Red Robe*, a film which the character of Richelieu seemed to dominate. Quite diabolically the "board" had clearly planned to frighten us wayward waifs into a severe early discipline by presenting to us one of history's toughest Headmasters. Naturally, in my case, their plan fizzled—my conduct and scholastic prowess disintegrated totally—but for a long time after, the image of that extraordinary face never left me. For it was a face not moulded just for horror—it was wise and devout; there was a gentleness in it, and a strength. It was a face carved from oak; drenched in melancholy; it had seen ghosts and war, sorrow and death. To a boy of ten it could terrify! As Cardinal Richelieu—it terrified!

All through that time its memory clung to me until one day—fifteen years later—someone introduced me to the Cardinal. The spell was shattered, the terror melted away, for under the Red Robe, which fell limply from his shoulders and vanished, stood a tall, dignified, kindly man wearing a delicious expression of perpetual surprise, with an infectious penchant for laughter, and about him the

*This is the face that frightened the ten-year-old schoolboy. R.M. as Cardinal Richelieu in the film Under the Red Robe, England, 1933.*

quite ludicrous and endearingly unexpected hint of a rather large, overgrown schoolboy. The menace was wiped away and there was left a twinkle and I knew, with one great surge of relief, that everything was to be all right! I had met a friend that day.

When people think of Raymond Massey they remember him for his famous and devastatingly touching Abe Lincoln on stage and screen; and on TV in the "Dr. Kildare" series, his crusty, kindly Dr. Gillespie. What they perhaps do not remember is that he has had a brilliantly varied career in all branches of entertainment which has spanned the greater part of this century. He has done everything there is to do around a theatre short of taking tickets.

As a director, he dared to help the great Augustus John to design a scene for the first production of Sean O'Casey's *The Silver Tassie*. He persuaded a reluctant Charles Laughton to waltz in a wheelchair in the same production; and most incredible of all, as a producer, he persuaded George Bernard Shaw to reduce his royalties for five productions of his plays at the Everyman Theatre in London. Well-documented rumour has it that the adamant Shaw never did this before or since.

At eighty-two Raymond Massey still possesses a soft, low, cultured speaking voice which can give a sustained musical cadence to the grandest of poetry and prose. But when aroused—or if an acting part calls for it—he can and does change gear and roar to rock the balcony.

I remember once we were trying to rehearse *Julius Caesar*, the American Shakespeare Festival's first production. We had been saddled with some ghastly, cumbersome cloaks, made from the heaviest of velvet—rendering movement of any sort almost an impossibility. I asked Ray—who was the "top-liner"—to say something in his own quiet, tactful way to the management to get rid of the damn things for all of us, including himself. Being a gentle and uncomplaining star, it took days of persuasion to get any action out of him. Finally, after merciless nagging by me, the rise came. Ray boiled over. He strode to the footlights, and no witch in his ancestral Salem ever rasped out a curse more archaic and imaginative. Gone, the beautiful voice, replaced by a roar which shivered the timbers. The offending costumes were described in a mixture of blasphemy and derisive comment wonderful to hear.

"Are we supposed to stick the guy through all this plush?"

The newly constructed floor of the stage groaned under my weight as I fell on it, helpless with laughter.

Raymond Massey has always been the complete professional in his work. There is no higher compliment in our profession. But he brooks no professional bondage. His is a full, unfettered view of life. Offstage there is nothing "actorish" about him—no frills, no posturing. He is gregarious, generous, jovial, gentle, an admirer of Trollope and racy limericks, and a hell of a lot of fun.

As I sat with him in his dressing-room watching him change for the street, it crossed my mind that this well-read, highly intelligent and merry man would probably have been successful at any pursuit in life apart from the theatre. But I am wrong. Raymond Massey belongs in the theatre and nowhere else. He would have it no other way.

By a quirk of circumstance and fate, my own father has always been a stranger to me and, presumptuous though it may seem, I have often secretly thought of Ray—more than anyone else—as being the most likely candidate to play the father I never really knew. Yet he mustn't be concerned—I wouldn't wish it on him, and besides he's too damn young for the part. So I shall simply continue, as I always have, to think of him with the deepest affection and to treat him with gentle irreverence, as a warm, talented, extremely lovable, slightly "naughty" bigger brother.

> Christopher Plummer
> April 1978
> Venice, Italy

# 1

In the early summer of 1922 I was a passenger aboard a small, aging Cunard liner eastbound for Liverpool out of New York. Smart luxury liners used Southampton as their home port but for me this was no luxury voyage and money was not to be wasted. I was on a highly problematical venture to try to become a professional actor or at least to find out if there was a working life for me in the theatre. I had made the final decision just three weeks before in Toronto.

My first twenty-six years had been busy and varied. Schools, four years of service in the Canadian Field Artillery in the First World War, an aborted try for a degree at Oxford, and an horrendous stint in my family's farm machinery business had given me little indication that I had any talent for the theatre. But my mother had sowed the early seed which grew into the determination which put me on that boat.

As the ship chugged up the Mersey I spent the final two hours leaning on the rail in an attempt to bolster my resolution to become a professional actor. Determination never wavered–and never has–but I thought I'd feel better if I could recall just a few occasions when even a school play had caused some outburst of enthusiasm for my performance, even from a captive audience of relatives.

My search was unproductive. Only a show I had put on during the war gave me solace, but it was a lovely bit of evidence. What it boiled down to was the realization that for once my big decision was mine alone, based on irresistible feeling and determination. Throughout my childhood, school days and army years, I had had to deal only with tactical questions. The strategy had been decided for me by others. A year earlier at Oxford I had been reminded by the Master of Balliol that I was now an adult. He had suggested that my facing the examiners in the History Schools in 1921 was out of the question; according to my tutor, I was unprepared. I should either put off the examination for another term or go down without a degree.

I impulsively elected to go down at once, an action which I still regret. I had lived Oxford life to the full, and loved it. There was great activity, not much of it scholastic, and a bit of rowdiness – perhaps not exceptional for someone tasting freedom after four years of military service, but definitely unbecoming to a man of twenty-three. And so I failed to exercise that self-discipline without which Oxford is a waste of time.

Following this mood of impetuosity I married an art student named Margery Fremantle whom I had met in Cornwall the previous summer. In this act we both displayed astonishing lack of judgement, and we were soon aware of it.

And three weeks earlier I made my third momentous decision. This one involved my father, whom I dearly loved, and to this day I marvel that he was not hurt by it.

As we steamed along the fogbound Cheshire shore my thoughts wandered – obviously ducking my attempt to make reason fit determination. Occasionally a gap in the fog revealed low hills behind which I knew was a village called Knutsford, whence my ancestor, Geoffrey Massey, had fled with his wife to join Governor Winthrop's expedition to the New World in 1630. Geoffrey was a Puritan, a victim of Laudian persecution. I wondered what my forefather would have thought of my expedition to go on the English stage. I do not think Geoffrey could have had much interest in the glories of the English Renaissance while he was clamped in the Knutsford stocks.

In the time of John Wesley, my Puritan ancestors turned Methodist, and Methodists are not exactly theatre lovers.

Only seven generations later Geoffrey's direct descendant, my father, Chester Massey, became head of the family business, a worldwide producer of farm implements which his grandfather had founded in 1847. He took over in 1900, when he was fifty years old and I was four. My mother, Anna Vincent Massey, was an American of Huguenot stock and, like my father, a Methodist. My brother Vincent was nine years older than myself. He was to be Canada's first Canadian-born Governor General. Our family lived in Toronto, where the main factory was, my father intent on his church and his business, in that order, with little thought of the theatre.

It was my mother who first told me about the theatre. It was in 1903 and I was seven years old. We were on a trip to Europe and had just arrived in London. Though a Methodist, mother loved the theatre and wanted to see some plays. Mother and Vincent went to see Beerbohm Tree in *Richard II*, and father took me to the zoo. I remember thinking that Vincent had the better deal. When we all got

14

back to the hotel I asked mother what this theatre thing was.

"It is a 'once-upon-a-time place' where people called actors and actresses tell stories. It's very mysterious, it's sometimes creepy, sometimes sad, sometimes funny, sometimes adventurous and exciting, and sometimes it's enchanting like those fairy tales I've read to you."

Then mother told me about the play she had just seen with Vincent. She had wonderful powers of description and her account of Shakespeare's tragedy stirred my childish imagination. She even made a pen-and-ink sketch of Richard in the dungeon scene.

"When you're a little older, Raymond, I'm going to take you with me. That's when we get back home."

But she never did. A few days later mother died from an appendectomy which had been delayed too long. Incredibly, the operation was performed in a house father had rented in Hampstead.

I loved my mother very much. She was tiny of stature and beautiful, with dark eyes and hair. She was always happy and her laughter was like singing.

It was a grief-stricken homecoming to Canada for father, Vincent and me. To the very young, death is especially shocking because of its unexplained finality. Those moments when mother spoke of the theatre had been the last I spent with her before her sudden illness. It was as if she had left me a whole new world of enchantment and delight to explore. For a long time it would remain a private world. I went to my own secret theatre as often as I could and dreamed stories just as mother had told me, funny, sad, happy and scary.

This was not the dawning of a playwright, nor had I any thought of being one of those people called actors. I was just preparing to be an insatiable member of the audience. A few years later, when I saw real theatre, I found that my imaginary one had not been so very unlike it.

Father had overheard mother's talk with me about the theatre. In his grief he pledged that he would keep her promise. Although he remained aloof from the theatre himself, he generously subsidized my attendance, during boarding-school holidays, at matinées at the two Toronto road-show houses, the Princess and the new Royal Alexandra.

I used to go alone and sit in the balcony. At first the plays would be selected by father, his parental guidance being of the most uninformed nature. But by the time I was sixteen or so, no questions were asked and I was able to see burlesque and vaudeville as well as the legitimate stage.

When I matriculated from school in 1914 I had seen most English and American stars in the classics and in contemporary plays. For me, Forbes Robertson, Martin Harvey, Beerbohm Tree, Nat Goodwin, E. H. Sothern and Julia Marlowe, Robert Mantell, Oswald Yorke and Annie Russell were idols to worship, not to emulate.

It was June 1914 and suddenly my school days were over. I had been in Toronto three days writing my honour matriculation exams and then in Cobourg for a day where I had been invited to ride in one of the jumping classes of the horse show. The owner of my mount was a horsey old lady, a friend of my brother's. To console me for a poor performance (I had a fall) she took me to tea at a nearby farm with some friends of hers.

"Their name is Tracy. You'll meet a perfectly lovely girl who's staying with them. She's from Buffalo."

The young lady from Buffalo was the most beautiful creature I had ever seen. She had a musical voice. Tall and dark, she had eyes like my mother's, big and far apart.

Her name was Katharine Cornell. At Mrs. Tracy's request she took me to see the barns that housed the Guernsey herd, the pride of the Tracy farm. Miss Cornell and the cows evinced a mutual disdain.

She asked me what I was "going to be."

"Oh, I think I'll make farming machinery or something."

She looked through and beyond the cows.

"I'm going to New York next fall. I shall become a professional actress. On the stage–on Broadway."

Bedazzled by this beautiful girl and her pronouncement, so calm and determined, the cows and great-grandfather and farm machinery went out of my mind, although later I did dutifully give the family business a fair try. I knew all of a sudden that somehow I too would be a professional actor and act with Katharine Cornell–on Broadway.

That dream remained my secret for a long time. It came true twenty-six years later when I starred with Kit on Broadway in the first of three plays we did together.

That was the moment, in a cowbarn in Cobourg. I had walked in my imagination through the pass-door from the front of the house onto the stage. I still had no idea whether or not I could act. But I now had that beacon which Kit had lighted and it stayed lighted.

The Great War had come. I remembered making the slow progress up this same Mersey in a troop ship in 1915 on my way to the trenches. About nine months later I had gone down the river on my way home. I had been wounded and shell-shocked in France and I

16

remember nothing about my return to Canada.

Medical boards, sick leave and boring training duties had followed, most of which I forgot, but in June 1917 I had been assigned as instructor in the gunnery of trench warfare to the Yale University Reserve Officers' Training Corps. In addition I taught the cadets how to ride. In subsequent years while touring in plays throughout the U.S. I have been impressed with the number of increasingly mature men who hasten to tell me they remember my admonition: "Sit back on your asses, gentlemen!" Since New Haven was reasonably close to New York I could avidly resume my affair with the theatre. But my play-going became different from the Toronto days. Now I felt I was watching future comrades instead of idols, and I could sense the comradeship which I would later find was the core of professional acting.

Katharine Cornell was then with the Washington Square Players and I had seen her several times. I even told her of my dream of going on the stage as she had done. She had not laughed.

I was particularly fascinated by the great comedians, Leon Errol, Fanny Brice, Johnny Dooley and, of course, Bert Williams, perhaps the greatest black comedian of all time. What I learned from seeing the great clowns and comedians of Broadway would soon come in very handily when I gratefully borrowed what I could remember of their acts for an army show in Siberia.

As I leaned against the rail of the old liner my thoughts travelled twelve thousand miles westward across the world and four years back to Vladivostok in eastern Siberia. I had gone there after my Yale duty with a mixed brigade of Canadians to help the White Russians against the Bolsheviks. It was March 1919, and we had been rotting in idleness in Siberia for months without having fired a shot. One day I was called to report at once to General Elmsley, our force commander.

Impressed by a little skit I had put on at the headquarter's mess, he ordered me to go to work and mount a full-length entertainment for the troops. He promised full backing and wanted it ready in two weeks.

"We're up against a situation that's tougher to handle than a fighting war," he explained. "I've got five thousand men with nothing to do in this cesspool of a place."

I decided on a minstrel show, the first half in the conventional blackface style, and the second a succession of vaudeville acts.

I worked all night with two brother officers writing the minstrel part. Among the three of us we remembered thirty-five gags. The vaudeville acts had been discovered in various units of the brigade,

17

my own gunners producing two professional turns from the Pantages circuit in the States. By the following night we were ready to start rehearsals.

Besides staging the show, I played an end man in the minstrel half, daring to do two of Bert Williams' routines, "The Solo Poker Game" and his great song "No-body." In the vaudeville half I gave imitations of Fanny Brice, Johnny Dooley and Leon Errol. The Signal Company commanding officer had written a dramatic sketch called "In Flanders Fields" which was pretty good. I wanted to try my luck in the leading part but was persuaded against it. My talents, if any, were thought to be in a slapstick style, so the author played it himself.

The "Road House Minstrels" were ready to open on the day set by "Gentleman Jim" Elmsley. We were a smash hit. Homesick soldiers in idle futility were not exactly critical audiences but we were not too bad. And how they loved the show! We played fifteen performances to audiences varying in size from three hundred to three thousand. General Elmsley saw it several times. As a rookie producer he was very proud.

My first production and direction job had not been professional but neither had it been amateur. There had been plenty of backing and no need to bargain with talent. All of us had been under orders to perform—at military pay. The Major-General's peremptory order had moved me a great deal closer to the professional stage.

My thoughts returned to the present and I cheered up. At last memory had provided me with one bit of solid accomplishment to bolster my determination to make my life in the theatre. The Mersey pilot now had the old ship close to the Cheshire bank. We were approaching a pier with a weather-beaten barn-like structure sitting on the end of it, atop a cluster of slimy, grey piles. It was ornate, though much decayed, and as we drew abeam a sign could easily be read: "Winter Gardens New Brighton." It was a theatre! I could see the flaking paint, the windblown playbills, a man pasting new bills on the boards. It was not only a theatre but a working one.

I watched the Winter Gardens recede into the mist. My mind wandered back to my year in the family business in Toronto which had followed Oxford.

The Oxford University Dramatic Society (O.U.D.S.) had been a disillusionment. After some difficulty because of my Canadian accent, I played two minute parts (one non-speaking) in the O.U.D.S.'s first postwar production: Thomas Hardy's *The Dynasts*—with an enormous cast. Common sense had told me that this disordered

18

affair was the essence of amateurism. The only real performance had been that of Maurice Colbourne, the society's president, in the role of Nelson. My own brief moment had been ghastly.

I had heard of Frank Benson, Arthur Bourchier and so many other great men of the profession who found their initial interest in the stage through the O.U.D.S. But I left the society, thoroughly disappointed, and my only other theatrical activity while at Oxford was in organizing a little group from my college to read plays every month in the manner of radio–then unknown.

I also rekindled my stage aspirations by a couple of London visits to see Katharine Cornell, then playing her first lead in a production of *Little Women* at the New Theatre.

Back in Toronto after my Balliol days, I had dutifully begun service in the Massey-Harris Company in good faith. My father, now seventy-two and in poor health, had set his heart on my joining the company. I was determined to satisfy his wishes, though still eager to go on the stage. The theatre would have to wait–or rather, I would have to wait; I did not think the theatre was panting for my services. There was no room for histrionics in the farm-machinery business.

The year in Toronto was frustrating and disturbing. My wife hated Toronto and rarely left our house. I started work at the main factory almost at once, changing from one department to another about every month. My reward for this drudgery had been set at twenty-five dollars a week and was almost immediately cut to twenty-two fifty.

I quickly realized that my attempt at following my father's and my uncles' footsteps was a failure. But immediate escape from the bondage of factory life seemed impossible.

Yet the theatre kept beckoning. My grandfather Hart Massey's residual estate before the war had been formed into the Massey Foundation by my father and my brother Vincent. Its initial project had been a students' centre opened in 1919 at the University of Toronto. An afterthought in this design was a small theatre under the Quadrangle. This was an irony which would have made my mother laugh– that father, the old Puritan, should have built, or rather dug, a theatre for the students. It was underground and still is the only theatre I know with a lawn on its roof.

I acted in three plays at the Hart House Theatre, after long days "making farm machinery or something," as I had told Kit Cornell that momentous day at the cowbarn. One of them was Shaw's *Candida*. I learned an important lesson in playing Marchbanks, which was never to rely on my own emotions in front of an audience. Bertram Forsyth, the professional director, had taught me this. But Hart House was essentially an amateur effort and I wanted to be a "pro."

At Toronto's Arts and Letters Club, whose members were writers, painters, journalists and various eccentrics, I played Smitty in *In the Zone*, one of Eugene O'Neill's short sea plays. It was my first taste of the new realistic theatre. For the first time since Siberia I worked with a cast who had vitality and enthusiasm, with that team feeling which I believed must be part of the professional theatre.

I began to learn that the theatre was not mere bricks and mortar, lights and scenery, but people who write, act and respond.

Just after this I saw the Broadway production of *The Circle* at the Royal Alex in Toronto. The great John Drew was Lord Porteous. I had never seen Mr. Drew before. He was the equal of Allan Aynesworth in London and I cannot give higher praise.

That night the Royal Alex was high comedy at its best. During the second act I made my sudden but irrevocable decision. The seed sown by my mother had been growing a long time. Now I knew I needed practical advice about the nuts and bolts of how to get a chance to work in the theatre. So after the final curtain I asked the stage doorman to take my card in to Mr. Drew.

Mr. Drew would see me!

I found myself in his dressing-room – a dingy closet of a room badly in need of paint. It still needed paint eleven years later when I used it on a pre-Broadway try-out of *The Shining Hour*. A shabby sofa (still there in my occupancy) and an open wardrobe trunk filled the little room. Mr. Drew, in a tatty dressing gown, sat at the dazzlingly lit make-up table.

I stammered my appreciation of the play and dried up.

"I'm sure you didn't come round just to tell me that," said Mr. Drew.

"No, sir," I plunged in. "I'm going to be a professional actor... and I'm bold enough to ask you if you would give me some advice as to how I might accomplish that."

"Are you any good as an actor?"

"I think I could be but I haven't done enough to know."

"If you don't know for a certainty, don't try it. You have to *know* you're good. What have you done?"

I told him. It was very little. He seemed impressed by the Leon Errol, Fanny Brice and Bert Williams imitations I had done in Siberia.

"Do you know what acting means – or do you? It's a bare stage lit by a work light a lot of the time. This kind of dressing-room for months and months. Hotels–trains. It's much worse here than in England. But if you really want to act, and you know you're good, there's nothing in the world that's better."

He reached for a big pot of grease.

"Don't try to start in New York. It's no place for a young man who is unknown. The competition on Broadway is heartbreaking for men. Go to London. There is so much theatre there and with your Canadian accent you can play American parts. You may have good fortune in London."

Early next morning I went to Charles Wisner, the general sales manager of the Massey-Harris Company and my boss at that time. The dapper little man, in vest and shirt sleeves with elastic armbands, was busy at his desk. Without looking up he grunted, "What can I do for you?"

"Mr. Wisner, I have now been with the company for nearly a year and I'm earning exactly twenty-two dollars and fifty cents a week. I'd like to know what I may look forward to earning in, say, five years' time."

"Repeat that."

I did.

"I would hazard a guess that you might be getting thirty dollars a week in five years."

"Mr. Wisner, that's less than I earned as a lieutenant in the army. I'm twenty-five, I've had a decent education, and I've served nearly five years in the army. At times I've been in charge of hundreds of thousands of dollars worth of government property and the lives of a hundred and fifty men. I think I know enough about this company to be entrusted with responsibility and the salary that goes with it."

"Huh?" said Mr. Wisner, who was now looking at me.

"I think you heard me, Mr. Wisner."

"Now listen to me, you young fellow, I don't care if you're Hart Massey's grandson or who you are. The fact remains that while you were in the army and fiddling at Oxford, other men have been learning this business and they are going to have the responsible jobs and the pay raises before you!"

"I'm quitting, Mr. Wisner."

I have nothing against Charlie Wisner. Indeed, I am very grateful to him, for he gave me the firm and final push towards the theatre.

Now I had to tell father. I was confident that he would be at least in sympathy with my quitting the company.

21

He just said, "By George, it's insufferable."

But I was not so sure how he would take the theatre. I told him about seeing John Drew and my decision to go to England and try to go on the professional stage.

There was a long silence. Then he got up from his chair and took my arm.

"I think you are quite right to go to England and to become a professional actor. I think you will be a very good one. I think you will be able to serve God as well on the stage as in the implement business which your great-grandfather founded.

"There is one promise I want you to make: that you will not act or practise on Sunday."

This was a tough situation. I knew, of course, that I could not and would not keep such a promise. But I had to give that wonderful old man peace of mind. I crossed my fingers and promised.

Then he knelt on one knee, the way he did for family prayers, and made a prayer to God for my success and honesty as an actor. He asked God to help His servant, Raymond, to avoid self-conceit, to appear in good plays, and to abhor indecency in the theatre. To the best of my powers, I have tried to do just that.

Vincent entered and father told him the news.

"What name are you going to use?" he asked.

I smiled and father smiled.

As I turned to look astern I was again smiling, as far away the Winter Gardens was in view again, for the mist had lifted on the pier at New Brighton. In the bright summer sun the broken-down old relic looked like the real theatre which she was.

Three weeks later when I got my first professional job on the stage, it was at the Winter Gardens on New Brighton pier. The play was *In the Zone*.

# 2

Bursting with determination and enthusiasm and without any idea of how to accomplish my purpose, I set about finding a theatre job.

I had letters of introduction to a number of people connected with the theatre, including two actor-managers, Dennis Eadie and Nigel Playfair. The letters contained phrases like, "wishes to try his luck," "has an ambition," "would like to learn something of the theatre," and generally suggested a stage-struck dilettante but I immediately sent them off. I won five fruitless interviews and three lunches which also drew blanks, although Dennis Eadie did offer me work in the box office of the Royalty Theatre of which he was the lessee. This I politely turned down.

Playfair advised a period of training at the Royal Academy of Dramatic Art but I was not keen on academies. My Oxford defeat was too fresh in my mind. Besides, I had an instinctive distrust of academic preparation for actors. I have never had any reason to change my mind. I believe the best way a young actor can learn his job is to act for pay before audiences who have paid for their tickets.

Everybody I saw in that first frustrating week of job-hunting asked what I had done in the theatre. My amateur experience did not mean a thing. It was obvious that in order to have a future it was necessary to have had a past, however humble. To get a job I would have to claim experience. So I neatly invented eighteen months of repertory and summer stock in the eastern states, performing in several of the O'Neill sea plays, Shaw, Ibsen (I never said what play) and current plays released for stock. True, I had actually played in *In the Zone* at the Arts and Letters Club in Toronto. This eased my conscience a bit, but to tell the truth, I was not much troubled by the creation of a mythical background.

After a fruitless interview with one of London's many theatrical agents, I decided to seek work on my own. The most active agents in the English theatre—and in America, too—have always been the actors themselves. As a profession actors are generous. Many laymen are convinced that actors are covetous and jealous. Not so. Competition for jobs is cut-throat, but once an actor is defeated for a part, he will do his best for someone else to get it. I have often heard an actor, painfully "at liberty" himself, boast of helping friends to a job. Three of my own best parts I was to owe to fellow actors.

I began my search for work at once, haunting West End stage-doors and pubs. I soon found the grapevine of casting news. Someone said, "Arthur Bourchier's casting three plays for a South African tour. There are three good bits still open – one's an American. Go to the Strand stage-door – the stage manager's name is Reggie Bach. Good luck!"

This was a plum. Bourchier was one of the few remaining actor-managers and one of the founders of the Oxford University Dramatic Society I had belonged to.

Reggie Bach was as nice as he could be. But, alas, Mr. Bourchier had changed his plans. The tour was off. He was going to do a new play at the Strand, but there was nothing in it for a long string-bean of a Canadian with nothing but repertory behind him. Bach wrote my name and address in a notebook.

"I'll mark you 'character actor.' What accents can you do?"

"I think I can do most of them, Irish, German.... But I have to work out an accent with the dialogue."

I could see Bach write "slow rehearser."

"What's your height?"

"Six-feet-two."

"What can you shrink to?"

"I don't think I can."

"Nonsense. I'm five-feet-ten and I can build up to six-four and shrink to five-eight."

He stood up to his full height and then literally shrank himself a good two inches. Returning to his book, he said:

"I'll put you down – 'can shrink to six feet!'"

It may seem odd that I can remember this conversation after over fifty years but Reggie Bach's Houdini-like ability to shrink was something you are not likely to forget.

In those first weeks in London there were a lot of these visits to stage-doors and rehearsal rooms. I learned later that such methods of job-hunting were highly unorthodox. But I found my way around the West End theatres and the way they worked. After nearly three weeks my name and temporary address were in a number of notebooks and I had met some kindly theatre people, but I seemed as far away from a job as ever. The Old Vic, where the redoubtable Lilian Baylis was running a permanent Shakespeare company, was out of the question. With my Canadian accent I would not have had a chance. There remained one outlying little theatre called the Everyman.

I had no difficulty finding it, close by the Hampstead tube station. It was not a prepossessing building. It looked like the small meeting hall it once had been. I could not find the stage-door, for the good reason that there was none. I was fumbling with a fire-exit door when the thing flew back against me with a crash and I found myself on my back on the pavement. I heard a shout from inside, "Mr. Carr, find out what that disturbance is." Someone, apparently Mr. Carr, knelt by me with the solicitude of one experienced drunk for another. I explained that I was just a trifle stunned, not stoned, and told him of my quest for employment. Rapidly I told my story of those eighteen months of repertory, ending with the O'Neill plays. As I came to *In the Zone* Mr. Carr helped me to my feet and led me into the theatre through the fire door. In a few minutes I was rehearsing the part of Jack, the American in *In the Zone*. It had taken just three weeks for John Drew's advice to work out, but I was now, I could tell myself, a pro.

It may not have been a glamorous job but it was my first. The man who had picked me up from the pavement and put me to work was the stage manager of the Everyman, George Carr. He became my close friend and associate in the management of that same theatre only four years later. It seemed that the actor playing Jack had that very morning left the rehearsal for a West End job.

Norman Macdermott, the manager of the theatre, was directing *In the Zone* and, without checking my credentials, accepted his stage manager's recommendation that he had better engage this man who had acted in the play in America since there was no time to find anybody else. Macdermott explained that the company which was now playing Shaw's *Arms and the Man* was to leave for Liverpool the following day, Sunday, perform the Shaw play for a week and open with a bill of three one-acters the following week. He would pay me three pounds ten shillings a week including rehearsal, and told me he was going to play the one-act bill for at least two weeks at the Everyman following Liverpool. Of course I agreed. It was even less money than I had earned in business but that did not dim the delight of my first stage job. Nor did the squalor of the Winter Gardens Theatre, on the end of that pier jutting into the Mersey at New Brighton.

The Winter Gardens had seen better days and probably larger audiences. Shaw's satire about a Balkan War did indifferent business, though excellently acted. The triple bill in our second week on the pier fared little better. The two light comedies which completed the bill were played by a strikingly beautiful young actress, Isabel Jeans, and an excellent comedian, Harry Kendall. About the end of the first playlet, a skit on psychoanalysis, set in the elegant office of the doctor, a large rat made an unexpected entrance causing Miss Jeans to utter a shriek which totally confused Harry Kendall, who hadn't seen this new character, and gave the audience the biggest laugh of the evening. George Carr claimed later that he had tried to engage this rodent scene-stealer for *In the Zone*. But, as he sadly remarked, "He was last seen leaving the sinking psychiatrist's office!"

The Merseyside audience loved *In the Zone*. On that crummy stage with the Mersey lapping below, every one of us thought of the crews of countless tramps and freighters who just a few years before had made it to Liverpool one more time through The Zone.

Back at the Everyman the triple-bill ran three good weeks. All the London papers sent critics and I won my first mention, a good one and in *The Times*. I read it over and over. The critic said that three of us gave admirable performances. I did not tell anybody that the critic was Charles Morgan, just appointed to *The Times*, whom I had known at Oxford where we had both acted for the Oxford University Dramatic Society. But I think he meant what he said. He would give me my quota of knocks in the next twenty years.

The Everyman was tiny, less than five hundred seats, and the stage itself had no flies and almost no wings. The actors' only access to the dressing-rooms, under the auditorium, was down a stairway in the lobby. The stage could be reached only by two narrow spiral stairs which made crinolines and hoop-skirts most hazardous. The up-and-down traffic demanded finesse, particularly on the part of the ascender.

A few weeks after *In the Zone*, during a performance of *Twelfth Night*, Herbert Waring, playing Malvolio, on his way upstairs became enveloped in the voluminous skirts of Margaret Yarde, the Maria, who was rapidly descending. Neither could retreat, Mr. Waring because of an arthritic hip and Miss Yarde by reason of her bulk. I was behind her and could hear Mr. Waring's muffled protest, "Goddamn it, I can't breathe!" His cue for an entrance was rapidly approaching. Asphyxiation seemed a distinct possibility. George Carr got a rope under Margaret's arms and four of us pulled her free just in time for Bertie Waring to play the letter scene in an entirely new and breathless manner which was most effective.

In 1922 the Everyman had been a legitimate theatre for only two years but already it had become a minor institution. It was not an experimental theatre. There was nothing avant-garde or arty about it. It was not really a repertory theatre either. Most of its productions had been revivals but new plays had also been staged. Financial success depended on the transferral of a new play to a West End theatre. To date none had left Hampstead, but during Macdermott's lease of the Everyman three substantial successes were launched: *Outward Bound*, *At Mrs. Beam's* and *The Vortex*, all of which had good West End runs and crossed the Atlantic to be Broadway hits.

The Everyman was a special boon to actors since it enabled them to play parts for which they might not be considered in the West End. As the theatre was in constant production of plays which would run only a few weeks, casting was always going on. The salaries were a good deal lower than in the West End except for the minimum rate which was the same—just awful. It is hard to believe that in England, the birthplace of trade unionism, the acting profession was not organized until 1935, thirteen years later. The minimum salary (not recognized by all managers) was still in 1922 the miserable three pounds ten shillings which had been contained in a so-called contract which a loose organization of a number of actors led by Sydney Valentine had failed to secure before the war. Inflation had made this seem ridiculous but there were managers who did not pay even that for small parts.

In New York in 1920 actors had secured decent minimum salaries, rehearsal pay and good working conditions by organizing themselves into a strong union called Equity. They had had to strike to get their contract recognized. Their example was not followed for years in England. Every Friday night when I pocketed my miserable three and a half quid, I swore I would be in there pitching when we achieved a union shop in England.

I stayed on at the Everyman for several plays, acting small parts and understudying. About the end of September Macdermott did the production of *Twelfth Night*. It was an early example of the return to a simple architectural setting for classic theatre. In the nineteenth century Shakespearean productions had been so cluttered with scenery that the plays had been lost. None of these plays had been written with time-consuming scene changes in mind. Such delays were as damaging as commercials are to dramatic material on current television.

The streamlined simplicity of the Everyman productions was not entirely by design, however. A light purse and the dimensional limitations of the stage made such methods mandatory–but the result was extremely effective. *Twelfth Night*, I think Shakespeare's best comedy, literally flowed along. Not a word was cut and the playing time was not more than the average modern three-act play. It was a tip-top company, Isabel Jeans in particular giving a delightful performance quite different from the usual stately Olivia.

I was lucky to be in it, playing Fabian. It was my only Shakespearean acting attempt before playing Hamlet in New York ten years later. Not that I lacked opportunity but I had been intimidated by the renowned Mr. Waring, who had declared to me over two double Scotches, for which I paid, "Never attempt the Bard until you have learned to speak from your diaphragm, my boy." I was to spend many hours declaiming Mr. S.'s soliloquies while lying flat on my back with twenty pounds of books on my stomach. I didn't get any Shakespearean roles but my voice certainly sounded a good deal deeper and better.

My first chance to act in the West End came in a play with the unfortunate title *The Heart of Doris*. It was not a good play and it only found its way to the stage because it was financed by one of the co-authoresses, a dear old, titled Scottish lady who gazed at the world through thick, roseate glasses. I have not the foggiest idea why I was chosen for the part–an aged, philosophical head waiter of a country inn. I knew nobody connected with the production and it is certain that nobody in the theatre at the time knew me.

In addition to the acting chore, I understudied the three other male parts, was assistant stage manager and unofficially helped the business manager. In this production the stage and business management were joined in one man named Henry Millar. An agreeable fellow, he was not unwilling to accept my assistance to the fullest extent. For these comprehensive services I was paid four pounds ten shillings for the week.

In other respects the production of *The Heart of Doris* was on a lavish scale. An excellent cast was engaged. It included Aubrey Smith, Frances Carson, a beautiful American actress making her first English appearance, and E. Holman Clark who, besides playing one

28

of the male leads, was also directing. I had seen him two years before give a delightful performance in the London production of *The Circle*.

All seven of us in *The Heart of Doris* knew that we had a weak, contrived piece of sentimentality to deal with. It was fascinating to me to see how professionals faced such a situation. Holman Clark, who was about as fine an exponent of high comedy acting as there was in England (and this was the time of Charles Hawtrey's greatness), must have felt much as Tilden or Borotra playing championship tennis on a bumpy vicarage lawn.

Early in rehearsal Holman Clark, to my surprise, thought it necessary to explain to the cast his function as director. "You know, this fellow called the director is quite a novelty in England," he said. "He has come on the scene because the old idea of allowing a good cast to find their way under the guidance of an egocentric actor-manager is over."

I knew that in America the director had been a vital force in the theatre for years. Frances Carson, who was from the American stage, was as astonished as myself at Mr. Clark's revelation. After all, on Broadway David Belasco, Arthur Hopkins, Winthrop Ames, were just as famous as the stars they had directed. Yet in Edwardian programs I examined there was no mention of anyone responsible for direction.

Holman Clark was a good director. Being on the prompt book most of the time, I got to know his methods and theories pretty well. One idea of his I have always remembered. "There should be one word in every sentence, one sentence in every speech, one speech in every scene and one scene in every act which in a good play is the dominant one, and the director's duty is to detect them and see they are duly emphasized. *Indetectably*–do not forget, indetectably–for if you make that emphasis obtrusive, young fellow, I will come back, like Banquo's ghost, and haunt you!"

I asked how the emphasis was to be made. He snorted angrily. "Do you know what tempo, tone, intensity, pauses, mean? I don't need to tell you–to each problem you meet, there is a fresh resolution. But," he whispered, "don't look for dominant points in this play. There is only one, and I wrote it, for myself."

We tried out for two weeks at Cardiff and Brighton. Business was not propitious. The 1,500-seat Cardiff Playhouse was a barn in which our little play was lost. Even so the customers who came to see us, though few, laughed and applauded to the slight extent that Henry

Millar could not restrain the old Scottish authoress from proceeding on stage at the second call and expressing her genuinely heartfelt thanks.

It was not customary in Cardiff to play a mid-week matinée, but we did, and our little company of seven outnumbered the paid admissions by the margin of one! Aubrey Smith claimed we had set a record. Henry Millar countered that he had been with a touring company which had topped the paid audience by two to one. "What was the play?" demanded Aubrey testily. "*Henry IV, Part II*," was the answer. I remember the old cricketer's reply, "Good God, sir, that play has a cast of thirty–two to one means an audience of fifteen. Ours is the victory– by a margin of nine, sir, nine!"

Aubrey Smith was then in his late fifties, handsome, rugged, a monolith of probity, wildly miscast as a philandering husband. In spite of his excellent performance, those who saw the play knew for certain that the virtue of Miss Carson as the other woman was never in jeopardy. Aubrey, a great cricketer, had captained the English Eleven on two tours. He was an ardent golfer too, and in the wings while waiting for his entrances he would practise short approaches with his stick and a ball of paper. On one occasion during a performance he chipped his paper ball through a window of the setting onto the stage. He was terribly cut up about it. I whispered that nobody would notice. He was one of those people who cannot whisper and replied in a resonant tone, "I know, but I shanked my shot!" It was always his custom to clear his vocal cords before an entrance. Sometimes the audience would be puzzled to hear offstage a distant voice booming "Hip bath! Hip bath! Hip bath!"

This was the only time I acted with Aubrey Smith on the stage, but years later I worked with him a great deal in Hollywood. Aubrey, a sort of Commissioner of the large British Colony there, handled relations with the natives with dignity and tact.

Henry Millar had engaged digs in Cardiff for himself, Phyllis Stuckey, who understudied the women, and me. They were pretty comfortable. About the third day it was my turn to do the shopping for supper after the theatre and I decided on tripe and onions which Henry had been lusting after for days. I came in for tea with the groceries and a loofah which I purchased for myself. A loofah, according to Webster's dictionary, is "the fibrous skeleton of a tropical fruit used as a sponge." The fruit is about the size of a marrow. I handed the bag to our landlady. Henry, who was with me, instructed

30

her how to prepare what he called the touring actor's delight.

After the play the three of us came eagerly home to supper. The landlady brought in a large, covered platter. Henry eagerly lifted the cover and gazed dubiously at an elongated form covered with egg sauce and bowered in a mass of small onions. The substance resisted knife, spoon, fork and invective; and Phyllis, Henry and I subsisted that night on shallots and egg sauce. I thought the loofah was improved for its primary use.

After a performance one night in Brighton I received another bit of unforgettable advice from Holman Clark. I asked him what had happened to a good laugh which normally followed a line of mine in the play.

"Tonight the line was a flop and I lost my laugh," I said. "What did I do wrong, sir?"

"What did you say you lost, my boy?"

"My laugh, sir."

"Never again refer to *my* laugh! It was our laugh, *ours*. Mr. Aubrey Smith's, Miss Carson's, mine and yours. The laugh was not heard tonight because I neglected to turn my glance from Miss Carson to Mr. Smith at the split second you finished that riotously funny line which the gifted authoress has written for you."

The next week, under the title of *Glamour*, which Holman Clark said was short and misleading, we opened at the Apollo Theatre in London for a short visit, closing after ten performances. But the old waiter and Mr. Clark had taught me quite a lot and a return to the West End was not far off. In the meantime I was back at the Everyman, singing and dancing blackface again. The play was called *Brer Rabbit* and was a children's musical based on the Uncle Remus stories of Joel Chandler Harris by Mabel Dearmer with exquisite music by Martin Shaw.

During the run the manager, Norman Macdermott, sent for me and asked if I thought I could play the part of a bumptious youth of sixteen. Of course I said I could. I was confident enough to assert that I was equal to essaying any male character within the range of Jaques' Seven Ages with the possible exception of the mewling and puking infant and I wasn't at all sure I couldn't handle that one! This seemed to impress Macdermott and he handed me a manuscript, saying that the name of the part was James Bebb. It was the first time that I had been allowed to read a play before accepting a role in it and I slunk off with the script like a dog with a bone.

From my first glance (to see if James Bebb was on at any of the curtains—he "had" the first), I knew it was a dandy part. There could not have been more than a dozen or so lines but they were good lines and the play itself was a very funny comedy of boarding-house life called *At Mrs. Beam's*. The moment I finished reading the script I knew this would be the first Everyman production to be moved down to the West End. I hurried back to Macdermott's office bursting with an enthusiasm which made certain that my salary would remain at that wretched four pounds a week, at least for the Everyman part of the run. But I did at last have a good part to play.

The boarding-house has appealed to many playwrights as a setting for comedies and dramas, and once for a morality play when Jerome wrote *The Passing of the Third Floor Back*. I think there was never a better boarding-house comedy than *At Mrs. Beam's*. The author, C. K. Munro, knew his boarding-house types to perfection, the protocol which prevails, knew the shifting jealousies, prejudices, loyalties and suspicions of the inmates. The play had a smell of boiled mutton and caper sauce about it and, even though you never saw the dining-room, you were conscious of the long, white-clothed table, the massive cruet and the odd, partly empty wine bottles marked with strips of paper.

The virtues of Munro's play were his triumphantly drawn characters. The principal role was a garrulous busy-body named Miss Shoe, played with a touch of comic genius by Jean Cadell. She was the leader of a hilarious collection of boarding-house freaks in building a case against two mysterious temporaries—a notorious and unapprehended Bluebeard and his intended victim. In the end the couple turn out to be cheap hotel thieves who vanish with all the valued possessions of the permanents. Not much of a story perhaps but good enough to occupy ten superbly drawn characters in the telling.

The play went well at the Royalty and the critics were magnanimous with all of us. We ran three hundred performances and I was on the stage of the Royalty Theatre, not in the box office, where Dennis Eadie, the Royalty's actor-manager, had invited me a few months before.

In some ways James Bebb was cast to type. Although I was twenty-six when I got the part, I had not yet shed my juvenile bumptiousness, and I understood James Bebb. This repellent youngster was on stage for the entire first scene, which played for half an hour, during which he was described by the author as "fiddling with a gramo-

*At Mrs. Beam's, a boarding-house comedy by C. K. Munro, which ran ten months at the Royalty Theatre, London, 1923. I am the obnoxious sixteen-year-old with the gramophone. Left to right: Fred O'Donovan, Dennis Eadie, Frances Wetherall, Jean Cadell, Elizabeth Watson and R.M.*

phone." I spent the half-hour stripping the gramophone to pieces and reassembling it in time to play a record which brought the curtain down. As I was placed down left almost on the setting line it was impossible to simulate the business. The instrument was a vintage, handcranked His Master's Voice with a lily-shaped horn and the audience could see every step of the stripping and reassembling. At a certain cue I would put the turntable back on its spindle, place on it a horrendous, cracked record of "Land of Hope and Glory," recorded by the band of the Coldstream Guards, and drown out Miss Cadell in one of her monologues. She got a chance to resume her story while I replaced a needle but the curtain would fall on a deafening cacophony.

Everything proceeded with matchless precision for nearly a hundred performances. Only once did human error intervene. As my cue to play the record approached, I saw a telltale little cogwheel on the stage cloth. There was no time to go back and insert the little gismo. I had prepared for such a disaster and when my cue came and the turntable was demonstrably motionless, I just said, "There's something wrong, but it goes like this," and I sang Elgar's triumphant lyrics in as fortissimo and off-key a fashion as I could manage. Herbert Chown, the stage manager, was not prepared for such vocalizing but he managed to ring down on my rendition of "...make thee mightier yet!" and the audience seemed more than satisfied. I thought Eadie would blow a fuse, but instead he was rather pleased. He told me after the show that the new curtain was possibly an improvement but that he did think that another emergency necessitating my singing Sir Edward's paean might endanger the Empire.

I shared a dressing-room at the Royalty with Fred O'Donovan, an Irish actor who played Mr. Durrows. A graduate of the Abbey Theatre and veteran of several tours of the Irish Players in America, Fred was a "darlin' man" and a first-rate actor, full of stories of Yeats and Lady Gregory, Synge and Lennox Robinson. My favourite was about Joe O'Rourke, one of the immortal Abbey Theatre comedians. Joe had a high-pitched nasal voice which was of tremendous comedic value. He was a favourite of Yeats who once miscast him in a poetic drama of Lady Gregory which he was directing. At the initial rehearsal Joe's shrill but guttural rendition of his first line, "Oy come from the hoigh king..." got a terrific laugh from the company. Yeats stopped the rehearsal.

"Ah—the adenoids, O'Rourke, a little less of them, please!"

"Yes, Misther Yeats, I know a doctor who wants to take them out."

"Ah–excellent, O'Rourke."

Joe was back at rehearsal in a few days. The Messenger's cue came and Joe delivered his opening line with full nasal force. Yeats held up his hand.

"O'Rourke, has the surgery been performed?"

"Yes, Misther Yeats."

"Ah. How sad. Return to your physician friend, O'Rourke, and have them put back!"

All the dressing-rooms in the Royalty Theatre were under the stage and auditorium, along the outside walls, with Eadie's large room in the centre. None had access to fresh air–if the atmosphere of Soho can be called fresh. They were ventilated by ducts fed by a large fan. The intake was in the rear of the theatre near the kitchens of two restaurants, one Armenian and one Greek. Fred O'Donovan used to say he never ate before a performance: two deep breaths at our ventilator and he was full.

Fred had frequently voiced opinions not entirely flattering to Dennis Eadie. I am afraid I had too. Fred sometimes gave a short impression of Eadie's performance in our dressing-room. One evening Herbert Chown stuck his head in our door and said, "Ray, Mr. Eadie wants to see you!" I crossed the corridor to the star dressing-room. Eadie sat at his make-up table. Not a word was spoken. But through the ventilator came the soft tones of Fred O'Donovan singing a lovely Irish song. Finally Eadie spoke. "O'Donovan has a good voice. But I prefer those Abbey Theatre stories. Tell him to do the O'Rourke one again!"

# 3

For the three years after *At Mrs. Beam's* opened, my gainful employment was chiefly at the Royalty, where we ran for nearly a year, and in the first production of *Saint Joan* which had an even longer run at the New Theatre. I am sometimes asked what actors do to pass the time during long runs. The answer in my case was that I nearly worked myself to death. In both plays I had lengthy waits and my roles were not so exacting as to prevent me from snatching some sleep during performances. During the days, and some nights after the show, I worked harder than at any time in my professional life.

In the early 1920s the Sunday play-producing societies were at their peak of activity. These organizations, mostly of post-war vintage, operated as showcases for actors and playwrights. Only one, the Stage Society, went back to Edwardian times: it had a long record of discovery of avant-garde authors including Shaw. The rest were frankly in search of good commercial plays, to be produced for a single performance on a Sunday night. There were about eight of these groups, among them the Repertory Players, The Venturers, the Interlude Players, the Play Actors, and the Phoenix which existed for the revival of non-Shakespearean Elizabethan classics and Restoration plays. Each produced three or four plays during the theatre year and there was a new Sunday production almost every week. The societies had the blessing of theatre managers who provided theatres at cost. But the miracle of the Sunday shows was the support of the newspapers. In a land which had created the country weekend, top dramatic critics regularly attended the Sunday performances. These extra-curricular "first nights" had almost the impact of regular theatre openings.

The actors worked for nothing. Only stagehands and "front-of-the-house" staff were paid. At least half the cast would be employed in current plays. The truth is that most actors, employed or not, would willingly have paid to act. I was involved in some capacity with all the groups, and once I worked in three productions simultaneously. I would stage-manage, assistant stage-manage, act anything and everything that came along, and after about a year I was directing. The day would begin at nine and end God knows when. The blessed sleep during my paid performances got me through.

During this three-year span I must have honed my stage experience in more than fifty Sunday plays. I never would have become a stage director without the experience as a stage manager in the Sunday shows, particularly with the Repertory Players, who finally let me direct a few productions. There was strong competition for acting opportunities in the Sunday plays, but stage managers were not plentiful. The regular stage managers wanted no part of it. The man who would stage-manage a Sunday show had to be a combination of conman, mendicant and scrounger. On a budget of two hundred pounds or less he was supposed to rent or improvise scenery, meet rehearsal expenses and bring in a production comparable to West End quality. I am by nature untidy-minded and forgetful; but in the theatre I am orderly in thought and have the instincts of a chartered accountant, perhaps a dishonest one. I was a good man for the job, welcomed by all the societies, usually with the bribe of a small part.

Women make excellent stage managers. I soon had a small list of stage Marthas, good housekeepers, who could keep an immaculate prompt book or rustle rare props, while the Marys on stage took the bows. Over the years as a director I have had my trials with temperamental actresses. I have consigned them in my mind to an eternal concentration camp. But then I remember the Marthas, devoted and zealous, lashing out at a slothful stagehand or calmly reminding a forgetful actor of what the author wrote, and I remain a convinced feminist.

My first real pay-dirt came unexpectedly after four or five Sunday offerings on the altar of experience. It was now halfway through the run of *At Mrs. Beam's* and I was promoted to stage manager of a Repertory Players production of a play called *Harwood Blood*. As usual I had received the bonus of a small part as a Canadian backwoodsman named Zick Hales. The director, Leo Carroll, allowed me to write a short offstage scene for myself and six husky sledge dogs (the first act was set in Alaska) in which I played all seven characters. I insisted on playing all six dogs to avoid my own three lines from being drowned out and to achieve consistency in the barking tone of the huskies. The result was surprisingly good.

That night I, a virtually unkown actor, won an entrance round of applause. The dog team had performed well and clearly. But the acting chore took second place to my interest in stage management. It was a heavy production, with elaborate lighting effects. All went well. But to my delighted astonishment the critics took Zick to their hearts. James Agate, in *The Sunday Times*, wrote, "Mr. Massey is to be congratulated upon one of the most spontaneous and deserved successes I have ever seen." I could hardly believe my eyes, for Zick had not seemed that good. I think the unseen dogs had helped.

I did not get anything much in the way of acting jobs from this Zick bit, but my housekeeping efforts paid off. My first chance to direct came shortly after when the "Reps" put on a play by the dramatic critic, Hubert Griffith. *Tunnel-Trench*, a war play with a big cast and a lot of scenes, was well written and a director's delight. I was even given money to build scenery. Griffith had served two years in the infantry and two in the R.A.F. He knew war and hated it. There were many anti-war plays at this time. I acted in or directed ten myself. Most of the cast were composed of ex-servicemen. Only one of the ten succeeded but they were all well received. I imagine that the public and the ex-servicemen, although they all detested the Kaiser's war, resented the idea that all the agonies had been in vain.

A few months after *At Mrs. Beam's* closed I found myself in a musical by William Makepeace Thackeray with a couple of songs and dances to do. This strange statement is true in substance. The play was a new musical dramatization of Thackeray's *The Rose and the Ring*, aptly described on the billboards as "a pantomime for great and small children." It was produced for a Christmas run at Wyndham's Theatre by Lewis Casson, who also directed. Hugh Sinclair and I played two modern youths interpolated into Thackeray's fantasy and Casson used two existing "star traps" for our initial entrance.

The "star trap" is a small platform about two feet square which can be lowered below stage level and by counterweights and manpower be used to propel an actor (rarely a star, for obvious reasons!) some six feet or so into the air usually accompanied by fireworks. This brings squeals of delight from the children out front and terror and injuries to the human missiles. During our eight-week run, due to minor bumps and sprains which I sustained on the trap, the time step Hugh and I were supposed to perform had to be eliminated from at least a dozen performances.

Lewis Casson, who was married to Sybil Thorndike, was somewhat dour but also a kind and gentle man and an incisive actor with much strength. The Cassons had acquired a new play about Joan of Arc by Bernard Shaw which promised to be the most important London production of the year. There had not been a truly great home-grown play on the London stage since the war. Rumour had it that *Saint Joan* might be the play the theatre had been waiting for. The Theatre Guild had produced it successfully on Broadway toward the end of 1923. But in London the script remained a tight secret. At last, in late January, a March opening date was set and the Green Room Club, of which I was now a member, was seething with casting rumours. Nobody knew a thing about the play itself. With customary pessimism I discounted my own chances of a job in it, thereby reducing potential disappointment. This time my philosophy paid off. I found in my box at Wyndham's stage-door a note from Lewis Casson with an enclosure. The note merely said that he had put me down for the part of Brother Martin, the Dominican monk who defends Joan at the trial. The enclosure was the "sides" for the part. I was to come to the New Theatre the following morning at eleven to meet the author, the note adding that it was not an audition but suggesting I be familiar with the lines.

I was word perfect in two long speeches by two o'clock next morning. The part seemed an actor's dream although it is difficult to judge a role from "sides" alone. (Only leading actors were supplied with scripts in the twenties, the rank and file being given only the cues and lines of the parts concerned. These were known as "sides.") In the case of Brother Martin they indicated a mighty good part.

At the New Theatre, Casson's selection for the English cast of *Saint Joan* was assembled, about two dozen of us. We all had a euphoric glow. I knew a few of the actors and recognized most of them – a goodly company. The stage was bare, with a table and some chairs down right.

Suddenly Bernard Shaw came through the pass-door, followed by Sybil Thorndike and Lewis Casson, and strode (he never walked!) to the table, where he sat in the central chair. Sybil and Lewis made a few casual greetings on the way and joined him. The rest of us drifted to the wings. Shaw's curls at each side of his high forehead looked startlingly like horns. I thought that Mrs. Shaw's curling iron must have helped nature. The horns suited two of his favourite roles, Satan and Moses. It would be Satan day for me.

Each of us was to be presented to Shaw, inspected and told to wait. Shaw knew most of us and the interviews were short and sweet. I felt confident as my turn approached; I had met Shaw a few months before at a rehearsal of *Captain Brassbound's Conversion*, when he had commended me on my performance of the American Captain Kearney in J. B. Fagan's repertory company.

At last it was my turn. I could hear Lewis Casson saying, "This is the young actor Sybil and I have in mind for Brother Martin."

Shaw exclaimed, "Lewis, are you out of your mind? Brother Martin should be good-looking!"

I stopped dead in my tracks. I was standing up centre stage, without a line to speak and twenty or so of the best actors in London watching me. I looked at Sybil Thorndike. She sat bolt upright, her eyes closed, looking suddenly pale. Lewis and Shaw were in vehement discussion. I said nothing.

Casson, after what seemed an inconclusive talk with Shaw, came over to me and said practically in a whisper, "As you see, Shaw has different ideas from mine about Brother Martin. But I give you my word you will be with us. Now, give me back that part and I'll call you when I've settled things."

A fine young actor named Lawrence Anderson got the part of Brother Martin which he played superbly well. We became close friends and shared a dressing-room during the long run of *Saint Joan*. Two other occupants of the dressing-room were Keneth Kent, who played the English soldier in the epilogue, and Robert Cunningham, the Archbishop of Rheims. I eventually received two small parts: La Hire, a tough, hard-swearing knight at the Court of the Dauphin, and Canon D'Estivet, the prosecutor at Joan's trial. Neither of these roles offered much acting opportunity but they kept me at work in an important play and I was able to pursue my Sunday adventures with the chance of some forty-five minutes sleep every performance. This opportunity was respected by my roommates.

Rehearsals of *Saint Joan* presented a strange split of authority in staging the play. Lewis Casson had already earned a high reputation as a director when such a functionary was still a novelty. Most of us in the company assumed that he was officially directing *Saint Joan*. But as we progressed two voices of guidance were heard and the voices were in continued disagreement. Author and director did not see eye to eye.

The main point at issue from the very start was pace. The play was very long. Shaw would not cut a line. It looked like three hours playing time even if briskly paced. Lewis had two good reasons to impose a smart tempo. He had to ring down the final curtain in time for customers to make suburban trains and he had to keep them awake. Shaw gave not a damn for such mundane considerations or said he did not. He cared only for the spoken word and he would not have his precious lines "gabbled," as he described the vitality which Lewis strove to get from a cast which had to deliver more marathon speeches than ever before.

The battle was on. We rehearsed for three hours every morning with Shaw sitting in the front row of the dress circle. He had a reading light and a clipboard on his knee. In the darkness out front he was featured in a pool of light. Finally darling Sybil, who had a giant part, could stand it no longer. She said to Lewis, "Please dim the light on G.B.S., I can't take my eyes off him!" But the notes came just the same, all of them pointing to the same thing, "Take your time," "Don't gabble," "Remember that pause," and so on.

Shaw's notes and comments were always given direct to the actor and not through Lewis as director, as the custom of the theatre demanded. The strain on the cast was considerable. Each of us knew that Lewis Casson was right. We wanted to do it his way, and we would do so but it is always difficult to brush aside the demands of the author, especially when he has devil's horns.

Shaw always went to lunch at half-past one. He never came back in the afternoon. Lewis would patch things up and get about five minutes out of the playing time of each of the seven scenes. Most of the company were seasoned players. They were not confused and the situation did not jeopardize the production. All our sympathies went out to Lewis. How that patient, skilful man stood the strain and developed his own brilliant performance of de Stogumber, the chauvinist English cleric, I do not know.

After some two weeks of rehearsal Shaw came backstage with his clipboard and notebook which he threw down on a prop table.

"Lewis," he said, "I don't think much good ever comes from these afternoon rehearsals."

"We must have more of them," said Lewis.

I think Shaw accepted defeat at that moment. After that he gave only token resistance to Lewis' efforts for pace.

One day Shaw left his large notebook on a prop table and was offstage on some business. I sneaked a look at the book. There were many pages full of his beautiful longhand. The last was hardly dry. It was, as I afterwards realized when the play was published, part of the preface to *Saint Joan*. He had been writing it during rehearsal!

Shaw, the original of his own Professor Higgins, was interested in my Canadian pronunciation. On several occasions he invited me to walk home with him at lunch time. I am well over six feet tall with long legs and I was pretty fit at twenty-eight, but only once did I get as far as the Adelphi Terrace where Shaw lived. The other times I was left panting at various stages of the way from the New Theatre to the Strand, while the great man disappeared in the distance. He was about seventy at the time.

By the way, an astonishing number of Canadians, men and women, have become stars in the theatre. Margaret Anglin, Lucile Watson, Marie Dressler, Mary Pickford, Walter Huston and Christopher Plummer come quickly to mind and the list continues to grow. The talent is varied but one quirk of speech has identified each and all as native-born Canadians. That remains the pronunciation of the vowel combination of "ou" as in "gout."

About four years later Shaw came to the opening of Sean O'Casey's *The Silver Tassie* which I directed. He was ecstatic about the play. A few nights later I saw his own new play, *The Apple Cart*, with Cedric Hardwicke and Edith Evans in the leads. I wrote to Shaw to tell him how much I had liked the play. In reply I received the following postcard which I subsequently framed. He uses "produce" in the English sense as "direct."

Ayot St. Lawrence, Wellwyn, Herts. 11/11/29

Yes, but I have a considerable grudge against you for letting me slave over *St. Joan* when you could have produced it as well as I or better. Why were those talents hidden? Producers are one in a million. Anybody can play La Hire or D'Estivet. Why didn't you tell me; confound you!

G. Bernard Shaw

So Shaw clearly takes credit for directing his play. In *Who's Who* Lewis Casson states that he himself directed it. The program of the opening night, March 26, 1924, does not name a director. It remains the only play I acted in without knowing who the director really was.

After we had been running some months my father came from Canada to see the play. This was a great occasion for both of us. He was now seventy-four but seemed older. With a couple of his lighter overcoats against the fickle June weather he sat in a comfortable chair in a box which Tom Kealy, the company manager, had arranged for him. It was only the second play he had ever seen. I had grave doubts that the old man would get much out of the Shavian dialogue so crisply acted. It can be difficult for seasoned theatre-goers. But my concern was needless. I met him at the pass-door. Father was not fatigued, bored or confused – he was enchanted. That is what the theatre is meant to do, to cast a spell. I took him to meet Sybil Thorndike. Sybil was wonderful with him. She realized that this tall, bearded Victorian was stage-struck. Father voiced his admiration and

42

announced that he was going to "Raymond's dressing-room."

"Oh, it's a dreadful climb – please sit here in my sitting-room while he changes."

But no, he wanted to meet Raymond's colleagues, and off we went up the four flights of concrete stairs. I had to negotiate those eighty steps four times every performance, twice in full armour. But I soon found out why my father made the effort. My "colleagues" were, indeed, a factor in his decision to make the ascent, but he really just wanted to see the sights.

On the first flight we passed a tall figure in a broad-brimmed hat. He was E. Lyall Swete, on his way to the Garrick Club, no doubt for his devilled bone or chop.

"Good-night, sir," I said.

"Good-night, my boy." He was gone.

Father murmured, "He was the Earl of Warwick, wasn't he?"

"Yes, father."

"A beautiful performance, beautiful!"

As we gained altitude we passed several open doors and descending figures. In awe-struck whispers various players in *Saint Joan* were recognized and their performances commended. But always the past tense was used.

"That was the Dauphin? The Inquisitor? That was Dunois?"

He had the right idea – the character remains in the theatre when the actor leaves it.

As we approached the open door of Room 16 where my "colleagues" and I dressed, the resonant tenor voice of the portly Archbishop of Rheims reached a deafening crescendo in the Pilgrims' Chorus from *Tannhauser* with new lyrics.

"The Lord Himself hath bought beer for the actorrrs..."

I stopped further blasphemy by announcing, "My father!" But my fears were groundless.

"You have a truly fine voice," said my father, speaking with the authority of a former chairman of the Music Committee of the Metropolitan Methodist Church. "Please continue. I would like to know how the Lord's hospitality was received."

On our way home to Kensington he put his great hand on mine and said, "That was a good play – yes, by George! – a very, very good play. I release you from your promise not to act or practise on Sunday."

During the run of *Saint Joan*, in October 1924, my elder son, Geoffrey Massey, was born at Hornton College in Kensington. Returning from a matinée I found him alone and awake in a basket on the floor in what was to be the nursery. For his age (about two hours) he was unusually quiet and composed, qualities which he still retains at the age of fifty-four, though not continuously.

The cast of *Saint Joan* was one of the best I have ever worked with, although some vagaries and foibles could be found even in this notable company. The role of the Inquisitor was acted brilliantly by O. B. Clarence. Instead of the grim fanatic of tradition, Shaw had written this character as a mild, elderly Dominican monk. "Clarty," as Clarence was known to us all, was in his early fifties but acted the part as a fragile old man. He had a skin allergy which prevented the use of grease paint and he made up with water colours. The result was most effective and he obtained gradations of colour and shade which were unobtainable with the grease sticks then available. But there was a drawback to the water colours. After they had dried, the delicate pigments would curl up on his face and flake off. As Clarty was onstage for nearly fifty minutes in the trial scene he seemed to develop a galloping dermatitis before our eyes.

Robert Horton played Dunois, the French Commander. Horton was an exponent of the new naturalistic acting, pioneered by Gerald du Maurier. He had never appeared in a costume play. He was very good indeed in *Saint Joan* but confessed that he never knew what to do with his hands when wearing full armour. The wardrobe mistress was kept busy removing hand make-up from his white surcoat, the result of his nervous search for non-existent pockets.

E. Lyall Swete, the Earl of Warwick, who had trod the boards with Irving, had no such problem. In Irving's time an actor studied gesture. His diction was a joy to hear and I believe he could have brought rhythm to a reading of a Bradshaw timetable.

The Dauphin of Ernest Thesiger was a memorable performance. Ernest was a master of eccentric character with seemingly unlimited versatility. Not only was he a fine actor but in private life an exceedingly good painter. At the outset of the First World War he enlisted as an infantry private and was one of the first citizen soldiers to see action, being wounded on January 1, 1915. Tendons and nerves in both his hands were severed. In order to restore their full use, after surgery, Ernest took up needlework. He became head of Queen Mary's Needlework Guild and a leading exponent of this art, writing a book on the subject, entitled *Adventures in Petit Point*.

Shaw declared during rehearsals that no man would ever top Joan in any of her scenes. He was correct in this prophecy. No man did. It

44

remained for a boy to accomplish the feat. The old pacifist had succeeded in writing a battle scene, for Joan and Dunois, the French Commander, and his Page, which was both intelligible and exciting, a rare achievement. The substance of this scene on the Loire River bank was the planning of the assault on Orleans, in which the direction of the wind was the decisive factor. The weather reports were in the hands of the Page to whom Shaw granted ten lines and a sneeze. But, armed with this meagre verbal equipment, a young actor of fourteen named Jack Hawkins acted with such exuberance and vigour that he invariably captured the honours of the scene. Jack went on to a fine stage and film career.

But Sybil Thorndike and Lewis Casson crowd other memories of *Saint Joan* from my mind. I worked as an actor with these remarkable people for nearly three years. Their active careers spanned the first six decades of this century. They established together a record of industry in the living theatre which probably will never be equalled. Everybody in the theatre has personal ambition but neither Sybil nor Lewis ever showed egotism. They seemed to be impelled simply by love of the theatre. I think Sybil's tour of the mining towns of Wales in Shakespearean rep meant just as much to her as a West End triumph.

The morning after we opened *Saint Joan* Sybil started rehearsals for a Sunday-night performance of *Masses and Men*, Ernst Toller's play, to be given by the Stage Society. Lewis was directing. I had a part in it, and I remember seeing Sybil, who had just scored an enormous success in a great play, sitting in the wings, script in one hand and a sheaf of press notices in the other. She was studying the script. The notices had to wait.

When *Saint Joan* closed after a year's run at the New Theatre, Sybil was already rehearsing for *The Round Table*, an amusing but unpretentious little comedy by Lennox Robinson, the Irish playwright. Again I was of the company and Lewis Casson was director. After the tempest of Shaw's drama the gentle breeze of the Robinson play seemed to some critics a bit of a letdown. But not to Sybil; I believe she enjoyed playing Daisy Drennan as much as Joan.

Both Dame Sybil Thorndike and Sir Lewis Casson were perfect examples of theatrical professionalism. They spurned pretence, vulgarity and showmanship. They were honest to the theatre, to themselves and to the fortunate people who worked with them. The theatre which Sybil and Lewis lived for had nothing to do with "show business."

# 4

Early in 1926, together with George Carr and Allan Wade, I took over a long lease of the Everyman Theatre. It was the first of two periods during which I was the lessee of a London theatre, although I have been a transient manager many times. Theatrical management under any conditions is an uneasy occupation but the bricks and mortar manager of a little theatre with about four hundred seats to fill is not inclined to sing at his work. Sometimes a new play had to be ready to open with only two weeks of rehearsal. We knew all this and we were not starry-eyed. We knew it would be rugged. What we did not know was how rugged.

As a managerial triumvirate we complemented each other pretty well. George Carr, who had literally lifted me off the pavement and put me on the stage, was the technical director. He knew the limitations and also the advantages of that crazy little theatre for he had been working as stage manager there since the end of the war. He and I had run a short summer season of four plays there in 1925. Allan Wade joined us with a long experience of the current new theatre, having been assistant to Granville-Barker for many years. The guiding spirit behind the Phoenix Society and the Stage Society, he had directed many of their Sunday productions. He had a sound knowledge of theatre economics, in which mystery George and I were not exactly experts. I was available as an eager Pooh-Bah to do anything, which resulted in my engaging in every theatre activity, including press-agenting.

It is the custom to describe any theatre project which is not located in the West End or on Broadway as experimental. It is a silly designation; every theatrical venture is an experiment. Our Hampstead adventure was an attempt to achieve a reasonable degree of quality over an extended period with a continuing number of plays. We had no set policy; policies become expensive. We had no extended plans. Mostly we saw no farther ahead than our next production. We had about three thousand pounds to work with, collected from various sources.

When half of it was spent we would have to quit. Some backers had been promised at least a return of their money. We expected to export some of our plays to the West End. That was where our hoped-for profits would come from.

Our reserve of plays would be from Shaw revivals and here Allan Wade, an old friend of G.B.S. from Edwardian days, proved his worth. Before the Granville-Barker seasons, in 1904-1906, when Shaw plays were the mainstay of the enterprise, Shaw was not a box-office author. It was not until after the success of *Man and Superman* which Robert Loraine produced in 1906 and *Pygmalion* with Beerbohm Tree in 1914 that Bernard Shaw became the only "15-percent-straight" author. Nothing would persuade him to reduce this figure. But Allan Wade, reminding G.B.S. of the old Barker days when he was glad of the 5, 7½ or 10 percent which the author normally gets, obtained the only concession Shaw ever made to a professional management—the Everyman Theatre could have Shaw plays at a straight 5 percent! I do not know how dear, gentle Allan pulled that one.

At the Everyman whenever we were in a jam and the spectre of the landlord appeared we did a Shaw. He always saved us.

The opening production which emboldened us to undertake our Hampstead venture was a ballad opera by Clifford Bax called *Mr. Pepys*. The first night was a rapturous justification of our choice of play and, it seemed to us, of the enterprise itself.

*Mr. Pepys* was an account of a typical day in Samuel Pepys' life with an enchanting score by Martin Shaw. Many old friends from the Diary took part. Pembleton, the dancing Master, the faithful Will Hewer, Mrs. Knipp, Nell Gwyn, Elizabeth Pepys, Deb Willett, Mr. P. and others. It was an unpretentious and rollicking evening, best described by a character called The Showsman who spoke the Prologue:

*If Mr. Pepys, for whose ungodly mind*
*A theatre held all heaven, were here today,*
*How he would rub those poor weak eyes to find*
*Himself the butt and centre of a play.*

Mr. Pepys was played by Frederick Ranalow who had not long ago finished his merry years as Macheath in *The Beggar's Opera*. Nell Gwyn was played by Isabel Jeans. Both were perfect, as was the whole cast, all of whom had to sing as well as act. Allan Wade's experience in Restoration comedy and his keen sense of humour assured fine direction for the play.

47

It has always amazed me that experts in obsolete musical instruments can be produced at need – instantly, ready and able to play spinet, theorbo or lute. The delicate effect of plucked strings is unobtainable from percussion instruments, so Martin Shaw assembled eight of these seventeenth-century virtuosi. As a double lute looks incongruous in the hands of a man in a dinner jacket, the musicians of *Mr. Pepys* were in wig and costume.

It seemed we had hit the jackpot with our first offering. The notices were all good and there were several nibbles from West End managements. The Royalty Theatre was soon to be dark and we decided that under our management *Mr. Pepys* would open there in four weeks' time. The transfer to the Soho theatre would involve no further production expenses, since the Royalty was virtually the same size as our own.

There were no plans for the Everyman. Right at the start the menace that was to haunt us for the next year, a closed box office with the rent to pay, was frighteningly close. It was now Wednesday of our first week and we took another chance.

On the following Sunday I was to play Robert Mayo in Eugene O'Neill's *Beyond the Horizon* for the Repertory Players. Nobody could foretell the fate of an O'Neill play but I knew it was a good one and the Reps had cast it well. Leslie Banks was playing the other Mayo brother and Joyce Kennedy was the girl in this New England tragedy of square pegs in round holes. Richard Bird was directing, most expertly. I persuaded George and Allan to bring the play up the hill to Hampstead immediately following the descent of *Mr. Pepys* to the Royalty, providing Leslie would continue in his part in the O'Neill play. This he gladly agreed to do. The rest of the Rep cast was also signed.

Just after we had closed this deal Joyce Kennedy was taken ill. The Reps were faced with a hard decision, postponement or substitution of another actress in a long and difficult role with only two days of rehearsal. They chose the latter course. Marie Ney, who took over, scored a major success in one of the most unsympathetic and thankless roles which only O'Neill could write.

Leslie Banks was one of the most resourceful actors I ever worked with. There seemed no limit to his versatility, or to his power. A birth injury had left him with one side of his face paralyzed and one eye sightless. This handicap he overcame with complete success by simply ignoring it – as did his audience.

*Beyond the Horizon* was a success at the Sunday performance and again for the three weeks we played it at the Everyman. It was a beautiful play, with O'Neill at his best; and Robert Mayo, the would-be poet who longed to wander, remains for me as fond a memory as any. Nowadays we are inclined to remember O'Neill for the marathon plays of his later years (*Mourning Becomes Electra*, *The Iceman Cometh*, *Long Day's Journey into Night*) and allow them to hide his glories of the twenties (*Desire under the Elms*, *The Hairy Ape*, *The Emperor Jones* and *Beyond the Horizon*).

As soon as *Mr. Pepys* had been launched at Hampstead and well before the O'Neill play had been brought up the hill we decided on another American play for our third production. It was *Hell Bent for Heaven*, a drama about the West Virginia mountains by Hatcher Hughes, a college professor who had won the Pulitzer Prize for its authorship. The play had already had a successful Broadway run.

There would be at least four weeks for rehearsal, a luxury which we never enjoyed again. I was to play the central character, a sort of hillbilly mixture of Uriah Heep, Hugh Peters and Tartuffe with a good bit of the author's own creative deviltry added. Rufe Pryor was as evil and detestable a character as I have ever met professionally and tremendous fun to play. Leslie Banks at once agreed to stay on for one more Everyman job and play the other male lead.

I directed *Hell Bent for Heaven*, a task complicated by the need to provide what a character described as "the daggonest rainstorm I ever seed" through the entire second and third acts. This torrential downpour could be seen through a large window in the rear wall of the single cabin set. At the first performance a burst pipe in the rain-effects plumbing brought the flood in awesome reality to the stage and to the front row seats some two minutes before the curtain was to fall. It did not prevent a wonderful reception for the play. I still remember an enthusiastic lady trying to applaud while pouring water out of her shoe. I would have liked to refill it with champagne.

The first nine weeks of our tenancy had exceeded our rosiest hopes. *Mr. Pepys* was in its sixth week at the Royalty and building nicely. The two American plays had both done well at the Everyman and the theatre had recovered from the first-night deluge in *Hell Bent*. There had been quite a bit of interest in bringing *Hell Bent for Heaven* to the West End. The new production, *Widowers' Houses*, Shaw's first play, looked extraordinarily promising under Allan's direction and was to have its dress rehearsal Monday, the last day of

April, after we closed the Hatcher Hughes play. I was not acting in that or anything else and for the first time in months I looked forward to having a bit of rest and a chance to see my son Geoffrey, now aged one-and-a-half, whom I scarcely knew. Instead, on Tuesday, May 4, 1926, I was wrapped in a single army blanket in cold discomfort trying to get some sleep on the floor of a huge shed at the Chiswick garage of the London General Omnibus Company.

# 5

The General Strike of 1926 was something every Briton would like to forget and most of them have. Coal miners were in the throes of a long strike for decent wages, a strike which they seemed to be winning, when the Trades Union Council made the staggering blunder of calling a General Strike in their support. The miners had the complete sympathy of the public but a General Strike is undisguised revolution. The government, a coalition under Stanley Baldwin, was cool and firm and the public accepted his leadership in the same spirit.

The immediate effect of the strike was paralyzing immobility. Not only were the transport workers solid in their support of the walk-out but instant and stringent restrictions of fuel supply emptied the streets. Together with practically all the theatre managers, we closed the Everyman and the Royalty.

I volunteered as a lorry-driver in answer to a wireless call for transport workers. At five o'clock that afternoon of the first day of the strike I had completed my tests as a bus-driver on the training course at Chiswick.

These tests were not perfunctory; regular instructors put us through a complicated obstacle course including mock-up streets covered with an oil slick to try us on skids. To put a big bus onto a well-greased patch of road at forty miles per hour and deliberately skid it around and get it straight again was not a habit-forming procedure. Five hundred of us were put through the course that afternoon and the "skid stretch" flunked about ten percent. As it was May and the weather dry for England it seemed that this elimination was excessively cautious. It also seemed a bit illogical that the losers in the skid test were immediately sent to the General Post Office as lorry-drivers who could look forward to much greater slippery hazards in the long mail runs than we did in London.

It was obvious that our efforts were meant to defy the strikers and not really to provide transportation. Regular bus routes would not be followed. We were to pioneer a single new route, a belt-line from Chiswick garage through the West End, via Hyde Park Corner and

51

Piccadilly to the City and back via Holborn, Oxford Street, Bayswater, Ealing and so to the garage, about fifteen miles in all.

We had come prepared for an extended visit and were issued with ground sheet, blanket and so forth by Army Ordnance. I spent a pleasant and mildly profitable evening playing poker with some friends in the Coldstream Guards.

A bus left Chiswick garage every five minutes beginning at seven next morning. Mine was to be an early starter but it took me ten minutes at the hand crank to get her to fire. Barring excessively weak brakes and a defective clutch which made gear changing sound like a jack-hammer, the bus had a good burst of speed in her. The conductor was a meek little civil servant who, as far as I could see, had passed into a state of shock when told by a police inspector that he was responsible for restraining suspicious characters from boarding the bus. As I never slowed down from a brisk and deafening thirty miles per hour, he was not immediately called upon to exercise his powers. There was a huge crowd at Hammersmith Broadway, a confluence of six roads, but the police had been able to keep a path open for the buses and I went through with the throttle wide open. There was no windshield and I was a sitting duck for numerous decaying vegetables, eggs and other missiles directed at us with extreme accuracy. I took these as evidence of hostility.

In Kensington we were greeted with cheers, but only two intrepid citizens came aboard. Our total patronage passing through Knightsbridge and Hyde Park Corner amounted to ten and we were empty again as we entered the Strand. For the rest of our run back to the garage it was a variation of jeers and cheers and no business.

There was plenty of fuel for a second run and we passed the Chiswick depot without stopping. It was now eight-thirty and there were a lot more people on the streets. There were so many in Hammersmith Broadway that we could hardly move. We came to a stop in the middle of a howling mob which packed the whole square. There were two buses a hundred yards in front, one overturned. Before I could get out from behind the wheel, two or three men lifted the hood and smashed the carburetor and cylinder heads with sledge-hammers. I yelled to the conductor to get away and tried to jump out myself but was held in my seat by two women armed with leeks. A sharp blow on my head convinced me that the ladies were in earnest. There seemed absolutely no chance of escape. I had to sit there, listening to a stream of obscenities from the women and watching the further destruction of the engine.

I could hear tramping on the top of the bus where a rope had been tied and we started to teeter violently. But efforts to overturn the bus failed. We remained unsteady but upright. Around the bus I could see nothing but a mass of howling madmen, at least ten thousand of them, and not a policeman in sight. I have been scared badly many times, but never have I experienced such terror as I did on Hammersmith Broadway that morning. This time it was the naked hatred of a mob that I saw and felt....

Suddenly a young man, smartly dressed, wearing a bowler hat and carrying a light bamboo walking stick, pushed through the crowd and jumped up on a fender. His appearance so astonished the rabble that for a moment there was comparative silence. A man who was urging the burning of the bus tumbled to the ground. The newcomer uttered only a few words in a shrill but calm voice. "What you people are engaging in is outright revolution. It is traitorous and wicked. This is not a strike. This is a rebellion. Go back to work. Leave this man alone! He's only doing his duty." He jumped to the ground, calling to me, "I'll get you help," and disappeared in the crowd.

It was an act of great courage. The crowd was subdued for the moment by the sheer audacity of the man but it was only a moment before his taunts had results. The arsonist remounted his rostrum on the remains of the engine housing and called for action. The fuel tank in this bus was just under the driver's seat. But my immediate danger came from the women. Three of them now renewed their attack. I could not hear the arsonist. I was trying to keep one of the leek women from knocking me out but she did deliver one blow which blurred everything. I was conscious of a horse's head tossing over my right shoulder, and a mounted policeman saying, "Can you ride?"

I said yes. I climbed from the driver's seat on to his horse, grabbing him around the waist. We started out, five mounted policeman, myself riding pillion in the middle. Groggy as I was, I was aware of those police horses forcing their way through a savage crowd, three or four hundred yards through a solid mass, apparently without hurting anybody.

At the police station just off the Broadway, I caught a glimpse of myself in a mirror. My face was a mass of scratches, one eye was nearly closed.

That afternoon I did two more trips round the belt-line. This time we were better prepared. I had a new bus with the engine hood secured with barbed wire. A spare driver and a policeman rode on the seat with me and there were two conductors. Steel helmets were worn. The whole effect must have been uninviting to passengers but we took on more than we had carried in the morning.

I slept one night at home and for the next ten days was in charge of mail convoys usually of six or more big lorries delivering mail all over the country. Round trips to York, Southampton, Bristol, Plymouth, filled in the rest of my strike duty.

A vigorous attempt to operate the railways was ineffective. The risk of sabotage was great. Road transport was easier to maintain. As far as the mail convoys were concerned the big streamers proclaiming that we carried Royal Mail proved a guarantee against most interference. We did not carry police or military protection, just a few extra drivers. We bivouacked in the country and drove all-out through populous areas.

Some bright moments remain in my mind: a smartly liveried chauffeur climbing a ladder to a lonely railway signal box with a large wicker luncheon basket for the white-moustached signalman sitting at his two huge levers, while an ancient Daimler touring car waits below.

At Liphook, a village in Hampshire, I remember a pause for coffee. "How are things in Liphook?" I asked the proprietor of the stall. "The unions 'ere have responded one hundred percent," he said. "The labour movement is solid for the strike to the last man. And there 'e is – picketing 'is own business." He pointed to a solitary man pacing up and down in front of a shop bearing a sign "E. Jones – Electrician."

In Brentford on the Great West Road there was a vicious narrow zigzag which had been an annoyance to travellers for several hundred years. The maximum hazard was the corner of a shed jutting close to the middle of the right-of-way. The last day of the strike a mail convoy was returning to London from a Bristol run. I was driving the leading lorry, a big Leyland. I entered the zigzag at a cautious 15 M.P.H. and misjudged the width of the load I had behind me. There was a rending, jolting crash. I braked to a halt and examined the damage. To the lorry there wasn't much but the jutting menace of the shed was a mass of rubble and the road was now almost straight. I could feel the gratitude of bygone travellers, Dickensian coachmen, brother lorry-drivers. But I didn't boast about my demolition when I got to the G.P.O. garage.

And then the General Strike of 1926 was over. It had lasted ten days, achieved nothing but chaos throughout the country. It had not helped the miners, who had won their battle on their own. The public survived the grim ordeal by sheer patience and guts. The strike breakers helped a bit but it was the people's will that licked the unions.

I believe in unions. I belong to three. I helped organize British Equity (The Actors' Union) and was a council member of both British and American Equity for over twenty years. What I hate is revolution.

# 6

I returned to the Everyman feeling like a truant. My partners were in a mild state of shock at watching the rent add up in a dark theatre. The Shaw play, *Widowers' Houses*, had gone into rehearsal the day I came back. Allan planned to have it ready in two weeks. Everyman would have been dark nearly four weeks. At the Royalty the news was no better. *Mr. Pepys* would re-open at once but Allan was dubious about its future. His doubts were justified, and the play ran only two more weeks at a loss. Due to the strike, over half our capital had vanished. The rest was inviolate, which meant that the Everyman would have to run without further loss. It did for another year.

We decided to stay with Shaw for another play. The price was right and G.B.S. had proved reliable box office at the Everyman. After the Shaw plays, Allan proposed that we revive *The Country Wife* which he had directed for the Phoenix a couple of years before. I was not too happy about this choice. Wycherley's play in my opinion was one smutty joke done to death, without any of the grace and style of Congreve. But I had no better suggestion, and we needed a Restoration or Elizabethan revival to balance the season.

The next day I was on my way to Toronto, deserting my partners for the second time. I had received a cable that my father had died.

Father's death was not unexpected. He had been in failing health for the past year but it was a grievous blow to me. He was nearly fifty years older than I and this gap in years made him more like a grandfather to me. But we were very close. I loved him, of course, but also I respected him deeply and held him in awe for his goodness. How many times I had looked to my father as a pattern of behaviour. Half a century after his death I still do. How many times the pattern has been out of reach.

When I got back to London *The Country Wife* was in its final rehearsals, with Allan directing it. Isabel Jeans was giving a delightful performance, but the play remained a leering succession of *doubles entendres* and innuendoes.

A successful opening drew a good press and business was excellent from the start. Everything seemed roses and pink lights. But in the long queue at the box office the second night appeared a formidable lady named Mrs. Hornibrook, president of the London Public Morality Council. This lady was well known to all of us in management. As press representative of our theatre, I greeted her cordially and expressed the wish that she enjoy herself at the play. She obviously did for she wrote a blistering attack on our production in the form of a circular letter to every London newspaper. This was printed by several of the papers. A brief quote from the letter indicates that as a sleuth in search of smut Mrs. H. had struck pay-dirt. "It is a perfectly obscene play and never ought to have been produced, the theme is a disgusting one to any evolved mind, and the theatre retrogresses when it has to rake over the dust bins of the Restoration period for a choice piece of garbage such as this."

Mrs. Hornibrook also tried to persuade the Lord Chamberlain to take action but Lord Cromer shied away. *The Country Wife* was written long before the Theatres Act was passed and required no licence.

By the same token the police whose aid Mrs. Hornibrook had sought refused to interfere. An affable inspector, who admitted that Wycherley was a bit obvious in his salacity and lacked the genuine wit of Congreve, confessed that he enjoyed the production.

The Bishop of London, a close ally of Mrs. Hornibrook in her pursuit of decency, did not visit the Everyman himself but wrote us a letter of protest based on a perusal of the text which, as the letter reached us the day after Mrs. H. had seen the production, must have been on the shelves of his library at Fulham Palace.

The lady did all she could to discredit our show. Nowadays one would say she did all she could to build up the box office. But in the 1920s such a campaign could be lethal to a play.

I took Mrs. Hornibrook to lunch at the Ivy in a vain attempt to persuade her to lay off *The Country Wife*. I got nowhere. She foretold the possibility of decay in the theatre with startling clarity. Looking back, I am struck by the accuracy of her prediction of nudity, sexual display and unlimited violence on the stage if uncontrolled licence were permitted.

I suppose there was always a strain of puritanism in me. I had never liked *The Country Wife* and found it difficult to defend it against charges of bad taste. It did have the longest run at the Everyman during our tenancy. But Mrs. Hornibrook's campaign scared off two managers who thought of taking it to the West End. Ten years later the play, in an uncut version, with Ruth Gordon in the leading role, was given a successful revival at the Old Vic, a theatre absolved from entertainment tax because of its "educational functions."

The Everyman tenancy rolled along with a succession of plays, most of which I hardly remember. With the exception of the two American parts which I played early in the season, my own acting was confined to a few small character bits. We had to offer the good parts as bait to attract good actors and actresses for short-term runs between regular engagements. We could not pay West End salaries but Everyman pay did not count as "taking a cut." Indeed, an engagement at our theatre was a professional plum. A constant trickle of first-rate talent defied gravity by flowing uphill to Hampstead for the acting opportunities we could offer.

Our Everyman venture came to an end as suddenly as it had begun. At the end of a year's operation we were barely afloat financially and when job offers in the West End came to all three of us we decided to call it quits.

When we closed, a set of obituary notices appeared in the dramatic columns, notices so impressive that I would not have dared to write them myself. Our tenure of the Hampstead theatre was described as "imaginative," "courageous," "adventurous," and as *The Observer* put it, "One went to the Everyman in the knowledge that one was going to see a play that was trying to be a work of art."

It was a heartwarming reward to the three of us, who knew that we had had only a rather desperate desire to stage a season of good plays and keep a reasonable distance ahead of the sheriff.

# 7

When the Everyman closed I had the satisfaction of receiving almost simultaneously three acting offers for West End productions. For the first time each offer was accompanied by a full script. Hitherto my jobs had come to me by way of a brief conversation with the manager, whose approach would be a mixture of selling the part and keeping the salary down.

This time I had been promoted to the script-approving elite. It was a privilege I never had to surrender and it soon became every actor's right. The time of blind decisions was nearly over. The offers were all pretty good and came from reputable managers but the choice was easy to make. As any young actor would do, I picked the offer with the best acting opportunity, deliberately disregarding the chances of the play itself.

The play I chose was *The Transit of Venus* and the author-producer was H. M. Harwood. I have only vague recollections of the other two plays, but one was an American importation which had quite a long run. Harwood's play was a failure, lasting only a few weeks. But my choice was right. My role was one of the best I had ever had and was the starting point of the most crowded and productive five years of my stage career. If *The Transit of Venus* had enjoyed a long run it would have been quite a different story, for my performance would have been forgotten long before I could have capitalized on it. It is the first-night audience, the five hundred or so critics, managers, agents, professional theatre patrons, who control the future of actors and directors, not the public. Young talent should be in the shop window over and over, should face that opening night ordeal as many times as possible. The long run can be a tomb for a young player.

Harold Harwood was one of two resident doctors at St. Thomas's Hospital in London who had abandoned medicine to become playwrights about the turn of the century. Somerset Maugham was the other, and with John Galsworthy this trio represented the old guard of English playwriting. They differed vastly in the content of their plays but they had one thing in common: they all possessed style. They wrote for a theatre which was a little larger than life, were not obsessed with "holding a mirror up to nature" and were not afraid of writing literate dialogue.

Although in the twenties these three playwrights were at their peak of success, the days of such plays of grace and style were numbered. The great Victorian and Edwardian plays had been comedies and dramas of manners and in the years immediately following the Kaiser's war there were already signs of that permissiveness, of "anything goes," which meant that such a theatre would be obsolete.

*The Transit of Venus* was not one of Harwood's best plays but it narrowly missed being a very good one. There was a serious theme mixed with a comic plot. In a British-mandated territory somewhere in the Middle East an aggressive intrigue is being carried out to make the Arab chieftain of a neighbouring territory grant concessions to a big Anglo-American oil company. The Arab chieftain, called the Khan Aghaba, resists the overtures of the oil men, being a somewhat old-fashioned Arab unlike his modern counterparts who are perfectly willing to part with their precious oil for 51 percent of the action, fleets of air-conditioned Cadillacs and high-rise hospitals. The Khan in Harwood's play was of a very different breed. He had had some acquaintance with Western civilization and wanted no part of its blessings which he knew would accompany the oil derricks if he allowed his desert to be exploited. Camels may not be air-conditioned but they seemed to him preferable to Cadillacs. He just wanted to be left alone.

Nobody could write political comedy better than Harwood and in this phase of *The Transit of Venus* he was at his best. The battle for the oil was joined with the British High Commissioner walking a stately tightrope of neutrality. It was a most interesting situation into which was introduced an amorous and predatory female, who, accompanied by her complaisant husband, arrives in pursuit of the High Commissioner's newly appointed aide-de-camp. The play slipped from serio-comedy into hilarious farce involving everybody in the cast including the Khan himself. The ardent lady of the title in her lustful quest nearly provoked the armed intervention which the oil people desired but it all ended with the return of Aphrodite to her weary husband, with the Khan's resistance to civilization remaining unresolved and everybody's chastity threatened but inviolate.

The author directed his own play. I did not know this until I read the program after we had opened. Rehearsals were informal social

60

*Athene Seyler and R.M. in The Transit of Venus by H. M. Harwood, at the
Ambassadors' Theatre, London, 1927. It is evident that the Khan Aghaba and
Lady Cynthia have dissimilar views on women.*

gatherings. Harwood conducted them in the manner of a shy but
solicitous host whose chief concern seemed to be that all his guests,
great and small, were at ease and enjoying themselves at his party. As
his invitation list had included four of the most skilled and stylish
players in England –Athene Seyler, Nicholas Hannen, Allan Aynesworth and Nigel Playfair–and the rest of us were not without experience, the production matured to opening pitch with a sort of concerted effort seemingly without guidance.

I was playing the Khan, who was an actor's dream. But he did

61

present a problem to me, as I had no notion of what accent he would have. Research on the subject conducted among the entire company, including Harwood, elicited nothing constructive. The stage manager, Stafford Hilliard, who was playing an Arab servant in the High Commissioner's household, was not helpful.

"The bugger I'm doing is going to talk just as if he comes from Earl's Court where I live."

Then I found that Archie Batty, who played the Commissioner's aide, had served with Allenby in Palestine. He was a regular, just retired from the Indian Army, and this was his first job in the theatre. He had known King Faisal in the war, and I got him to read some of my lines to me. He sounded pretty authentic although some tones were strangely reminiscent of the garment district of New York. I avoided this pitfall carefully and eventually Archie's impression of English as spoken by a cultured Arab received some small acclaim by the press. Some years later Alexander Korda cast me as Faisal in his projected film of the T. E. Lawrence story. He had remembered the Khan Aghaba. Unfortunately for me this picture was never made.

On the first night the Khan Aghaba walked away with the notices. Critics and first-nighters loved the serious theme but resisted the farcical side of the play, although the laughter was loud and genuine.

There is a wondrous thing about the theatre. The full satisfaction of acting is as complete in failure as in success. When you have worked hard for weeks of rehearsals, when you have belonged to a theatre "family" which has struggled to get a play on, and when you have faced an audience and done your best, that is all. It does not matter whether you close on Saturday night or run a year; you have had much of the joy the theatre can offer.

My next acting job came, as I had hoped, from *The Transit of Venus*. It was my first West End leading role and it was in another Harwood play called *The Golden Calf*. The two other principal parts were acted by Margaret Bannerman and Nicholas (Beau) Hannen. I played a Levantine financier with an acute sense of market value in stocks and feminine honour. It was a good acting part, but again the play failed. Ominously the critics attributed the failure to an outmoded theme and one of them actually dismissed the idea of a woman's honour as a valid issue in the scheme of a play.

The character I played in *The Golden Calf*, Reuben Manassa, required a make-up which took me nearly an hour to do. Being basically a character actor I have had many elaborate nose-putty and beard jobs

62

*R.M. as Reuben Manassa in H. M. Harwood's drama The Golden Calf, at the Globe Theatre, London, 1927.*

in my time but this was one of the most difficult I ever had to do. Some actors love making up. Laurence Olivier will give himself a new nose just for the hell of it but I just hate it. In *The Golden Calf* I had to mould a putty nose and apply a small trimmed beard. The year was 1928 and rubber noses and rubber make-up aids were far in the future. Every performance required a modelling job from scratch and time had to be allowed for failure and a fresh start.

About the third or fourth performance I was laying on the initial strip of putty when to my horror I seemed to have two noses and four hands all blurred together. I tried to tell my dresser to get me a brandy but I could not speak. My dresser was smart enough to call Beau Hannen who had the next dressing-room, and I was able to pantomime my desperate need of strong drink. Beau understood and I got a great slug of whisky down the hatch. I knew that alcohol dilates the blood vessels. Sure enough, in a few seconds I could speak, although the double vision persisted. Beau Hannen, God love him, although he never had to use make-up himself, being about the handsomest man in the theatre, put that nose in with his own inexperienced fingers. By the time it was powdered down I could see well enough to apply the beard and finish the job myself. I now had a splitting headache back of my eyes, but my brain seemed clear enough. I got through the performance pretty well, though the headache was awful.

Beau came into my room after the show. He had been watching me from the wings like an anxious mother.

"Have you ever had one of these attacks before?"

"No."

"Did your mother or father have them?"

I remembered mother having what she always called "sick headaches" when I was a little boy and I told Beau about them.

"This sounds as if you might be a migraine victim. You had better see a doctor. For God's sake, don't tell anyone in the theatre. It mustn't get around."

It did not. I saw a doctor the next morning who confirmed Beau's diagnosis. He gave me some pills and approved my therapeutic alcohol. I have had many attacks since. They have come at all times of the day. There is no accountable reason for their occurrence. In old age the attacks are much less severe and there is now no subsequent headache. These pills have always restored normal vision rapidly. But the menace of that frightening blurring of sight and the threat of that loss of speech at the Globe Theatre have stayed with me.

# 8

One of the first things I learned when I came to London in 1922 was that Gerald du Maurier and Gladys Cooper were the King and Queen of the English Theatre. I heard them so toasted in a pub opposite the Duke of York's Theatre on Charing Cross Road. Without a qualm of disloyalty to our lawful sovereigns, King George V and Queen Mary, I downed the remains of my half-pint of bitter in accord with this affectionate demonstration, no doubt prompted by the announcement of du Maurier's knighthood in the Birthday Honours list that morning. Honours were not lavishly bestowed on the acting profession at that time. When I resumed my search for a job that afternoon, I marvelled at the tribute which had just been paid to two leaders of what I hoped would soon be my profession. Next day I was lunched at the Garrick Club by an old friend of my brother's. We had a table for two next to another at which sat a solitary member.

"That's Gerald du Maurier," Vincent's friend confided. "He's a tremendous fellow in the theatre but I'm new here and I don't know him." I just looked at Sir Gerald from a six-foot distance.

Six years later my good friend Nigel (Willy) Bruce telephoned me to say that Gerald du Maurier wanted me to come up the following Sunday to Cannon Hall, his house in Hampstead, for tennis. I demurred. I had hoped for this meeting for years and did not want it messed up by a game I loathed. But Willy said he would look after me and I would fit in beautifully.

Cannon Hall was a lovely house, Sir Gerald and Lady du Maurier delightful, as were their three daughters (Daphne, just twenty, had yet to write her first novel), and the tennis was agony for me and everybody else. After du Maurier had extricated me from the tennis court with a couple of drinks, he guided me to a garden seat.

It was not for my tennis that I had been invited. Du Maurier had a question.

"What was the trouble with Dennis Eadie in that production of yours at the Royalty some months ago?"

I had directed a thriller called *The Crooked Billet* for Alec Rea with Dennis Eadie in the leading part. After a few rehearsals Eadie had been replaced by Leon Quartermaine. The incident had not gone un-noticed by the press. Eadie had died quite recently. He had been, with du Maurier, one of the last two active actor-managers in England.

"The press release was unfair to both of us," I said. "Eadie wrote it himself claiming he had withdrawn from the cast owing to a dis-agreement with the director."

"It certainly left the issue open to a variety of conclusions. What was the disagreement about? Rumour around the theatres had it that the issue was Eadie's performance."

"That was fact, not rumour," said I.

There was a pause. Sir Gerald spoke more slowly.

"I had hoped – I still do – that this new job of directing – or produc-ing, as we call it here – will not become too powerful for its own good or the good of the actor. I believe that the actor should be in com-mand of his own performance."

"I agree with you entirely. I am an actor before I am a director."

"I'm afraid we'll have that dictator type of domination here. And it is not for England."

"Sir Gerald," I said, "I dislike dictators as much as you do. How-ever, I believe the theatre must have some ultimate authority. The theatre is full of unprecedented, unique situations. I think in this instance the author, Dion Titheradge, topped the order of control. Remember *Bulldog Drummond*?" The play I referred to was a thriller by Sapper which du Maurier had produced and starred in.

"I recall the play and the part," he smiled. "The play ran for over a year just after the war."

"Titheradge had written a good run-of-the-mill thriller," I went on, "with a horrible collection of wicked scientists worse than your Drummond crew. It was made into entertainment by a light comedy detective – the same formula as the Drummond play. For this part, Alec Rea had cast Dennis Eadie."

"That seems a good choice. Eadie was a first-rate light comedian. He had a big range of talent."

"I daresay you won't believe this, but for five days of rehearsal Mr. Eadie deliberately ignored the comedy. He insisted on playing the role dead seriously – I mean dead. At first I thought he was feeling his way. But by the third or fourth day it was clear that he was going to unload the comedy. He even started to tinker with the script. Of course, I could have none of that, and Alec Rea replaced Mr. Eadie with Leon Quartermaine."

I added that a few weeks later I was invited by Mr. Eadie to direct his production of A. E. W. Mason's play, *The House of the Arrow*, in which he was to star. His untimely death intervened in these plans but Dennis Eadie's gracious offer closed an incident, painful to us both, in a professional manner which I will never forget.

We strolled back towards the tennis court. I wondered what impressions my remarks had left on du Maurier. Very soon I knew.

"Speaking of A. E. W. Mason reminds me about the King George Pension Matinée," he said. "It's due in about a month's time. Mason will be there as usual with the King. I'm doing Bulldog Drummond. Would you like to play the young American? It's not a long part but it's quite effective."

Like all actors, I had been called on for numerous charity shows. Charity leaned heavily on the theatre for support between the wars, but this would be my first time in one of the big so-called "command" performances. King George was not fond of the theatre. He paid his annual visit to his Actors Pension Fund Performance, grimly determined to do his duty in the best tradition of the senior service in which he had served with disctinction. Queen Mary, on the other hand, was stage-struck in her regal way, genuinely enchanted by the theatre.

Command performances were at that time revivals of full-length plays produced for one occasion only and inevitably under-rehearsed. Gerald du Maurier did dozens of them both as actor and director. It must have been agony for him, the most meticulous of actors, to take part in such untidy operations. They were forced on him. Usually, the shows squeaked by without incident and were forgotten. But not this performance of *Bulldog Drummond*.

Rehearsals had gone well. There were four of the original cast in the matinée production including Gilbert Hare, Alfred Drayton and Ronald Squire. Hare had retired from the theatre after the play had ended its long run and for five years he had been engaged in biochemical research at Cambridge. He now returned to the theatre to play his part of a wicked biochemist, Dr. Lakington, in the command matinée. He seemed very nervous.

We were to play at the Adelphi, a huge theatre in the Strand. As the young American millionaire kidnapped by the bad guys, I made my first entrance in the second act supposedly drugged to the extent of semi-consciousness and with my arms pinioned, led by the arch-villain, Dr. Lakington. I got myself trussed up by props and, a good five minutes before the cue, took my place by a scene door which opened onto the stage.

In the darkness I was relieved to see Mr. Hare – his luxuriant wig identified him – standing near the door. I thought to myself, What a professional! All ready for our entrance! As our cue came closer, I whispered, "Here I am, Mr. Hare." The figure turned and to my horror it wasn't Gilbert Hare, but a stagehand waiting to hand some props to him.

I rushed to the prompt corner and told the stage manager. The stage wait was the time it took to bring Hare from his dressing-room on the second floor. I suppose it was only two or three minutes, but in stage time it seemed eternity.

Edith Evans and Alfred Dayton were on stage. They had been warned of a delay. Back at the door I heard our cue. I was helpless. I felt like a traitor. I could do nothing without Hare. Through a peep-hole I watched Edith Evans keep things going in one of the most astonishing improvisations I have ever seen. She was playing a fake Russian countess, and she started off with a stream of Russian double-talk which so bewildered Drayton that he panicked and left the stage. Alone, she proceeded to toy most seductively with a long cigarette holder while softly humming snatches of "The Volga Boat Song." The audience apparently was in her hand. All, that is, but the Royal Patron of the Pension Fund. Just as the breathless and shattered Gilbert Hare was about to make his belated entrance, the Monarch's quarterdeck tones were clearly heard – "Mason, is this one of your damned, dramatic pauses?"

The King received Sir Gerald in his box in the second intermission, there was an ovation at the final curtain and it looked as if a good time had been had by all. I finally managed to get Sir Gerald alone in his dressing-room.

"I feel I'm partly responsible for Gilbert Hare's missed entrance. I should have verified who the man was with the hairdo that looked like Hare's. I'm damned sorry, sir."

"My dear fellow," was the reply, "you must not judge these special shows by the same standards as we apply to regular productions. Thank you for your help – I hope you'll do some more for me."

I knew Gerald for just five years. I worked with him only once in a regular production, when he directed me in a rather poor play in 1933. But I saw a good deal of him during those years and we became

68

close friends. Hearing Gerald talk of the theatre was one of the great privileges of my professional life.

It was a rare one too, for like most professional Englishmen of his generation (Gerald was fifty-seven when I first met him) he was reluctant to discuss his own vocation even with a fellow pro. I suppose my transatlantic proclivity to discuss a subject of common interest may have overcome the taboo against talking shop.

Anyway, we often talked openly about theatre, mostly at the Garrick Club where Gerald had proposed me as a member in 1928. For my friend, the theatre was an intensely personal matter. It was as an actor that Gerald du Maurier made theatrical history. Almost alone, and unwittingly, he inspired the revolution in English acting which took place in the 1920s.

Even before the First World War Gerald had evolved for himself a new low-keyed style of acting because, as he told me once over lunch, "I couldn't do some of the plays–realistic plays, like *Alias Jimmy Valentine, Raffles*–Good Lord! *Drummond* if you like–*The Dancers, The Ware Case*–in that declamatory style which everybody had been using since David Garrick. I had to find another way."

Even in Edwardian days that seemingly simple, easy manner had been developed, a style critics admired and accepted as Gerald du Maurier's own. "Relaxed," "casual," "light," "engaging," "natural," "realistic," "smooth," "easy," were adjectives trotted out annually. They took no account of the painstaking effort which had produced the apparent spontaneity of his performance.

All through the twenties the theatre in England was undergoing an important change. Stylized, mannered plays were giving way to realistic dramas and comedies, and actors had to make some adjustments in their acting style. For older and more experienced players, this was not difficult. But many of the young ones, principally men, adopted the new naturalistic playing as a cult, like the long hair of their grandsons. They sometimes dropped all pretence of diction. They threw lines away in mumbling inaudibility and conducted themselves much in the manner of some of the "Method" actors thirty years later in America.

These incidents were few and mostly in rehearsal when directors were able to keep them in check. The public knew little about them. But the fact was that inaudibility, practically unknown in the Edwardian theatre, was now present, a result of the pursuit of naturalism by actors who lacked the technique for it. The sad truth is that this acting offence is still often with us in the English-speaking theatre.

These rebels, some of them untrained but others with ample experience, ironically claimed du Maurier as their leader—much to the dismay of that gentle conservative. Despite this embarrassment, Gerald remained the pattern of English acting of any school or mode.

Most of the acting profession thought of Gerald du Maurier as the perfect examplar of spontaneity and instinctive reactions. But those who knew him and his work recognized that the smooth naturalness of his performances came from laborious preparation. He told me that he sometimes rehearsed ordinary bits of business, such as lighting a cigarette or mixing a drink, at home in front of a long mirror for hours at a time. "Little things like that don't come easily to me," he said.

To quite a few of us it was reassuring to know that there were things that did not come too easily for the best player in our profession.

Clubs flourished in England between the wars, and two of them—the Garrick and the Green Room—played important parts in the lives of actors and theatre men. The Garrick had been founded in the 1840s with the declared purpose of allowing actors to meet gentlemen. Eighty years later this laudable intent was still in practice although most of the actors to be submitted to gracious society seemed to be of fairly advanced maturity. Gerald du Maurier proposed Willie Bruce and me for membership in 1928 and we were the youngest members of the club at that time. Neither of us used it at first unless we were sure that Gerald would be there, when we would brazenly walk straight to his table in the dining-room.

Some of the most pleasant hours of my London years were spent at the Garrick. I always found it fascinating and on occasion enchanting. The building is a beautiful example of early Victorian architecture, exactly as it was when the club moved there in 1862. Since it was founded, practically every great actor of the English stage, the actor-managers who ran the theatre, the great dramatists who wrote the plays, have all been members of the Garrick, along with many of the leaders of arts and letters and the bar. There has always been a great feeling for the past, and a sense of history.

The English actors who visited Toronto during my boyhood days, like Forbes-Robertson, Martin Harvey, Cyril Maude, were great heroes to me. Just after I was elected to the club in 1928, Sir Johnston Forbes-Robertson came to see *The Constant Nymph* in which his daughter Jean and I were playing our first leading roles. The old gentleman came backstage after the show, one of the great moments of my life.

Soon after that, there was a supper in his honour at the Garrick and of course I went. Gerald du Maurier presided. It was an impressive affair. The dining-room was packed and there were many fine speeches, witty and affectionate. Finally Sir Johnston rose to make his remarks. I still think that even at eighty he had the most beautiful voice ever heard in the theatre, a voice with the quality of a violoncello. He spoke well without notes, describing many amusing or moving incidents in his life, and in his peroration referred to the lovely ladies with whom he had had the privilege of acting, mentioning four or five of them by name. "How those dear names crowd in upon me!" he said, citing Mary Anderson, Madame Modjeska, Kate Rourke, Mrs. Patrick Campbell, Genevieve Ward. "And last but, oh, not least," he concluded, "the lovely lady who has been my inspiration and my comrade in so many theatre ventures, my dear wife— eh—" But this name did not crowd in upon Sir Johnston. The tall, noble figure stood straighter than ever, surprise on his face. There was silence as we waited. Was this magical occasion to fizzle out with a missed cue? No. With perfect timing, from the other end of the long table came the gentle prompt from Gerald du Maurier: "Easy does it, Forbie—Gertrude Elliott!" Sir Johnston's surprise turned into a smile. All of us stood and cheered. I understood Sir Johnston's predicament. I have had trouble remembering names all my life. I once forgot my brother's given name—forgot it in public!

# 9

In the twenties and thirties when I was working in England I kept in close touch with the American stage, read all the Broadway news and reviews I could find in London papers and even made short trips to New York to see plays. Broadway had become almost as familiar as the London West End before I got my first American job.

I often wondered why there weren't more producer-directors in England. There were a great many in America–David Belasco, Sam Harris, Arthur Hopkins and many others who combined producing and directing. But in England the only one I knew was Basil Dean. He never worked in the United States, as far as I know, but his methods were much like those of American directors I knew later. Basil Dean gave the leadership to his productions which I believe is the prime duty of any manager.

The trouble with the London theatre between the two world wars was managerial incompetence. True, there were some excellent managers active in London in those years: C. B. Cochran–there was never a better producer than Cocky–Basil Dean, Alec Rea, Gerald du Maurier, H. M. Harwood, Gladys Cooper, Sybil Thorndike. There were more, but there were never enough. There were also, however, a number of time-serving lease-holders concerned only with profitable occupancy of their theatres. These so-called managers totally lacked the initiative, imagination and leadership essential to theatrical production. Only too often the play chosen by this type of manager reflected nothing more than a timid attempt to anticipate public taste.

By 1928 Basil Dean had become the ablest English director. After the war he had five successful years at St. Martin's Theatre in managerial partnership with that amiable theatrical angel, Alec Rea. This management had a record of productions which included *R.U.R.*, all the later Galsworthy plays and, in truth, was unique in the contemporary theatre. The Basil Dean list of plays directed outside St. Martin's management had been equally impressive. In some of these ventures Dean had assumed managerial duties as well.

I was awed when Dean engaged me to work under his direction in an American play by S. N. Behrman called *The Second Man*. It was a witty, cynical comedy, with a cast of four: Noel Coward, Zena Dare, Ursula Jeans and myself.

Instead of the eternal triangle, life in Behrman's play was presented as a quadrangle, or rather a quadrilateral, though with the two women each stalking one man at a time, it threatened to revert to the conventional threesome.

The numerical balance of the play was complicated by a confession made by Noel, playing a second-rate literary adventurer. There was in him, to quote from a letter of Lord Leighton, "another strange second man, calm, critical, observant, unmoved, blasé and odious, who constantly interfered in his emotional life."

As the other male in the quartet, I also had an alter ego. So in a way Noel and I doubled. My substantive character was a wealthy gentleman, a humourless scientist, and my "second man" was a violent romantic. Zena and Ursula did not have these complications but they were spirited players of Behrman's mixed doubles.

Rehearsals were bumpy, particularly the early ones. *The Second Man* was not just another job for any of us. Noel Coward had just suffered two serious setbacks as an author in the failure of two plays: *Home Chat* and *Sirocco*. The opening night of the latter had been the occasion for a battle between Noel's partisans and those who resented his dazzling success as actor, playwright and composer.

I will never forget the first night of *Sirocco*. I sat on the steps of the dress circle during the second act and saw three different fist fights. The second interval was tumultuous and the last act pandemonium. At the final curtain it was impossible to distinguish catcalls from cheers. The stage manager assessed the din on the plus side and raised the curtain for a call. This only increased the noise and the curtain fell. About four or five curtains had been taken in this manner when Basil Dean, who never saw his own first nights and had been in a nearby restaurant waiting for the curtain, entered the theatre by the stage-door. He made the same judgement of the uproar as the stage manager had and came onstage to take a call himself. He was not able to speak at all but he went upstage, grasped the hand of Frances Doble, who was playing the lead, and led her down to the footlights. Basil held up his hand and miraculously there was silence. Miss Doble made an immortal comment: "This is the happiest moment of my life."

They mercifully kept the curtain down after that.

I found Noel sitting in his box with a rather sad smile on his face. "Isn't it charming?" he said. "Such enthusiasm."

After *Sirocco*, the critics almost unanimously decided that Noel Coward was now washed up as a writer.

He had seriously considered a temporary retreat from the theatre in all his capacities. But Basil Dean, somewhat battle-scarred himself from *Sirocco*, would have none of this.

Zena Dare as Kendall Frayne, the rich and charming widow of *The Second Man*, was making a timorous return to the stage after eighteen years of retirement following a decade as an Edwardian queen of musical comedy. Ursula Jeans, with much talent and little experience, faced her first important West End role as the spirited flapper, Monica Grey. As for me, I was trying something I had not attempted before in the role of Austin Lowe. Each of us had an awful lot riding on that play. As none of us could be classed as placid types, the tension at the early rehearsals was just short of the snapping point.

Noel turned up at the first rehearsal word perfect in the part of the writer, Clark Storey. He ostentatiously closed his script as he sat down at a table for the first reading, always an uncomfortable experience for me as an actor. I am a slow study but I have found out it is best for me to learn my lines after my initial attempt to read them at rehearsal. As a director I had observed that most actors tackle a part the same way, and I had always encouraged it. But Noel was substantially at first-night pitch at that first reading. I was certain I would be fired.

Basil Dean put us on our feet that afternoon. He seemed rather dictatorial but he certainly knew what he wanted. Before we quit, he had plotted out the whole first act for moves, and the next day we dealt with the second act in the same mechanical fashion. There was no thought of performance and even Noel was no longer sparkling. Featherweight comedy seemed leaden chatter while we marked down crosses and rises and sits in our scripts.

There was one scene between Noel and me in the last act which I knew at once would be difficult. It was a quarrel over the usual thing men quarrel about. The gentle scientist was to give place to the emotional romantic who, spurred by primitive jealousy and a glass or two of champagne, takes a potshot at the second-rate writer. The scene came perilously close to farce and could be kept within the bounds of

*Noel Coward, R.M. and Ursula Jeans in The Second Man by S. N. Behrman, at the Playhouse, London, 1928.*

legitimate comedy, it seemed to me, only if my part were acted with simple sincerity.

When we came to this scene in the process of mapping out our moves, it seemed more formidable than ever. Then I heard Basil say almost confidentially, "Remember, the man is drunk in this scene. Don't underplay it." I was shocked. But I wanted very much to play Austin and I did not like the thought of being fired. So I told Basil my misgiving about the danger of farce. He made it clear that it was what he wanted; I put off the showdown and cooperated.

After some ten days of rehearsal, my performance satisfied Basil but embarrassed me painfully. Behrman arrived from New York and although we were quite unready for the ordeal, Basil decided to show the author a run-through.

The essence of comedy acting is timing. Timing is not only an individual accomplishment, it is a good measure of coordination, which can only be perfected in rehearsal and finally with the help of an audience. The first time any cast is put through its paces from rise to fall, with the director, who is also the producer, and the author out front, is an ordeal for everybody concerned. When the play is a comedy, it is agony, for proper timing will not have been established at that point.

This run-through was the most painful I can remember. The complete silence in the stalls continued through the first two acts. In the short interval, Noel reported that both Basil and Sam Behrman were still alive and apparently breathing. In a few minutes the stage manager said, "All right, third act."

This started with what everybody now referred to as "the drunk scene." I took a deep breath and made my entrance as if straight from skid row. I was now determined that either the drunk performance or I would go. We had played about a quarter of the scene when we heard audible evidence of life out front. I stopped, as did Noel. Behrman came through loud and clear. "This is awful—the man is not drunk."

"I quite agree," said Basil.

"And I quite agree," said I.

I stood there waiting for the thud of the axe, but there was no thud. Instead, Basil said, "We'll work on this scene this afternoon. Now go on from the end of it."

I decided to push my luck. "Can we start the act again and let me play it straight?"

There was no applause from the two out front. But when we broke for lunch, Basil grinned, "We'll do it your way."

*The Second Man* fulfilled all our hopes. It was a delight to act and the success of the play was a reassuring reward for the apprehensive four who had faced that first-night audience. In these days of try-outs and previews it is hard to believe that we opened "cold" at the Playhouse. Our opening performance was the first time we had acted the play before an audience of any kind. Since the actor gets his final lessons in timing from audience reactions, we were, in effect, attending school and graduating at the same time. In any event, the opening was a stunning success. One critic said, "All plays should have a cast of four. No more and no less!"

We did have fun for the first five months we played *The Second Man*. It was the only time I ever acted with Noel, although we were close friends. He was Godfather to my son Daniel. After Noel's crushing defeats as the author of *Home Chat* and *Sirocco*, the press went overboard to extol his performance in the *The Second Man*.

I was the sole witness of a well-known incident in Noel's dressing-room after the second performance. An obnoxious fellow named Hannen Swaffer entered unannounced. A critic and theatre writer on *The Daily Express*, he had been insufferable in his abuse of Noel (and of me too). As usual, he was wearing a large black hat, black satin stock and cape liberally sprinkled with dandruff. "Nowley," he sneered in his assumed cockney accent, "I've always said you could act better than you write."

"And I've always said the same about you," was the instant reply.

Apparently Basil bore no rancour against me for our disagreement in rehearsal, for a few months after *The Second Man* closed he rang me to ask if I would play Lewis Dodd in the revival of *The Constant Nymph* which he was going to do at the Garrick Theatre. Just two years previously the play had ended a run of nearly six hundred performances at the New Theatre. Noel Coward had played Lewis Dodd for three weeks, and for the long pull the role had been acted by a young John Gielgud. Each had scored heavily in performances which, differing considerably, had literally taken possession of the character. I'd seen both and watched Edna Best in her beautiful performance.

Basil had collaborated with Margaret Kennedy in writing the stage adaptation of her novel and had produced and directed the play. On all accounts, it had been his greatest achievement to date. When he asked me to play Lewis in the revival, I naturally had misgivings.

Noel gave me the strongest possible advice to reject the offer.

"Basil is co-author and he will give you far more trouble in rehearsals of Lewis Dodd than you had with *The Second Man.* I've played the part and I know. Lewis Dodd is a bastard and inevitably you will try to put some charm into him. I can see Basil's face when you try to do that!"

Noel could be excessively vehement when giving advice. I remember once in my house he reduced Gertie Lawrence to tears when he heard she was contemplating an English movie. The gist of his advice was that her talents were not suited to the movie medium. I had to ask him to go home. The wretched woman was in a state of shock. As far as Lewis Dodd was concerned, Noel was wrong, at least half wrong. Basil convinced me that he was putting on the play again because he wanted fresh performances in the two leading parts and expected me to play Lewis Dodd the way he and I would determine in rehearsal.

I had no difficulty in deciding to accept the offer. I would have been mad not to have done so. Dodd was the most difficult and interesting part I had been asked to play up to that time – and anyway "caution" is not a theatre word.

Basil's choice for the role in the revival was Jean Forbes-Robertson, Sir Johnston's youngest daughter. The director was determined to have a new Tessa who would not try to challenge the memory of Edna Best. Jean's was a more serious, a more intellectual, a more sophisticated Tessa than Edna's, though she had her human moments too. Jean had an ethereal quality. She would be vastly different from the very human, touching schoolgirl Edna had made her own in the original production.

Florence Churchill, Dodd's wife, had been played by Cathleen Nesbitt and was now to be performed by Frances Doble. There would be more emotion and less edge from Frances – I could see that. A discovery was made when Basil cast a former schoolteacher named Madeline Carroll as Paulina Sanger. She was a most beautiful young creature who, after this engaging stage debut, went off to films which she adorned for years.

I had a relatively peaceful time working out my Lewis Dodd. As Noel had prophesied, I did try to make the character a bit more likable. Basil's face did not glower, it glowed; he seemed to welcome a kindlier streak in Dodd.

Acting with Jean, I thought she was transcendent. She was not easy-going: she disagreed quite a bit with Basil Dean in rehearsal.

The revival justified itself. We ran our limited eight weeks and almost all our notices were extraordinarily good. Ivor Brown explained it best in his notice:

The new *Constant Nymph* is new, indeed. I never saw Dodd I, who was Mr. Noel Coward. Dodd II, Mr. John Gielgud, showed genius, harsh and livid. Dodd III, Mr. Raymond Massey, brings an amiable waywardness. It is the rough wind which shakes the darling bud which is Tessa, it is not an east wind but a wild, rough, westerly caress. He has tenderness as well as abruptness with the result that his being so loved is more credible and his conduct at the party less unnatural. Miss Jean Forbes-Robertson, Tessa, assists in this lifting of the play, for she, as we know, acts in an unterrestrial way, and we suddenly see how right the word "nymph" has become.

Many plays I have acted in remain in my memory in the person of the character I played. These images are quite distinct from myself. Their visitations vary in frequency. Some are close friends. Some are mere acquaintances. A few remain strangers whom I never really knew, once embarrassing to me and hostile. Now I find them faintly amusing. One thing is clear, they do not leave me. I do not forget them and I do not regret them.

One of the most persistent of these strangers is the preposterous Randolph Calthorpe, leading character in a play called *The Black Ace* which was offered to me in early 1929. It was a terrible play—and my first impulse was to turn it down. I had just had a fabulously lucky year with four leads as an actor and five directing jobs. I could be choosy—indeed I really could not afford not to be. And apart from the play itself, the credentials of the offer were good. It was to be directed by Basil Dean, then at the peak of his career. The manager was Sir Alfred Butt, a highly successful producer and hard-headed theatre man. The play would get a first-rate production. The author, Dorothy Brandon, already had one hit to her credit (*The Outsider*), and her collaborator was Negley Farson, an American journalist of some repute.

But there remained the script. I could not imagine what had induced Basil Dean and Alfred Butt to touch it. Both men were far too firmly established to act as figureheads in any adventure. They had reputations to protect as well as solid financial interests. It was all very puzzling.

Whenever a drama critic wants to damn a play, he gives a capsule version of the theme or the plot. No play, good or bad, can stand up to a summary of what it is about, least of all *The Black Ace*. Its premise that Negroes do not like being black was an erroneous assumption even back in 1929. Reviewers could not resist summarizing the plot, more or less as follows.

In a spirited prologue, an old French scientist, at Berebe on the Gold Coast, is about to inject a Negro with a serum that will change his skin from black to white. The black guinea-pig, a deserter from the Foreign Legion, has been rescued from a firing squad by the scientist. As the needle is inserted, number 22, as he is called, declares, "Make me white and make me free!"

When we next see number 22, he is Randolph Calthorpe, a shining member of the English bar and Oxford graduate – in fact, a graduate of my old college, Balliol. He is in Alabama visiting Colonel Warrington's plantation, a beautiful, white-columned house surrounded by live oak and magnolia. There is a large black plantation staff who constantly break into the harmonious rendition of spirituals. With Calthorpe is a young Englishman, an erstwhile buddy of Foreign Legion days, who does not recognize number 22 without his black pigment. Both are courting the beauteous and very white daughter of the Colonel. She favours the young Englishman.

All goes smoothly until the end of the first act, when the old French scientist arrives and warns the Colonel that one of his English visitors is a Negro and may turn black at any minute. (The serum has proved to be unstable in its effect.) The scientist has a fatal heart attack before he can disclose which of the two will find black patches on his chest. In those modest days this was an area of the body not generally exposed in public.

There follows an astonishing succession of melodramatic improbabilities. News is out that there is a white nigger in the Colonel's house. The Ku Klux Klan is aroused. Both the Black Ace and his fellow visitor are suspect. The Black Ace at first resolves to let his friend be sacrificed. His friend fails to pass the test of a voodoo trial.

But in the end our hero's noble conscience will not let him betray his innocent rival. He bares his darkening chest to the assembled multitude and goes out to meet the bullets of the K.K.K. At all events there are a lot of shots and spirituals and a loudly-voiced theory that "he's swimming the river."

The bare facts of the plot were not helped by the dialogue. A few gems were quoted by one critic: "When I hear the love call, I shall follow it, even to the ends of the world"; "This house has got hold of my heart like two old, worn and beloved hands"; and "Can't you see his beautiful, white soul looking out from his black body like a Star of

Bethlehem on Christmas Eve?'' These lines were delivered by a courageous and highly talented young American actress named Carol Goodner, who was making her London debut in this play. Her wonderful sense of humour added much to their effectiveness. The effort to suppress a giggle would bring tears to her lovely eyes and when she spoke of the Star of Bethlehem, the laughter would burst through as the most enchanting of sobs. Her successful years in London were assured.

James Carew, who played Colonel Warrington, was also American and shared Carol's weak tearducts and sense of fun. Watching these two rehearse, I saw that we were all sitting on a powderkeg of burlesque. I caught Basil Dean after he had been struggling with a particularly horrible scene of mine, and suggested that we might be missing a bet by playing the thing straight instead of as farce. He just gave me his frightening, toothy smile and asked if I wanted to be fired.

Probably I was wrong. Nothing could have saved this script; but years later when I was playing Jonathan Brewster in the movie of *Arsenic and Old Lace*, I kept thinking that Jonathan and Randolph Calthorpe had something in common. After all, it was a widely held belief that *Arsenic* had started life as a serious script about euthanasia.

The critics murdered *The Black Ace* but the first-night audience gave us a rapturous reception, possibly in recognition of our bravery in facing them. In any event, our courage was not required for long and *The Black Ace* passed into oblivion as soon as the closing notice could be typed.

In spite of the disaster, I won some of the best acting notices I had ever received. Embarrassment did not last long. In a few weeks I could go into the Garrick or the Green Room without being asked about the dark spots on my chest. Randolph Calthorpe has become quite a friendly ghost after fifty years. But I never want to be seen in public with him.

# *10*

Late one night in September 1929 I found a large envelope when I got home from rehearsing a play I was directing, a romantic comedy by Ivor Novello. It had been a long day. Ivor, who was playing the lead, liked to rehearse at night, and I was nearly asleep on my feet. I was about to fix myself a drink when I gave the envelope a double take. It bore the magic name of C. B. Cochran. I tore it open.

I could scarcely believe my eyes. The envelope contained the script *The Silver Tassie*, the new play by Sean O'Casey. In a short note, Cochran asked me to read the play with a view to directing it. It was to open in about six weeks. Suddenly I was not sleepy at all. This was an offer from England's greatest showman to stage the newest play by the astonishing dramatist from the Abbey Theatre.

O'Casey's *Juno and the Paycock* and *The Plough and the Stars* had both been shown successfully in London; at the Everyman we had presented *Juno* for a few weeks after its London run, with Arthur Sinclair, Sara Allgood and Maire O'Neill. *The Silver Tassie* was something of a mystery. It was known that the Abbey Theatre people, in particular W. B. Yeats, had rejected it for production. Nobody knew why. The Abbey had announced that the play had been returned to the author for "revision," a weasling statement, as I was soon to learn, that had infuriated O'Casey.

But what did all this matter? Here was the new play in my hands and it was only midnight. I read it and then I read it again, and went to bed to lie awake, wondering how on earth it could be staged.

Of course I would take on the job. But the play presented problems of staging that I had never met before. I called Cochran at his home and told him I would direct the play. He asked me to come to his office at 49 Old Bond Street. On the way I thought, as I have so often after making a decision, what a fool I had been. Here was a play in four acts with no consistency of mood or style, unaccountable changes of character, and riddled with irreligious and sometimes blasphemous matter. It was a bitter anti-war outburst, unreasoned and prejudiced. It was, as O'Casey would say himself, a new type of play which would burst the bonds of the conventional theatre, a play of mood, plotless and formless.

*The Silver Tassie* had almost baffled me at my second reading. The first act appeared to be realistic, although there were symbolic intrusions such as a chanting crowd offstage, as if O'Casey were preparing his audience for the outright expressionism of the second act. Three soldiers on leave from the front are celebrating the victory of a Dublin football team in which the hero of the play, Harry Heegan, has scored the winning goal. Through most of the act the second soldier, Teddy Foran, is heard in the tenement above in furious battle with his wife. The third soldier is trying to capture the attentions of Jessie, Harry's chosen colleen. There is a sort of chorus of two comic old O'Casey reprobates who at first glance seem quite disconnected from the main theme, but are in fact a vital part of it. A number of vividly drawn Dublin slum types also seem extraneous but are nevertheless essential to O'Casey's theme. A battling wife, a religious fanatic and several other vivid characters appear in this puzzling act which ends with a woman's ironic sigh of relief as the three men leave for the front: "Thanks be to Christ that we're after managin' to get them away safely!"

The second act is outright expressionism, a fantastic and ferocious satire on the war, and mostly in verse to be chanted. Although the three soldiers from the first act appear in this scene, all the characters are ciphers and have no connection with the rest of the play. At first reading this act appeared to be parenthetical. I realized that the integration of this scene into the play as a whole would be one of the chief problems in directing it.

In the third and fourth acts the author returns to apparent realism, though they are anything but realistic. This mixture of poetry, symbolism and riotously funny Irish comedy is not for tidy minds.

Calm, confident and dapper as always, Cochran greeted me with something of the air of a French aristocrat addressing another as they climb into the tumbril. He introduced the author, who at once informed me in his soft Dublin brogue that he could be of no help to me in that second act. Cochran smiled. I confessed I was still in a state of shock from my initial encounter with the play. I really was not prepared to discuss the problems. Cochran smiled again. He looked at a calendar on his desk. "I would like to open at the Apollo six weeks from tomorrow night," he said. I rather liked to work under pressure and admitted I could be ready. "So all right," said Cochran, "let us

*"The Silver Tassie"*

*The second act of The Silver Tassie as designed by Augustus John, at the Apollo Theatre, London, 1929.*

talk of scenery." I loved him for using the word "scenery." It was frowned upon in the 1920s as belonging to the dead days of Irving and Mansfield, the latter having been managed by Cochran. The modish terms were "settings" and "designs." But Cocky was a theatre man, a showman, and it would always be "scenery" to him.

He went on, "I have made two commitments for designers before sending for you, Ray, and I hope you will agree. Sean has a great desire to have Augustus John design the second act scene and I have secured his agreement to do it."

Of course I was delighted. But the thought of this tempestuous genius working in the theatre gave me a shock. I asked if John had ever worked in the theatre. Sean said no. I murmured that the six weeks had already become considerably shorter. Cocky asked me when I could talk to John about ground plans and the like. I said, "Tomorrow morning. Who's going to do the other three acts?"

"Gladys Calthrop," he told me.

This pleased me. Gladys had designed many of Noel Coward's plays and I knew her versatility would be equal to the job. I made one request, which Cocky instantly granted: that Alick Johnstone, the scene painter, and Ted Loveday, the scene builder, be engaged. For the second act I had a premonition that these, the best men in the scenery field, might be needed.

The music then came up for discussion. Sean said the chants and songs had all been arranged by Martin Shaw, who had written the music for *Mr. Pepys* and *Brer Rabbit*. This too was perfect. Martin was a patient and effective teacher. It was essential that the war scene be cast with careful regard to the musical capability of chanting plainsong in the Gregorian manner. Both Cochran and the author agreed. The chanting was to be as musically perfect as in a cathedral choir. Thanks to Martin Shaw, that was the standard we eventually achieved.

We talked about casting. Arthur Sinclair was an obvious choice for Sylvester Heegan, the number one old comic reprobate, but O'Casey said he had a better idea—an Abbey Theatre actor named Barry Fitzgerald. O'Casey said he had had Fitzgerald in mind when writing Sylvester. That is how Barry Fitzgerald started his professional career with the great Hollywood success waiting for him. The Abbey Theatre was semi-professional and most of the cast held part-time jobs. Barry, I think, worked in the post office. Sidney Morgan would be the other comic. We cast other parts at that meeting and scripts were sent to Ian Hunter, Beatrix Lehmann, Una O'Connor and several others.

85

They all accepted. Charles Laughton would play the role of Harry Heegan.

Cochran arranged for me to see Augustus John at his studio the following morning. I was also to see Gladys Calthrop about the three other scenes and have a session with Martin Shaw about the music. Since I wanted to talk a great deal more with O'Casey, I took him off to lunch at the Ivy.

I asked him about the inconsistencies and inaccuracies as to the war. Were they, as I assumed, intentional? This question raised his ire. I told him that his would be the fifth war play I would have directed in the past few years. It was, however, the first which was in a symbolic or expressionistic form; the others had demanded complete authenticity. Sean with obvious anger said that of course the flouting of authenticity was intentional. It was done for dramatic or satirical effect. The character switch in the role of Susie—a religious fanatic in the first act and in the final two acts a gay party girl—was justified by the play's development.

O'Casey made it quite clear that he was dramatizing the war exclusively from the Tommies' viewpoint. He knew he was being grossly unfair to all other ranks and, indeed, to civilians. His farcically inane staff officer, the asinine visitor, and the surgeon of the last two acts were all fantasies of real characters, projected in the private soldier's prejudices. They provided comic relief. In the sweep of the expressionistic scene such distortions would be accepted. He would stay with his play as written.

Although O'Casey said nothing about the Abbey Theatre's rejection of his play, it was clear that he had been deeply hurt by it. What had galled him was the accusation that he did not know the realities of war and the soldier. W. B. Yeats, on behalf of the Abbey Theatre, had written him a letter of rejection, which O'Casey would quote in his autobiography *Rose and Crown*: "You are not interested in the Great War; you never stood on its battlefields, never walked its hospitals, and so write out of your opinion. You illustrate these opinions by a series of almost unrelated scenes, as you might in a leading article."

"Oh, God," O'Casey would comment, "here was a man who had never spoken to a Tommy in his life chattering to me who had talked to them all, infantry, cavalry and artillery...." As for me, I was soon aware that Sean O'Casey had a knowledge of the war and the soldier that few civilians have had.

I had not learned much about expressionistic theatre after my lunch with O'Casey, but I certainly knew that there was no room in it for balanced opinion. It was all out and no holds barred. I read and reread the second act, and each time it became clearer to me that O'Casey was right, that there could be no compromise with reason. The emotional range was supreme and the act was no interpolation but the core and substance of the play.

I was still in the throes of directing the Ivor Novello comedy, and *The Silver Tassie* had to wait its turn. The conflict of two productions overlapping was not as difficult as it might seem. The Novello play had an excellent cast and was in good shape for a four-week try-out in Manchester before the O'Casey play started regular rehearsals. Barring one or two visits to Ivor's play I could still find time for the *Tassie*. Not that it was easy.

Augustus John did not mind early hours, so I was at his studio on Mallord Street bright and early. I had hoped to find him with an open mind about the scene and I was a little surprised to find not only an open mind but a blank one. I had never met Augustus John before. He seemed to me distracted if not actually nervous. We talked about the scene in question but I did not get anything out of him.

O'Casey's delineation of the setting, running to more than a page of script, went far beyond the brief indications usually made by playwrights. It was obvious that John felt hampered and frustrated by the mass of detail. Suddenly he went to a cabinet with wide shallow drawers and took out some large charcoal drawings which he said were part of the collection of sketches he had made at the war front for the Canadian government. I had seen some of them on exhibition in London a few years before and thought then that John had succeeded in revealing the horror of trench warfare more effectively than any other artist. Most of the drawings he showed me now were of ruins, shell holes, wrecked equipment, wire, mud, desolation and destruction. He had concentrated on inanimate objects rather than man. John put one particularly stunning drawing on the top of the pile. "That one is vaguely like it, perhaps?"

It was, indeed. There was the ruined wall of a chapel with the window at the right and a broken archway to the left. That was about the only resemblance to O'Casey's description, but the effect of the drawing was remarkably close to what the script called for.

John looked relieved.

I said, "If you agree, I would like to raise this whole mass stage right and have a ramp coming down to right centre to bring on the group of soldiers at the beginning of the act." I asked for a pencil to show him roughly what I had in mind. I had made some ineffective strokes when I burst out laughing and threw the pencil down.

"Why do you laugh?" John said.

"I just remembered my old drawing teacher, Ernie Casselman, rapping me over the knuckles and saying, '*Dumkopf*, never will you draw a line that means anything.' And here I am trying to explain something with a pencil to the greatest living draughtsman!"

John looked at my effort and said, "Mr. Casselman was not right – I can see what you mean."

He took five minutes to draw a rough pencil elevation of the scene. "Does that meet your requirements?"

"Yes," I said, "and the gun would be here." I pointed to the centre of the drawing.

"Oh, I'd forgotten the gun. What will we do about that?"

I thought it should be a howitzer, a big, squat, toad-like gun. John agreed. He also liked my suggestion that the gun should increase in size in all three dimensions as the act proceeds. "I would like to see a six-inch how gradually become a twelve-inch," I said.

"That's fine, but how do you draw a growing gun?"

"Mr. John, draw the big one and let me and the carpenter and painter work out how it grows."

John promised to finish a fully detailed and coloured sketch of the scene in two days. I said I would like to bring along the scene painter, Alick Johnstone, when I came to the studio to see it. We set a time.

I had a feeling that Augustus John was not at ease in the theatre medium. I wanted to have Alick Johnstone thoroughly prepared to take over the "staging" of the sketch. I knew Alick would be perfectly able to put Augustus John's five-minute pencil drawing on the stage, even without the promised sketch.

When I returned with Alick Johnstone, John seemed worried as ever but he had made two big sketches, one rather more detailed than the other. Both were superb. Frightening, grizzly and jagged, O'Casey's scene was there in both the sketches. Alick was tongue-tied, awed by the great artist.

I told John I preferred the simpler design. In both the sketches the window was merely a vague concentration of colour. It was to be a figure of the Virgin and it was agreed that John would paint it himself at Alick's studio when the scenery was delivered there by the builder.

John was reluctant to let one of the sketches out of his hands, claiming that they were not finished. I insisted, pointed out that he still would have the second sketch. I was about to offer our help in preparing the scale drawings. "Don't worry," he growled, "I'll have your damn plans ready for you – just give me a few days."

Off we went to 49 Old Bond Street with the big sketch. I told Alick he had better be ready to make a model. I felt pretty sure we would get nothing more from Augustus John.

Cochran was delighted with the sketch. I suggested that we tell Alick Johnstone to go ahead with the model, and that we proceed with the job without waiting for John. As always, Cochran was wise and unflappable.

"We must be patient with John. The theatre is strange to him. And remember, we haven't anyone to paint that stained-glass window," he said.

"And what about the crucifix?" I asked. "He's forgotten to put it in the sketch."

"He is not a sculptor. We'll get Frank Dobson to do it."

Dobson was one of the best sculptors in England and Cochran commissioned him by telephone.

"Cocky, you wouldn't fire me if I did get Alick and Ted Loveday going on this sketch? We have precious little time, as it is, without waiting for John."

"I'll fire you if you don't."

Rehearsals for the first week were smooth. Expressionistic plays were not easy for English actors, accustomed to realism. But I had a first-rate cast who were afraid of nothing.

The Gregorian chanters of the war scene, self-dubbed "Cochran's choir," rapidly became expert in plainsong, to the delight of Martin Shaw. The same group eagerly accepted the stylized movements and groupings which we devised.

Some parts still remained to be cast. I had expected a plethora of beauty from the Cochran office from which to choose a Jessie, the lovely colleen who deserts the paralyzed Harry Heegan for his lusty rescuer. But Cocky's casting facilities presented nobody for the first couple of days of rehearsal. Lunching at the Ivy restaurant the third day I saw a lovely girl at a nearby table and without hesitation sent her a note: "Are you an actress? Raymond Massey." She scribbled an answer: "I'm not sure but I think I am." It was signed "Binnie Barnes." She was rehearsing in the *Tassie* that afternoon. So started a bright, fruitful career on the stage and in pictures in Hollywood and England. She had been a nightclub crooner with a husky, Broadway voice, though she was English. But she did not want to sing; she wanted to act. And act she did, in dozens of Hollywood movies. Binnie Barnes has been for many years the wife of the eminent Hollywood producer Mike Frankovich.

That same afternoon a young Welshman, newly down from Oxford, wandered into rehearsal and asked if anything was open. After a brief conversation, Emlyn Williams joined our company as the messenger in the second act. So, with Barry Fitzgerald, Binnie Barnes and Emlyn Williams, three fine careers virtually started with *The Silver Tassie.*

About the end of the first week Cochran reported that Augustus John was away from home. Three days later Alick Johnstone was ready with a model of the war scene. It delighted the company, O'Casey and Cochran. There was an ominous empty space where the stained-glass window should be.

Gladys Calthrop's sets were also well in hand. As for the gun, Ted Loveday came to the theatre with a working model. A triumph of mechanical skill, the six-inch howitzer could grow to a twelve-inch in any desired time. The change in silhouette would be almost imperceptible to the audience but the gun would grow. The gun and the Madonna of the window, both untouched in the hideous ruin of the scene, would dominate everything.

So we moved on to the four dress rehearsals. The day of setting up came. The scenery looked frighteningly awful in the bare work lights. We set up the second act and lit it. As we were still behind schedule we decided to work all night. Since Augustus John was still missing, Alick Johnstone was to paint the window, copying a Giotto Madonna. It was nearly midnight when Alick was ready to start work on it. Suddenly there was a cry of "Ray–wait!" and Cochran hurried down the aisle from the lobby. Gesturing towards the front of the house, he hissed, "John is in the lobby! He's very drunk!"

"Alick, hold everything!" I called.

We all turned to look as Augustus John, his great black hat cocked over his forehead, sauntered down the aisle. He was indeed gloriously drunk. He climbed unsteadily onto the stage, and with a cordial wave to Alick and me, swept to stage centre and surveyed his scene in silence. In the harsh work lights it looked like a bone yard as it was meant to. The artist slowly moved towards the window frame lying on the stage, took up Alick's stick of charcoal and made a firm stroke on the oiled silk.

He worked as though possessed and for more than two hours he

90

never looked up. Cochran, Sean, Alick and I and the crew watched in fascination. At last he was done. He moved to the side of the stage and stood waiting. Without a word, two stagehands lifted the window piece and braced it in position. The master electrician connected the cable and set the lights for act 2. And there shone the Madonna of *The Silver Tassie* as Sean had described her, as genius had painted her. It was nearly three in the morning. We cheered Augustus John. He did not hear us; he just stood there looking at his scene. He was pleased with it. He left, swaying slightly.

The first night was better than I had prayed for. Our heaven-blessed company outdid themselves. Laryngitis, the endemic curse of the English theatre, took an unusually light toll. Charles Laughton had had literally no voice at ten o'clock in the morning. With the aid of a throat specialist, Geoffrey Carte, he started with half his voice and gave a glorious performance.

Young Emlyn Williams turned up at six o'clock unable to whisper. Since no understudy was ready I had no alternative but to do it myself. I had a pitch pipe to give me the key and was reasonably confident. As the second act progressed, I stood at the top of the ramp, stage left. My cue approached and I stealthily blew through the pipe. Not a sound. I was in a state of terror. The inevitable result was that I started the Hymn to the Gun sharp, about five tones higher than was ordered. Ian Hunter, who had to follow me in a higher pitch, looked up with the pathetic rebuke of a wounded spaniel, lowered my pitch by an octave and went on, the audience none the wiser.

In the newspapers the next day Emlyn won two good notices for his performance of the messenger, much to his annoyance.

The critics were astonishingly favourable and, most important, the comments were understanding and intelligent. The one-time critic, Bernard Shaw, returning to his early vocation, summed it up. "A hell of a play!" he shouted as he stood in the cheering stalls.

"It's the proudest failure I ever had!" Cochran said when we closed after twenty-six performances.

I returned to the theatre the morning after the final performance. Cochran had told me I could have John's Madonna. I wanted to take it home. I watched two stagehands carry the huge frame from the centre of the stage to the wings. Somebody called me and I turned. There was a crash behind me. Turning back, I saw the whole frame flat on the stage, the window pierced by the rock on which it had fallen. The painting was in shreds. *Sic transit gloria fenestris Johannis.*

In a letter to me, Sean said, "I hope that English dramatists will abandon their faith in the 'as it was in the beginning, is now and ever shall be' of Drama, and give you–now and again, even–plays that will give you a chance to 'sing a song and show the stuff you're made of.'"

*The Silver Tassie* was such a play.

# 11

Following *The Silver Tassie* I faced the realization that my marriage of seven years was a failure. My wife and I both wanted to end it. I sailed for New York for a short visit, leaving instructions with Sidney Hall, my secretary and dresser, to find a service flat for me when I returned.

Broadway always raised my spirits. I saw about eight plays, most of them successes, but the one that impressed me most was *The Sacred Flame* by Somerset Maugham. It had failed badly and I saw the closing New York performance.

It was a well-constructed play, written with objective detachment, with all Maugham's story-teller's skill; but unlike any of his previous work, completely devoid of the cynicism and the wit we had been led to expect from him.

Instead, the author told an astonishing tale of human frailty with sincerity and unexpected commiseration. It was not a pleasant story which he told.

Maurice and Stella Tabret have been married for five years, during all of which time he has been a helpless paralytic as the result of an airplane crash. During the last year Colin, Maurice's brother, has been home and he and Stella have fallen in love. Maurice is found dead. His nurse of five years insists that he has been murdered. Suspicion points ominously at Stella who confesses that she is to be the mother of Colin's child. Mrs. Tabret, the mother of the two young men, avows in the shocking denouement that she had given her poor son release from the suffering of knowing of his wife's and brother's love by administering an overdose of a sleeping potion.

The mother's fearful act is not justified; it is merely explained. Its tragic impact affects everyone in the play.

As the nurse and the mother, Clare Eames and Mary Jerrold had towered over the rest of the seemingly bewildered cast.

The play interested me as a director, but since Gilbert Miller had presented it in New York and staged the production, it seemed certain that he would perform the same function in London, if the play were produced there.

I read in the *New York Times* the next day that Gladys Cooper, the London actress-manageress, was going to present *The Sacred Flame* at her theatre, the Playhouse, and would star in the part of Stella Tabret, the wife. No director was mentioned. I was sure Gerald du Maurier would get the job. Gladys Cooper had been directed by him in Maugham's *The Letter*, which had run for a year.

So I resigned myself to returning to London without a sign of a job, either as actor or director, and moving into a flat in Pall Mall which Hall cabled he had found for me.

I sailed a couple of days later in a half-empty Cunard liner and after sleeping for twenty-four hours, went for a stroll on deck before luncheon. Also strolling was Clare Eames, who had given such a powerful performance of the nurse in the Maugham play in New York. I introduced myself and told her how much I had been moved by her playing of this role and by the play itself. She seemed a bit distrait. Gladys Cooper had offered her and Mary Jerrold their New York roles in London; hence their presence on board.

"If we get good direction – du Maurier perhaps – I think we'll do well," she said. She knew the London theatre, having scored a big success a year before in *The Silver Cord*, which her husband, Sidney Howard, had written.

We were interrupted by a page boy. "Marconigram for you, sir." I opened it and silently handed it to Miss Eames. It read, "WOULD LIKE YOU DIRECT SACRED FLAME REHEARSALS START NEXT WEEK PLEASE REPLY PLAYHOUSE GLADYS COOPER."

There was no comment from Clare Eames as she handed the message back to me.

"I know you're disappointed, Miss Eames," I said. "Nobody is as good as Sir Gerald, but I believe I can help."

"I am not disappointed," said Miss Eames. "I'm intrigued." I wired my acceptance at once.

I had never met Gladys Cooper. I found her to be a discerning producer and a most unselfish one. Stella Tabret was by no means the best acting role for a woman. It was the type of part which many actresses shun, a foil for more showy characters. But Stella was the pivotal character in three key scenes which demanded from a player that rare power of expressing thoughts without words. Miss Cooper had that ability. And there was her striking beauty.

Maugham, fresh from his disappointment in New York, attended

94

most of the rehearsals. I had heard that he could be difficult to handle – a disgruntled author can be a meance to any production – but he proved a reticent and appreciative observer. At the end of a full week's work, he expressed satisfaction with the production. His only concern was the integrity of his script; that the actors should read their lines exactly as he had written them.

He was one of the few remaining playwrights (Galsworthy and Harwood come to mind and, of course, Shaw) who still wrote literate dialogue and disdained colloquial realism. His plays were structured and written in a style that rejected the naturalistic chatter favoured by many of the new dramatists.

Low-keyed, realistic acting, the then-current style of underplaying, would have made much of Maugham's formal dialogue seem artificial. However, the cast which we had chosen, including C. V. France, a fine actor of the old school, Richard Bird and Sebastian Shaw as the two sons, were quite able to tackle style. The women, I found, were perhaps more at ease with the author's austere lines than were the men, and of the three leading actresses in the company, the most facile in this regard was the American, Clare Eames.

We had been rehearsing for a full week when Clare failed to show up on a Monday morning. Nobody knew where she was. Neither her agent nor any of her English friends had been in touch with her. She had told her hotel on the Saturday that she would be away for the weekend and left no address.

On Monday we rehearsed as best we could without Clare, her understudy standing in. It was an alarming situation. Although I had not seen Clare on the voyage after our first meeting, it had been evident from the start of rehearsals that she was under some emotional strain.

The next day passed with no news and G. C., Maugham and I had a talk. I said that if Miss Eames rejoined the company during the next three or four days and was able to work, we could open as scheduled. Otherwise, we would have to postpone the opening and recast the nurse's part. I pointed out that although Clare Eames's performance was set, it still remained for me to integrate that performance with my directing scheme. I took no stand on the question of replacement nor did Willie Maugham. In spite of his medical training and experience, he made no prognosis of Miss Eames's condition. Gladys Cooper was not unprepared for her decision. As I always found her to be, she was unflappable.

"I believe that Clare's performance is essential to this play. I am betting that she will come back to us and that she will give a better performance than she did in New York.... I don't know what the trouble is. I don't think she knows herself. But I'm certain that her best hope is to give that superb performance in Willie's play. I believe that the poor woman will find a safe refuge in work." She smiled as she added, "And before this week has ended."

Gladys was right. Miss Eames came back to us, at the Saturday morning rehearsal. She gave a performance surpassing her achievement in New York. Every member of the little company served the author faithfully. G. C. was perfection in what was still a secondary part and in her curtain speech gratefully acknowledged "her debt to her two leading ladies" as she took the hands of Mary Jerrold and Clare Eames.

Clare played the long run of *The Sacred Flame* with courage and distinction. A year later she died in England, aged thirty-four.

The London performance of *The Sacred Flame* was a victory for Maugham, the story-teller. In this production he had resisted any temptation to cleverness that could be out of character, relying solely on his narrative genius to tell his disturbing and startling tale.

I had to conform to this austerity in my direction. Roughly speaking, my problem was to make the play as realistic as I could while preserving the author's style and his characters as he had written them. Only Maugham himself could properly pass judgement on the extent of my success in solving it.

Beyond the formal felicitations mutually exchanged after the opening performance, Maugham withheld any comment on my contribution to the production. But a few weeks later I got a long letter from him, ending with words which I wish I had the talent to set to music–"You brought out everything I had seen in the play when I wrote it and despaired because I could not get it in New York."

Gladys was the second actress-producer I worked with. I had already been under contract to Sybil Thorndike for two years and acted in three plays under her management. With Gladys, I acted in and directed six plays during an association which lasted four years. Later I acted opposite Katharine Cornell in New York in three of her productions–in all, twelve major productions I worked in were presented by actresses in management. I have never worked with a male manager who could have done a better job than any one of these three ladies.

Meanwhile, the long divorce proceedings were over in 1929. When the decree was finally granted, it was a matter of relief to us both. My

96

wife promptly married Major Giles Sebright, a very pleasant fellow. About a year later our son Geoffrey, then five years old, whom the court had given to the custody of his mother, was transferred to my care at the suggestion of his maternal grandmother.

My second wife was the clever and talented actress Adrianne Allen. She is the mother of my children Daniel and Anna, who both went on the stage as soon as they were able.

I had a small difficulty in "casting" the two witnesses for my wedding to Adrianne.

I found Tottie Harwood at the Garrick just before lunch one day in September and asked him to be a witness. The civil ceremony was to be at the Westminster Registry Office at noon, October 30.

Tottie's great jaw thrust out as he consulted a small notebook.

"Can't do it, old fellow. I'm down for a tennis court at Queen's that morning. Courts are the very devil to get this time of year. By the way, I'm sending you a new script of *The Man in Possession*. I've fixed up the last act considerably. Read it, will you?"

I quite understood. First things came first with Tottie. I recast the witnesses with Edna Best and Herbert Marshall.

The last act of *The Man in Possession* was indeed improved.

# *12*

In these permissive and tasteless days censorship is an anachronism, as hateful to the world of the theatre, both to layman and professional, as was the Inquisition to the Protestants. Up to the fifth decade of this century, theatre people had always paid lip service to the idea of a completely uncontrolled and free stage. But many of us, and I certainly include myself in this accounting, were thankful that in the times between the wars we had in England an agency which would maintain a standard of taste and morals in the plays which were to be presented on our stage.

It was in the Theatres Act of 1843 that England had devised a censorship system which proved viable for nearly ninety years. It was a simple system whereby all new plays would be licenced for production. The granting or withholding of such a licence was placed in the hands of the Lord Chamberlain of the Royal Household, a functionary whose chief duty was the conduct of Court procedure and ceremonial. The office was happily outside of politics and had a dignity and independence which no bureaucrats could have. Of course, whether the system would work really depended on the man himself who was the Lord Chamberlain. Frequently it didn't, as the records show.

For most of the years between the wars the office of the Lord Chamberlain was held by the second Earl of Cromer, a nobleman whose urbanity and dignity concealed the fact that he was stage-struck. Lord Cromer had a genuine respect for the theatre. He was an avid playgoer, and in the countless decisions he had to make as censor (a word he detested) he was guided as much by his concern for the playwright as by his duty to protect public taste. As a stage director I got to know him quite well. In fact, on one occasion Lord Cromer proved that he himself could have been an adroit director.

Early in 1930 I staged *The Man in Possession*, a play by H. M. Harwood. It was witty, cynical and for that time a daring farce in which Isabel Jeans played a lady of pliable virtue and I, the title role.

*Isabel Jeans and R.M. in* The Man in Possession, *at the Ambassadors' Theatre, London, 1930.*

As author of this play, Tottie Harwood was at his best. It was as good a farce as ever came out of Paris and brilliantly constructed.

During the first week of rehearsal, cuts had reduced our playing time to about an hour and a half, and although the play was now finely paced, that is dangerously short for London audiences. I urged Tottie and Alec Rea, who were producing, to put in a curtain raiser and suggested my old standby, *In the Zone*, O'Neill's little masterpiece. They agreed and the O'Neill play went into rehearsal at once. This time I played Smitty, as I had done eight years before in Toronto.

It was a fine double-bill. We opened to a unanimously good press and were a solid hit. We settled in for a long and merry run at the Ambassadors'.

There is, of course, at least one seduction scene in most farces. Nowadays we are almost invariably treated to a realistic demonstration of the *fait accompli*, with extensive beds, bare shoulders and drawn-out disrobings. In my direction of *The Man in Possession* (so named from the fact that the seducer was a bailiff's man) I staged the scene on the proven theory that the "unhooking" of a lady was a deal more intriguing than a progressive "striptease," especially when the seducee was the lissome Miss Jeans encased in one of Norman Hartnell's tightest gowns. The curtain fell on the second act as I struggled with the last recalcitrant hook, and rose after the interval with the entrance of the lady's maid carrying a torn garment which she displays to a moderate laugh from the audience. I kept wondering why that laugh wasn't bigger.

We had been running for a month or so when I got a call from Lord Cromer to come and see him at once. When I passed the sentries at St. James's Palace I was in a bad state of jitters. Lord Cromer wasted no time.

"What is the garment which the maid displays at the opening of the last act?"

He didn't even mention the name of the play.

"I don't know what they call it—I think it's a chemise, or slip or something."

"Exactly. I saw the play again the night before last—it's an *intimate* garment and that is not what is mentioned in the script which I licenced."

He read from a copy of the play he had in his desk. "The maid is carrying *some garments*...there's nothing about 'intimate' or 'under-clothing' ... and that's not good enough, Massey. I am having

100

*For the third time I acted in* In the Zone, *which was used as a curtain raiser to* The Man in Possession. *This time I acted Smitty again. Left to right: Charles Farrell, R.M., Tom Reynolds and Paul Gill.*

a deuce of a time with Mrs. Hornibrook and the Bishop of London. . . ."

I suppressed a smile at the thought of my old friends of *The Country Wife* episode being on my trail again.

" . . . and there are a lot of other letters too!"

"I don't know what to do about it, Lord Cromer. I've got to convey the impression that these two people acted by Miss Jeans and myself were not just holding hands and looking at old photograph albums after the second-act curtain! After all, I've played fair with

101

you as to those garments the maid brings in . . . I don't see that a torn shoulder strap is so awful . . . and remember I couldn't undo the last hook!"

Then the man who could control the mode of fashion in the Royal enclosure at Ascot gave me a lesson in the direction of risqué farce. Quite deadpan and in a confidential tone, he offered this suggestion: "What about the maid carrying on a replica of Miss Jeans's dress which you had tried to unhook? It could be . . . oh . . . eh . . . appropriately damaged."

I could hardly wait to get to Hartnell's. I wanted to put Lord Cromer's direction in the performance that evening. It was already past noon but Norman Hartnell was as eager as I to get the job done. There was enough of the material left and two seamstresses finished the duplicate by 5:00 P.M., when the famous couturier and I together "appropriately damaged" his creation. I took it over to the Ambassadors' Theatre and rehearsed the action with Ann Codrington who played the maid. That night and on every subsequent performance of a long run, the damaged dress got a shout of laughter.

I wrote a note to Lord Cromer thanking him for his help and seeking his collaboration in the event that I should undertake to direct another bawdy comedy in the future. He replied with modesty, "I am glad to think my suggestion is an improvement and has in no way wrecked that passage of the play."

The Lord Chamberlain's office was much concerned with the reduction of profanity in the scripts submitted for licencing. Most of this laundering was carried out by the chief reader, a man named Street, for Lord Cromer only dealt with major issues. Mr. Street approached his task on a strictly mathematical basis, a routine order being "Eliminate one-third of the references to the Deity." All such references – rated equal, requests for divine forgiveness, blessing or punishment – counted the same. The assessment of the "Gods" and the selection of the eliminations would be left to the director or producer. It was quite satisfactory if a few "Thank Gods" and "God knows" were rubbed out and "God damn you!" remained. Even though Shaw had emancipated "bloody" in *Pygmalion* in 1914, the expletive was still taboo twenty years later. In the early thirties I bargained the loss of a number of "Gods" for the retention of one "bloody."

My warmest memory of Lord Cromer is his enthusiasm for what would be my favourite play, if I went in for superlatives. It was called *Spread Eagle*, written by two American journalists, George S. Brooks and Walter Lister, and was a bitter satirical melodrama, an anti-war play with force and validity.

Specifically, Big Business in the shape of billionaire Martin Henderson of New York has a mine in Mexico (the time was 1927 before oil interests became the villains of commerce) and badly wants American intervention in that unstable region. His right-hand man, Joe Cobb, is an ex-doughboy, embittered and disillusioned with his present chief. When the son of an ex-president of the United States, one Charles Parkman, asks Henderson for a job, Joe's sarcasm comes readily.

"If they should have the bad taste to kill you, the United States would have an army on the way down there inside of ten minutes—" Joe stops his speech in mid-air but Henderson has picked up the inadvertent suggestion.

Parkman is sent to the mine and Henderson promptly finances a revolution by a stupendous ruffian of the Pancho Villa type, named General de Castro. Besides creating chaos, the revolution is intended at least to place the American princeling in danger and at most to rouse the United States to war.

It comes off. The former "White House Baby" is murdered together with assorted mine officials and a priest. War is declared. With the aid of films, we see for a few minutes the "whoop-de-do" of propaganda at work. Since his mine interests are thus officially protected, Henderson can afford to become a "dollar-a-year" chairman of the Committee on National Defense, with *Spread Eagle* achieving blistering irony in depicting the public sainthood of an unspeakable traitor.

In the last act, Henderson, his daughter and Joe are "discovered" in Henderson's private train at a railhead in Mexico. Joe is getting more and more disgusted with the whole thing when young Parkman turns up wounded, clothes in ribbons, but alive and all too ready to give Henderson's game away. Joe, by playing upon Parkman's love for Henderson's daughter, and questioning his honour in abandoning the victims to Castro's brutality at the mine, silences the fugitive hero.

Using his reserve army status, Joe abandons Henderson and comes back in a private's uniform; and as a band outside the car plays the "Star Spangled Banner," Joe tells Henderson exactly what he thinks of him in five crisp words: "You son of a bitch! STAND UP!"

In 1928, with Tottie Harwood and Alec Rea as partners, I bought the English rights to *Spread Eagle* and at once submitted the play to

*Ben Welden, Fritz Williams and R.M. in Spread Eagle, at the New Theatre,
London, 1928. The plot to bring military intervention to salvage millionaire
Henderson's mining interests in Mexico is hatched in New York.*

the Lord Chamberlain for licencing. It had been produced in New
York by Jed Harris who had been one of my cadets at Yale and was
already known as the "boy wonder of Broadway." *Spread Eagle* had
been his third production and though it had a magnificent press, it
had only a modest run of eighty performances. I was to play Joe Cobb
and also direct the play in England.

I was a little apprehensive about the tag line getting Lord Cromer's
approval and when a message came requesting my presence at St.
James's Palace, I took no chances and brought my partners with me.

Lord Cromer lost no time in confirming my fears as to the reason
for the summons.

"Sit down, gentlemen. With regard to *Spread Eagle* ... an excellent
play if I may say so ... has a theme similar to your *Transit of Venus*,
Harwood, big business rattling sabres and all that ... needs a bit of

cleaning up...too many references to the Deity...remove half of them... And, of course, I cannot allow that last line..." (He looked at the script.) "You son of a bitch! STAND UP!"

He mouthed the tag with a prophylactic delicacy which made me think he was trying to gargle. With tactful disregard of Lord Cromer's views on the multiplicity of "Gods" in theatrical scripts, I took over the discussion. "My God, Lord Cromer, you can't take out that line. It must be a shocker, a profanity, the summation of a man's disgust at hypocrisy and dishonesty!"

The battle was on and went on for a very long time. The three of us eloquently relieved each other. Lord Cromer, with the patience which much service at the foreign office had taught him, listened, parried our attacks and never gave an inch. Finally he ended the discussion by rising and crossing to the large central window of his office and turning to us, "Gentlemen, I cannot allow the word bitch to be spoken on the English stage...except denoting the female of the canine kind."

I replied, "Very well, we won't produce the play. We have signed no contracts yet and it's not too late to call the whole thing off. I won't play Joe Cobb with some gutless, insipid tag line. Do you agree?" This last to my partners. They did. We walked to the door where we were stopped by Lord Cromer.

"Gentlemen, please come back...sit down."

We complied. He remained standing by the window.

"I cannot be responsible for preventing the production of this play...it's a fine play, an important play...it must be seen in London." He returned to his desk where he stood facing us.

"Would 'goddamned bastard' satisfy you, Massey?"

Once again Lord Cromer had come through for the theatre. His suggested substitution had been offered with a tender reticence which I did not employ when I delivered the tag to a delighted London audience some six weeks later. But it proved his genuine theatre sense.

It is ironic, but a demonstration of Lord Cromer's belief that his actions as censor should reflect current public taste, that some five or six years after this incident in 1928 he allowed Marie Tempest to call another woman a "bitch" as the curtain line of the second act of *The First Mrs. Fraser*. This on the stage of the Haymarket where Mrs. Patrick Campbell had triumphantly uttered Eliza's "not bloody likely" in 1914.

*Spread Eagle* was the greatest disappointment of my theatre years. Although the play and the production won the unstinted acclaim of the critics and an ovation from the opening-night audience, we had one of those moribund three-week runs. With most plays the reward of a successful opening, the conquest of a play well done and the acknowledgement of critics and audience, is a sufficient guerdon. The long run is icing on the cake. But the failure of *Spread Eagle* at the New Theatre box office really hurt. I loved that play and still do.

# 13

In September 1930 I gave up my role in *The Man in Possession* because of ill health. I had played this Harwood comedy for eight months, at the same time staging two other productions, and I was exhausted. I entered a clinic in the Midlands for a cure of what the doctor who ran it diagnosed as colitis. This Harley Street physician was not the usual sympathetic salesman of beds in his sanitorium but a former army doctor with a fierce resentment of malingerers. He ran his London practice on the lines of a magistrate's court. Verdicts would range from summary sentences of ten to sixty days in the "home" to instant discharges. His success with what he considered deserving cases had given him an envied reputation for honesty.

I was sentenced to thirty days in his Gothic morgue. After ten days of bland dieting, sleeping and reading Trollope, I was feeling much better. Life in the clinic was becoming unbearable.

A telephone call from Harold Harwood triggered my determination to escape. In partnership with the Shuberts, he was going to produce *The Man in Possession* in New York in November; if I wanted to play Raymond Dabney on Broadway the part would be mine again. He was going to get Isabel Jeans to play Crystal. This was a chance to make my first Broadway appearance in a play in which I had already proved myself as an actor and director. It seemed likely to repeat its London success.

I decided that my cure was complete and made my escape from the clinic. Though I had not said yes to Harwood, I was pretty sure I would.

But once home I found a script waiting for me. It was called *Topaze*. The accompanying telegram read: "WILL YOU CONSIDER PLAYING TITLE ROLE LONDON PRODUCTION TOPAZE CO-STARRING WITH DELYSIA. PLEASE PHONE EARLIEST POSSIBLE. ANGUS MACLEOD, DANIEL MAYER COMPANY."

Alice Delysia, a French star who had played in several revues in London, was a great favourite.

I knew something about this play by Marcel Pagnol. It had been running in Paris for nearly two years but had only scored a modest hundred and fifty performances on Broadway the previous season. As a satire on French politics *Topaze* was likely to be poison in any London box office. I saw no reason to reconsider my inclination to make a first try in New York in *The Man in Possession*.

Still, I would have to read *Topaze* before I declined it. Benn Levy's adaptation proved entertaining reading but it did confirm my doubts about its chances on the English stage. At the same time, the character of Topaze was any actor's dream to play.

A hard choice had to be made. Personal considerations usually settle such questions. But which job did I want—the old, safe one in New York or the new one in London? After three days I chose the London job. It proved a disastrous decision.

The blue-ribbon cast assembled for the first rehearsal of *Topaze* was suffused, as always, with high spirits and optimism. Even veterans like Frederick Lloyd, Frank Cellier, Martita Hunt and Delysia herself were enthusiastic, I with them. Only Reginald Denham, who was to stage our play, remained intent on his script. Directors must be realists and Reggie foresaw the problems.

*Topaze* exposes dishonesty—but not to condemn it. On the contrary, dishonesty is shown to be the only possible virtue for anyone with sense. Even in the light of satire at its wittiest, this was in 1930 a bitter pill for the Anglo-Saxon conscience.

An obviously honest schoolmaster becomes the tool of a crook until he acquires the art of deviousness himself; then he turns the tables on his master and inherits all the fruits of knavery, including his former chief's lady friend, rich food and clothes.

I became increasingly aware of the difficulties I faced in the interpretation of Topaze. I did not envy Reggie Denham his job as director. I sought his guidance.

"I find that I'm doubling two contrasting parts. No connection between the schoolmaster I play in the first act and the crook I'm supposed to act in acts 2 and 3! What the hell do I do about identification?"

"Ray, we're doing a French play. The French don't give a damn about character progression. They're only interested in what you do when you're there, not how you got there. I can't help you. You've got to consider your role as divided into two unrelated parts, Topaze 1 and Topaze 2. Vive la France!"

Reggie was right. I suppose I had known it ever since I had first read the play.

For the last week of rehearsals we were on the stage of the New Theatre, which was to be our West End house.

We opened there on the Wednesday following a week's try-out in Glasgow. Arriving at the stage-door for the first of two dress rehearsals on the Monday, I saw to my dismay that about a hundred people had formed a queue. My dresser told me there was an equally long gallery line in St. Martin's Lane. Two hundred people were going to wait forty-eight hours, seated on folding stools and huddled in blankets, to see us. Next night their numbers had doubled. A delighted press agent had Alice and me photographed serving hot coffee to the fans after the second dress rehearsal.

To this day I shudder at the memory of the London opening of *Topaze*. It is painful to recall the extremes of approval and derision which the audience displayed on that incredible occasion.

The first act, which tells most of the story of Topaze 1, the innocent schoolmaster, brought forth such an ovation of bravos and cheers as I have seldom heard even at a final curtain. Stagehands had already started to strike the first act set when the producer, Rudolph Mayer, told Delysia and me to take a call. "Take the call through the curtain!" He pushed us downstage. The applause had died down with the house lights.

Delysia and I were thrust through the curtain in comparative darkness and silence. The sudden switching on of the footlights revealed two embarrassed players whose one thought was: How are we going to get back through that curtain?

The ill-timed call after the first act was a sad mistake but I doubt whether it was responsible for the doom in store. In the try-out performances, audiences had all loved the first act and Topaze 1. They had merely tolerated his successor, Topaze 2, and the cynicism of the last two acts. With this audience there was no tolerance – only open resentment of a play which failed to hang together.

The second act was received with polite reservation. The performance was subdued and, as so often when nerves are taut, the pace was slow. Early in the act an unfortunate miscue led to the omission of nearly four pages, including the first entrance of Frank Cellier, playing the chief crook. I managed to restore the cut, or most of it, and probably nobody but the players knew what had happened.

The third act was in two scenes. Open hostility broke out in the first scene with both pit and gallery joining in the dialogue and shouting derisive comments at the actors. None of these interjections seemed to have the slightest effect on the individual performances. In the

Act 1 – big success.

R.M. in Topaze, at the New Theatre, 1930.

Acts 2 and 3 – big flop.

final scene of what had now become a disaster the baleful "count-out" of the prize-ring referee came from the gallery. "One, two, three...nine, ten—you're out!"

A few minutes later the chant was heard again, this time from the pit. A short time before the curtain fell the combined efforts of pit and gallery produced a third count-out, the loudest of all. Alice Delysia, to the delight of her admirers, resorted to the conventions of revue, belting out her lines to the front, and bouncing her jokes off the teeth of the opposition. Cowed into submission, the recalcitrant pit and gallery had no more fight in them. There was no post-curtain demonstration. The production died with some dignity.

The post-mortem disclosed disagreement as to the cause of death. Some critics held me responsible for the murder of the comedy, citing my inability to link together the two characters of Topaze. Others blamed the author's text.

There was truth in both opinions. As Charles Morgan said in *The Times*:

> Mr. Massey gives two extremes—an absolute innocence in the poor schoolmaster, an absolute coarseness and greed in the blackmailer that he becomes.... Brilliant though Mr. Massey's separated performances are, they have not the connecting link that might have made of them a representation of one continuously recognizable human being.

I had to acknowledge that I had been miscast as Topaze. My selling ticket as an actor was sincerity, in whatever kind of part I was cast, villain, hero, wastrel or zealot; and I had ignored the fact that there are roles, and Pagnol's Topaze was one of them, in which there can be too much of that virtue. There should have been a suggestion of self-delusion in my schoolmaster and a hint of realized futility in my blackmailer which would have linked the two aspects of Topaze.

I read and reread the indictments of my performance. Although my notices were not all bad, the consensus was that I had stumbled as an actor. In the collapse of a play, anyone playing a leading part comes out of the disaster in a battered state. I knew I could not expect much in the way of acting or directing offers until the dust had settled. At such times a visit to New York had often proved lucky. I was about to call a travel agent when my phone rang. It was Gerald du Maurier.

111

# *14*

"It's too bad about Topaze, old chap. Just don't try satire again – until the next time! But I didn't call to offer advice," he said. "Some film people have asked me to play Sherlock Holmes in *The Speckled Band*. One of these talking pictures. I don't want to do it. There's nothing wrong with the offer – it's a fair script, there seems to be plenty of money lying about, but I feel rather tired. If you feel you would like to do it, I'll try to push it your way."

My one thought at that moment was that with luck I had a job again. I thanked him most heartily, and asked him to go ahead.

At any other time I would have weighed Gerald's suggestion very carefully before accepting it. In 1930 anything to do with motion pictures was highly suspect. Before the talkies came in the late 1920s, English stage actors paid no mind to the flicks. Moving pictures meant Hollywood and only a few made the trek west. The British film-making business was nearly dead. A theatre man would turn up his coat collar, pull down his hat brim and look both ways before he entered one of those warehouses where English silent pictures were filmed. I have unpleasant memories of squalid ventures in British films about 1928: An unsuccessful silent test for Lewis Dodd in *The Constant Nymph*, my mouth crammed with cotton wool because I looked too thin. Playing a bit in the first all-talking English movie which was shot at night to avoid traffic noise. And there were other murky incidents, each touched with a bit of the madness that seems to go with movies.

That English movie-makers were trying to entice Gerald du Maurier to make a picture was a good sign. But the thought of that supreme perfectionist of natural acting, who would spend an hour before a mirror finding a better way to light a cigarette, being thrust in front of a camera with scarcely enough rehearsal to find his foot marks fills the mind with horror. I think Gerald knew this, although his getting the part for me was one of the kindest acts I ever knew. Seven weeks later I had finished my first talking movie.

It was inevitable that I would go into movies sooner or later. But to take this step with the sponsorship of the leader of my profession in England was a reason for pride and confidence which I have never forgotten.

Some three hundred and fifty weeks, or seven years, of my professional life have been spent in the actual filming of motion pictures. I have acted in nearly seventy movies made for theatre exhibition (i.e., other than television pictures). Though not a large number for an actor who plays the field these days, it amounts to a sizable slice of my working years.

Yet the experience of those years in the movies counts for very little to me as a stage actor. When I entered a film studio and acted before a camera I was in another profession, distinct from that of a player in the theatre. The actor who works on stage and screen must accept the sad truth that he is following two professional paths which do not converge.

I am not a theatre snob who looks on movie work as a form of slumming. I detest such snobs. I love the theatre, acting is my profession, but I have genuine respect for the mechanized theatre, including movies. I am grateful for all the work I have been able to do in front of cameras, and to the public who enjoyed it. I am saying only that the two kinds of acting are different.

Gerald du Maurier had described the film script of *The Speckled Band* as "fair." He was a shade generous. To start with, both in narrative and character the producer had introduced some novelties. The casting of du Maurier or myself for Holmes was unorthodox, to say the least.

It was not only in physical appearance that my Sherlock Holmes deviated from Conan Doyle's original. The film-makers would have

*R.M. as Sherlock Holmes in one of his famous disguises. The Speckled Band, filmed in England, 1930.*

*Athole Stewart as Dr. Watson and R.M. as Sherlock Holmes in The Speckled Band.*

nothing to do with the calabash pipe, the tobacco in the Persian slipper, Mrs. Hudson and the enchanting disorder of Baker Street, the violin and the hypodermic needle. Instead Holmes was given a magnificent suite with glass flowers and modern art furniture, typists, secretaries, dictaphones, card indexes and mechanical devices which predated IBM by a quarter of a century. I could not avoid a sense of guilt at my participation in this travesty of a classic.

It did not console me that all the other characters were cast and played in a style that would have satisfied the most critical Holmesian purist. Lyn Harding as the villainous Dr. Grimesby Rylott and Athole Stewart's Dr. Watson were straight from Conan Doyle's pages. Lyn had created his role on the stage years before. The young lady in jeopardy in Dr. Rylott's house was played by Angela Baddeley, many years later to be lovingly known to the world as Mrs. Bridges of *Upstairs, Downstairs.*

One of the few incidents which I remember in the shooting of *The Speckled Band* was a glaring example of the denial of adequate rehearsal to a performer. In this case even a perusal of the script was withheld. Instead, on the advice of the player's agent, the director decided to risk a "take" relying solely on the technical resource and instinctive emotions of the player, an eager and conscientious Alsatian dog, weighing some 150 pounds and deprived of all sustenance

114

for twenty-four hours prior to performance. All that was required of the performer was that he should attack as Holmes approached Dr. Rylott's house in the guise of a plumber. Once the attack was in progress there would be a cut to the wicked doctor and the canine performer's job would be finished. As far as I could see, having observed my prospective adversary from a distance, so would I.

To prevent this untoward culmination to my movie career I wore a "bite-proof" trenchcoat to which was attached a sort of necklace of meat fragments to divert my friend to a meal more attractive than my skinny frame provided. This being a night scene, Fido's ingestion of the meat would seem to indicate my personal demise.

All was finally ready. Both of us were at extreme emotional tension. (I was scared stiff.) Two cameras rolled. "Action!" was called. The huge beast bounded out of the shadows—was my coat tough enough to stand those fangs?—then suddenly I realized that my colleague hadn't read or couldn't read the script. Jumping on his hind legs and towering above me, he threw his great paws around my neck and smothered my face with kisses. I was a "dog person" and he liked me. Then as suddenly as it had started, his passionate greeting was over. He remembered his hunger and there was something to satisfy it. With great delicacy and with the deft aid of a forepaw, my friend nibbled the meat off the string, stopping once or twice and looking at me as if to say, You think of everything!

I tried to simulate a struggle but finally I gave up. I threw my arms around the dog and we staggered round in a dance of mutual admiration. The cameras continued to roll and the crew roared approval.

Jack Raymond, the director, wiped the tears from his eyes. "The pooch is a good romantic actor and we cast him as a heavy."

I was finally given a new entrance to the Rylott house without any canine assistance. In spite of my misgivings the old Holmes story was good enough to carry the picture to fair success in England and America.

*Angela Baddeley, the future Mrs. Bridges in Upstairs, Downstairs, as the heroine in The Speckled Band.*

115

# 15

Following my first film adventure I sailed for New York, arriving on December 28, 1930, in time to see the closing performance of *The Man in Possession*, which had enjoyed a profitable run of one hundred performances. My old friend Leslie Banks, in my part, and Isabel Jeans had both scored successes, as had the play. My regret at the *Topaze* decision may be imagined; also the strength of my desire to find a good play to bring back to London.

The next day, Sunday, on the peremptory order of a doctor named Bertram Eskell, to whom I had been referred by Alfred Lunt, my angry appendix was removed at the Park East Hospital to the long-range benefit of my health but the immediate curtailment of my search for a play. However, with the insistence of Bertie Eskell that I "get on my feet as quickly as possible," I was making the theatre rounds five days after surgery, still unable to stand up straight.

It was now January 2, and the first play I saw in my un-straightened circumstances was *Five Star Final*, which had opened a few days before. As I crawled out of my cab at the Cort Theatre I caught a glimpse of the marquée, which bore the words A. H. WOODS PRESENTS twinkling in electric lights. This meant that I would not find a play that evening as I knew Albert Herman Woods would never have any dealings with me. I had unwittingly crossed him when directing one of his productions in England and I knew that Al Woods neither forgot nor forgave. However, *Five Star Final* was a hit and it would be worth seeing.

As I sat in pain in the back row of the orchestra and watched this gripping, fast-moving, bitter, gutsy melodrama unfold, I knew that whatever happened or had happened I must have it for London to act the lead and direct. A big production, revolving stages, nineteen scenes, a castigation of sensational journalism, the play had everything for a London triumph.

Driving back to the Park East Hospital for my last night there, I traced back the trouble I had been through with Al Woods.

116

I had staged several plays while I was acting in *The Second Man*. One of them was a melodrama entitled *Blackmail* by a young English writer named Charles Bennett. I have a great liking for melodramas (the only play I ever wrote was a melodrama), and the co-producer of *Blackmail* was this famous American manager who by his own count was responsible for the production of 409 plays during his fabulous career. Most of these plays were sensational melodramas and broad farces. Woods knew his business. He believed in the American idea of managerial authority. He had quite recently presented three quality productions on Broadway, the Guitrys in *Mozart*, Katharine Cornell in *The Green Hat* (her first starring role) and Florence Reed in *Shanghai Gesture*.

He was a no-nonsense professional who did not take kindly to any interference with his responsibilities as a producing manager. Al was thick-set, with a shock of white curly hair and a wall-eye, and called everybody "Sweetheart" regardless of gender. He was usually soft-spoken, but when crossed in any way he could be really mean. He was in his late fifties at this time.

His English co-producer was Sir Alfred Butt, a desk-man, who in this case left everything of a backstage nature to "Sweetheart."

The play was the story of an artist killed by a model in self-defence after a ball in Chelsea; the track-down of a ne'er-do-well blackmailer who is suspected of the murder; and the confession by the model after her detective lover has connived at the charge against the blackmailer. Rather his life than hers, he argues.

The model was to be played by Tallulah Bankhead, starring in her sixth play in London and at the height of her solid success there. Tallulah was hugely talented but at this stage of her career, brash and undisciplined. She was not yet twenty-five and she was having fun. The crowd of sycophants who surrounded her offstage, and who had nothing to do with the theatre, had slightly turned her head which, fortunately, was not an empty one. Tallulah had been prone to express her opinions about scripts, casts and other production affairs with undue emphasis in previous plays, but in the English theatre, which was a little more easy-going than the American, it hadn't disturbed anybody too much.

In the *Blackmail* job she was dealing with a different kind of manager, and Al Woods began to bristle. Her frequent suggestions about improving the script had irked "Sweetheart" and a few days before rehearsals started he told me to see Miss Bankhead and reassure her about the healthy state of the script. His words, as I recollect, were like this: "Get that Bankhead broad off my back – you're the director of this play, not her. Tell her to learn her jokes and not bump into the furniture." This made sense to me.

Accordingly, I arrived at Tallulah's house in Farm Street by appointment, armed with the script of *Blackmail*, and was immediately taken upstairs by her maid and shown into her bathroom, where her lovely head and shoulders were dimly visible through the dense steam and soapsuds. I sat on a stool and for about ten minutes listened to Miss B.'s views on the care and feeding of theatrical managers and dramatic authors. These indicated that far from dismounting from Mr. Woods's back, Miss B. would use spurs in future. When I left Farm Street, my script a mess of pulp, and dizzy with the heavy scent of bath salts, I realized that I had scarcely uttered a word.

I reported my failure to Al Woods, and the next day, Saturday, I had some minor surgery on an infected toe done after the show. Consequently I had to play Austin in *The Second Man* for a few days with one foot in a black felt slipper. I got through the Monday-night performance fairly well.

The reading of *Blackmail* the following morning was plain sailing but I didn't look forward to being on my feet all afternoon blocking out the first act. I was sitting in an aisle stall with Tallulah next to me, an open script on my knees, when Al Woods appeared.

"Well, Miss Bankhead, can we go ahead with the rehearsal?"

"Buzz off, Sweetheart, I'm talking to the director."

That was more than Al could take. He grabbed my cane, which was hanging on the seat in front of me, and in making a violent gesture at the script on my lap he brought the weapon down on my bad toe. I yelled. Tallulah leapt at Al across me, stepping on the toe in the process. Another yell, and Tallulah shouted, "You wall-eyed old bastard, you've hurt him!"

She followed Sweetheart up the aisle and they disappeared into the lobby. She returned shortly and handed my cane back to me, murmuring, "All right, darling" – the Bankhead equivalent of the Woodsian "Sweetheart" – "let's go. Sweetheart will be quite tame tomorrow."

He was, we did go, Tallulah was impeccably professional throughout rehearsals, but despite an excellent performance by her and the cast, *Blackmail* failed.

I asked Tallulah what she had said to Al Woods in the lobby after the fight. Without batting an eye she told me. "I just said to the old pirate that I was young and inexperienced, that I couldn't stand violence, I just wanted peace and love and understanding, and would Sweetheart please for God's sake leave me alone and let me work it out with you, darling!''

I lay there in the Park East Hospital as I remembered Tallulah's words, which seemed to have cooked my goose as far as getting *Five Star Final* for England.

I don't know if the Broadway bruit that Al Woods had been cleaned in the 1929 crash was true or not. But I do know that in spite of the magic of ''A. H. Woods presents—'' and the fact that the new play at the Cort was already a smash hit after a few performances, Al was nowhere to be found. I was told the next day at the theatre that Mr. Woods would not be in his office that day. Finally I tried the stage-door of the Cort and I was given a number on Broadway in much the same secrecy as a tourist was given the address of a bootlegger.

The Broadway number turned out to be one of those ''honky-tonk'' set-ups with which Broadway has always been filled. Pornography, records, notions, there was no limit to the State Fair midway variety which Broadway has always housed. The address I went to was called *Movie-of-You*; and as I gathered from the advertising outside, a clip of some fifty printed movie frames, which could be flipped by the fingers to convey the movie impression of the subject, was offered for sale at a price of seventy-five cents.

I entered and found the place lined by about a dozen curtained booths, where one or two patrons could be photographed. I spied Al Woods at the rear of the ''studio'' in his shirtsleeves, sitting in a chair. I approached him, my hand outstretched. ''I'm Ray Massey, Al. Remember *Blackmail* in London two years ago?''

Al made no move and stared at me in silence. I decided on a frontal attack. ''I want to buy the English rights to *Five Star Final*, Al.''

''You can't,'' he replied. ''You let me down – you sided with Bankhead.''

He went back to his copy of *Variety* and I decided on a retreat.

I couldn't make it out; the producer of a current Broadway smash – selling flip-card movies. It made no sense.

When I got back to my hotel I found a message to call Noel Coward. Apparently he had just arrived for the Broadway production of *Private Lives*.

''Don't tell me about your squalid search for work or your wretched appendix. I am aware of your activities.'' Noel became serious. ''I need your help. I've just heard that beloved Constance is in trouble and I'm going to see her tomorrow morning. If you'll come with me

119

I'll pick you up at your hotel at ten. All right?"

"Of course," I said, and he hung up.

It was like Noel to arrive in New York for the production of his most successful play so far and to make an errand of kindness his first duty. Constance Collier was more than a very fine actress; she was a kind, gentle, generous human being and the friend of all of us in the profession who knew her.

On the way to see Constance, Noel briefed me on the nature of our mission.

"Just before you called last night, Martha, that selfless, devoted creature who has dressed and maided Constance for years, phoned me and told me that for three months Constance has been holed up at the Royalton, has seen or communicated with no one—completely cut herself off from life outside. It's not a new story . . . particularly in New York, which can be lonelier than a desert island. When *The Matriarch* folded after about ten performances, Connie was very depressed and shut herself up in her hotel . . . refused to take calls. In a few days there weren't any calls. People thought she had gone back to England. Her isolation was complete. She left the hotel where she was . . . left no address and moved to the Royalton where we're going now."

"Why didn't Connie go back home?"

"Oh, the affair with B—— had ended and the last thing she wanted was to be where he is. She's been at the Royalton for three months and only goes out for walks at night."

"How's her health?"

"It's all right. The trouble is not health or money or drink. It's just bloody, gnawing loneliness."

"Does she know we're coming to see her?"

"Yes, Martha told her. Constance had forbidden her to communicate with anyone and Martha was afraid there would be trouble when she let Constance know that I was going to call on her."

"Was there?"

"No, she's quite passive. Martha is no mean psychologist. She told me that nothing in the way of work, a part, or hospitality will do any good. The only thing which could pull her out of this depression or whatever it is would be the chance to help somebody else. . . . What about you? I see you aren't as upright as you usually are."

"Oh, I'm getting on all right. That surgeon of Alfred's is a wizard – Eskell, I mean. Oh, I saw a play night before last that I would give my eyeteeth to act and direct in London. It's called *Five Star Final.*"

"Well, go ahead and get it. What's holding you?"

"It's a production of Al Woods. He just told me yesterday to go to hell! You remember the run-in I had with Al when I was directing *Blackmail* with Tallulah . . . when *The Second Man* was running?"

The taxi was drawing up to the Royalton as Noel exclaimed, "I've got an idea . . . I believe it will do the trick!"

It was a shock for both of us to see our friend. Connie was no longer the warm, cheerful companion we had known. Instead we found cold, apathetic dullness. She greeted us formally from her chair. We must have seemed to her to be remote figures from the past.

Noel's conversational powers, I believe, were limitless, but on this occasion it was impossible to arouse Connie's interest. We babbled on about current theatre news.

"*Private Lives* scored a triumph at the Phoenix," said Noel. "The only setback we encountered was that Ray here went to sleep at the first reading of the play at his house."

No reaction from Constance.

"Gertie, the Oliviers and I arrived yesterday on the Q.M. Adrianne didn't come. She's doing a play in London."

Still no reaction. Noel tried some personal approaches.

"*Hay Fever* will probably be done on Broadway . . . very soon, I think, and Judith would be quite perfect for you, my very dear Constance."

No dice. It was my turn.

"Elsa Maxwell's throwing one of her parties tomorrow night. What do you say to coming with us?"

This laid the largest egg of all. Noel decided to play his trump.

"Would you like to help Ray?"

To my astonishment, as if someone had turned on a switch, Connie's eyes sparkled and she was attentive, her listlessness gone. The word "help," as Martha had promised, did the trick. Noel poured it on, told Constance the *Blackmail* story, which he knew as well as I did, and I told of my efforts to get *Five Star Final* for London. I finished up with, "I can't understand what the producer of a smash hit can be doing with a tin-horn proposition like *Movie-of-You*."

"Don't you see?" said Constance with a smile for the first time. "Both operations are on Broadway. What's the phone number of *Movie-of-You*?"

I got it from Information, and soon Noel and I were watching the old Constance at work. She was very moving.

"Al, this is Constance Collier... So are you, Sweetheart...Oh, I've been resting...taking it easy... Al, Ray Massey wants to do your wonderful smash hit play in London–Five something something...Oh! Al, that is not true... He did his best for you, dear Al, under frightful odds, injured and... He really struggled for you, in those dreadful days in London, Al... He was not against you, Al... He wasn't, eh, tied up with Tallulah... Al, oh, Ray is not a two-faced... Oh, how could you say that, Al... Now, listen to me...if that dear boy doesn't get that wonderful play in London I don't know what will happen to him, Al... Oh Al, dearest Al, I knew you would... Yes... He'll come to 277 Park Avenue tonight... Thank you, Al."

It was a great job.

Releasing the flow of Connie's goodwill and generosity was all that was needed. She did go to Elsa's party with Noel and me as her escorts and dressed in one of Edward Molyneux's best. She soon was a great success in Noel's *Hay Fever* and fully resumed her rightful place as a gracious, talented lady of the stage. In truth, only Noel, Martha and I knew that Constance had ever forsaken it.

That night before the party I called at Al Woods's apartment at 277 Park Avenue. His greeting was, "You're a smart son of a bitch to put Connie Collier on to me. She always makes me cry."

He spread some papers on a table.

"Here's a letter giving you the rights to produce *Five Star Final* in London. I give you a year." He pointed to the letter. "I'm only charging you 5 percent on your gross, which is very generous"–it was–"and I don't want any advance. You sign both copies." I did, as Al went on. "I'd have given you a free *Movie-of-You* if you hadn't been in such a hurry. I still think you're a two-faced son of a bitch but I think you'll give the play a good production. Here are a couple of scripts of the play and some blueprints of the scenery. Good luck."

My amazement at Al Woods's benevolence continued through the successful opening and run of *Five Star Final* in London, but was slightly tempered when at a party in New York, where I was rehearsing another play in the fall, William A. Brady, the producer, asked me, "When am I going to get that 10 percent on the gross of *Five Star Final* in London?"

About mid-morning of the next day I was awakened by a telephone call.

"This is your agent, Noel Coward. Listen to me. I have just declined an offer to play the title role in what promises to be a somewhat eccentric production of *Hamlet* by W. Shakespeare, which Norman Bel Geddes is to design, produce and direct on Broadway next fall. I have explained to him that I do not wish to act again this year after *Private Lives*. I have also told him that there is in New York at this moment a specialist in indecision, vacillation and anxiety who could portray these characteristics of the Dane to perfection. I have given Geddes your number and you will hear from him. You will, of course, say yes and worry afterwards. I'll see you in London in June. Happy vacillating!"

I had not said a word. The telephone rang again. It was Norman Bel Geddes, who asked me to lunch at the Plaza Oak Room in half an hour.

At the Plaza I was warmly greeted by Norman Bel Geddes and introduced to his partner, Courtney Burr. Geddes was a chubby, dimpled extrovert with a midwestern twang; Courtney Burr, a genial, racquet-club type. The table was littered with sketches of ground plans and elevations.

Geddes announced: "Noel Coward is one hell of a booster for you, but I've heard of a performance of yours in London – *Spread Eagle* –which sounds exactly what I want for Hamlet." I murmured thanks.

Manhattan cocktails were served to us in coffee cups, though no one had ordered them. Norman Bel Geddes plunged into his sales pitch.

"Gee, this play *Hamlet* has everything. It's an action show. Think of that duel scene – four characters dead at the end of it. . . . I've got a cut version that plays just over two and a half hours, plus two intervals. Tried it out at Skowhegan last summer and it runs like an express train. I billed it as a melodrama."

"Who played Hamlet?" I asked.

"Howard Lindsay. I used the stock company that was there for the summer; Howard was their leading man. He was just dandy. Of course, I didn't have enough rehearsal time."

"You put it on as part of the stock season with just a week's rehearsal?"

"That's right."

Geddes went on to explain his *mise-en-scène*. The setting would be a fixed architectural arrangement of angles, planes and levels. Although a proscenium theatre would be used, there would be an apron stage jutting into the orchestra. The method of staging would be what was then known as "presentational." Changes of scene were to be

123

accomplished by variations of lighting; the action would be completely continuous. Geddes's idea was that the play be presented with the "flow of a motion picture."

I thought of some of the Hamlets I had seen – the grace and beauty of Forbes-Robertson's Prince; of Walter Hampden's, in similar mould, sonorous and noble; E. H. Sothern's tortured student; the ranting but somehow exciting Robert Mantell; John Barrymore's scintillating actor's Hamlet; Colin Keith-Johnston's vibrant youth in the London modern-dress revival. They seemed a frightening company to follow.

Geddes was folding up his lighting plan. After a silence he said, "Do you want to do it?"

I had muffed one opportunity to act on Broadway and was determined to avoid another mistake. Yes, I wanted to do Hamlet. I knew what was probably coming: I would be the instrument of a highly talented designer. As for my performance, I would be on my own.

Courtney Burr took over. Rehearsals would begin in late September. After a two-week try-out there would be an early November opening in New York. On our way out Norman handed me a script. "My cut version," he said. Later I found that the cut text was typed in prose form. It annoyed me that such an elaborate attempt had been made to disguise the meter.

I walked over to Brentano's and bought a little Temple copy of *Hamlet* and marked the Geddes cuts in it. I never looked at the prose script again. Next day at noon I sailed for home on the *Aquitania*. In my deck chair, bundled in rugs, I read *Hamlet*. These lines would be entrusted to me. My emotions were mixed but fear predominated.

Traditionalists and pedants would eventually scoff at Geddes's butchery of the play, but in fact his cut version was little shorter than most recent acting versions. Nothing of "great pith and moment" was missing. The great soliloquies were untouched. Given the stress on action, the editing was consistent and effective. It certainly moved, as Geddes had claimed. I closed the little book with the realization that for the moment I could not afford the luxury of dreaming about Hamlet. That was still months away. Meanwhile there was plenty to do on *Five Star Final*.

In my cabin there was a cable from the Gatti brothers, who owned the Vaudeville Theatre. They wanted me to direct a revival of Somerset Maugham's *The Circle* as soon as I landed. I decided to do that too.

# 16

In London I had *The Circle* in rehearsal before the end of January. We opened cold at the Vaudeville on March 2, 1931.

*The Circle* had always held a particular interest for me. It is perhaps Maugham's best comedy. He thought so himself and the public agreed. It is a romantic comedy in which a worldly father tells his son, husband of a restive wife, that the way to keep her is to treat her so well that she will be ashamed to leave. But love laughs not only at locksmiths, it laughs at unlocked doors as well.

Only one of the original company was in the revival, Allan (Tony) Aynesworth, as Lord Porteous, the elderly victim of romance. His partner in this enchantment was dear Athene Seyler, and as the dry-witted father we had Sir Nigel Playfair. I had acted with all three in Harwood's *The Transit of Venus*, and I knew their ability to play in the major key, which Maugham's comedy demanded.

Of the three players of the younger generation, Celia Johnson as the recalcitrant wife would present no problem. About Frank Vosper as her priggish husband and Peter Hannen as the lover I was not so sure. I knew I would face problems which occurred whenever the older and younger generations were together in the same play. Actors who had learned their craft before the First World War used the major key; post-war players used the minor. The latter were natural but they had no attack. Their elders possessed assertive technique; they pointed their sentences; they understood emphasis. They were not afraid to be actors. As rehearsals proceeded, a hint or two brought Celia to perfect harmony with the play.

The conversion of Frank Vosper and Peter Hannen to the style of their senior colleagues was not so easy. Not that their talents were unequal to the task. The trouble was that their performances were in a smaller dimension than those of the older players – they were out of focus. They seemed to have an irresistible impulse to discard their lines. Inaudibility is to me intolerable in any style of acting.

Maugham arrived towards the end of the first week of rehearsals. I

125

sat with him in the stalls and let the first act run its course without interruption, just making notes. Maugham, as usual, made no comments, although he seemed more pleased and relaxed than he had been at *The Sacred Flame* rehearsals. I asked him what he thought of the cast. He just stammered, "I think everybody is v-v-very good. I couldn't hear a damned word Vosper or Hannen said."

I crossed the rehearsal gangway and quietly repeated Maugham's exact words. I added, "Let's run the first act again." There was no mumbling this time.

Maugham was delighted. "Let's get Tony Aynesworth and have some lunch at the Garrick. It is a good play. D'you know, I've never seen it acted before?"

It was true. In 1920 Maugham had been on one of his many jaunts to the Far East and had missed the London and Broadway productions.

We sat at the long table at the Garrick.

Just as we were about to leave, a familiar Garrick figure took his seat on the other side of the table. It was Sir Arthur Pinero.

"Pin, when are you going to give us another play?" Tony asked him.

The answer was instantaneous.

"I shan't write another play. There are no more rules to break."

Sir Arthur's lament was of little substance. The comedy of manners was not based on laws and customs, but on human behaviour. Maugham himself was a teller of tales, not a moralist. *The Circle* is timeless.

I remember the decorum which pervaded rehearsals. Everybody in the cast dressed with some formality: neckties and polished shoes for the men; hats, attractive dresses for the ladies. The great moment was the arrival of Mr. Aynesworth, invariably immaculately tailored in browns or greys. A true Edwardian dandy, he favoured double-breasted suits accented by waistcoats of the most sensitive hues. Tony was sixty-six at this time and the double-breasted jackets concealed his slight corpulence. His buttoned boots glistened with polish. One morning he made a most impressive "up-centre-fancy" entrance, bowed to the ladies and seated himself in a beautiful Chippendale chair which Laurence Irving, the designer, had not meant to be used. We all waited for the groaning masterpiece to collapse. Old Tony fingered the handkerchief in his breast pocket, sensing something horribly wrong. He withdrew the offending article.

"My God," he muttered, "my shaving towel!"

126

The chair survived Tony's shock.

Ivor Brown, writing in *The Observer*, described *The Circle* as "an admirably adroit piece. Tight in its workmanship, spare and muscular in Mr. Maugham's distinctive way."

It was a joy to direct. Even with the postponement of the opening performance because of Tony Aynesworth's flu, the company were at concert pitch for the first night. All six did the play proud. It still makes me shudder to think of how comedies that needed the timing of a delicate watch were often submitted to an audience for the first time at an actual opening performance. *The Circle* was a hit in 1931, just as it had been in 1921, and would be many times again.

On the voyage home I had read *Five Star Final* carefully, three times. I liked the play better each time I read it. But it was not going to be easy to find a management to put it on the London stage. It would cost a bundle to produce, it would be expensive to run, and there were only four theatres in the West End with stages large enough to take the necessary three revolving stages.

As soon as I got *The Circle* into production I turned my mind to *Five Star Final*. Of some forty producers then active in the West End of London, I could think of only two men with the means and the guts to undertake such a venture. One was C. B. Cochran and the other Alec L. Rea. Cocky could always find money and Alec always had it. Both possessed courage and followed their own instincts. I flipped a coin and it came up Alec.

I knew Alec Rea intimately as a friend and as a manager. I cannot recall a moment when he was not beaming. He did not smile; he beamed, because he loved the theatre and he was having a wonderful time. He used to say to me, "Sometimes the flops are more fun than the hits—remember *Spread Eagle*?"

On the way to St. Martin's Theatre, where Alec had his offices, I passed several newsstands displaying banners which read "Raymond Massey slams the managers." I bought a copy of *The Era*, the trade paper in question. It featured an interview I had given about a week ago on my return from New York. It was a scorching attack on London producers for their timidity and apathy, expressing my admiration of their Broadway counterparts for daring enterprise. I had pulled no punches and was accurately quoted. I was satisfied with what I had said but was not sure that this was the best time to have said it.

Alec was at his desk, *The Era* in his hands, E. P. Clift, his partner, seated nearby. Alec was still beaming.

Clift said, dead-pan, "I heard the West End Managers' Association is going to give you a testimonial dinner."

I placed the script of *Five Star Final* on Alec's desk and started my spiel. "Alec," I concluded, "it really is a humdinger."

The little man was really beaming. He had been leafing through the script and was now gazing at the list of scenes – twenty-seven of them! He was not scared.

"It will have to be called *Late Night Final* in England. We don't use this *Five Star* term here," was Alec's first comment.

I felt sure he was going to take it on. But first he made a counter-offer. He would read *Late Night Final* if I would read a play called *Lean Harvest* by Ronald Jeans. He wanted me to direct it.

Within a few days I had agreed to this, while Alec had decided to back *Late Night Final* in partnership with Sidney Bernstein. I was to direct that too, as well as play the lead. Meanwhile I also undertook to direct Edward Knoblock's stage version of Vicki Baum's novel *Grand Hotel*. I was committed to playing Hamlet on Broadway. . . .

Now I was really in for the whole thing. In slightly less than six months I would have to direct four major plays, three of them multi-scene productions, and in one of them I would be acting the leading part. I knew the preparation and rehearsals of these plays would be complicated beyond belief. I would have to struggle to keep the productions distinct. When I was actually at work on the three big ones the conflicts, confusions and overlappings were so involved that I seemed at times to be staging one mammoth impossibility with sixty-eight scenes and a cast of one hundred and one! Even telling about these six months makes me dizzy.

Staging the Maugham play had been a pleasant and simple task. *The Circle*, so perfect in form, with its gallery of lively portraits and one handsome setting, had come to life at the Vaudeville, to prove that high comedy was still flourishing in England.

I had added an extra week of dress rehearsals for *Grand Hotel* as well as for *Lean Harvest* and *Late Night Final*. The schedule would involve me in confusing, overlapping effort. Why had I taken on such a backbreaking schedule? I was confident I could do a good job and I knew that all three plays offered opportunities I could not afford to lose. And although I work best under stress, I admit there were moments during those five months when I had qualms.

A director must have a designer he trusts and can work with. For *Lean Harvest* I had Laurence Irving. A grandson of Sir Henry Irving and son of H. B. Irving, he had theatre in his blood. A first-rate artist,

128

he was as good a stage designer as we had in England. Only Aubrey Hammond could compare with him in inventiveness.

We were to produce the play at the St. Martin's Theatre. The stage was terribly small. Laurence and I decided revolving stages were out. The proscenium was too narrow. The wings on both sides of the stage were roomy enough, allowing nearly fifteen feet for two jack-knife platforms to pivot to the proscenium setting line. There was also enough depth to permit a third castored platform. Laurence was satisfied that he could make do with the three platforms.

It was late at night, halfway through rehearsals, when we decided on the platforms. But before I saw Laurence again, I had my first session with Max Hasait, the German engineer who was to design *Grand Hotel*.

Herr Hasait was not like Laurence Irving. I still think he should have stuck to lighting, his true vocation. There seemed to be some thought in his mind that he had risen to the rank of Herr Direktor. I could never quite dispel the idea.

By late February only a rough scenario had been delivered but on the strength of it Hasait was to submit sketches and plans for a revolving stage. Hence his first English visit.

The Adelphi Theatre, where *Grand Hotel* was to be produced, had by far the largest stage of any London theatre normally used for dramatic shows. It was available to us from mid-July, giving us time to install the 35-foot revolving stage and allow at least two weeks' rehearsal in the theatre. Adelphi lease-holders agreed to share the cost of the revolving stage, if it was to be a fixture.

Hasait had returned to Berlin and *The Circle* had opened successfully before I could go back to planning the *Lean Harvest* production with Laurence Irving. He had already made scale models of the platforms and sets. At his studio we went through the entire script timing, as best we could, including the moving of the platforms and resetting of the stages. It worked. No scene change during an act would take more than half a minute; most would take fifteen seconds or less. (When *Lean Harvest* opened, our estimates proved right on the button.)

"Laurence, you've put that whole production on a stage half the size of the Adelphi one—and there's room to spare!"

"Yes. A fourteen-scene show on that postage-stamp stage and the sets will look as big as yours from Deutschland!"

"Gilbert Miller made that Hasait deal."

"And it will bust him. Our platforms will cost about a hundred and twenty-five pounds. That thing from Berlin will cost five thousand pounds."

Eddie Knoblock's script of *Grand Hotel* arrived next day. I thought it very good. It was much more of a melodrama than the New York version and called for a far bigger production. Eddie enclosed a note that he had kept the number of speaking characters down to forty-two, less than in Max Reinhardt's production in Berlin, and quite a few more than in the Broadway version by Herman Shumlin. The play had not done well in Berlin but it was still running in New York. Eddie Knoblock had been right to expand the spectacular side of the play.

"Soap opera" was a term that had not been invented in 1931, but that is what our London *Grand Hotel* was, an enormous, scrumptious soap opera. I was going to have a lot of fun directing it.

Right now, though, I was worrying about *Lean Harvest*. The physical production did not worry me as much as the play itself. It might be described as a witty sermon on the evils of money-grubbing. Would its fourteen separate little plays be accepted as a single creation? Then blocking out the actors' moves, I realized that my first reaction had been right. These fourteen scenes were packed with entertainment, with enough satire, humour and wit for ten plays. To hell with the rules!

Laurence Irving's effects in the death scene were an enormous help. He succeeded in creating an interior that shrank and became distorted. Playgoers would rub their eyes and blink as window frames went askew, columns tilted and walls converged.

*Lean Harvest* was something new for the theatre, a morality play which would make people laugh. We had an ideal company to act it, led by Leslie Banks, Diana Wynyard, J. H. Roberts and Nigel Bruce.

I have seldom read such ecstatic reviews as we won for the play and performers. This innovative, episodic sequence of little plays gave the first-night audience entertainment they had not found in a straight play for years.

Now I had two in the bag and two to go. *Late Night Final* was next.

It was early May, seven weeks before we were to open at the Phoenix. *Late Night Final* would need every minute of rehearsal time. If Sidney Bernstein (now Lord Bernstein of Granada Television) had not promised us the Phoenix stage for two full weeks before our opening date, I could not have had the show ready. As it was, careful planning and rehearsal for four weeks followed by a week of dress rehearsal brought the performance to the public in the best condition of any play I ever directed.

There is nothing more heartless than a newspaperman's love of human interest. *Late Night Final* was a play by Louis Weitzenkorn about the seamy side of American newspaper life. The *Evening Gazette*, a sensational tabloid, is suffering from a depressed circulation, ascribed to the high-brow tendencies of its managing editor. The publisher insists on raking up a twenty-year-old story which he believes will sell his newspapers. The innocent victim of an old scandal is hounded to suicide.

Louis Weitzenkorn had written the play after quitting the *Daily Graphic*, a long-defunct New York tabloid. His play is painfully authentic.

Casting an American play in London has never been easy. There were twenty-eight speaking parts and nearly all of them demanded the authentic dialects of New York City. I had agreed to cast the play from talent to be found in London. In the end I did bring Allen Jenkins to England to repeat his hilarious performance of Ziggy Feinstein, the competitions editor of the *Evening Gazette*. But he was the only import.

For the ten principal parts we cast Louise Hampton, Eliot Makeham, Francis Sullivan, Carol Goodner, Charles Mortimer, Rosemary Ames, John Gordon and Beatrix Lehmann. About fifty auditions supplied the remaining parts. We were a fair company in our command of New York dialects.

After three weeks of rehearsal, performance was close to opening pitch. All that remained to complete the readiness of the company was what I have heard described as "a look at the scenery."

We had been working in a big rehearsal hall. We were to move to the Phoenix stage the following day. There we would meet the complicated production for the first time. Ten days later we would open.

We were finished for the day. The company had been dismissed and the stage management, all four of them, and "props" were gathering up our rehearsal clutter to take it to the Phoenix.

Louise Hampton beckoned me.

"Ray, why have you brought this company to performance pitch so soon? You've got us ready to open day after tomorrow and we'll still be ten days from first night!"

"You're right, my dear. We could open tomorrow. That's the date I had aimed at."

Louise was tired. "You haven't answered my question. Why have we got to wait nearly two weeks more to open this play?"

"Because it's going to take at least a week for you all to get back to the state of performance you're in now. You've got a backbreaking experience to go through. It'll rub off all the glint and sparkle I saw this afternoon, and I want you to have it all back when we hit London."

Louise and I were veterans of Sunday shows and talk of a week to spare made her laugh. Many of those shows were produced, rehearsed and opened within a single week.

"What do you mean by 'backbreaking' experience?"

"Let's have dinner at the Ivy and I'll tell you."

We walked the short distance in silence—two very tired people. Mario took our order. Drinks arrived.

"I'm waiting," said Louise.

"Instantaneous scene changes are like cuts in a movie," I said. "That's where the backbreaking experience comes in. I've got to coordinate the crew with the company. It will mean lethal boredom and monotony for you and the cast—mostly learning how to keep out of the way. It's going to take two, maybe three, days but the result will be practically instantaneous scene changes—six or seven seconds—the time it takes to turn a revolving stage ninety degrees."

"Isn't it a mistake for the stage to compete with the screen in action and narrative, which can be so much better done on film? And here we are trying to beat the movies at their own game."

"I don't agree that films have any exclusive hold on action, Louise. When the stage is given the chance to tell a fast-moving story in realistic terms, it can do a much better job than any camera can— because there is a darn sight more drama in flesh-and-blood acting than there is in celluloid! In our play Weitzenkorn has used simultaneous action with terrific effect. When Luella Carmody climbs into your apartment with the photographer, finds your dead body on the floor, phones me at the *Gazette* and I call the city desk and tell Brannegan to get that story in the late night final, there are three scenes going at once. No screen cutter can do that!"

I seemed to have persuaded Louise.

*The five stages of Late Night Final. These multiple acting areas did not merely accelerate scene changes. There were several occasions when two scenes overlapped with fine dramatic effect, and at the end of Act 2 the action occupied three stages for over two minutes. But never were four or five seen at once, as in this photograph.*

132

After dinner I had to go on to Gilbert Miller's office for a meeting about *Grand Hotel*.

The sketches were pretty good. Gilbert had wanted German atmosphere and that was exactly what his German designer had given him: opulence but not elegance. I think Gilbert was quite right too. This hotel was no graceful Ritz but a grand hotel, enormous, brash and lusty.

Much to my surprise, Gilbert accepted my suggestion that we use a replica of the hotel façade as an act drop, a built piece, allowing a character to climb from a window to the floor below and into another room.

It was an expensive idea which I never expected to realize, but I got it and it worked.

Another break I got at the meeting was that Gilbert made Eddie Knoblock technical adviser to the director. He would run interference for me against Max Hasait.

Next day I was back with *Late Night Final*.

The cast met the scenery at the Phoenix with appropriate joy.

We of the cast were thirty in number; the crew came to eighteen, not counting four electricians and the stage management.

I had hired a young American actor and theatre man as my production assistant, Irving Rapper. One of his responsibilities was to keep an eye on my own performance, along with those of the whole cast. It was impossible for me, with a long part, to keep in touch with the whole production. Lewis Allen, stage manager, would concentrate on the technical side.

While we were in the throes of lighting rehearsals at night, and drilling the stagehands and the cast in the daytime, perfecting the continuity and flow of the play till its mechanical execution went without a hitch, I had to turn my attention to *Hamlet* again.

Norman Bel Geddes and Courtney Burr had arrived in London to cast some parts. Norman was well informed about English actors and gave little trouble, but I had to help. Two of my suggestions, which were followed through by Norman, were Colin Keith-Johnston for Laertes and Celia Johnson for Ophelia.

The King came up for discussion at our first meeting. My theory that Claudius should be a dashing leading man, not a villain, did not prevail. Norman chose David Horne in the conventional manner. I got George Carr the part of first grave-digger.

Norman wanted Leon Quartermaine for Horatio, and that delighted me. I hoped some of his classical know-how would rub off on me. At our first meeting I had warned Norman that his prose script would offend English actors. A vehement discussion had followed. Norman was pained when I told him that English actors regarded Shakespearean experience as equivalent to a university degree; his prose version of *Hamlet* would be considered on the level of *McGuffey's Reader*. He was unconvinced but agreed not to show his prose script to any English actors until they were safely signed up.

The casting meetings made the *Hamlet* venture real for me. It was a disturbing thought that in just under two months I would be re-hearsing it in New York.

The opening performance of *Late Night Final* was like a beautiful dream. The hours of technical rehearsals paid off and the scene changes all seemed instantaneous. The play moved with a rhythm which I know the author had intended, without a single hesitation. The cast, without exception, regained the peak of performance after the ordeal of rehearsal with the crew, and played superbly.

The audience reaction was everything we had hoped for – intense and understanding. So were the reviews – Ivor Brown in *The Observer* expressed the concensus:

> This play may be described in the vernacular as a whale of a show. It splashes, lashes, spouts and generally churns up the fouler waters of American journalism ... the multiple stage is here used to excellent purpose ... to frame the essentially multiple scenes ... it makes great drama, coarse, vehement, relentless, as the theme demands.

We had an immediate hit on our hands.

The morning after we opened I received a call from a friend, Lady Furness. "Ray, congratulations on your hit at the Phoenix. A certain someone and I would like to see it tomorrow night. Can you get us two front-row dress circle with an empty seat each side? No publicity about this, you understand?"

"Yes, Thelma, you won't get any publicity from us. But with H.R.H. and yourself tucked away in the front row of the dress circle with empty seats on each side of you, that isn't exactly an incognito visit."

I sent four tickets to the lady's house.

The visit of the Prince of Wales coincided with that of the victorious cricket team of Harrow School. The Prince and Lady Furness left

135

*Late Night*

halfway through the first act. Next day Thelma Furness said, "You promised there would be no publicity. But there was an enormous round of applause when we came in."

"That, Thelma, was for the members of the Harrow Cricket Team. There were a lot of Harrovians in the audience. But your exit during the first act has brought us bad publicity. 'Prince Walks Out of American Play,' and that sort of thing."

A few nights later the Prince came back. He bought his own seats, and with his aide-de-camp, Major "Fruitie" Metcalfe, came to my dressing-room after the final curtain. Nobody had more charm than the Prince of Wales. I believe he really enjoyed the play; for ten minutes he talked about it with genuine understanding and appreciation.

As a gesture of thanks to the London newspapers for their support, I suggested to Alec and Sidney that a special midnight performance of *Late Night Final* be given for journalistic charities. "The critics have been incredibly good to us but I think a midnight gala, say on Friday week, that's eight days off, would be a good promotion. What do you think, Alec?" Alec and Sidney jumped at the idea. I went on. "John Van Druten called me up early this morning and says he would write a fifteen-minute burlesque with an all-star cast as a teaser for after the show."

"Ray, you'll be working on *Grand Hotel*," said Alec. "Don't take on too much."

But it was not too much. On July 17 we played *Late Night Final* at midnight to a packed house, and a quarter of an hour later we did John Van Druten's burlesque, *Late Night Special*. The cast included Lilian Braithwaite, Maisie Gay, Cicely Courtneidge, Leslie Banks, Nigel Bruce, Gordon Harker, Morris Harvey, Naunton Wayne, Nelson Keys, Jack Hulbert, Leslie Henson, Sybil Thorndike, Edgar Wallace and myself.

We were able to give the journalist charities over seven hundred pounds. Every working actor and actress in the West End was able to see the show at midnight, and did.

One note I treasure, dated July 13, 1931: "My dear Ray, I came to see you last night in *Late Night Final* and thought the whole thing magical, in fact, first class all around, and you, superb. Yours ever, Gerald."

*Late Night Final, at the Phoenix Theatre, London, 1931. Randall, editor of the Evening Gazette, gives instructions to Rev. Vernon Isapod, religious editor and a defrocked minister, to resume his clerical garb and get a story on the suicide of Nancy Vorhees. R.M. as Randall and Francis Sullivan as Isapod.*

At the midnight show, as on the opening night, I led on Irving Rapper and Lewis Allen for a call. They got tremendous applause at the opening, and at the gala, a standing ovation. Only pros could realize what they had done.

The direction of *Grand Hotel* was not going to be as pleasant a job as the one I had just completed for Alec Rea. I would have to deal with a divided management, Gilbert Miller and Mary Leonard's Syndicate, and I never found out who had financial control. I had a designer who was opinionated and prejudiced. Of the eight principal characters, three had been cast against my wishes. But I had a good script and Eddie Knoblock, the author, had been appointed my assistant. I was determined to steer my own course as director.

It was now early July. I had just six weeks to prepare *Grand Hotel*. A first night had been set for August 27. As installation of the huge revolving stage had just begun and would take three weeks to complete, we would have the Adelphi stage for only a week before dress rehearsals began. I still had forty speaking parts to cast.

It was the mechanical side of the *Grand Hotel* production that very nearly floored me. Actors, God love them, always come through and I had three dozen good ones in *Grand Hotel*. The performance never worried me in rehearsals. But the huge, travelling revolving stage, which had been made and installed by German mechanics, nearly drove me out of my mind. Eventually it caused a total of four days postponement of the opening at the Adelphi Theatre and only began to work with any semblance of efficiency when British workmen took it over.

On opening night we rang up at 7:45 and I was able to watch the curtain go up and see the telephone operator scene and the first big lobby scene before leaving for the Phoenix. I was already made up for Randall in *Late Night Final* and had a car waiting. I was standing by Herbert Chown, the stage director, in the prompt corner. The first two changes were smooth as silk. The big lobby scene was dimming, the black cloth scene drop came down – nothing happened. A murmured, calm voice out of the dark came. "Fuse on the revolve motor's burned out, Chownie."

"All right, put on the drag ropes."

The big stage, with twenty-two people riding on it, started to turn with eight men on the ropes. The lateral motor was now cut in but it was too slow. It seemed an eternity. I remember to this day that I thought of dear Chownie's trouble with the turntable of the gramophone in *At Mrs. Beam's* which gave him his cue for a curtain. Seven

*One of the nineteen scenes in Grand Hotel, and forty-five of the fifty-one in the cast at the Adelphi Theatre, 1931.*

years later it was a much bigger turntable. In emergencies you can think of the darnedest things.

"Let me know at the Phoenix how things are going, Chownie." I was gone. When I got to my theatre the stage doorman gave me a message. "Mr. Chown says to tell you everything is all right. The new fuse is in and we gained a few seconds with the drag ropes."

The moment the curtain was down on *Late Night Final* I got back to the Adelphi amidst a tremendous, tumultuous reception which seemed to go on forever. I had received two messages during our show from Chownie, one at 9:15 and the second at 10:10, both saying the same thing: "It couldn't be better. Chown." There was pandemonium at the Adelphi. I'm told they shoved me on for a call. I don't remember. I do know that all the seventy people of the cast and the crew were simply wonderful. In spite of the frustrations and the uncertainties they faced, they never faltered. They were never overshadowed by a lavish, pretentious production; they proved that in the end the theatre is indeed flesh and blood.

The unbelievable had happened. The four productions which I had directed—*The Circle, Lean Harvest, Late Night Final* and *Grand Hotel*—had all been staged within seven months and had all been successes.

Best of all, Randall, my part in *Late Night Final,* was safe in the skilled hands of Godfrey Tearle.

But I was not sanguine about *Hamlet.*

# *17*

I sailed for New York aboard the *Bremen* a week ahead of the English actors. By the time I landed I had learned my lines, using the Temple edition. Norman Bel Geddes met me with a new prose script, remarking, "I've altered the script a bit." He and Courtney Burr had come out in the press boat to Sandy Hook and I could not in the presence of reporters tell him what to do with his wretched script.

At the first rehearsal five of us from England met the American members of the cast. We were very pleased. Mary Servoss, a beauteous young woman with a lovely voice, was the Queen. She was reading from a printed text as Shakespeare wrote it—another rebel. Polonius was to be played by John Daly Murphy, probably the only actor ever to go from Ziegfeld's Follies to *Hamlet* in the same season.

At the rehearsal a tall, stoutish man had been introduced as Clayton Hamilton. His presence had not been explained. Later he was formally introduced as literary adviser; he was also the "drummer" or publicity representative. Clayton was a sound Shakespearean scholar who knew the theatre and loved it. He had written several theatrical biographies. A specialist in nostalgia, he could tell you when Richard Mansfield had taken a full breath in any soliloquy. He had a thorough knowledge of the cut versions used by all the Hamlets of the past forty years. He knew their idiosyncracies, but he was no director. When it came to developing a new interpretation he was not effective.

Norman himself had the makings of a good director but was limited by his absorption in the visual side of the production. The play to him was something to be seen and if there was time he would be able to work with actors but this was going to be "a hell of a thing to see" and that came first. Rehearsals as in the movies were a matter of keeping to marks for lighting.

The New York Producing Association, Norman's company, started with one hundred thousand dollars which was to finance three plays, *Hamlet* being the first. The money had been put up by the charming Nell Cosden, wife of Joshua Cosden, the oil millionaire. In 1931 the sum was quite enough to finance three reasonably budgeted productions, but by the middle of the second week it was obvious that Nell Cosden's hundred grand would not cover Norman's Elsinore venture, let alone two more plays. What it finally cost to open *Hamlet* in Philadelphia, where we had the Walnut Theatre for a week of dress rehearsals, I do not know. But Mrs. Cosden remained radiantly cheerful.

After a few days Norman fired the Ghost. The same afternoon we were rehearsing the rampart scenes in act 1. The Ghost had not been replaced. When we came to the point where Hamlet's father first speaks, Norman called from the orchestra, "All right, stop here!" But I did not feel like stopping. I always seemed to know the other fellow's lines better than my own, so I went right ahead speaking the Ghost's lines as well as Hamlet's. For the Ghost's speeches I froze in whatever position my cue caught me.

I got through the Ghost's lines:

> *I am thy father's spirit;*
> *Doom'd for a certain term to walk the night.*
> *I could a tale unfold whose lightest word*
> *Would harrow up thy soul, freeze thy young blood,*
> *Make thy two eyes, like stars, start from their spheres,*
> *Thy knotted and combined locks to part*
> *And each particular hair to stand an end,*
> *Like quills upon the fretful porpentine:*
> *But this eternal blazon must not be*
> *To ears of flesh and blood. List, list, O, list!*
> *If thou didst ever thy dear father love—*

Hamlet then interrupts the Ghost with "O God!" and the Ghost continues: "Revenge his foul and most unnatural murder."

HAMLET: *Murder!*
GHOST: *Murder most foul, as in the best it is,*
*But this most foul, strange, and unnatural.*

I had fallen on my knees at the interjection. Then putting my hands over my eyes spoke the "Revenge" line almost to myself and motionless. Well, it was a good gag and I said, "Norman, I charge extra for it that way!"

I could hear conversation out front. I sat down and lit a cigarette. Strangely enough "Leo" Quartermaine, the traditionalist, came over

142

*The duel scene in Norman Bel Geddes's Hamlet. R.M. as Hamlet and Colin Keith-Johnston as Laertes. The duel played just over five minutes and both Colin and I were scared every time we did it. Due to the violent contrasts of light, we never could quite see what we were doing.*

to me and said, "It makes more sense than some of the things being done around here." Suddenly Norman shouted, "Ray, it's terrific—we'll do it that way!" I was horror-struck. I bounded down the rehearsal steps to Norman's seat in the tenth row of the orchestra and said, "Norman, I was kidding. I don't like the idea—please, let's have a talking ghost like Mr. Shakespeare wrote it!"

I turned to Clayton Hamilton for support and shuddered as he agreed with Norman. He was obviously racking his brains for any precedent for this Freudian trick. Norman was in full cry by this time. Here was a new and provocative idea. He was going to adopt it and nothing I could say could dissuade him.

He won his point and on opening night I spoke the Ghost's lines to a floating, silent, disembodied head! Some of the traditionalists became cardiac cases at this blasphemy but some customers actually liked it.

Norman wanted the duel between Hamlet and Laertes at the end of the play to be a real fight and genuinely exciting. He had suffered, as we all had, those safe exhibitions of fencing which had put the play to sleep in recent revivals.

Albert van Decker was to stage the duel. Besides being a first-rate swordsman, he was a fine actor. He made the most of his chance to set up a rousing fight. He chose *épée-de-combat* as the technique of the duel and the foils had rather heavier blades than usual.

143

Decker had the resource and showmanship of a movie stunt-man and when he had finished with the carefully staged routine the duel played just over five minutes. Colin Keith-Johnston was a fairly practiced fencer but I had had little fencing experience and we worked at the duel at least an hour every day. For our own safety it was essential that every thrust, lunge, slash and parry be in proper sequence. The foils had rubber buttons and our doublets were of heavy material but the blades were stiff enough to make a successful lunge uncomfortable. The single "palpable hit" was to be delivered upstage, apparently causing a flesh wound.

The duel played considerably longer than the dialogue connected with it. I wondered whether the fight itself might lag when carried out with patches of silence. But with numerous audible reactions from the courtiers—and gasps from the audience—the duel did hold. We could have made it longer.

Norman, who directed me in all the soliloquies with great imagination and resource, had a strange reservation about Hamlet plunging cold into "To be or not to be." He therefore suggested that, coming onstage via the tunnel, I should speak four or five lines inaudibly and as I entered the actual speech would become clear and distinct. The tunnel lines were chosen from a portion of the play which had been cut. But the result was that several critics accused me of mumbling "To be or not to be"! I tried to persuade Norman to drop the device but finally succeeded only after two first nights in Philadelphia and New York had shown its futility. I can't repeat those beautiful lines to this day without a twinge of headache and a hunch of my all-too-round shoulders.

The principal hazard for actors, particularly tall ones, was a tunnel through the superstructures in which the cross-struts gave only 5'-8" clearance. I suppose for a first run-through in the set, with lighting, costumes and props, things weren't too bad. Most of the mishaps had been in the blackouts, none had been serious, and those carried out of the tunnel, including this writer, rapidly regained consciousness!

An unexpected diversion came in the second scene of act 3, the Players scene, when the King, the Queen and the Court enter for the play, joining Hamlet and Horatio. Shakespeare notes "with the Guard carrying torches," and when Mr. S. gave instructions concerning "props," Norman always paid attention. During the weeks of rehearsals in New York we had been told of these torches which were going to supply a good deal of the actual light for the scene and also would simulate, by means of a motor operating on some coloured silk, the actual flame of a torch which, of course, was not permitted by the fire regulations. These torches, in their long shafts, would contain storage batteries to drive the motors and supply the light. They had cost nearly two hundred dollars each and weighed some fifty pounds. There were to be eight of them.

The moment came for the Court to enter. As Horatio says of the King, "If he steal off the whilst this play is playing/And 'scape detecting, I will pay the theft."

Hamlet replies, "They are coming to the play, I must be idle/Get you a place."

But I could not hear my own words nor had I heard Horatio. There was a noise as of the greatest swarm of bees ever heard. The Court entered with the torchbearers. The torches looked wonderful and they were deafening. We struggled on but the torches had dominance. It was useless and Norman mercifully called a halt. "Cut the motors—if only there was no dialogue they would be great!" So the torches became visual, and bereft of motors they still looked great.

A requisite, it seemed, for participation in a Geddes production of Shakespeare was a certain amount of climbing experience, for as the dress rehearsal progressed I found myself in the inky darkness climbing a perpendicular ladder, a heavy broadsword at my side, to a tiny, unexplored plateau which I knew would be fourteen feet above the stage—twenty feet if I were to stand upright and count from eye level! But I was certain I could not.

At last I felt myself on top of this tower, trembling on my hands and knees, feeling for the edges, gasping for breath, my sword caught between my thighs. Down below, bathed in light, was David Horne declaiming that "my offence is rank, it smells to heaven. . . . "

My cue was close. I struggled to my feet. That soft, uncertain padding added to the dizziness. With a struggle, my sword was disengaged from its entanglement and I drew it from the scabbard. I was now actually standing up in the black darkness, on the tiny platform only four feet square, a little pool of light far below. I heard David Horne say most unconvincingly, "All may be well," and then a blinding light hit me full in the face. I could see nothing. The King might be down below, but I couldn't even see my feet. Yet the lines stayed with me:

*Now might I do it pat, now he is praying;*
*And now I'll do 't.*

The speech is finished. Again, in a second, it is black as pitch and I

*R.M. as Hamlet and Leon Quartermaine as Horatio.*

*R.M. in the Norman Bel Geddes's Hamlet, at the Broadhurst Theatre, New York, 1931. "Now might I do it pat."*

crawl down the ladder while the scant seconds flee. Polonius speaks to the Queen, my cue comes to speak offstage and a moment later I am into the closet scene! Polonius has been run through, standing behind an arras which was placed there as I sweated in dizzy fear on the tower. This scene with the Queen was almost a rest for me, for I was standing on the stage and the heights had been for a moment abandoned.

... And so to Horatio's blessed flights of angels singing me to my rest!

The Broadway first night, due to Nell Cosden's popularity, was somewhat of a social gathering. I was warned that it would be a difficult audience, but as far as I was concerned they were wonderful. The audience certainly was there, practically onstage, when the curtain silently rose in the darkness. In our production, during the first scene, the whole Court is assembled in the darkness and Hamlet lies on the stage wrapped in his black cloak. As I lay motionless on the stage, Leon Quartermaine stood over me. I could hear the murmur of the audience through the curtain. I could also hear Leon muttering to himself. The audience stilled as the house lights dimmed. There was the faint rustle of the great curtain as it slid upwards. The stage was black, the house was black. I could just hear "Leo," six feet above me, murmur, "Forgive us, Master Will, for what we are about

146

to perpetrate!'' The lights go up on the ramparts: ''Who's there? Nay answer me: stand and unfold yourself.''

Well, we would make it somehow.

The Philadelphia critics were enthusiastic, though none showed much knowledge of the play.

Philadelphia loved the production, the play and, in all humility, the cast as well. The play literally spilled out into the orchestra, ignoring the proscenium bounds and the presence of huge lamps all over the front of the house. Yet its impact was received with enthusiasm by audiences not given, as St. Paul's Athenians were, to accepting any new thing. In 1931 our production was radical, suspect to most of the theatre establishment. The intimacy which the apron stage permitted between player and audience was too inviting for some. My seven-year-old son Geoffrey, at a matinée with his Nanny, greeted the first grave-digger with, ''Hello, Uncle George!'' and tried to climb the steps to investigate the grave.

The Geddes *Hamlet*, of all the parts I have played in the theatre, was the most physically exhausting. Of course, under any conditions the role is no toboggan slide. I had a dressing-room on the stage and snatched a few moments of rest in the intervals and the Laertes break, but each performance exhausted me. Hamlet has two most beautiful speeches before he dies: in my breathless state after the duel it was agony to do justice to them and, after ''The rest is silence,'' to remain completely still.

It was also my first shot at Broadway. I knew little of New York's first-night theatre. To me it was a wonderful audience and the performance the best we had given. All the hurdles were cleared in stride, the lighting, more complex than ever, was flawless and all my own pitfalls were avoided. My only blunder was in misjudging the curtain line after crawling back upstage after ''The play's the thing with which to catch the conscience of the king.'' Two long black legs were still protruding when the house lights went up for the interval!

There was a warm reception at the final curtain and a lot of calls. At two o'clock, at supper, we read the first five dailies, two blistering slams and three really good ones. With the four evening papers, the count read five good. There was brisk movement in the box office.

The weeklies and magazine notices were a little more favourable. The intellectuals disliked the production. In 1931 they were fewer in number than today. I am not sure that their subsequent proliferation has been an unmixed blessing. Robert Benchley, writing in the *New Yorker*, said:

My only criticism of Mr. Raymond Massey in the new Geddes production of the great tragedy would be that he is not enough of a ham. . . . Mr. Massey is quite natural, his voice is the voice of an ordinary man (an ordinary man who doesn't like actors) and he gives the impression of being just what Hamlet probably was: a very young man with something on his mind. . . . Norman Bel Geddes has done another of his majestic lighting-setting-standing-sitting productions, which, at times, eliminates Shakespeare entirely (and O.K. with me) but which is always something splendid to look at. . . .

The box-office story of this *Hamlet* was a record of high promise not quite fulfilled. Broadway has always been a blue-chip gamble and has no time for partial success as London has.

On our final Saturday after a four-week run both matinée and evening performances were sell-outs. After the matinée my dresser announced Robert Sherwood, and all six feet seven inches of the playwright entered my tiny room. He was accompanied by Geoffrey Kerr, the actor. They sat down on my cot and not a word was spoken. After an agonizing pause, Sherwood slowly said, "This is . . . absolutely . . . terrific. . . . I am coming again tonight . . . if I can get a seat!" Geoff Kerr agreed and they left. After the curtain fell for the last time that night Sherwood was back again. He asked, "Would you like to play a young Abe Lincoln?" I said yes. "I think Mr. Lincoln was something like Hamlet," Sherwood said.

But it was six years before the script was ready.

# 18

After *Hamlet* closed at the Broadhurst I was "at liberty" with a vengeance. Being out of work is never pleasant but in New York it is intolerable. It was November 1931, mid-season both in London and on Broadway, with production at lowest ebb. There seemed little chance of any stage work in New York, which was where I would be for quite some time. My wife Adrianne had opened in Harold Harwood's play *Cynara* at the Morosco just before *Hamlet* and it was certain to run through the season until June. Adrianne had scored an acting triumph, giving a beautiful performance, and at once the movie offers started to arrive. Within two weeks of her opening she had four big studios bidding for her. She chose Paramount, with a contract for two pictures a year and five annual options for a delightful salary which was at once mentally spent.

Still it was a good contract and looked extremely attractive to her unemployed husband, who had nothing to do in the evenings but go to the movies. One of these I was familiar with: *The Speckled Band* was currently showing at the Warner Theatre. Fortunately its reception in America had been better than in England, where James Agate had remarked: "Mr. Massey is delightful but is no more Sherlock Holmes than I am Little Red Riding Hood." It was hardly an ideal recommendation for Hollywood should I choose to go there.

The agent who handled Adrianne's deal was a charming young man named Leland Hayward who was in a perpetual state of emergency. At this time he was the New York man for Myron Selznick, the redoubtable brother of David O. Selznick, the movie producer. Myron and David were known in Hollywood as the Fighting or Biting Selznicks. Though usually on cordial terms, the brothers sometimes came to blows over their professional interests. It was said that at least once they had used their teeth.

I knew nothing of this when Leland came along. He had arranged Adrianne's film tests, which I had directed and acted in. There had been four separate tests as the film companies refused to share one.

After the Paramount deal was closed Leland asked me if I would be interested in directing pictures. Cool as I was towards the movies, it did seem that a move to Hollywood would be an escape from idleness in New York. I gave him the green light. I promptly found a job directing a play called *Collision*, to open cold at the Hudson in about four weeks' time. A translation from the German, it starred Geoffrey Kerr and June Walker.

It was a pretty bad play. I knew almost at once we were headed for disaster. At this point Leland Hayward reported an offer from Universal Pictures which he described as exciting. I did not know then that "exciting" is agentese for "this is the best I can do and you had better hurry up and take it." Universal offered a long-term contract for my services as director and writer at a low starting figure.

"They're not interested in you as an actor," he said, "but they want you right away for directing and writing. Can we pry you loose from this *Collision* job?"

I wanted out from *Collision* anyway. But I told Leland that Lew Gensler, the producer, was a litigious character who would not release me voluntarily. So Leland got on to his lawyer.

Sure enough I was out of *Collision* next morning. But I had chosen this moment to come down with jaundice. My doctor enjoined bed for at least two weeks. Leland brought me the contract to sign, phoned the New York offices of Universal and got a reluctant agreement that I should report to the Coast studios in two weeks' time.

A jaundiced look at the contract was not comforting. It bound me to perform the services and duties pertaining to anybody connected with the motion-picture industry in any capacity whatsoever for as long as the company cared to continue my employment up to seven years. The only function not mentioned was acting. Directing and writing were specified, though my writing experience had been nil. A sinister reference to something called "maintenance" led me to suspect I might have a spell at plumbing.

I boarded the 20th Century a couple of days before the deadline of two weeks had been reached. Leland claimed to have received a telegram urging my speedy departure for the West Coast a few days before. I never found out who sent this wire, Universal or the Selznick Agency, or if it had been a figment of Leland's urgency. I suspect the last.

After three days and four nights in a Pullman compartment I crawled off the Santa Fe Chief at Pasadena feeling like death. Nobody turned up to meet me. I took a taxi to my hotel in Hollywood and had a bath. I should have called my agents and reported to the studio under proper escort. But I felt so rotten that I was determined to deliver my wretched body to Universal myself.

Another long taxi ride over the hills took me to the main gate of Universal. The guard said, "Whaddya want?" I had forgotten the name of the head of the studio. I said, "Take me to your leader!"

This enraged the security guard.

"Listen, wise guy, we're used to nuts like you."

I got out and started to tell my strange story. I was still talking when a young man alighted from a car behind my taxi and identified himself.

"I'm Harry Mines—you're Raymond Massey, aren't you? Where's your agent? He should be here with you."

"Well, there's been some mess-up."

"Lower the drawbridge, boys! This is Raymond Massey reporting for a term contract. He should go straight to Junior."

The police seemed mollified. Just then a stout little man drove up flashing a card and loudly declaring, "Dave Bender, the Selznick Agency. I've got to see Mr. Laemmle."

I almost shouted that I was his man but Harry Mines hissed at me, "Let him make his own excuses to Junior. You make your own entrance. I've got a neat little story out of this."

He had. His by-line, which appeared in *The Mirror* next day, did nothing to endear me to my agents or the Studio. But Harry has been my friend for over forty years. He's still a busy movie press agent.

He guided me to the bungalow of Carl Laemmle, Jr. and left, chortling with glee.

Ushered into the presence, I found Junior an agreeable but self-conscious youth who seemed about eighteen years old. He was actually twenty-one. His first words to me were, "We're glad you're here. We hadn't expected you so soon."

Before I could reply, Bender, the agency man, after hastily greeting me, resumed the altercation which had been taking place before my entrance. I did not hear one word of truth spoken by employer or agent. I did gather that Junior had known nothing of my contract before that very day. With a toothy smile he exclaimed, "We have great plans for you."

I was somewhat perturbed when this announcement was followed by the question, "Are you an actor?" I said I was, but Junior preferred to go by the contract.

He got somebody called Henry on the telephone.

"Henry, I have a young writer in my office. He's from the East. He's under contract to us. I'm going to put him on Ernst's picture—yes, *Ngana*. You have a story conference on it this afternoon. Oh, it's going on now? I'll send him right over."

I left Junior's office with Dave Bender who said, "Junior has great faith in you."

Henry turned out to be one Henry Henigson, the executive producer who virtually ran the studio. In his outer office I could already hear the din of the story conference. Henigson greeted me perfunctorily, introducing me to four other men who paid no attention but continued to shout at one another. Suddenly one of the men shouted an impassioned announcement of his severance from Universal Pictures. He then made a vigorous exit and was never seen again on the lot.

The meeting broke up. Henigson introduced me again to Ernst Laemmle, Junior's cousin. I was to be attached to the *Ngana* production. Ernst suggested I walk back to his bungalow. In his inner office he poured me a stiff Scotch. "You must need this. You are, of course, bewildered and exhausted. I'm going to speak with frankness."

In his middle thirties, he spoke with a slight German accent.

"Before I came here two years ago I was in London for quite some time. I know your work well. I have seen *The Silver Tassie* and several other plays you have directed. I have seen *The Second Man*, *The Man in Possession*, *The Constant Nymph*. . . . You have proven talent as an actor and director. You have just done *Hamlet* in New York and some liked your performance. Now you are here at this studio, with your hat in your hand like a beggar. What in the name of reason possessed you to come to Universal Pictures on one of these catch-all contracts?"

He rose and stood by his desk.

"My dear Massey, at your first opportunity make your escape and go home—to the theatre!"

I knew he was right.

My Hollywood writing career lasted six weeks. I wrote two lines of leonine dialogue—the growls of an off-camera king of beasts transcribed as, "Grrrrr," "Grrrrr." This creative writing may have been the reason for my summons to Junior's office.

In the six weeks since I had met him Junior had aged visibly. He now looked all his twenty-one years. He motioned me to sit down.

"Now, what are we going to do with you? You seem to be unhappy as a writer."

152

"I have never had any experience in writing."

"We have great plans for you. I am going to attach you to William Wyler who is to direct one of our new pictures. It will be a stimulating experience for you."

It was instructive if not exactly stimulating. Willie Wyler was directing a routine police melodrama. He was already one of the best film directors in the industry. I was with him throughout the production. We became friends and I learned an important fact from him. I found out that I did not want to be a film director.

What has always fascinated me in stage direction is the collaboration of actor and director. Cooperation and mutual trust seem implicit in most theatre adventures. But the screen director must be a dictator whether he likes it or not. In movie-making there has to be a boss. The actor becomes a puppet with his strings in the director's hands. In turn the director is the bondman of the camera, a demanding master, not always as easy to satisfy as it might seem. As I watched Willie Wyler in his lonely task, shouldering the responsibilities of player, producer, cameraman, writer and a dozen other functions, I decided that directing a movie was not for me.

Once the Wyler picture was finished I found myself uneasy in subsidized idleness. And without Willie Wyler or Ernst Laemmle to give me the hospitality of their offices, there was nowhere on the lot where I could sit down.

So when my old friend Walter Wanger suggested that I fly up the Coast with him and his wife Justine for a weekend at the Hearst Ranch at San Simeon I eagerly accepted.

Walter was a movie producer I had met in London. His wife, the famous Justine Johnston, had been Florenz Ziegfeld's most beautiful showgirl. She had made the unusual transition from Ziegfeld showgirl to research biochemist and was now working with Dr. Sam Hirshfield, my physician and friend.

We flew the two hundred and fifty miles in a single-engined airplane in a few minutes less than it would take by car. I was too frightened to appreciate the beauty of San Simeon as we swayed past the house. I heard the pilot's comments after our goony-bird landing. "There's another San Simeon drop I can walk away from!"

I was relieved when Walter promised we would drive back to Los Angeles.

It is the California custom to crown every hilltop with a house, often a sprawling, Spanish bungalow. San Simeon is a refreshing exception. This so-called ranch house is a lofty, twin-towered building in the ornate style of an Italian sixteenth-century church. There was a great deal of elaborate terracing and landscaping; the whole effect from the western approach was enchanting. The inland aspects of San Simeon were not as impressive. The hindquarters of this highly wrought building were simple concrete. I thought of the Hollywood backlots where the façades of a white-columned Southern mansion or a French château would be backed by wooden buttresses.

The party which kept arriving through the afternoon numbered about twenty. There were four or five journalists, two of them editors of Hearst newspapers, and several non-movie Californians. The rest were tied to the camera in some way. Marion Davies, who received us on arrival, was responsible for the presence of most of the movie people, including me.

With its heavy Renaissance furnishings, rich Italian ceilings and ecclesiastical atmosphere, San Simeon was not exactly a merry-looking place. The settings called for Borgias and poisoned wine.

The thought persisted as we went to dinner in the great hall. Designed around the beautiful set of sixteenth-century Italian chancel stalls which lined the two long walls, it contained a refectory table, the longest I had ever seen, with benches on each side. The only lighting was from candles on the table in fabulous silver sconces. In the shadows overhead were heraldic banners. The silver and plates could have served the Medici. The only signs of reality were the Lea & Perrins Worcestershire Sauce and Heinz catsup bottles.

Mr. Hearst had invited me to sit near him. As he talked with his friends he seemed to have donned the scarlet silks of a Cardinal. When he turned to me with a question about the English theatre, I almost replied, "Your Eminence, it flourishes. We have a playwright in Her Majesty's company whose fame will spread over the whole world. His name is Will Shakespeare." Instead I found that Mr. Hearst knew a great deal of the London stage.

After a session of parlour games and chatter I wandered out on the terrace. There was a full moon and a generous supply of yew trees. Yews are magical by moonlight. I must have stood there for fully five minutes. As I turned, a light in one of the towers caught my eyes. A figure stood in the window. It was Mr. Hearst. He was beckoning me to his eyrie. I obeyed.

At last I reached the large room filled with drafting tables, sketches, models and blueprints. I happen to be interested in architecture and landscaping and I must have shown my pleasure at being invited. Hearst plunged into a fascinating exposition of his plans for San Sim-

154

eon. He was a true builder. He knew his schemes down to the last detail. He described his projects for terraced gardens, colonnades, waterfalls, pools, grottoes, tree planting. Did he realize, I wondered, that the fulfilment of all his plans was impossible? Like many great builders, he had planned more than he could finish. He could not even finish telling me of his plans. Abruptly he broke off. "Thank you for listening. I must go to bed. It's two o'clock."

At breakfast next morning with the Worcestershire sauce and catsup bottles in sole command of the long table, the cold light of day brought the word "ranch" into clearer focus. After we had ridden to a picnic lunch about ten miles over the hills, the Italian feeling was far away. Mr. Hearst had ridden with us, on a beautiful Palomino mare. Despite his great weight, he rode well. I noticed his gentle hands.

He was also a surprisingly expert swimmer and diver. It astonished us to see this pear-shaped figure in a loose Victorian bathing suit dive off a six-foot board and cleave the water like a javelin.

Walter Wanger and I and one of the Hearst editors stayed on a few days at Hearst's invitation. Every day I rode that beautiful Palomino which Hearst had put at my disposal. The housekeeper gave me a new room every day so that I could enjoy different Italian ceilings. Universal Pictures seemed far away.

Back at the studio Junior announced that he was going to give me an opportunity to act. But the long and colourless juvenile part I was given did not permit much acting. The picture was based on a mystery by J. B. Priestley called *The Old Dark House*. Benn Levy had written a good screenplay. James Whale, who had staged *Journey's End*, directed. Most of the cast were British, with Charles Laughton, Ernest Thesiger, Boris Karloff, Brember Wills and Eva Moore all being very sinister. The good guys were Melvyn Douglas and myself. Gloria Stuart and Lillian Bond jointly carried the burdens of beauty in distress.

It was the first of nearly fifty Hollywood movies I would make. It turned out to be a good one. Or so I was told. I never saw it.

Through most of it I had been hiding a bandaged finger. After working on the picture about a week I went to a Sunday cocktail party at Walter Wanger's beach house at Santa Monica. Before I could speak to anyone a furious fight broke out between two little dogs at my feet. Countess di Frasso threw herself at me screaming, "Stop them! Stop them!" Instead of kicking the little beasts into the swimming pool as any normally intelligent man would have done, I pulled them apart with my hands. I felt a sharp pain. The second finger of

155

my left hand had been bitten off at the base of the nail. Everybody was commiserating with the Countess who was nursing her little darling. I saw my doctor, Sam Hirshfield, and hollered, "Sam, do something!"

"What a beautiful clean job," he said. "I wish we had the tip. I know just the man to put it back."

Gary Cooper found the missing fingertip at once. "Get a cocktail glass and put it in," Sam said. "I've got some alcohol in my bag."

Sam did a deft job of cauterizing and fixing me up, assisted by Justine Wanger. "It's a good thing that little beast wasn't hungry," he said. "Now, where's that glass, Coop?"

Gary Cooper looked embarrassed. "The bartender says he threw a half-finished Gibson down the drain. That must have been it."

Although my part in *The Old Dark House* did not give me much chance to act, I thought it might lead to something else. It did not. I went on picking up my weekly cheque and reducing my golf handicap to twelve, my all-time lowest.

Adrianne finished two pictures at Paramount. The lease of our house was about to expire. I was in a familiar dilemma, whether to cut and run back to the theatre or sit out another option. The money was now attractive and there was no job in sight in London or Broadway.

A telegram from Kit Cornell settled it for me. She wanted me for a lead in Sidney Howard's new play, *Alien Corn*, which she was going to put into rehearsal for Broadway as soon as possible. I wired back an emphatic acceptance—"yes" nine times and "love" once. I did not care about script or money or billing or anything. I was going back to the theatre to fulfil an ambition which had its origin in a cowbarn near Cobourg, Ontario, eighteen years before. I was going to act with Katharine Cornell.

I walked out on Junior and his great plans.

My first brush with Hollywood had ended in defeat. But at least I had learned a lesson—never to sign a term contract. There was another important lesson which I never did learn—never to sign for more than one picture.

Once in New York I was on top of the world. But not for long. Kit and her husband, the director Guthrie McClintic, had had to change their plans and *Alien Corn* was postponed for at least six months. I could not bear to wait for it in New York. We continued our eastward journey home. The ambition to act with Kit, though strong as ever, would have to wait another eight years for fulfilment.

156

# *19*

Back home in London after the fizzle of Hollywood, the theatre welcomed me with a succession of five plays which kept me busy through the following year of 1933. Four of the plays were failures but one of them, the third, had a good run and I was working on the stage again which was what I wanted. The movie business was closed to me even in England until my truancy from Universal had been forgiven or forgotten, whichever came first.

The first job came from Sir Alfred Butt who had a new Frederick Lonsdale comedy which he wanted me to direct or play the lead in as I wished. It bore the title of *Never Come Back*, a bit ominous for me at that moment, but I read it with delight for it was vintage Lonsdale and the part that Butt suggested I might act was fine – a mysterious American named simply Smith. He was a modern Robin Hood, committing wrongs and righting them, light-hearted and light-fingered and, of course, I opted to act him.

All the ingredients of a Lonsdale success were there: scrumptious settings on the Côte d'Azur and Leicestershire; a large gallery of obnoxious, amusing, blue-blooded freaks of both sexes; a wealthy American social climber attempting to marry her daughter to a title; an entertaining detective; the aforementioned Smith; and a peripatetic diamond necklace.

I played Smith. Adrianne was a charming heroine, Frank Allenby a most diverting detective, and as I remember, the necklace found its way back to Mrs. Social Climber. The first-nighters joyously received the latest Lonsdale offering but after six weeks of disappointing business, Butt withdrew the play. *Never Come Back* was a near miss, a painful kind of failure.

The next offer was to play in an English adaptation of one of Louis Verneuil's plays, *Doctor's Orders*. The comedic idea of this piece of gallic entertainment was a genuine kidnapping, which is not a really sound basis on which to generate laughter. I did not like the script.

"Never Come Back"

Besides, the *Topaze* disaster had supposedly given me life-long immunity to the temptation to act in French farcical comedies.

I saw nothing but trouble ahead. Nobody could save this script from disaster—not Yvonne Arnaud, the Belgian comedienne with her invincible ebullient attractiveness, not Gerald du Maurier's direction skill.

I should have turned it down. But I did *Doctor's Orders* and in spite of a fine performance by Yvonne and resourceful direction by Gerald, we failed badly. In poor health at this time, Gerald did not spare himself, instilling confidence in a company who really knew what was in store for them. This was the only regular production I ever did with him.

After the *Doctor's Orders* fiasco I had some time off. One night in London I found myself at one of the evening parties I have always tried to duck. I remember practically nothing about this affair, who the hosts were, or why Adrianne and I were there. A vague impression remains that it was a second-grade diplomatic party; there was an ill-assorted collection of nationalities present. All were on their self-conscious, best behaviour and excessively dreary.

At about 10:00 P.M. I found myself marooned in a corner of a large but overcrowded drawing-room with Adrianne and an attractive American brunette whose name, of course, I had forgotten. I procured some champagne and as the hour was still too early for departure, decided to sit it out.

The American lady, after a period of silence, announced that she had run out of conversation; but before we could be of any assistance in her frustration, she slipped to her knees extracting a large pair of dice from her evening pocketbook and bounced a sweet, natural seven off the nearby wall.

"That's more like it," the lady said. The evening bag was emptied of its ample contents of silver and notes, and blowing on the "bones" in her hand, she looked up at me. "I can't shoot craps alone, now can I?"

I had about ten pounds on me and faded the ten shillings which she put up. Another natural took that and she let it ride.

The lady was a beautiful crap-shooter, fast and accurate. She read the dice like a book. It's hard to believe, but in twelve throws, she

*Adrianne Allen and R.M. in Lonsdale's Never Come Back, at the Phoenix Theatre, London, 1932. Diamonds are usually persuasive but nobody knew who owned these.*

rolled four naturals and made her point seven times before a pair of box cars finished the run. Eleven passes!

I was cleaned before I ever held the bones and Adrianne was down to her mad money. Several local crap-shooters joined the session but they had none of the empathy with the bones which the American lady had. Their spurious exhortations to the "bouncing dominoes" to deliver a pair of shoes to the suppliant were frequently disregarded while the soft Maryland tones of the lady from America were rewarded substantially.

At last I tore myself away from this casino in spite of itself. In the cab, for which we had just enough left to pay, Adrianne said, "That's an awfully nice woman, that American. Her name, which you had forgotten, is Wallis Simpson—her husband is a Canadian...in the city. I've asked her to lunch next week. Gladys Cooper and a few of the girls will be there. I want her to meet Thelma Furness. They're both Americans."

Mrs. Simpson, who would later cause King Edward VIII to abdicate, did meet Lady Furness at the luncheon at 21 Wilton Crescent. They became fast friends. When Thelma Furness left for a trip to the United States she entrusted the care and entertainment of another good friend to Mrs. Simpson. This commission was faithfully carried out. Things in England were not quite the same after that.

During my Hollywood stint I read a novel called *The Rats of Norway* which I thought would make a good play. The author was Keith Winter, twenty-three years old. I had written offering an option, meaning to get an experienced playwright to adapt it for the stage. Winter wrote back that he wanted to dramatize his book himself. With some misgivings, I agreed. Six months later I received his script—a first-rate drama, the first of the two Winter plays which I would direct for Gladys Cooper and act with her.

*The Rats of Norway* was a queer, powerful and continually arresting play about the private lives of the staff of a private school, known as Fallgates in Northumberland. The boys were never seen. It was no ordinary school, not even the usual ex-stately home. It was a gaunt and Gothic monster with yew trees that flout the sky and a peacock wandering on the terrace.

The strange drama was played out against a background of school routine, as viewed from the masters' angle, the author's premise being that there was in some sense a curse upon Fallgates preparatory school.

160

*Gladys Cooper as Jane Clayden and R.M. as Hugh Sebastian in The Rats of Norway, at the Playhouse, London, 1933.*

Two ill-starred, contrasted love affairs told the story of *The Rats of Norway.*

One was a sordid intrigue between Jane Clayden, the wife of the headmaster of Fallgates, and Hugh Sebastian, a nerve-wracked drunkard, broken by the war, who taught classics. Thwarted passion and hatred were mingled and ultimate tragedy was clearly discernible.

The second affair involved a young newcomer to the staff, Steven Beringer, and Tilly Shane, a poor relation of the Claydens. But for them too unhappiness lay in store. Tilly, who taught the smaller boys, loved too deeply and possessively and her well-intentioned efforts to fall in with Steven's wishes only served to aggravate the young man's nerves as his affection waned.

Gladys and I played the sordid intriguers, Jane and Sebastian, fully aware of the troubles which lay ahead for both of us in these roles. But our efforts were received more warmly than we had expected.

As always with Gladys as a producer, the play came first and she cheerfully allowed the better and larger of the women's parts to be

161

*R.M. as Hugh Sebastian and Laurence Olivier as Steven Beringer in The Rats of Norway.*

played by Helen Spencer, a young actress of much talent.

The chaste affair of Steven and Tilly, to my surprise, met more critical resistance than did the outrageous characters whom Gladys and I acted. This, in spite of the immaculate performances given by Laurence Olivier and Helen Spencer.

We found that the gloom of Keith's play was much less oppressive than we had feared. Although we opened to an unresponsive audience, we got a very good press and the play ran for six months at the Playhouse, being the last production in Gladys' six-year management of that theatre.

*The Rats of Norway* was the only play in which I acted with Laurence Olivier. I had worked with Larry several times in Sunday shows in our early days, directed him twice in regular stage plays, and our professional paths had crossed in Hollywood and England in the movies.

For over half a century we have been close friends. Larry has long since succeeded to the unofficial leadership of the acting profession in England left vacant by the untimely death of Sir Gerald du Maurier in

162

*R.M. as Rittmeister Kurt von Hagen in The Ace, at the Lyric Theatre, London, 1933.*

1934. He has fought and won two tough battles: one for his life in the defeat of disease and the other for the establishment and success of the National Theatre in London.

Although blessed with every attribute of a star, he continues to dominate the English-speaking stage as a character actor who simply tries to find out what he can do for the characters he has to act. As an artist in his craft he has no equal.

Just after *The Rats of Norway* closed I appeared in a play called *The Ace*. It had been banned in Berlin by Hitler as being offensive to the memory of Baron von Richthofen, the great German flying ace on whom the leading character in the play was clearly based. Written by a kinsman of von Richthofen's, Herman Rossmann, the English adaptation was the work of Miles Malleson who also directed the London production.

Comparison between *Journey's End* and *The Ace* may seem unfair, for the German author had never seen or read Sherriff's play, but to me it seemed inevitable. The German author had transplanted the Sherriff scene from the British dugout to a château behind the Ger-

163

man lines where a fighter squadron was quartered. The commander of the squadron was Rittmeister Kurt von Hagen. He was a fine officer, beloved of his men – like Stanhope of *Journey's End*. He drank heavily in order not to think – like Stanhope. He was afraid that he might be afraid – like, well, Stanhope. Among his officers was an elderly, kindly man nicknamed Daddy. And there was an elderly, kindly man in the Sherriff dugout; he was called Uncle. There was also a youth who gave way to all the fears that von Hagen is conquering. And I remembered the coward in *Journey's End*. Finally there was the German equivalent of a cockney batman, and the play ends as *Journey's End* did with the heroes going out to meet the deaths they had experienced so often in their dreams.

*Journey's End* was intensely moving because its author merely opened up a British dugout and showed the inside, without trying to dramatize what may have been too strong to be successfully unfolded. *The Ace* perhaps did not grip one's throat as its predecessor did because it was written from the head rather than from the heart. *The Ace* failed, but it was a great role for me.

The first Robert Sherwood play I acted in was his first flop. It was called *Acropolis* and was a study of Periclean Athens. It was produced in December 1933 at the Lyric Theatre in London where I had just played *The Ace*. It was elaborately and beautifully staged, produced by a charming and intelligent American named Paul Bonner, played by a good cast, and it showed Sherwood at his best as a dialectic writer. The play was well received by the critics, yet it ran for only eleven performances.

I believe for once Bob Sherwood ignored his own dictum – "the theatre is heart rather than mind." It must deal with human beings and their emotions. *Acropolis* presented a conflict of values, not a conflict of people. Bob knew of this weakness and had taken a calculated risk in constructing his play as he did. In all his other plays he was careful to base his plots, motivations and conflicts on the characters themselves, their emotions, and superimpose the intellectual values. *Idiot's Delight* was a perfect example of his ability to do this. His characters in all his other plays were living human beings first and foremost, but in *Acropolis* they were too often mouthpieces for ideas. After we started rehearsals it was too late for major repairs for we were to open cold without a try-out.

The task of staging this essentially literary piece was in the hands of Marc Connelly, an American who seemed baffled by the job before we started. Instead of getting the play out of the library and on to the

*An early rehearsal of Acropolis by Robert Sherwood, London, 1933. Left to right: Gladys Cooper, R.M., Bob Sherwood, Ian Hunter, Marc Connelly and Paul Bonner. It is evident that Marc has just picked up the scent of a "fresh major handicap."*

stage, he seemed intent on keeping it on the shelf by his didactic method. We players needed broad, sweeping direction and we got meticulous coaching. Our performances were competent but we could have been better.

In England most directors come to the first rehearsal with the play "blocked out"–that is, moves tentatively set–and immediately the play is "put on its feet." There may be one reading, rarely more. In *Acropolis* we sat around for four days and as we had only four and a half weeks to opening, most of the cast were getting jumpy. Gladys Cooper, who played Aspasia, was particularly restive and during a break she said to me, "Ray, dear, when are we going to get on our feet and start to work? Do something!"

So I went to Marc and told him that English actors weren't used to readings and sitting around and that we all wanted to get the moves set. Marc said that he would start plotting the moves beginning the next day. But when we arrived for rehearsal the following morning the damned table was still there and the chairs gathered around it. We all sat down and Marc Connelly adjusted his glasses and delivered himself of an immortal line which is graven on my memory: "Now, this morning we will deal with the minutiae of the first scene of the second act and then we will search for fresh major handicaps."

165

After lunch the table and chairs disappeared and we found that the various scene plans were taped out on the stage. The play was to get on its feet! The first scene was "Before the steps of the Parthenon" during its construction. It was soon evident as we progressed that the search for the handicaps was on, in addition to the plotting of the moves.

In fact, it was open season for handicaps, major and minor. Almost at once a large, hairy handicap, at least a handicap for me, presented itself. I was playing Cleon (in 1933 the Nazi movement was in full swing and Bob had patterned Cleon on Hitlerian lines). In the first act I had a long speech to the populace stating my views about killing Spartans and making the intellectuals and artists of Athens do something productive instead of building pretentious temples like the Parthenon.

I was stammering along trying to wing it for the first time and doing pretty well when an actor, who had a small part as a stonemason, appeared down left carrying one end of a ladder. The ladder was a long one and I stopped my speech to watch the operation. There is always something funny about the concerted effort of two men doing something. A tandem bicycle reduces me to helpless laughter. Besides, I wanted to know who was at the hind end of the ladder. Everybody on the stage was laughing. About twenty-five feet of the ladder was onstage when the action came to a halt with a loud crash from the wings. The hind legs of this monstrous intrusion had run foul of a lamp standard. Marc announced that he wished to indicate that work was actually in progress on the Acropolis but he added, "I'm not sure that this is the right spot to bring on the ladder." I led him aside.

"Marc, dear Marc, I have a suggestion for the ladder. Bring it on in the interval between acts 2 and 3. That runs ten minutes which is just about what it will take to get it across the stage and the iron curtain will be down!"

That was the last of the ladder, but it was not the last of the handicaps. All through the final week of lighting and dress rehearsals there had been trouble in making entrances down left because of a large spotlight which was in our way. Aubrey Hammond, the designer, had finally eased the problem by raising the lamp on its standard so that we could pass under it.

On the first night, I was made up with my Grecian nose, breast plate, greaves, sword and buckler, pacing up and down by this crucial entrance. The call boy was giving "Overture and beginners!" and the men on the big lighting board were giving their cue sheet a final once-

166

over. Ian Hunter, as Phidias, was fighting nausea in a corner of the wings. Gladys was in a cold fury of determination. I was trying to keep my knock-knees from knocking. (I always have hated parts in which my legs showed.) Others in the company wandered about in the shadows. The orchestra started the overture. Way down left the pass-door to the front of the house suddenly opened and Marc Connelly, in immaculate white tie and tails, came furtively onstage. He didn't know how he was watched at that moment. He moved to the spotlight and placed a white gloved hand on the vertical adjustment crank. With a cry of rage I drew my short Greek broadsword and rushed at the unsuspecting director. Marc was through the pass-door and into the arms of Bob Sherwood before my sword could cut him down. Bob told me afterwards that all Marc said was, "Ray seems very nervous tonight!"

A few years ago Marc celebrated his eightieth birthday with the well-deserved acclaim of his fellows of the theatre. I don't think he ever realized how close he came that night at the Lyric Theatre in 1933 to missing that eightieth birthday by thirty-seven years.

# 20

In late November 1933 the scripts of the play Keith Winter had promised to write for Gladys Cooper and me were delivered to us at the Lyric Theatre just before the second performance of Bob Sherwood's *Acropolis*. I was squeezing my putty, Grecian nose into shape when Bob entered my dressing-room. The script was lying in full view on my dressing-table with the title, *The Shining Hour* by Keith Winter, plainly visible. Bob looked down at it and murmured, "The Marines have landed and the situation is in hand." With mendacious reassurance I said, "Oh, that won't be for some time." Bob muttered, "We know the worst now and it's no easier to take because it's my own fault." This failure had hurt Bob.

Tired as we were, Gladys and I read Keith's play that night and, as agreed, I phoned her when I finished. It was about three o'clock in the morning.

"I think it's a first-rate drama and I want to play David. How about you?"

"I want to play Mariella," said Gee. "And I think it's a fine play. I want to produce it in partnership with you, Ray, and I want Adrianne for Judy and please take up the options or whatever we have to do and I can hardly keep my eyes open ... good-night ... and, oh, you will direct, please, and I am so sad about *Acropolis* ... poor Bob ... I think he's such an angel to take the blame for what's happened to his play ... I ... " I think she was asleep.

Brooks Atkinson was to describe *The Shining Hour* aptly in the *New York Times* after we had opened on Broadway:

The Lindens are English country-folk; they are gentleman farmers who live in an Elizabethan farmhouse in Yorkshire, keep a respectable stable, and enjoy in a stuffy way the beauties of the countryside. After having been away for several years Henry returns with his bride, Mariella, who is only half English and is not sure that she likes the surly country breed. But she likes her brother-in-law,

168

David, and presently she loves him, despite the high regard she has for his wife. *The Shining Hour* is the story of the heartbreak and the agony this spontaneous love wreaks upon a closely woven family. Mr. Winter carries it off with fastidious and fervent emotion.

This emotional stress, as we have been led to expect from Keith Winter, extended beyond the fastidious, if not the fervent, to the self-immolation of Judy, David's wife, in a burning cowbarn at the second-act curtain; and in the last act, to the most intense hysterical outburst I ever had to exhibit as an actor.

Adrianne, of course, loved the role of Judy, and for the third time in my own experience Gladys, without hesitation, had put the play first and taken the secondary woman's part for herself. For the third time she was right, for the role of Mariella needed the inner passion which Gladys could express so well.

Her lease of the Playhouse, where so many of Gladys' successes had been produced, had lapsed, and she was no longer tied to a theatre. We both had the idea of an American opening for *The Shining Hour*.

To rehearse a play in England, take it out to New York and, after a U.S. try-out, open on Broadway, was a reversal of the usual order of things. But I thought it was a sound idea. One thing was certain: neither Gladys nor I could handle the Broadway management, nor did we know of an American manager who would be receptive to such a scheme.

Jack Wilson, Noel Coward's manager, seemed to be a mind-reader for he called me up just at this time and said that he along with Noel Coward and the Lunts were forming a producing company to do exactly what Gladys and I had in mind. What is more, he said he had read the Winter play, as had Noel, and wanted to produce it as the pilot venture of his plan. After a long talk with Gladys at her house in Highgate it all seemed to boil down to the control of the production.

"I don't want to go through another leaderless ramble like we had in *Acropolis*," she said. "I think we are in agreement that we do this one ourselves, you and I. How much do you think our English production will cost?"

"I think I can ring up for a Broadway dress rehearsal for – oh – four thousand pounds. That's on the high side," I said. "Let's be safe and call it a five-thousand-pound nut. Now who's to be the nice, tame American partner to handle the Broadway details?"

We called Jack Wilson and told him we wanted to have *The Shining Hour* on Broadway by the end of January. But Jack reported that Noel and the Lunts would be in London for the rest of the season. The next season would be too late for us. We needed a Broadway partner, and Jack suggested Max Gordon, who had already read the Winter play. I didn't know Gordon, but Jack assured me he was just the tame kind of manager we wanted.

Gladys was delighted. We got Gordon's New York number from Jack Wilson, and by a miracle at that time the call came through in just under half an hour. In between bursts of crackling static, Gordon welcomed us to his management, agreed to business details, and set an opening date of February 14 at the Booth Theatre on Broadway. He would try for a Toronto try-out a week earlier. That meant that I had just over four weeks to rehearse the play, get a set designed, built and painted, and be ready to embark for New York.

Aubrey Hammond, the designer, read the play that night and gave me a working sketch the next morning. I made two or three suggestions and the blueprints were in the hands of the scene builder in two days' time. The remaining three members of the Linden family were cast that afternoon. We got Marjorie Fielding for Hannah, the spinster sister; Cyril Raymond, as the middle brother, the husband of Mariella; and Derek Williams, as Mickey, the youngest brother. The afternoon of the following day we were rehearsing in earnest.

Keith Winter was a playwright who wrote from his imagination, not his experience. His plays were good theatre; they were emotionally true, but he was no slave to actuality. I doubt if Keith himself had ever met any people remotely resembling the Linden family. He liked to put his characters, authentic in themselves, in incongruous situations. *The Shining Hour* was not a faithful picture of Yorkshire rural life any more than *The Rats of Norway* had been a careful study of life in a typical English preparatory school. He chose these rather inconsistent backgrounds for the telling of his tales because he was led there by his unfettered imagination. As a director I faithfully protected and furthered the author's intent and matter in both productions.

David Linden, whom I played, had evidently spent much of his youth at the piano, at the expense of the reaper and the plough. It was inherent in the plot that he be an accomplished musician. Mariella's passion is instantly stirred by his playing. To this end I engaged a talented young pianist through the Guild Hall School of Music, to play offstage several pieces by Chopin and a lengthy portion of

170

Rachmaninoff's Fourth Concerto. I don't play a note myself but I was determined to avoid the dreadful ceiling-gazing and heaving shoulders of the onstage exponent of the pianoforte with the hidden keyboard. I arranged to place my small grand piano with a dummy keyboard downstage at an angle which permitted most of the audience to see my hands. I spent hours with the pianist learning the fingering so that I could give a reasonable simulation of actually playing. Amplification of the offstage piano could be placed under the instrument onstage. It worked well, but in Toronto I received two bad notices for indifferent playing of the Rachmaninoff concerto.

Our dress rehearsal at St. James's Theatre came at a time when we were sadly in need of an audience. I was much against showing the play to any sizable gathering. I wanted it to be as fresh and as unknown as possible for London after our Broadway run, whatever happened there, so we played *The Shining Hour* just for our patrons—Noel Coward, Lynn and Alfred Lunt and Jack Wilson. That was as exciting an audience as could be wished for, and as discriminating. Our performance won their approval.

Two days later we sailed for New York on the *Aquitania*, with our scenery and props. Daniel, my younger son, who had been born October 10, accompanied his parents on the voyage in a Moses basket in charge of Nanny Burbidge. Nanny, who had newly encountered theatre life, was already imbued with its loyalties, enthusiasms and hopes. These feelings remained very real to Nanny all the years she was with the family. As her charge lay in his basket on the deck, I well remember her reply to one who admired the somnolent infant. "This little man is making his first theatrical tour and he's not three months old yet. There's an actor if I ever saw one." Nanny's anticipation turned out to be correct, for forty-five years later Dan is a leading player in the National Theatre Company.

We were met at quarantine by Max Gordon and his staff. Max welcomed us as his favourite entry for the Broadway stakes. I would soon find Max to be an ardent horse-player. These devotees of the pari-mutuel windows do not usually know one end of a horse from the other but they often have an unaccountable talent for detecting equine quality, and in Max's case this extended to an ability to detect worth and distinction in a play probably without reading it. As we passed up the harbour to our dock, Max explained that two of his entries were off and running already with great success on the main stem. They were a comedy by Clare Kummer, *Her Master's Voice*, starring Roland Young and Laura Hope Crews; and *Roberta*, a musical by Jerome Kern featuring two young comedians named George Murphy and Bob Hope.

At Customs Max Gordon's voice increased in volume with his growing enthusiasm and he held a considerable audience of passengers waiting to confess their purchases abroad.

"The two odds-on runners that are going to make it four hits at the same time on Broadway for me are you three in *The Shining Hour* —we're going to open there at the Booth on the thirteenth—and Walter Huston in *Dodsworth* coming into the Shubert a week later. You are both certainties."

I shuddered superstitiously, preferring to think of *The Shining Hour* as a long odds outsider with good blood lines which with a bit of luck might be in the money. We would see.

We never had a proper dress rehearsal at the Booth or at the Royal Alex in Toronto. The lighting was very important and it took most of my time, so that when we rang up for the Toronto opening it was the first real performance we had given since playing the show for Noel and the Lunts in London. Toronto turned out an audience which was a joy to play to. Their Excellencies, the Governor General and the Countess of Bessborough, were in a box with the Vice-Regal party. Lord Bessborough was an ardent theatre enthusiast. He had sponsored an annual Dominion Little Theatre competition, which was to prove a great boon to the Canadian stage. The Lieutenant-Governor of Ontario and Mrs. Herbert Bruce were out front and, of course, my brother Vincent and Alice, his wife, who gave a big party for us after the show.

Toronto in the thirties was a great show town and the audience proved it that night. I think the play went very well; certainly the reception was enthusiastic, even rapturous. They gave Gladys an ovation on her first performance outside of England and the rest of us were correspondingly warmly welcomed. I was appearing after twelve years as a professional and the cheers were gratifying. Keith Winter made a speech. I really thought that Max Gordon, who was there, may have had something in his selection of us as a winner.

The next morning we read the local critics. They were very good to Gladys, Adrianne and myself, and they were indeed kind to the rest of the cast. But they bombed the play without mercy.

Max Gordon telephoned about ten.

"I've just been talking to the box office at the Royal Alex here. We're going to sell out this week . . . it's unbelievable for a try-out!"

"But you read the papers, Max. They're terrible for the play."

"Oh, forget about the notices. The evening papers are worse. Will you and Gladys have lunch with me at the hotel? One o'clock? See you then."

Sure enough, the *Telegram* and the *Star* were even more carping than the morning papers had been. Of course they had a right to their opinions as to what were the faults in the play as they saw it. Bad reviews are hazards which all players and authors must be prepared for. But all these writers had gone beyond the bounds of ethical criticism by indulging in gleeful anticipation of our imminent Broadway demise, conjecturing what abuse the Broadway critics would heap on us. Augustus Bridle of the *Star*, most destructive about *The Shining Hour*, was an experienced and knowledgeable theatre man. Bridle, or Gus as everybody called him, had been a critic and theatre writer for years, had a fine sense of theatre history, knew all of the great English and American stars of the last four decades, and had actually been of some influence in getting me to go on the stage. But his Cassandra-like prophecies of Broadway doom for our play were really pretty amusing.

Lunch with Gladys and Max Gordon restored my equanimity.

"Glad," Max said (Gee loved his blossoming familiarity), "they just loved you out front last night. I thought the big mogul in the box was going to bust himself cheering, and they're going to love you still more at the Booth."

"Thank you, Max," said Gee.

"As I told Ray, we're going to sell out tonight and we're solid through the rest of the week. So I'm going back to New York tonight. Don't give the slams of the play a thought. I talked to Keith Winter and he's fine—I don't think he gives a damn as long as the box office moves."

"Have you anything to suggest I should do with the show, Max?"

"The show is yours and Glad's here. You two are in charge. My advice is leave it alone as is."

No cuts or alterations were made nor would there be before the opening at the Booth.

Our first night was a smash. It gave Max Gordon his third hit as he had scheduled it, the quartette being completed a week later by Walter Huston in *Dodsworth*. A cable went off at once to Noel and the Lunts in London.

The critical verdict in the New York dailies which in 1934 still numbered nine, like the U.S. Supreme Court, was seven in eloquent and fervent favour of *The Shining Hour*, and two in reasoned though

"Shining Hour".

subdued opposition to it. It was a remarkable acceptance of a play which certainly had a controversial theme.

The press in New York was wonderful to us, as it would be later on when we went back home. Those of us who had the good fortune to work on the English and American stages in the years between the wars should be grateful to the dramatic critics both in London and in New York. Today there are precious few critics like Ivor Brown, Charles Morgan, Brooks Atkinson, Percy Hammond–men who could consistently write literate, perspicuous notices sometimes against 1:00 A.M. deadlines and frequently turn out a literary gem in the doing. They could write favourable criticisms which were constructive and not full of clichéd effusions, and they could write a bad notice which could help and didn't hurt–too much.

New York always has been a heavenly place in which to have a little spare time. Literary and stage folk and sundry notables would assemble at the bidding of such leaders of thought as Herbert Bayard Swope, the publisher, and Alexander Woollcott, the columnist and wit. There were others, of course, but these two salons were the ones to which we were beckoned, much to my surprise and gratification. Any resemblance to those Parisian salons of the nineteenth century was coincidental–there was no elegance or formality about them; but for wit, humour and debate I'll bet they'd stack up against those affairs of Mesdames de Stael and Recamier any day of the week.

Swope's gatherings were held at his big house at Sands Point and Woollcott's at any house he happened to rent for the summer. Both assemblies gathered by invitation but there were no fixed dates or hours, and meals were served in buffet fashion.

At both assemblages croquet of a savage nature and some form of card-playing were practised, but the principal activity was the playing of word games of a highly varied nature. These contests were genuine tests of erudition and were carried out with fierce intensity. At Woollcott's, the scene frequently took on the air of a Marx Brothers movie, which was accounted for by the inevitable presence of Harpo Marx and frequently a brother or two, but the Swope sessions were really serious at times and hotly contested.

Once at Swope's when I was playing a game called Hearts, very popular around New York, with Frank Adams, the much-loved

*R.M. and Gladys Cooper in The Shining Hour by Keith Winter, at the Booth Theatre, New York, the St. James's Theatre, London, and a provincial tour in England, 1934 and 1935.*

175

F.P.A. of the *Herald Tribune*, a word game was in progress in an adjoining room. All I can remember about this game next door was that a contestant who had scored some point had the right to ask a question as to the identity of some personage of historical or contemporary significance, such a person's name having to start with a certain letter. The answer had to be a definite description in three words, like "French medieval warrior." Swope, Bob Sherwood, Marc Connelly and others were playing. There were time limits of several seconds for both questions and answers. Suddenly the stentorian tones of Herbert Swope boomed in a triumphant "Who was Kleist?" There was a very short silence and F.P.A. shouted, "A Chinese messiah!" as he laid down a winning hand in front of me.

Not only was this my American debut as a director, with the exception of staging a revival of Strindberg's *The Father* in 1949, *The Shining Hour* was the only play I ever directed on Broadway. Many times I've wondered why I allowed my experience in staging plays to lie fallow in the United States. I suppose a strong reason for neglecting what was for me the most fascinating activity in the theatre was my involvement in the movies. But that was only half the answer. I regret my failure to continue stage direction in America. It was a very bad mistake.

*The Shining Hour* closed at the end of June after a most satisfactory run of 125 performances. It was exactly what we had hoped for. And the play had closed to virtual capacity at the Booth.

We sold the movie rights to Metro-Goldwyn-Mayer for a handsome sum. Then we headed back to England to play *The Shining Hour* in London at the St. James's, the theatre where Gladys and Gerald had acted *The Last of Mrs. Cheyney*, one of their greatest hits. We had taken the plunge and leased that lovely theatre from Gilbert Miller and we were now a full-fledged London management team.

But our return to England was not entirely a happy one. On April 11 Gerald du Maurier died, a victim of cancer. He had been too ill to see our play in England. His death was a sad blow to all of us, to all in the theatre who knew him. But particularly so to Gladys Cooper. For years Gerald had been her close friend, her professional guide and inspiration. Although I had known Gerald for only six years, and worked with him on only one occasion, I owed a tremendous debt to him for all the help, advice and friendship he had given me. Gerald was a great man of the theatre and to this day I don't think that many people really appreciate his great contribution to the English stage.

# 21

Our London first night repeated the acclamation of the Broadway opening. English audiences are rather more demonstrative than American, I think, because of the existence of the pit and gallery in most London theatres. These ardent first-nighters have a pent-up head of steam which is not usually to be found in patrons in the more expensive seats. It must be released either in appreciation or rejection of a play. When you have sat outdoors on a stool for twenty-four hours and more, possibly through a cold night, waiting to see a show, you have pent up quite a lot of reaction. At the St. James's on September 4, 1934, the cheers and the curtain calls were loud and prolonged. It was a great opening.

The "library" men – ticket brokers – consumed the statutory four bottles of Scotch and inked in the largest deal that the St. James's Theatre had had for several years. We were set for six months at least.

As soon as *The Shining Hour* opened I started work on my first movie for Alexander Korda. It was *The Scarlet Pimpernel* and I was cast as Chauvelin. The picture was shot at Elstree, about an hour from the West End, allowing for traffic, and Alex promised to let me leave the studio in time to get to the theatre an hour before the curtain rose at matinées and evening shows. He also let me have a limousine and driver to myself so that I could sleep.

The two good hot meals prepared by Quaglino's and served onstage to us during each performance of *The Shining Hour* at matinées and evening performances, plus the sleep which I had going to and from Elstree Studios, kept me fit and rested for the first three and a half months of the run at the St. James's, although I was working an average of more than fifteen hours a day.

When Alex Korda told me that he wanted me for Chauvelin almost as soon as *The Shining Hour* had opened, I was afraid that Gladys might take a dim view of my doing films during the run of the play. So I telephoned her to get her permission. But before I could

*The Linden family at the second of two Yorkshire high teas which were served in The Shining Hour. It was the "eatingest" play I was ever in and was known as "the dining hour" in theatre circles. Clockwise: Marjorie Fielding, Derek Williams, Cyril Raymond, Gladys Cooper, R.M. and Adrianne Allen.*

178

speak she asked if I'd mind if she did a picture with George Arliss starting almost the same time as mine would. I told her about my problem and said Adrianne also had a picture she wanted to do and why didn't we all say yes and get on with it. We did.

As usual, plenty of charity calls came in although we had to decline most of the requests for benefit performances owing to the movie work. There was one which was a must, although it would mean midnight rehearsals and three movie studios would have to spare us for an afternoon. This was a Gerald du Maurier matinée for his beloved Actors' Benevolent Fund, a sort of memorial tribute to Gerald, who had during the three decades before his death worked harder for charity than any other actor before or since.

It was an ambitious show attended by the Duke and Duchess of York (later King George VI and Queen Elizabeth). It consisted of the first acts of *Trilby* and *Dear Brutus* and the ballroom scene from *A Kiss for Cinderella*. Gladys appeared in *Dear Brutus*, and I was in *A Kiss for Cinderella*. J. M. Barrie's plays are most difficult to do with adequate rehearsals and they are terrifying when hopelessly under-rehearsed, as ours was.

The *Cinderella* cast included Yvonne Arnaud, June, Laurence Olivier, Douglas Byng, Haidée Wright, Adrianne, Sam Livesey and a bevy of beauties. There we were, about to act a famous scene from a famous play, most of us with only an amateurish impression of what we had to do, some of us meeting each other in the scene for the first time, trying desperately to remember what a harassed director had told us, and thinking what a beating the Royal Family has to take for the sake of sweet charity.

And then suddenly the curtain was up and we were on and the miracle of the charities show happened again. Somehow we all remembered that we were professionals and that there had been no way of doing this job any better, and so it was done. And I could hear Gerald's voice, as I had so many times before, "Thank you for your help—I hope you will do some more for me."

Another appeal to which the theatre had responded with great generosity was the Lord Mayor's Fund for the widows and children of the appalling Gresham colliery disaster.

The only way that Gee and I could answer this call was by a midnight performance, so we arranged such a showing of *The Shining Hour*.

Then Leslie Henson, that glorious musical comedian on whose busy shoulders Gerald's mantle had begun to settle, wrote, with the help of Reginald Purdell, a very funny burlesque of our play called *The Dining Hour*. The theme was the devastating effect of gluttony on the players. Leslie directed and played my part, with Yvonne Arnaud as Mariella and June as Judy, whose death in the skit was, as I remember, caused by a gastronomic mistake. Viola Tree was hilarious in Marjorie Fielding's role, and Morris Harvey, Bobby Howes and Stanley Holloway were extremely mirthful additions to the Linden family. The skit was presented after the midnight performance, as had been done in the *Late Night Final* benefit.

The six of us from the regular cast watched *The Dining Hour* from a box. I found Leslie's exposure of my mannerisms hilarious, especially when I played David next night.

All through the autumn months following our opening at the St. James's, a long, drawn-out struggle between British Equity and the Society of West End Managers was approaching its climax. At stake was the very existence of the British Equity Association, as the organization of actors and actresses was called after its American counterpart. The immediate issue was the recognition of Equity by the managers as the sole bargaining agent for the actors, and the consequent establishment of Equity as a closed shop. When I had come to England in 1922 to try for a job as an actor, just twelve years before, I had been shocked at the wretched salaries being paid by some of the London managers. I had been lucky in my employers, so this had not been my experience. There were many reputable managers but I was amazed that there was no standard contract with minimum salary and working conditions spelled out. Now as an actor, as a member of the council of British Equity and as a member of the Society of West End Managers, I was literally in the thick of this conflict.

About the middle of October Adrianne and I were invited to spend a weekend with Noel Coward at Goldenhurst, in the company of, among others, Prince George and the Greek Princess Marina.

We arrived at Noel's half-timbered compound in Kent about 1:00 A.M. and found the little house party happily engaged in some word game which we joined. This was soon followed by some songs by our host, who had quite a talent in that area.

The Duke of Kent and the Princess Marina were a delightful couple. The youngest son of King George V and Queen Mary, he was the only member of the Royal Family besides his mother who really loved the theatre and the arts generally. He was rather shy but possessed of a gentle wit and much intelligence. The Princess Marina of

180

Greece was very beautiful, a trifle shy too, but she had a sense of humour to which she gave free rein. They were obviously very much in love, and the exchange of family visits which royalty have to endure must have been most irksome to both these young people. Noel had been a friend for some time and Queen Mary, being a theatre addict, must have smiled on this brief interlude at Noel's sanctuary. As far as the public knew, the young Duke's romance was nothing but rumour.

For a month after this weekend visit to Goldenhurst my days were filled by Chauvelin at Elstree, David Linden at the St. James's, and endless phone calls, discussions and meetings about the Equity struggle any time they could be worked in, chiefly at midnight.

One night late in November I got out of the studio car and a voice from the pit queue nearby shouted, "Oh, Mr. Massey, you are going to have quite an audience tonight!" Sure enough, as I walked up the alleyway to the stage-door, the red carpet was being laid out from the private entrance to the royal box to the curb on St. James's Street. Charlton Morton, our business manager, was in my dressing-room. He had his dinner jacket on.

"Queen Mary and a party will be in the royal box tonight. I put the rug out. I've an idea it's something to do with the Duke and this Greek Princess. Anyway, I've notified Hitching and I told Rose to play 'God Save the King' after the reception – is that right?" Hitching was the press man and Rose the orchestra leader.

"Yes, yes, break right into it. We're a bit thin with just those strings we have."

"Rose has got a bull fiddle and a trumpet and a drum in for tonight. There are bouquets for the Queen and Princess Marina and Princess Micklas, I think it is, her mother . . . well, that's what I was told . . . in the lobby of the box. I told Miss Cooper. I'd better be out there waiting for them. I told the palace fellow that we ring up at 8:40 but of course I would hold the curtain if there was any delay."

From the prompt corner you could get a good view of the box and we all managed to see the entrance. You could hear some cheering on the street, for the red carpet had attracted a crowd, and at 8:37 Queen Mary stepped to the front of the box and the audience stood and cheered for what seemed to be a full minute. Then she turned and led Princess Marina forward, and the cheering redoubled. The Queen now left her future daughter-in-law alone in the middle of that huge box. She looked just lovely and was obviously touched by the welcome from her new countrymen. She waved at the audience and the

Duke of Kent joined her, and then Queen Mary on her right side. Rose timed "God Save the King" perfectly. The reinforcements to our little string group made it sound like a band, and when they finished the old anthem the cheering broke out again. But Queen Mary, with her regal smile, took her seat and as she gazed intently at the stage the house lights dimmed.

The audience was now in an exuberant mood, reluctant to be harrowed, but they were wonderful to play to and I think we gave them one of our best performances.

At the start of the second interval Gladys and I were called to the anteroom of the royal box (there was a special door at the end of the dressing-room corridor) by an equerry. The royal party were all in the best of spirits in spite of the harrowing scene which they had just witnessed, in which Judy, played by Adrianne, has walked into a burning barn. All three showed that objectivity which experienced playgoers always seem to have, and they made some pertinent comments about the play and the performance. They seemed to be enthusiastic.

Queen Mary had that perfect sense of timing which royalty must have. She just said, "And now, Miss Cooper and Mr. Massey, will you please give us the last act?"

I bowed and as I lifted my head my eyes caught Queen Mary's as she added, "There seems to be a great deal to be straightened out." As I left the anteroom I feared that the straightening out in our play would hardly be to this Queen's taste. Queen Mary's ideas of marriage were not flexible, as she would make manifest to her eldest son.

One of the thousands of gifts which Princess Marina received at her marriage to the Duke of Kent was a riding crop and thong with a silver band, engraved: "To Her Royal Highness, the Duchess of Kent, from the players of *The Shining Hour* at the St. James's Theatre, November 24, 1934, when the British public first met their lovely, new princess."

At the turn of the year the theatre war had reached a rancorous stalemate. The Society of West End Managers and a mass of disorganized independent producers chose to present a defensive front of disunity to the actors who were unable to find anybody to bargain with. I believed that any sign of unity on the part of the producers would be favourable to Equity. My old friend Alec Rea informed me that there was to be an unprecedented meeting of the society and the independents to be held the following day and urged me to be there as a member of the West End Managers. I jumped at the chance of meeting the whole clutch of producers and asked Leslie Henson to come with me as an independent.

About forty-five producers were present. After a few speeches I sensed a conciliatory attitude which I had not noticed in the society's meetings before. When called upon to speak I stressed the urgency of the managers making some reconciling move and quitting their head-in-the-sand tactics. I also warned against provoking an actors' strike, such as American Equity had needed to win in 1922.

Leslie had been busy writing on his knee and when called to speak he wasted no time in preamble. "The managers must make the next move in this struggle; they must do it at once, and I've written a resolution which will put us – and I say us, because Ray here and I are both managers as well as actors – on record as to our intentions." He then read the resolution he had just written:

This meeting of London theatre managers notes with satisfaction that the Minister of Labour is using his good offices to promote a satisfactory settlement of the difficulty existing between the British Actors Equity Association and the West End Theatre Managers and Producers. It welcomes the good offices of the Ministry and pledges itself to use its best endeavours to assist in promoting a settlement.

Beyond the efforts of a ministry man named Leggett to find out from Equity council members what the dispute was all about, Leslie Henson knew nothing of the minister's willingness to help, nor did Godfrey Tearle, Lewis Casson, Peggy Webster or anybody at Equity, nor, I believe, did the minister himself. Leslie had used a gamesmanship ploy with great skill years before Stephen Potter developed and codified the practice. It worked.

The reaction of the meeting to Leslie's resolution was astonishing. It was passed unanimously by this unorganized collection of managers. Accord was unexpected in that gathering; this sudden desire for peace was completely unforeseen. The acceptance of "the Ministry of Labour's offer to help" could rightly be considered a gesture of accord between the managers and Equity on the big issue of the closed shop. There were meetings and rallies before and after this occasion, when the excitement was greater, but I think peace came to the theatre when the managers agreed to get together with the actors.

We now had a union with strength and determination. There would be no strike. Forty-four years later British Equity is still the actors' union in all fields – stage, wireless, television, the screen and variety. It has done a good job. I am very proud that I was able to help a bit at its introduction.

Just what my father would have thought of his younger son's part in this victory of trade unionism had he lived through 1935, I can only conjecture. I think his smiling comment would have been, "By George, that's comical!"

The New Year disclosed a glow at the St. James's box office which augured a continued residence of *The Shining Hour*, at least until June.

The filming of *The Scarlet Pimpernel* was finished and so was the Equity war. What was I going to do in the daytime? It seemed that two goals of mine, to beat Nigel (Willie) Bruce on the Moor Park Golf Course and to win the Stage Golfing Society monthly medal, were both within my grasp. My twelve handicap and the vivid memories of breaking ninety on several occasions made me a warm candidate for these honours in my own estimation.

But this halcyon prospect of days on a golf course and evenings on a stage soon vanished. In truth, such an ordered simplicity was no longer a reality in our profession, which now practised its craft in all fields of entertainment. Once again I was to face one of those gluts of employment such as had piled up a few years before, when the four productions came almost together in 1931. The actor's lot is feast or famine, and his appetite is voracious. He must store up fat like a bear for the lean times.

Early in December Gee and I had read two new Keith Winter scripts. One, called *Ringmaster*, we rejected, but we optioned the second, a broad, farcical comedy called *Worse Things Happen at Sea*. It seemed a possible follower for *The Shining Hour*, presumably in June, for it was a funny play and a good bet for the summer months. As we now held the immediate lease on the St. James's, the thought of the theatre being empty was an awesome one.

Gilbert Miller had bought *Ringmaster* for London production at the end of January, cast it with Laurence Olivier in the lead, and then found himself tied up in New York. He asked me if I would take on the directing job. I didn't like *Ringmaster* but once more, "no" was not one of my words, and, anyway, it would be fun to direct Larry.

By mid-January I was well on the way with the staging of *Ringmaster*. It was an early example of the anti-hero play, so popular in the fifties and sixties. Larry's role was as repellent as I have ever seen – a crippled former actor who ran a guest house and, wheeling himself about in an invalid's chair, took a fiendish delight in probing

184

the sins, which were great, of his clients. Larry was delighted with this part and rehearsed it with the same gusto as he would show years later as Archie Rice in *The Entertainer*.

Just as we entered the final week of *Ringmaster* rehearsals, a blockbuster fell. My agent, Bill O'Brien, told me that Alex Korda wanted me on the first of July to play the dual leading roles in *Things to Come,* his film production of the novel by H. G. Wells. Bill said Korda had told him I would be working on the movie for a year, thus setting an all-time record for accuracy in such predictions.

In talking to Gladys about this bombshell I hastened to explain that although the picture was supposed to be one of several contract films, I could get out of it as my agreement with her took precedence. She said, without a moment's hesitation, "Of course you must do it. We'll close *The Shining Hour* in March. It will have had a six-month run, and we can get in a ten-week provincial tour before you have to start the Korda picture."

"What about the St. James's?" I asked.

"When could you have *Worse Things Happen at Sea* ready for a try-out?" That was the Winter farce we had optioned. We would not appear in it.

"In four weeks, that's the second week in March. Gilbert's in London and he can ride herd on *Ringmaster* for the Oxford week. I don't feel very happy leaving our play like this."

"Don't worry about taking off our show too soon. I never have too much faith in guesses on what business will be two or three months ahead. The bottom can fall out of any play any time. We can lose everything we've made by trying to stretch a run too far."

At the St. James's, rehearsals of *The Shining Hour*'s successor showed it to be lively, witty and very funny farce, with Yvonne Arnaud, Frank Lawton, Athole Stewart, Eileen Peel and three welcome arrivals from the Liverpool Repertory Theatre—Ena Burrill, Robert Flemyng and Harry Andrews.

Gilbert Miller led *Ringmaster* to its Oxford try-out and its brief visit to the Shaftesbury in London.

We took both the Winter plays to Manchester, where we played the Palace and the Opera House, being in the unusual situation of the same author and the same management having two productions playing as friendly rivals in the same city. Both were warmly received.

We laid off the tour for the following week so that Gee and I could see how *Worse Things Happen at Sea* fared with the London first-nighters.

The results of this confrontation were to me, and to all of us – the company, Gladys and even some of the critics – quite incomprehensible. I was as confident as I could be that we had a solid hit on our hands before the London opening. The Manchester audiences had been big and boisterous, and they loved it. At the St. James's, they laughed loud and long and hated the play. Standing at the back of the stalls, Gee and I could hear the roars of laughter mixed with sneers and derision. I saw one man, guffawing and slapping his thighs, get up and walk out, wiping the tears of laughter away and snarling, "What utter nonsense!" I believe that a considerable portion of that audience had come to the theatre determined to bring a smart young writer to his knees, just as they had done with Noel a few years before.

The critics were quite good to the play – "A gay and amusing piece"; "... domestic riot"; "An extremely clever light comedy" (it was not a light comedy!); "It is slick, witty, mad, satirical ... fine entertainment. ... "

But there was no life in the play and it closed after its eleventh performance – a bitter disappointment. The tour of *The Shining Hour* continued for another ten weeks to packed houses, but the sting of defeat hurt, all the more because of the initial success of our management. We decided to get rid of the remainder of our lease of the St. James's as we had no plays in hand. Gilbert Miller resumed his tenancy. Gee and I intended to continue our production partnership as soon as we found a suitable play, but as it turned out neither of us ever was to be in management again, either together or singly. I regret that, for we worked well as a production team. As a producer, Gladys had calmness, courage and good judgement – the prime qualities of a theatrical manager.

# 22

Alexander Korda was the first English movie producer whose pictures could compare with the products of Hollywood and Berlin. Alex was Hungarian, imaginative, intelligent, extravagant. Although lacking business sense, he had an uncanny ability to find money, and he also had an uncommon feeling for quality.

Alex Korda had two brothers, Vincent and Zoltan, a designer and a director. Vincent was pretty close to genius, but his artistic skills were sometimes overshadowed by his resemblance to Harpo Marx, both in character and appearance. As Zollie looked like Chico, it was natural to consider how Alex stacked up against the immortal Groucho. I thought there was common ground. The ten-inch Havana cigar, the outsize walking stick, the wavy hair, the elegant but crumpled clothes and the wry humour did suggest Groucho Marx, Hungarian style.

I never had such fun working in a movie as I did in *The Scarlet Pimpernel*. Of all the heavies I have played on the screen, the most wicked and the most fun to do was Chauvelin. I have been in pictures as good or with comparable actors, directors, cameramen, designers or producers, but only this once did all these elements function perfectly in unison. Come to think of it, even here there was not perfection. Alex loved to direct, but as he often had several films in production at the same time, it was impossible to find time to direct them all. So he was accustomed to ride herd on his directors a good deal more closely than other producers.

Alex hired Rowland Brown from Hollywood to direct *Pimpernel*. Brown had walked out of more studios than any man in Hollywood. It was said that one studio had installed a revolving door to ease his way.

At the first day's shooting Alex watched Brown shoot a scene and commented that he was directing it like a gangster film. Brown announced he would direct the way he liked or walk out. Alex said very sweetly, "Please walk." And he did. Alex himself directed the scene and by two o'clock that afternoon a new director, Harold Young, was watching Alex carry on. The next day Young ostensibly took over, but the direction throughout the months of shooting remained an unofficial but smooth collaboration. Thanks to the patience and competence of Young, there was no confusion and he retained the respect of actors and crew.

Alex was the first producer to exploit the beauty of the English countryside. British film producers had been afraid that sound recording would not be satisfactory on location. English weather was too fickle to plan outdoor shooting. Sunlight was believed essential to good photography.

Extravagance never bothered Alex Korda. He was determined to shatter the myth that exteriors were impossible in England. So he imported Harold Rosson, one of the great Hollywood cameramen, to supervise the photography, and Ned Mann to handle special effects.

*The Scarlet Pimpernel* was a beautiful, action-packed period piece which demanded exteriors. There were more outdoor sequences in the final cut than in most Hollywood Westerns. Hal Rosson, who became a life-long friend, used to welcome the cloudy days of the English autumn. "I can make sunlight anytime with a few arcs," he would say, "but I can't make clouds like that–look at them!"

The picture had some of the most perfect photography I ever saw. It was, of course, a black-and-white film. Even so, it was utterly lovely to look at.

But Korda's picture had more than beauty. The stirring story from Baroness Orczy's novel tells of the mysterious leader of Regency bucks who rescues French aristocrats from the guillotine just as the blade is about to fall and smuggles them to England.

The mystery man is Sir Percy Blakeney, fop, wit and scallywag. In his more thrilling moments he is the Scarlet Pimpernel, arch-enemy of the Terror and of Chauvelin whom he outwits in sundry encounters.

The "Frenchies" yell for the head of the Pimpernel, which they very nearly obtain. There are dark deeds, spying, conspiracy, disguises and, in the movie, much wit and humour.

The novel had not been blessed with humour. Korda had dared to have plenty of it in the screenplay. It was considered risky to infuse levity into so well-known a romantic drama. But Korda was right. The audiences of the 1930s loved the pepper in the treacle. The famous duel of brains between Chauvelin and Blakeney at the Granville Ball is all the better for some humour.

The Prince Regent, given a touch of Colonel Blimp as Nigel Bruce

*Leslie Howard as Sir Percy Blakeney (The Scarlet Pimpernel) and R.M. as*
*Chauvelin in the film made in England by Alexander Korda, 1933.*

played him, may not have been historically accurate but this was
rousing melodrama, not history. Everybody in the theatre knows that
the· secret of success in melodrama is the contrast of laughter and
tension.

No producer in Hollywood had been able to make such a picture,
so faultless in every technical detail. It is true that Korda had used
American camera experts. But he had shown what a producer can
contribute to the making of a great motion picture. Those wide
glimpses of English countryside, of Regency London, of Paris during
the Terror, the thousands of period details which made *The Scarlet
Pimpernel* a visual triumph, needed the imagination and taste of a
great producer as well as a cameraman to put it all on the screen. The
genius of Vincent Korda was also necessary to design this movie and
help make it a work of art.

189

When a band of good English actors is brought together in a costume play with a first-rate script, witty dialogue and plenty of time for rehearsal, success is assured. Korda had assembled some twenty-five players, with Leslie Howard as Sir Percy Blakeney and the lovely Merle Oberon as Marguerite. There was a spirit in that company, a feeling of confidence, a sort of *élan* which I have often found in the theatre but never sensed in any other movie.

*The Scarlet Pimpernel* flourished at the box offices of the English-speaking world. It was a ringing success forty years ago. I've often wondered how a remake would fare now, granted there were a Korda to produce it.

I have a grandson named David Huggins, Anna's boy, now an exhibitioner at Queen's College, Cambridge. Some years ago, at the age of ten, to use his own words, David was "much concerned" with thrillers, mysteries, spy stories and the like. He had made an in-depth study of the lurid adventures of James Bond, whom he regarded as "super." I cannot share that opinion although I respect the scholarship on which it is based. In a rating of the principal characters in the novels of this genre, David placed Sir Percy Blakeney (the Scarlet Pimpernel) fifth or sixth just ahead of Sherlock Holmes. He explained this running order because the Pimpernel and Holmes were too "slow moving" to catch .007 but he admitted that both of them had more "style."

David's estimate wasn't a bad one. I agree with it and I think that "style" is still the most important ingredient in the pot from which comes a finished movie. And I won't attempt to define "style." I think David would and maybe could. I know you can feel it, see it, hear it, and you can smell the lack of it.

When a character has a line like Sir Andrew Ffoulkes had in answer to a question put to him by Suzanne de Tournay – "What is the Scarlet Pimpernel, mademoiselle? It is a humble, wayside flower and it hides the identity of the best and bravest man in all the world" – that is Style.

# 23

After nearly two years with *The Shining Hour* I spent one whole year working in Alex Korda's film of H. G. Wells's *The Shape of Things to Come*. This was the biggest and most difficult film I ever worked in. I had read Wells's novel, fascinated by its humour and the earthy humanity of its characters. It was a huge canvas of adventure. I was thrilled by the news that I was to play the two roles of John Cabal and his grandson Oswald, and so travel through the whole century of Wells's prophecy, the next war, the age of dark frustration and anarchy, the new world of science.

But when I saw Wells's script I was appalled. Every trace of wit, humour and emotion, everything which had made the novel so enthralling, had been cut and replaced with large gobs of socialist theory which might have been lifted from a Sidney Webb tract. Although Wells often declared he was not a teacher or a political theorist, this was exactly what he had become. Not only had Alex Korda given Wells complete control of the script but he had contractually agreed to his interference in every phase of the production, in the direction, design, cutting, even in the promotion of the finished picture. Wells was not boasting when he referred, as he frequently did, to *my* picture, *my* production and *my* editing; he had a contractual right to do so. When he would say, "I chose to make this picture," he was just stating a fact. No writer for the screen ever had or ever will have such authority as H. G. Wells possessed in the making of *Things to Come*.

Having secured these dictatorial powers, Wells soon found out that he was unable to exercise them. He knew virtually nothing about film-making. His experience consisted of a visit to Walt Disney's studio in Hollywood, where activity was at that time confined to producing animated cartoons, and an early and abortive attempt on his part of making a silent short. He discovered that Korda and his production team were masters in their various departments and needed no help from him.

After watching a few scenes being shot Wells realized how little he knew about the cinema. "Many of the sequences," he said, "which slipped easily from my pen when I wrote the scenario were extremely difficult to screen and some were impossible." He quickly subsided into the normal dimensions of a screen writer. Some of the errors in the script were rectified. Not all, but he left the screening to people who knew how to do it.

Wells was constantly on the set but his only active participation in production was a close attention to the costumes of the female members of the cast. He would adjust a fold of a skirt or a casual pleat with the touch of a couturier and much more enthusiasm. But except for these activities he remained a fascinated onlooker, bug-eyed at the wizardry of the technicians.

The picture was fantastically difficult to act. Wells had deliberately formalized the dialogue, particularly in the later sequences. The novel's realism had vanished from the screenplay in which we delivered heavy-handed speeches instead of carrying on conversation. Emotion had no place in Wells's new world. I had a marathon acting job, playing a young airman through the war with which the picture begins and then through thirty years of anarchy which follow. I was also playing his grandson, who leads the men of science to control the new world.

It is these men of science, the engineers, the airmen, who save the world in Wells's story. And it was the technical experts who saved *Things to Come*—the special effects genius Ned Mann, the camera crew under Georges Perinal, and the designer, Vincent Korda. There are some technical achievements in the film—miniature effects, illusions, camera tricks—which have seldom been equalled since.

The moon-rocket sequence which makes the finale of the story is an astonishing anticipation of the NASA Apollo vehicle. This was no coincidence: the spaceship in Korda's production was designed by the German rocketry experimenters who twenty years later were brought to America to work in the NASA jet-propulsion laboratory. In the Second World War they had designed the V1 and V2 weapons for Hitler; their base at Peenemunde on the Baltic had been the target of several bombing raids by the R.A.F. In 1935 some of the same scientists had been working for Korda.

*Things to Come* was a difficult job for all of us. We were always the puppets of Wells, completely under his control. Like all socialists, in

*R.M. as Oswald Cabal and Margaretta Scott as Rowena in the film Things to Come, England, 1935.*

192

his forecast of man's future Wells saw nothing but authoritarianism. A bad dictatorship would be followed by a benevolent one. A benign big brother was bound to be a bore. He was the fellow I played in the futuristic part of the film. I could only act Oswald Cabal as calmly and quietly as possible and, as the saying goes, "Everybody was very kind."

Unquestionably the costumes in which we suffered in all the extremes of English weather bring up the most disagreeable memories of that twelve months spent on making *Things to Come*. In all phases of production, in the initial war period, in the subsequent "Age of Anarchy" and the final futuristic third of the film, the costumes gave proof that the spirit of the Marquis de Sade was alive and well and working as a designer for Alex Korda or, rather, for H. G. Wells. In the unusually balmy autumn months of 1935 I spent my working hours in heavy black woollen tights, with a papier-mâché breastplate and a huge formica bubble or headpiece.

Following this discomfort, we faced in 1935-36 the most savage winter England had endured for some half a century, with several blizzards which covered the southern counties with snow and ice and with appropriate temperatures of near zero, during which we wore the abbreviated skirts and Tudor-like doublets of foam rubber and pleated buckram. For six months my skinny legs, bare and knock-kneed, were photographed for posterity on unheated stages and freezing locations.

Then came the relief of an unusually warm summer, in which I found the foam rubber and the buckram – or whatever the stiff, metallic material was – to be intolerably hot. In all fairness to the memory of the Marquis, it would be impossible to place the blame for the discomfort of those cursed costumes on any individual, even Herbert George Wells, who approved of them.

Men and women through the ages have followed the dictates of designers with abject submission. Why should actors complain of their guesses about the future?

The film was a success all over the world, certainly the most ambitious production ever attempted in England at that time. It is still frequently shown on television, almost unrecognizable on the faded prints and unintelligible from being cut by one-third. But it still holds up, not because of Wells's prophecies or the acting but because it is a moving picture that moves, a perfect example of film wizardry in action.

194

# 24

One evening in September 1935 I came home to Wilton Crescent exhausted and bored. I had been working all day on the filming of *Things to Come*. For more than a year I had been involved in it and I still had no idea when I would be finished. I longed for the theatre again and particularly for Broadway.

On my way upstairs to the living-room Adrianne called out, "I'm going to play Elizabeth–it's all set. I'm sailing on the *Aquitania* on Tuesday. I talked to Max on the phone this afternoon–isn't it wonderful?"

"It certainly is. Congratulations! *Pride and Prejudice*, eh?" I came into the room as Adrianne went on, "Here's Ruth Gordon. She's in London on a short visit."

The diminutive, sparkling creature held out her hand. "Well... Ray Massey! We've never met and it's high time. So I have asked myself to dinner."

Adrianne rarely stammered but she did this time. "Why that's not...not..."

"No, Adrianne, I thought of it first and you had no alternative."

By this time I was armed with a martini. "This is a meeting I can drink to."

These immortal words drove Miss Gordon to a large chair by the fire. She was the only human being I ever knew who could lounge energetically.

"Yes, sirree," she said with a look of expert approval, "you are Ethan Frome for my money."

Rumblings of a struggle to dramatize Edith Wharton's novel for a Broadway production had reached England and prompted me to re-read it. I had finished it that morning on the Korda set.

"And Mattie Silver is for you and only you. Isn't that so?"

"I won't disagree with you." A firm smile which didn't reach her eyes signalled that what Ruth Gordon wants Ruth Gordon gets. "You have read the novel? I know you haven't read the play."

I nodded. "Now that you've settled two sides of the triangle," I asked, "what about the third?"

"I've decided on her too. She is not unknown. She had a great success in an O'Neill play–can't you guess?"

"Lovable Zeena...." I wanted to guess right. "Did she play Anna Christie?"

"Right on the button–Pauline Lord. Now there are the three stars. I've decided on the whole production.... I want Max Gordon to produce. He likes good things and he's got plenty of movie money. You and Adrianne know him from *The Shining Hour* and Adrianne's going to be with him in *Pride and Prejudice*."

"Yes, Max would be fine. Who's your director?"

"Guthrie McClintic. He would be—"

"Perfect! And your designer? This should be the toughest and most rewarding job he ever had–whoever he is."

"I would like Jo Mielziner—"

"Perfect again! You're quite a producer, Miss Gordon. But is there a play? Is it on paper? If so, who wrote it and who owns it?"

"Oh yes, there is a play. It's awfully good. There's a copy in the hall for you to read. By Owen Davis and his son Donald–I don't know who actually owns it. I hope Max Gordon will. All the rest of what I've said is dreams."

At dinner it seemed that Ethan Frome accompanied us to the table.

Ruth went on. "When the Davises finally got a script out of the Lowell Barrington try at it, Jed Harris—"

"Wait a minute. Who is Barrington?"

"Oh, he had written the first play. Ned Sheldon helped him a bit but it wasn't right. So Owen and Donald Davis got to work on a new script. They're acknowledging the help they got from the Barrington version. He's really a man named Louis B. Christ, Jr.–and that was months ago, maybe years–but Jed Harris—"

"Hold on–before we get to Jed Harris, did all these people have permission to—"

"I'm getting to that.... Jed had worked like anything with the Davises to get their adaptation right. He's had three options to produce it. I want to play Mattie more'n I want to go to heaven, and that's all right with Jed. But he can't or won't cast Ethan...."

"You mean he can't see me playing Ethan Frome?"

"Jed can't see anybody in that part."

"I can quite understand Jed's turning me down for Ethan. He knew me at Yale when I was a Canadian officer with British overtones, instructing in gunnery and trench warfare. The only things he could have seen me do in New York were the Geddes *Hamlet* and a very English gentleman farmer in *The Shining Hour*. At no time did I link up with the Connecticut countryside."

"Jed has turned over his current option on *Ethan Frome* to me. You are Ethan to me. He has to be homely and long with big hands and feet but he's no yokel."

Next day, on Korda's time, I read the Davises' play of *Ethan Frome*. It was just about the best dramatization of a novel ever to be seen in a theatre. The authors had brought the novel so completely to dramatic form that it didn't seem to be a dramatization at all, not in the Broadway sense of hacked-out pages and chapters.

It is forty-three years since *Ethan Frome* came to Broadway, and many readers may be unfamiliar with Edith Wharton's novel and the play. John Anderson in his *Journal* notice wrote:

The play begins where the novel does, with the gray-haired, gnarled and broken Ethan taking a stranger to a neighboring village through the snow, and it ends with the deep and festering rancor that bound him bitterly to the two women inside his bleak farmhouse. These two scenes enclose in tragic parentheses the twenty years of mortal torment that made up the life of Ethan Frome and the lost hope that was lingering tragedy.

The play concerns itself with the loveless marriage Ethan Frome made with his mother's nurse. It was winter when his mother died and he didn't want to be alone.

If it had been spring, maybe... but that is only a half-hidden speculation, made when young Mattie Silver comes to live with them and helps Zenobia Frome with her housework. Mattie lets him see the happiness he might have had, and in the brief absence of Zenobia Frome the touch, the rapture that might have been theirs.

But Zenobia returns, and being suspicious, sends Mattie packing. Mattie and Ethan decide to die together on a toboggan slide, crashing their lives out against an elm. They fail even in that, and so end their days broken in body and soul, by the fate which has stricken all three.

Told in ten scenes, it was compact, vividly dramatic and heartbreaking. There was no decision to make. If the role were offered to me, of course I would accept it.

I returned the script to Ruth Gordon at her hotel with a note saying

*Transatlantic voyages were usually merry affairs in the twenties and thirties, but this time Ethan Frome rehearsals were going to start the day after we docked in New York.*

I loved the play and wishing her a pleasant voyage home. I resigned myself to continuing work on *Things to Come*, even if it stretched into the hereafter. And I tried to put *Ethan Frome* out of mind. I found that impossible to do.

The Wells movie seemed stalled in daily retakes, minds were being changed with the regularity of the guard at Buckingham Palace, Adrianne departed for New York. Ruth Gordon's visit seemed to have been a tantalizing fantasy. Then one evening about the end of September the telephone rang. After several minutes of static the amplified voice of Max Gordon could be heard indistinctly: "Ray, I've got the hottest property that's coming to Broadway this season and I want you for the title part. It's the Davis play called *Ethan Frome*. I've got Pauline Lord and Ruth Gordon for the women and—"

"Guthrie McClintic to direct and—"

"How the hell did you know?"

"And Jo Mielziner to design."

"Yes, you and Ruth and Polly will be co-starred above the title. Will you do it?"

"Try and stop me!"

The astonishing thing was that the dreams of Ruth Gordon had all come true. Ruth Gordon's "dreams" usually did.

More vacillation as to the shaping of *Things to Come* caused a hair-raising postponement of my departure for New York, but I did arrive just in time for the first rehearsal on December 4, 1935. This was a reading of the play with the full cast and Max Gordon and the two Davises present. I detest readings. No actor, if he has any brains, will attempt a performance at a reading, and no director or producer can possibly anticipate a player's merits or demerits from his efforts at such a ceremony.

My ship having docked the previous night, I had had no chance to talk to the director before rehearsal. I did not know Guthrie McClintic very well but he had married Katharine Cornell and on that score alone I rated him pretty high. Max Gordon was a tough Broadway producer with an instinct for spotting quality plays and an obsession to produce them. Max was a desk producer; this would probably be the only time the cast would see him before dress rehearsals. Of the Davises, father and son, I knew little except that papa had won the Pulitzer Prize with *Icebound*, a New England farm drama, and that their adaptation of *Ethan Frome* was superb.

I was whispering congratulations to Ruth on her getting *Ethan Frome* into production her way when Guthrie got us seated in a semi-circle of chairs facing the producer, director and authors at a table. We were on the stage of the National, where we were going to open in just over six weeks. Guthrie took out his watch. "There will be no stopping for intervals or anything. At least we can get a rough timing. I'll read the stage directions. All right, CURTAIN!"

It was a cautious reading for all of us, particularly for me. I did not want to attempt a New England accent as Ethan. I knew the horrors of imitation Yankee talk. I took refuge in the cadences which the genuine idiom and style of the Davises' dialogue suggested, and ignored the accent. I felt a little more easy in the speech as we heard the tag of the play. There was a rhythm which was a joy to speak.

"The Fromes 're tough, I guess...the doctor was saying to me only the other day–'Frome,' he says, 'you'll likely touch a hundred!'"

I was gazing at my script and thinking of a superstition of the English theatre that deterred actors from speaking the tag line until the opening performance: it would mean bad luck to all concerned if the curtain line were heard at rehearsal. I was thinking that *Ethan Frome* would not be a suitable production to test this superstition when I became conscious of indistinct but vehement conversation at the director's table. Guthrie, his head tilted slightly to one side, just listened, as did Max. The talk was coming from the Davises. One line came through quite clearly: "This man is an Englishman!" There was silence.

Guthrie rose and looked at his watch. "That was two hours and eighteen minutes–about what I thought it would be. All right, lunch one hour! Everybody back at two and we'll block the prologue and the first act, I hope. Jo Mielziner will have the scene models here this afternoon."

He turned to the authors. "I'll see you in two weeks' time." He walked quickly off the stage.

When Owen and Donald Davis returned from exile a fortnight later no mention was made of the incident. It seemed that seven generations of forbears in New England and Canada had compensated for my recent English defection.

Before we started work that afternoon Guthrie said, "Ray, don't try for that damned New England accent–just what you were doing this morning is fine. You'll find your own way."

The models of the six scenes were now on a long trestle at the side of the stage. Guthrie led us to them. He looked at the models with loving admiration. "Take a good look at these sets, all of you, and memorize them if you can ... they tell a good part of the story ... and I believe that scenery means more to this production than to any play I've ever done."

The scenes were extraordinary. Jo Mielziner had caught the mood and temper of the play in his dingy kitchen, the cramped discomfort of the bedroom, the icy exteriors, and the grandeur of the snowy, star-lit hilltop. These settings seemed to call forth the very people who would be within them. Jo had indeed outdone himself, for our impressions came from half-inch scale models!

In staging *Ethan Frome* Guthrie McClintic had as tough a job as I have seen any director face. The theatre does not take kindly to reticence, but the essence of Mrs. Wharton's novel was New England reserve. Her characters begrudged words as a miser regards money. It wasn't that they were inarticulate; they hoarded speech. Although when the Davises dramatized *Ethan Frome* they supplied words and

*R.M. as Ethan and Ruth Gordon as Mattie in Ethan Frome, at the National Theatre, New York, 1936.*

200

*Ethan Frome*
*New York*
*193*

invented episodes and movement to satisfy theatre needs, they wisely preserved much of the essential austerity of the novel.

To observe and respect this feeling of reticence, of reserve, and at the same time to develop the interpretations of the three principal characters, without adding or altering a syllable of dialogue, was the seemingly impossible but completely successful accomplishment of Guthrie McClintic.

I quote from Brooks Atkinson's notice in the *Times*.

> In order to tell the gaunt story of *Ethan Frome*, which arrived at the National last evening, the management has hired Ruth Gordon, Pauline Lord and Raymond Massey, who are hereby nominated to immortality.... The actors have told a story of hope, bewilderment and anguish that is likely to make your heart stand still more than once during the evening. In the tones of their voices and the apprehensive look in their eyes, they have found incandescent words that no dictionary contains.

The dean of American dramatic criticism did not attend the rehearsals of *Ethan Frome* and could not know that in these few words he had paid tribute to the direction of Guthrie McClintic as well as to the players. But Pauline knew it and Ruthie and I knew it.

Guthrie orchestrated the three characters of the triangle with great skill. The reticence which I mentioned as pervading the play took different forms. In Ethan, it was taciturnity; in Zeena, an oblique meanness, frequently sarcastic and venomous; and in Mattie, it was often a frightened, irrelevant gaiety. None of us could be described as communicative, but under Guthrie's guidance we managed to make ourselves understood, with or without words.

Since I had first read the Davises' dramatization of *Ethan Frome* in London I could not rid myself of a vague suspicion that in its play form Mrs. Wharton's novel might suffer from the glut of books and plays that her masterpiece had inspired. In the quarter century which followed the publication of the novel, an astonishing number of plays about rural life in New England appeared. One or two of the plays were of tragic stature and there were some fine dramas and a few comedies among them. But the sombre mood prevailed. Owen Davis himself was an early contributor in *Icebound*, his Pulitzer Prize-winning play about the people and land of his own state of Maine. There were the O'Neill farm plays, *Desire under the Elms*, *Beyond the Horizon*, and scads of others. I had read many of them and acted in two of the O'Neill plays, which we did at the Everyman in London. Natur-

202

ally, authors took many different courses in their plays but over the years there had been complete accord on one point – with its tribulations, calamities and gloom, farm life in New England was an unattractive proposition.

This misgiving as to the future of *Ethan Frome* on the stage was entirely distinct from my rehearsing *Ethan* in the Max Gordon production. My faith in the play and my devotion to my job never wavered for one moment. I believed that the Davis adaptation was as near perfection as any such transferral of a novel to theatre form could be. I believed in my ability to give a good performance of Ethan. I was certain that Polly and Ruth would triumph and I had absolute trust in Guthrie. My doubt was quite private and concerned the extraneous effect of prejudices and misconceptions outside any professional consideration. I never mentioned my suspicion to anybody. As it turned out, I was not quite alone in harbouring such an idea.

Anyway, my misgiving persisted. The Yankee farmer, with his dourness and his Job-like misfortunes, had long since emerged on the theatre scene as a comic stereotype, and the manifold adversities which had plagued New England rural life in so many plays could, on occasion, bring laughter rather than pity from their very familiarity. I pushed the thought away but I could not make it vanish. The knife-edge line which separates tragedy, with its exaggerations and its unreality, from satire and burlesque can be crossed with one bad laugh, and a great play can so be lost. That chance was remote perhaps, but possible.

The advent of the scenery for the dress rehearsals at the Garrick in Philadelphia was for *Ethan Frome* a coming-of-age party. Models and sketches of sets cannot give a true impression of scenery. Jo Mielziner's scenery for this play had to be seen to be believed. Almost at once, when I saw the grandeur of those winter exteriors and the expressiveness and the character of the bedroom and kitchen, some of my private worry about the possible effect of the New England syndrome on the future of our play was removed. Nobody could laugh very loud at anything so glorious as that star-lit hilltop scene, no matter how hysterical they were.

This beautiful scene and the church sociable exterior were backed by a cyclorama with the appropriate constellations, each star twinkling a blue light with its individual motor.

The so-called dinner scene in the third act, when Mattie and Ethan have their evening meal alone with Zeena away overnight to see the doctor at Bettsbridge, had been an agonizingly difficult twenty minutes of pauses, glances, silences, cooking, eating, plumbing repairs and so on, in which we really played a love scene of intense passion, a scene I never thought I would master until the first dress rehearsal in Philadelphia, when we first met that matchless scenery and it all came together.

Of all the love scenes I've acted I think this one remains the most deeply moving to me. It was the only time that Ethan felt for a few moments the ecstasy which might be his. He felt it through a mess of a broken pump, smashed dishes, eating stew, and he never touched his lover except maybe his fingers were mighty close to Matt's once and he didn't express his ardour very vehemently except when Matt asked him, "What was it you were just too lazy to say, Ethan?" and he replied with unaccustomed passion, "I don't know...mighty peaceful tonight, ain't it, Mattie?" Just the same, if I do say it myself, there was more chance of the snow melting on the sills of the Frome kitchen window that night than if Ruthie and I had put on one of those bare shoulder exhibitions that are routine in the theatre these days.

Aunt Philura Maple's pickle dish was a peculiarly repulsive imitation cut-glass object which played a significant part in the third act. Bequeathed to Zeena in what looked like an act of revenge, the dish had an intrinsic value of rather less than $1.50, but in the recipient's eyes, its beauty put it beyond price. As Guthrie impressed on us, "It's worth more than the Portland Vase–and look where that is! I wouldn't know–but the pickle dish is 'it'–and when you break it (and we've got to get a way of dropping it so that nobody out front can tell who did it) that is about the end of everything!" The dish is broken while Ethan and Mattie wash up after the supper scene, Mattie having taken it from its hiding place at the back of a shelf to "spruce up" the supper table.

The pickle dish was, of course, an expendable "prop." A gross of copies of Jo Mielziner's obnoxious design had embarrassed the Corning Glass Company's artistic integrity but conscientious precaution had been taken to ensure satisfactory fragmentation on the slightest of impacts. Several tests and two dress rehearsals at the Garrick Theatre in Philadelphia had resulted in beautiful breakages. Then the unbelievable happened. At the opening performance in Philly, after a perfect drop, the pickle dish lay between us in its pristine solidity, unscathed and, I swear, grinning. Our horror was a perfect reaction but Ruth's first line was, "Oh, Ethan, it's broken!" My instant reaction was to stamp on the monster, which I did. It took three stamps to kill it, or break it. It was entirely out of character for Ethan to show such savagery but it had to be done. And to my astonishment and intense relief, there was absolute silence from a spellbound audience. I kept my relief to myself.

All sorts of counter-measures were taken against a repetition of no breakage. A large metal plate was placed under the stage cloth to secure a hard impact and breakage. A complete set of fragments was placed under the sink and I planned to shove any intact surviving dish out of sight and display the fragments. I actually had to do this during the third performance of the try-out. But the most monstrous of all mishaps was the failure of the damned dish to break on opening night in New York. On both first-night performances, in Philadelphia and in New York, I had to makeshift for the real thing, but both times we held them in a vice. That glorious play won, hands down.

Nevertheless, my little fears were groundless. The play was a triumph and the critics were unanimously in favour.

Several days after we opened, Robert Benchley's notice in the *New Yorker* appeared. It was entitled "An Event." It seemed that I was not quite alone in my apprehensions.

In the twenty-five years since Edith Wharton's novel, *Ethan Frome*, depressed and at the same time excited a complacent world, we have had more than our share of books and dramas following the course she set through the miseries and futilities of farm life, especially in the rock- and snow-bound district of New England, where jest nothen' seems ter go right ever.

In fact, one false step in bringing *Ethan Frome* before the public in play form, one too many dishes broken, one too loud a moan, an extra tremolo on the "Miserere" or even one bad actor, and Max Gordon could easily have had a burlesque on his hands, not because *Ethan Frome* is not wrought of pure gold, but because we have had so many imitations of it that the formula of "no fun on the farm" has become a dangerous one.

It is, therefore, all the more to the credit of everyone concerned that as a play *Ethan Frome* emerges with all its pristine and devastating irony. Owen and Donald Davis have brought their own New England accents to the dramatization, at the same time maintaining a fine reverence for Mrs. Wharton's story. If you want to see

*I don't care what the credits were. I'll always think of Ethan Frome as Ruth Gordon's production.*

what a real play can do to an audience, just hang around up back some evening and feel the shock that runs through the house at that one moment in the epilogue when God turns out to be the heavy...

Bob Benchley did not know about Ruthie's prophetic make-believe production of *Ethan Frome*. Nor did Max Gordon. Come to think of it, Ruthie herself had no mind of it once she had that glorious performance of Mattie in hand. When there is acting to be done, Ruth Gordon does not think of anything else.

206

# 25

I spent nine months of 1937 working on two Hollywood movies and the rest of the year back in England on a Korda job. My agent, Myron Selznick, had sent me to the Coast to work for two good producers, one of them his brother, David O. Selznick, and the other Samuel Goldwyn. Both were independent producers and the deals were each for one picture only.

Although the great studios were then in their prime, with most of the top directors, writers and actors tied up by contract, it was the independents like De Mille and Chaplin, Selznick and Goldwyn, who were most likely to turn out quality films. The big studios, which had to make about 150 feature pictures each year in addition to an equal number of so-called B's, could not always match the product of the autonomous producers. There were exceptions, of course, but movie-making is a creative and personal operation and does not fit the assembly-line process. The independent producers were an elite minority in the movie industry in the late thirties. In the seventies they would control what was left of it.

The David Selznick picture I was engaged for was *The Prisoner of Zenda*, the big daddy of all the Ruritanian stories that had been so popular at the turn of the century. It was not an original selection for filming in 1937, having been made twice as a silent and once as a talkie. But that did not deter David. He believed that a good story, well told, will remain popular, in whatever medium it is displayed. He was right, and saw to it that the old Anthony Hope story got as good a telling as it ever had. The picture had all the thrills, the humour, the tears and romantic flow which had made the novel a favourite half a century before and it was as beautiful to look at as a great camera-man, the late Jimmy Wong Howe, could make it. For a couple of hours one could forget current realities such as Hitler, Mussolini and the Depression, and watch Ronald Colman shaking hands with himself and substituting for his drunken royal cousin.

The story of how the Elphberg dynasty kept the throne of Zenda through the gallant efforts of the Englishman, Rassendyl, needs no telling here.

David Selznick picked most of his cast from the British colony in California. There were only two Americans in the picture, young Douglas Fairbanks, Jr. as Rupert of Hentzau and Mary Astor as a French adventuress. I was Black Michael, the black-hearted heir-apparent and villain-in-chief. Ronald Colman was the star, doubling as the Englishman, Rudolph Rassendyl; and his distant cousin, King Rudolph of Zenda. Madeline Carroll played Flavia, the king's betrothed, and was everything a Ruritanian princess should be, being about the most beautiful girl then in Hollywood.

The British Empire may have been a bit torn at the seams but in 1937 the British Colony in Hollywood was at its flourishing peak of professional activity and vehement loyalty to the Crown. Its leader was dear old Sir Aubrey Smith, who played Colonel Zapt in our film. He controlled his colony with firm dignity, his only problem being the erotic antics of Errol Flynn, who after all was, in the opinion of a stalwart member of the colony, "not really an Englishman but an Australian, old boy!" Similar activities, conducted with greater discretion, on the part of a young actor named David Niven, were viewed with tolerance if not envy by the elder brethren of the colony. In *Zenda* David played a rather colourless aide-de-camp, a part he infused with a brand of comedy that was entirely his own and was eventually to make him famous.

John Cromwell directed *The Prisoner of Zenda*. He had come to Hollywood after many successful years in the theatre as an actor and director. Like many others with a stage background he had at once been obsessed with the camera. He carried four or five lenses on a string round his neck and I do not think he ever looked at anything with his unaided eyes while he was shooting. Nevertheless, he did a first-rate job with *Zenda* and it looked superb.

A fine horseman, John was determined to make the most of his riding scenes. He did not want us to look as if we "were agoin' that-away to Zenda gulch." When we were to shoot the procession to the cathedral for Ronnie Colman's coronation he cast the horses as carefully as the actors. David Selznick had spent a terrific amount for this sequence, a glass coach with six horses and postillions, a squadron of cavalry and dozens of carriages and outriders. A Ruritanian street and the façade of the cathedral had been built as was customary in those days, and the Zendanian citizenry was present by the hundreds.

*My splendour as Black Michael in The Prisoner of Zenda is inspected by Sidney Howard (centre) and David O. Selznick. Sidney was unimpressed but D.O.S., who had paid for it, was overwhelmed.*

David Niven as Fritz von Tarlenheim was given a skittish and handsome mare to ride and I got a big, black stallion. Both of us wore our dress uniforms, "Chum" Niven with an eagle-topped helmet and I with a great Hussar busby. We both carried sabres in slings and in addition I wore the Hussar dolman or empty jacket over my left shoulder and a long sabretache with four straps hung from my sword belt. To cap it all I had a monocle. In short we were loaded like Christmas trees. In tassled boots and long, goose-necked spurs we were scarcely able to move.

I mounted with some difficulty. My horse was nearly seventeen hands and I must have been carrying a handicap of fifty pounds in medals and accoutrements. The wrangler said rather ominously, "Don't get too close to the mares if you can help it." I rode off to get acquainted with my mount. I found him handy and agreeable and he seemed ready to put on a quite effective little show.

As I trotted back to our set I spied Chum fixing things up with his mare and making her prance like a kitten. He spotted me and shouted coyly, "Keep your distance, sir!" Apparently he had been warned about my big friend.

The assistant director marshalled us through an enormous megaphone (there were no bull-horns in those simple days) and we took up our positions. Following a band, some infantry and a troop of cavalry, came the coach and six. Inside sat the lovely Madeline as Flavia and on her right Ronnie Rassendyl masquerading as the King. Both wore ermine robes. At Madeline's side rode Chum Niven and about five lengths behind, and alone, I followed with a troop of cavalry and some carriages. Five cameras were shooting this take.

A dry run proved satisfactory. The assistant director bellowed, "We'll try for a take!"

The movie actor is a creature of impulse. There have been rare occasions when the private emotions of the film actor have invaded the area of professional activity with unfortunate results. And this time there was such a breach on the part of a humble player, my horse.

Through the megaphone came a further instruction, "Before we shoot, Ray, will you move about ten feet closer to David Niven?" From Chum came over his shoulder, "I wish he hadn't said that!"

I complied.

"Roll 'em. . . . Speed. . . . ACTION!"

The cavalcade moved slowly forward as rehearsed – but not my poor horse. His professional task forgotten, at the command of "Action" the great beast plunged forward. Snorting with determination he leapt at Chum's mare. I must have nearly broken his jaw with the curb, shouting, "Look out, Chum, jump, jump!" He had already done so, and his mare was almost as quick in her getaway. My horse missed her, hitting the coach full on. Madeline received the full shock of his arrival, the huge head thrust through the open window and the bit rattling in her face. As for me, I landed on the roof of the coach, sword between my legs, busby over one eye but the monocle secure in the other, as embarrassed a horseman as I could be as I waited for a stepladder to make an inglorious descent to mother earth.

Nobody was hurt, not even the principal culprit. But stallions do not belong in parades, especially movie ones. I did not ride him in the next take.

# 26

*The Hurricane* was my next picture, the only film which brought together two movie giants, Samuel Goldwyn and John Ford, as producer and director. It was not a happy association, for both men were autocrats, but a fine movie came out of it. I did not know John Ford but Goldwyn and his charming wife, Frances, had been most kind to me during my troubles with Universal five years earlier. I had dined at the Goldwyns' house several times and was looking forward eagerly to working on the movie.

Everybody knew Sam for his whimsical assaults on the English language. Some were convinced that his malapropisms were contrived. I do not agree. I think Sam was a happy warrior against conformity, happiest of all when accidentally committing solecisms.

After dinner one night at the Goldwyns', Sam was reminiscing about the early days of hand-cranked cameras, of the times before covered stages when the light of the sun was all a movie-maker had, when he had to borrow a hundred dollars to get another day's work done on a two-reeler, and so on. His guests were fascinated. Gary Cooper urged Sam to continue.

'Oh well,'' he said in his high-pitched, still faintly Russian speech, "that was in the old days when Los Angeles only had a hundred and fifty thousand circulation.''

There was laughter and Sam looked pleased.

"What's the matter? Have I said something funny?''

"Sam,'' said Coop, "you said Los Angeles only had a hundred and fifty thousand circulation!''

"Oh, give a little – it may have been two hundred thousand.''

On the Goldwyn lot during *Hurricane* I met Sam outside his office. He had just returned to the studio after a week's absence due to a broken arm which was in a sling. I asked him how he was feeling.

"Oh, I'm fine.'' The injured arm moved slightly in the sling. He pointed at it with his free hand, saying, "It's hard to talk.''

Although I was set for *Hurricane* the contract had not been signed.

One day I went over to Goldwyn's office with Jimmy Townsend of the Selznick agency to settle things. In those days the client would accompany his agent on such errands, a practice which often led to the embarrassment of the wretched actor and has long since been mercifully discontinued.

Jimmy Townsend was handsome, gentle-mannered and reputedly the most honest man in the agency business. Together we entered Goldwyn's office and there was the usual small talk. Jimmy took a small scratch pad from his pocket and put it on Goldwyn's desk.

"It's a one-picture deal, Sam. There's my memorandum."

Goldwyn read it and snapped, "I never agreed to that!"

In the agency world the memorandum, a brief note of the verbal agreement, has the sanctity of the Ten Commandments. Questioning the veracity of a memorandum means war.

The ensuing battle was not long but furious from the start. Invectives were exchanged with increasing emphasis. I soon realized that my job was not the issue, but Jimmy Townsend's veracity. Not one word was addressed to me or about me; the insults shouted back and forth all referred to that precious memorandum. At last, when Goldwyn's legitimacy and Townsend's honesty had been impugned to the point of extinction, Jimmy played his high trump. Marching to the door he called, "Come on, Ray, let's get out of here!"

I saw the reason for my presence then. It was a good ploy to dramatize the threatened withdrawal of a client.

"James–come back!" cried Sam. It was the first time Goldwyn had used Townsend's first name. It was an olive branch.

"You have a deal, James." Goldwyn picked up the memorandum. "Ray, I want you to know you are my first choice for this role. I have not approached anybody else for De Laage, the governor."

Jimmy Townsend coughed. Sam looked at him. I looked at him. He was grinning. Sam continued, "Excepting only Baysil Rettbone. He hesitated because De Laage is unsympathetic. Baysil felt that at this stage of his career he should be acting romantic roles, not heavies. . . . Not that De Laage is a heavy, but in short–Baysil f——d the deal."

Goldwyn looked at Jimmy who was still grinning. Basil Rathbone was also his client.

John Ford directed *Hurricane*. Many people claim that Ford was the best director the movies ever had. I know that I never worked with another movie director who knew as much about acting as he did or cared so much about performance. Starting as a property man, he had worked in every job in the business except actor. Yet he could

*The five Europeans who lived on the doomed island of Manakoora in Hurricane, the Goldwyn movie, Hollywood, 1937. Left to right: Sir Aubrey Smith, R.M., Mary Astor, Thomas Mitchell and Jerome Cowen.*

guide an actor through a difficult characterization with much skill. Like other great directors, Ford had produced many of his own pictures. In any event he believed that, during the shooting, producers should be neither seen nor heard. He was a professional loner.

Goldwyn was also a loner. He proved it when he exploded himself out of Metro-Goldwyn-Mayer in the early days of that mighty company. For some years he had made his own pictures in his own studio with his own money, acting as his own producer. He believed that a producer was responsible for every phase of movie-making and he was able to make his ideas stick.

Like most of the great spectacle pictures, *Hurricane* told a simple story. It was based on a novel by Charles Nordhoff and James Norman Hall who had written *Mutiny on the Bounty*. *Hurricane* contained many of the ingredients of the *Bounty* story–idyllic South Sea settings, happy natives, tyrannical oppression and cruelty–and the screenplay included a relentless, duty-ridden governor of a Polynesian island. The story presents a long struggle between a native hero and the implacable governor who might have been a member of a French branch of the Bligh family.

Before the Second World War high-budget films were almost always shot entirely in studios in the Hollywood vicinity. Even pictures which demanded exotic settings such as the South Sea island in *Hurricane* were produced "at home." That lovely atoll of Manakoora with its cottages, huts, church, swaying palms and broad beach washed by gentle rollers was built on three acres of Goldwyn back lot in the shadow (literally so in the early morning) of a huge gasometer of the Southern California Gas Company across Formosa Street. Only low-cost B pictures went on location to avoid expensive scenic construction.

The Polynesian island which Sam Goldwyn had built on his back lot was a photogenic masterpiece. Its peaceful beauty, however, could be exploded and re-exploded at will. It had a controlled climate which no natural location could offer. Winds up to 150 miles an hour could be concentrated on the whole or any portion of the beach and village. Foaming breakers could devastate the island at cue. Tanks of water totalling 150,000 gallons could be poured on various points of action at will. When the hurricane sequences were shot the effect on those of us who were actually in the scenes was terrifying. It was indeed in 1937 the grandmother of all screen disasters but we had months of work on Manakoora before we faced the devilment of the special effects department.

Jack Ford shot the picture in sequence, a unique experience for the eight principals in the cast. It is a great help to play scenes in proper order. Three of us had come straight over from *Zenda* to Manakoora: Aubrey Smith, bereft of his time-honoured moustache, to play a priest for Sam; Mary Astor, now my screen wife instead of my screen mistress; and myself as De Laage, the governor. Thomas Mitchell, an old stand-by of Ford's, was with us as a philosophical doctor of amiable inebriety and Jerome Cowan as a stout-hearted sea captain. The Polynesian hero and his bride were played by a handsome newcomer named Jon Hall and the beauteous Dorothy Lamour.

The story was a bit shopworn, the characters were off the movie stockpile, and the success of the film would largely depend on the effectiveness of the special effects department. But Jack Ford put freshness and tension into the plot. He managed to infuse some originality into the stereotypes we had to play. Finally he succeeded in

214

preserving us as human beings, and not just bodies, in the hurricane sequences. That was no mean achievement.

Jack's method of direction varied with each situation and with the people involved. To me he rarely made a direct comment or suggestion. It was mostly brief innuendo, laced with Irish wit and always constructive, frequently confidential. If you could not laugh at yourself, Jack was not your boy and you certainly were not his. Everybody had to take a healthy amount of ribbing. Mary Astor became the sacrificial goat in this respect, most of the time a happy and willing goat.

Jack was in his element in the hurricane sequences. He was particularly adroit in directing vivid action. The storm, which amounted to twenty minutes of edited film, took more than five weeks to shoot and sank the plot without a trace along with most of the cast. No miniatures or doubles were used and stunt-men appeared in only a few shots. Although the principals played most of these strenuous scenes the only one hurt was Aubrey Smith, then seventy-six years old. He sustained two broken ribs when hit by a fast bowler while playing cricket at San Diego on a Sunday during the shooting of the hurricane sequences. He was embarrassed because he missed half a day of shooting while the doctor was X-raying his rib cage. Jack Ford said he was not responsible for youngsters going off and engaging in dangerous sports while working on one of his routine pictures.

After four and a half months on *Hurricane* we were all pretty tired. I had been in Hollywood since January and it was now nearly August. I knew that Bob Sherwood was home in England, finishing his new play about the young Abraham Lincoln. I was pretty tired of the South Seas and I wanted to go home where my daughter Anna had just arrived.

My last shot in the picture was in the can by mid-morning of a day in late July. I knew there might be an added shot or possible retake but it did seem nearly over. I went back to the Riviera Country Club where I was living, played eighteen holes with Basil Rathbone, beat him two up and was on cloud nine when I picked up a message calling me in to make-up at seven the following morning for an added scene. I was surprised to read that I would receive the dialogue at the studio on arrival.

When I arrived at my dressing-room the facts about the added scene became apparent. The make-up man laid on a beardless Lincoln make-up, correct in detail, including the wart. Requesting me to strip, he applied a rather mangy but unobtrusive chest wig. Wardrobe

*The big gag we never showed Sam Goldwyn. R.M. and Jack Ford.*

then fixed an abbreviated sarong on my then very-skinny waist. Finally a stovepipe hat was securely fastened on my head. The assistant director handed me this script.

### Added Scene

Front of Church–Massey struggling.

Long Shot–in surf effect using tanks A, B and C.

Medium Shot–Massey emerges from surf and advances towards camera.

Close Up–Massey waist up.

MASSEY

Four score and seven years ago we started *Hurricane*. For God Almighty's sake, Sam, let me go home!

FADE

It was Jack Ford's way of telling Sam Goldwyn to cut the cackle.

After the ordeal I went back to the Riviera for another round of golf and a new summons to appear at the studio at nine the next morning. This time there was no added scene or retake to be shot but

216

an announcement, in the Goldwyn manner, to the principals. It was the only time I remember seeing Sam Goldwyn on a sound stage. He was in his most ebullient spirits.

"Yesterday I saw a first rough-cut of this picture. I'm delighted. I'm proud. I am so excited with what you and John Ford have done that I'm going to shoot all the interiors again with new dialogue. I will carry you all. The new scenes will begin shooting in two weeks."

I remember the look on Jack Ford's face. I believe this was the first Jack had heard of Goldwyn's decision to scrap the work of Dudley Nichols and Oliver Garrett, two of the most literate and accomplished writers in Hollywood, in favour of a rewrite by Ben Hecht. Jack was not happy but his first reaction was to prevent Sam from seeing our effort of the preceding day. He got the cutter on the phone and told him to pull the Lincoln gag sequence from the dailies which Goldwyn was about to see.

Next day I could not walk and my doctor hustled me off to the hospital where I was bedded for two weeks with a blood clot in my leg. This was serious at that time as no anti-clotting drugs were in use. But after lying for a week on the deck of Jack Ford's big schooner I was able to do my work with Hecht's new scenes seated in a wheelchair. Everything I did had to be in close-up so as not to show the chair.

The doctors let me go home to England on condition that I remain seated for a further six weeks. I observed this admonition with as much respect as possible but I was defiantly ambulatory at my daughter Anna's christening without ill effect, and this gave me the courage to start a picture for Alex Korda almost at once. It was called *Drums* and entailed a certain amount of riding. Right after *Drums* I was busy with my dancing for *Idiot's Delight*. Since I came through these activities unscathed, it would seem that my doctors in Hollywood had been over-cautious.

# 27

It was six years after Bob Sherwood mentioned the possibility of his writing the play that I received the script of *Abe Lincoln in Illinois*. During those years we became close friends. I saw him constantly in England and America. I played in two of his plays in London but he did not return to the subject of Lincoln and of course I never brought it up. I had an idea that the project had not been abandoned for I would see well-thumbed copies of Lincoln books around his house. But I think he was afraid he might be forced to abandon the project and did not want to commit himself.

Long after the play opened, Bob told me it had been the most difficult project he had ever attempted. He felt he had engaged in a collaboration, a task he had always avoided, and that Lincoln himself had written some of the play.

Most actors who have played in Bob Sherwood's plays will agree that he was the actor's author, but only his close friends knew what a great sportsman he was. His specialties were horse-racing, bowling (the American alley kind), croquet and knock rummy. There was also close harmony of the 2:00 A.M. beside-the-refrigerator type, and soft-shoe dancing. This latter was always combined with a solo rendition of "The red, red robin goes bob-bob-bobbin' along."

For someone who never went near a race track he was one of the most assiduous, consistently misinformed and joyously unsuccessful horseplayers of his time. His wagers were small; they were spread so as to preclude any substantial profit and usually based on the blind-fold placement of a pin in the list of starters. His amazing good fortune held his losses to an average of six or seven pounds a week.

Horseplayers, or punters as they are called in England, have pseudonyms which they use when placing bets with their bookmakers. Bob's was "Old Savoy." It was a pleasure to hear him on a public telephone whispering "This is Old Savoy.... I want ten bob on Skinny Girl to win in the second at Kempton Park.... Yes, Old Savoy.... No, no...that's me.... The horse is Skinny Girl.... 'S'

like in sibilant, 'K' as in kerosene.... No, that *is* spelt with a 'K'....
Oh well, put it on the next horse.... That's Little Arthur."

Once a flunky came into the Savoy Grill at lunch and announced,
"Call for Old Savoy!" Bob bounded up to his six feet seven inches
and was on the telephone by the hat check booth in seconds. The
thought of some ten shillings on the wrong horse (or maybe the right
one!) was more than he could bear.

Bob was a very good man with a bowling ball. He could roll in the
neighbourhood of 180-190 quite often and with his height and reach
he could lay down a fine ball. In New York we used to bowl at the
alleys opposite Radio City Music Hall on Sixth Avenue.

One May afternoon in New York in 1936 we were bowling away
and Bob said, "This is one thing we won't be doing this summer."
Every year Bob Sherwood and his wife Madeline spent the summer
months at Great Enton, their house near Godalming, in Surrey. I was
due to close in *Ethan Frome* in about six weeks and go home to England and face a pin-less summer too. Bob rolled down a beautiful
strike and turned to me."Let's take an alley back with us!" Right
then we went down to the Brunswick people and bought twin alleys
with pins and balls and so forth, and six weeks later it was assembled
and ready for play at my place in England. We chose my place because
there was no level ground at Great Enton. The alleys were dandy,
smooth and true. They were housed in a long cowshed and I put a
thatched roof on it, thus creating the only bowling alley which could
truthfully be called "Ye Almost Olde Thatched Roof Lanes."

We opened the alleys in July with a bunch of friends present
among whom was a Royal Naval captain who shall be nameless. He
looked at the lovely maple surface and said, "Skittles, by Jove! Used
to play 'em at Malta!" Before we could stop him he took one of the
big, heavy balls–not a duckpin ball–in the palm of his hand and
heaved it down an alley. It was airborne halfway to the pins where it
landed with a sickening thud and so into the trough at the side. We
could all see the ghastly crater left in the alley even thirty feet away.

Except for a groan of agony from Bob there was silence. The gallant captain was unruffled. "Haven't quite got the hang of it!" he
declared. Bob took a ball from the trough and handed it to him.

Then with one of those soft snorts I knew so well, Bob said in his
lowest and slowest tones (once described by Alfred Lunt as logs tum-
bling over a waterfall), "Captain, these balls have three holes for the
insertion of the thumb and two fingers to prevent what you just did!"

The captain took his instructions and hefted the ball. "Jolly good, I see!'' he said. Then with a savage run he swung the ball with what appeared to be quite perfect form. But to our horror he failed to disengage his fingers and literally hurled himself down the alley. A solicitous group found two loosened teeth and a cut upper lip. Sherwood was not one of the group. He was sadly measuring the crater in the alley.

It was Robert Sherwood who elevated croquet from a cramped form of billiards on a manicured lawn to the stature of a broad sweeping battle over hill and dale. What Segovia has done for the guitar, Bob did for the game of croquet. Some will claim that Alexander Woollcott, others that Samuel Goldwyn, Herbert Swope or Harpo Marx, took croquet from the bustled Victorian ladies with their wire ''hoops'' and put it on the battlefield. I have played the Woollcott brand, the Goldwyn code and the devious Marxist rules and I know that Sherwood's game was of Homeric proportion compared with these lesser masters.

At Great Enton there was on the side of a low hill a grassy area that resembled a relief map of the Annapurna range of the Himalayas. It was here that Bob Sherwood laid out his croquet ''course'' as he called it. It was here that The Old Savoy Croquet Club conducted its tournaments, battles and ceremonies through the thirties. And it was here that old friendships were temporarily suspended by the competitive venom which only the Sherwood brand of play could arouse. Membership in the O.S.C.C. was exclusive and rarely exceeded ten members of both sexes.

The Founder drew up all the rules, arranged all team combinations and very rarely suffered defeat. Mixed play, in which women members engaged, enjoyed no relaxation in competitive spirit and, if anything, was more vehement and dishonest than in the all-male matches. Visitors at Great Enton had full playing status but were expected to play as directed and were seldom allowed to engage in strategic or tactical discussion. ''Theirs not to reason why'' was a lesson soon to be learned by anyone honoured by an invitation to Great Enton. No wagers were allowed as the Founder felt that the game was defiled by financial gain or loss. Besides, it was dishonest enough without financial incentive.

Before a match Bob would move the wickets (they were never called hoops) with devilish cunning so as to cause fresh hazards. One morning my phone rang and I heard the Founder say, ''You will play with me today against Bird and Kerr''–Richard Bird and Geoffrey Kerr. ''I have moved the third wicket so that it's next to impossible but I know how to get through ... but Bird will be driven mad!" The last was a hiss. That afternoon the match, which we won, was played in two and a half hours, a short game; and poor Dickie, dead on every ball, never got through the third.

An annual club event was a tournament played in the top hats and accoutrements of early nineteenth-century cricket. This was supposed to be a festive occasion when some of the Founder's rigid rules could be relaxed. But the customary adrenalin always flowed and the normal vicious spirit of the game was upheld. I managed to take a picture of a top-hatted argument in full heat with a little box Brownie but a few minutes later a mighty "kill" from the Founder's mallet finished my camera and its contents.

On the flyleaf of my treasured copy of *Abe Lincoln in Illinois* Bob inscribed:

To my beloved fellow-member – Raymond Massey.
All for none and none for all,
Everybody's dead on everybody's ball,
We'll knock for forty off
And never, never crawl,
That's the song of the O.S.C.C.
                    – The Founder

The "knock for forty off" is a reference to "knock rummy," an O.S.C.C. after-dark pastime at which Bob was a master. In his rummy operations he was able to offset his racing losses. Looking back on those mad, reckless devil-may-care days it would seem that I, an extremely poor rummy player, really subsidized Sherwood the horseplayer.

# 28

It was not until 1938 that I acted in another of Bob Sherwood's plays. It turned out to be quite a Sherwood year for me. In February I opened in *Idiot's Delight* in England and in October in *Abe Lincoln in Illinois* in New York. I had seen *Idiot's Delight* early in its long run on Broadway when I was acting in *Ethan Frome*, and made up my mind that I would play the part of Harry Van (which Alfred Lunt was playing) in London or cut my throat!

Harry Van was the part of a lifetime, one of those dream characters that makes every actor green with envy. A tough, wry, wise-cracking vaudeville hoofer, Harry Van had everything, including a cabaret act. Alfred was giving a beautiful performance, as was Lynn Fontanne as a mysterious Russian adventuress. I begged Bob for the part in London. He promised that if Alfred did not want to act Harry in London, I could play him.

Nothing was decided for a year and I had gone to Hollywood to do the two pictures, which certainly filled in 1937 for me but did not lessen the suspense. Eventually Bob cabled me in California that Alfred and Lynn were going to play in *Amphitryon 38* in London in 1938. The part and the play were mine.

I could not believe my luck. I remember wondering how Alfred could bear to give up a part like Harry Van. But I myself left Harry after playing him only six months. The truth is that the length of time you play a character is not what counts. What matters is having found a character, wrestled him into submission and achieved a fine performance. Naturally it is nice to have a box-office success, but I have rarely completed the long run of a play. Two roles which I enjoyed enormously and which gave me much satisfaction I played for only a week in summer stock, Sir Robert Morton in *The Winslow Boy* and Josiah Bolton in *Second Threshold*. Some of the disappointingly short runs of plays like *Spread Eagle*, *Never Come Back* and *The Ace*, flops at the time, remain precious memories outliving some of the successes. They recall old friends—Joe Cobb, Smith and Kurt von

Hagen. I knew them well, if not for long.

Delighted as I was at the prospect of acting Harry Van in London, I had to admit that there were several small clouds on the horizon. American successes were tricky propositions in England and more often than not failed to survive the transplant. Also, *Idiot's Delight* was an anti-war play and not only that but what Polonius would categorize as tragical-farcical. This is closely related to satire and the English do not like satire unless it is written by an Englishman, or by an Englishman whose family has lived for a generation or so in Ireland. War is a solemn matter and should not be indicted in a spirit of levity. The serious Englishman does not like to have his edification diluted with what he considers irrelevant humour. He prefers a neat potion which will probably bore him to death. He will suffer pacifist polemics levelled at him in unintelligible verse and chanted by a flat-chested choral group singing sharp, but will reject the most pungent comment on war's mass murders if it prompts a smile.

I also remembered, without trepidation, that of the seven American plays I had acted in or directed in England, only two—*Late Night Final* and *The Second Man*—had been box-office successes. But what did that matter? I had the play and I would open in London. But I very nearly did not, thanks to the Secretary of State for Foreign Affairs.

Henry Sherek had told me that if I got the English rights to *Idiot's Delight* he would like to join me in producing it. He had a healthy lack of concern about what the public wanted and was only interested in doing plays he liked. When I cabled him that I had the play, he joyfully started the wheels rolling.

Going home after *Hurricane* I established some sort of record from Los Angeles to Southampton, flying from the Coast to New York in sixteen hours, catching the *Queen Mary* and making the whole six thousand miles in under six days. After the christening of my daughter Anna, who had arrived three weeks previously, I found Henry had booked a try-out tour for four weeks during February, and had lined up a London theatre, the Apollo, for a March opening.

By mid-December I was deep in the pleasing job of casting *Idiot's Delight*. I know of no more pleasant task than casting a play with a lot of good acting parts. Actors are born optimists, as they must be in a profession so full of disappointments, and every part, good or bad, at once becomes the end of the rainbow. Bob's play provided twenty good parts, as varied a bag of characters as actors could wish for. It

223

was set in a hotel in the Italian Alps where four countries meet, and Versailles had created some ethnic faults. From a big window you would see Switzerland, Austria and Bavaria. In the twenty-four hours before the next war begins, the farce and the tragedy take place and the twenty characters face their common predicament–how to get home. I had to cast a German professor, a French radical, an English honeymoon couple, an armament magnate, his Russian mistress, a sextet of chorus girls and their manager and at least ten more interesting characters as only Sherwood could write them.

I had been lucky in getting every actor I wanted. Franklin Dyall was cast as the German scientist, his son Valentine Dyall as the young Englishman. For the armament tycoon I cast the highly personable and courtly Hugh Miller; while from New York we brought Tamara Geva, a Russian-born former member of Diaghilev's ballet company, to play the tycoon's mistress, Irene. Some critical eyebrows were raised at the choice of Hugh Miller. Some people feel that a heavy should have horns and a tail.

The scenery by Aubrey Hammond, my friend of so many productions, was almost ready, the casting completed save for two of the chorus girls, and everything set for regular rehearsals to begin in a few days, when the Lord Chamberlain informed us he could not grant a licence for *Idiot's Delight*.

I was holding an audition when my partner gave me the news. I refused to believe there could be any real difficulty. It was too outrageous to consider. However, when we reached the Lord Chamberlain's office at St. James's Palace we found he was serious. The Foreign Office had raised objections to the play because of the bitter anti-Fascist speeches which ridiculed and vilified the dictator countries. Those were the days of appeasement. To put it bluntly, the Foreign Office was scared pea-green of offending the Nazis and the Fascists. The play was no Ruritanian farce. I gathered that the Lord Chamberlain–who was Lord Cromer, my friend and "collaborator" of nearly ten years before–was as distressed as we were. He held out strong hope that the difficulty could be solved. He was determined that the play should go on.

I telephoned Bob in New York. Naturally he was angry and declared that he would not make alterations to satisfy anybody. The chief objection to the play, from the point of view of diplomacy, arose from the naming of the countries about to declare war and the locale of the action. I thought if the nations were unnamed we could get by.

224

Reluctantly Bob agreed, and the program eventually noted that the scene was "the Hotel Loda on a mountain peak in the Continent of Europe in any imminent year."

It seemed a very slight obstacle. I saw to it that by every device I could think of as director—uniforms and the like—the locale of the play would be pictured as northern Italy at a point where the Tyrol, Bavaria and Switzerland could be seen. We soon forgot that there ever had been any difficulty. When we opened for the try-out there was no doubt where the action was set: Ruritania had no part in it. Although I knew little about it, there had been a real battle between the Lord Chamberlain and the Foreign Office as to whether or not Bob's play should be licenced.

Thirty-two years later I was playing in Robert Anderson's *I Never Sang for My Father* at the Duke of York's Theatre in London. After a performance some visitors were chatting in my dressing-room and *Idiot's Delight* was mentioned. One of my guests, who shall be nameless, declared: "What a play that was! I don't believe you know, Massey, what a close run thing it was"—he used Wellington's words about Waterloo—"as to licencing it. The Foreign Office were very jittery about offending Hitler and Mussolini and brought all the pressure they could on the Lord Chamberlain to refuse a licence. I was in the F.O. at the time and I know what a fight the Lord Chamberlain put up for the play. It's probably the only time that office was used to enable a production instead of prevent it."

*Idiot's Delight* featured a cabaret act with dancing and singing, and this was a prime concern of mine. Henry Sherek had the best night-club show in London—*Les Girls*—running at the Dorchester Hotel. The star of the show was the greatest acrobatic dancer in the world, June Taylor. She had choreographed *Les Girls* and Henry had arranged for her to stage my night-club act in *Idiot's Delight*. It was a formidable task, for I was no great shakes as a customer dancing on a night-club floor, let alone as a performer. My previous experience as such had been confined to the barracks of Vladivostok twenty years previously. I had grown tired of being told that Harry Van was a third-rate vaudevillian and it wouldn't matter how bad I was at song and dance. I know that was as wrong as could be, for there is a vast difference between the tarnished technique of a professional and the ineptitude of an amateur. Any uninitiated customer in an audience would sense it. It takes talent to satirize.

June Taylor understood the problem at once. She devised time

225

steps for me which permitted a seemingly slithering, careless execution which showed a deteriorating technique rather than a frustrated attempt at being good.

I had cast the six girls for their acting ability (three had quite effective roles to play) and only two had had chorus experience, but June drilled them to Rockette standards. Her choreography was brilliant, the kind of cabaret numbers that would have a chance in Bucharest, Belgrade, Omaha or Oklahoma City. The girls were perhaps a shade too pretty for the troupe as described by Bob but one doesn't go broke making a profit. However, after we opened in the West End I found to my amazement that we rated amongst the young and raucous scions of the peerage as a musical, and one with the smallest and most alluring chorus in London. The stage-door of the Apollo was as busy as those of Daly's, the Gaiety or the Palace. Not only backstage was the lure of my young ladies to be in evidence, but out front an upper stage box was somehow secured for the second week of the run and the vociferous applause which greeted every word and movement of Beulah, Shirley, Francine and the others, to say nothing of the noisy somnolence which could be heard throughout the theatre when these charmers were not on, created a small problem. There was no way to prevent the sale of the box or any seats in the house to anybody who would pay for them, and the removal of over-hearty patrons by request or force was not desirable.

Fortunately our stage manager, Stanley (Tolly) Brightman, was a seasoned musical-comedy man. He said the only way to handle the problem was to make the girls individually and collectively responsible for the conduct of their swains out front. It worked like a charm, and a member of a wolfpack from the Guards Club remarked to me at the stage-door, "It's a jolly good show—we've certainly got to fight those bloody Krauts!"

This was hardly the message which Bob had intended his play to carry but the young Guardee's reaction was by no means unique. My own feeling on first reading *Idiot's Delight* was anti-Nazi, anti-Fascist rather than anti-war. I suppose the British Foreign Office saw it that way too. Later on when the war grew close, the play died in London. There was no more time for either a warning or a rallying call.

*R.M. and the girls in Idiot's Delight, at the Apollo Theatre, London, 1938. Alfred Lunt, who had played Harry Van in New York, wouldn't come to see me in the play. He said it would be like watching somebody use his toothbrush.*

226

Shortly after our London opening Bob Sherwood was asked to comment on the timeliness of *Idiot's Delight*. Bob replied, "*Idiot's Delight* appears unpleasantly as a creature of the moment. But I'm still thinking of the parent play, *Acropolis*, still hoping that the Athenians of the world will have enough sanity and unity and strength to resist the massed force of Spartans...."

We opened to an ovation, the try-out weeks having been virtual capacity, and from the start the play was a solid smash in the West End. The press was mostly ecstatic. They loved the play and the production but there were two important dissidents. Charles Morgan, in the majestic anonymity then imposed on its dramatic critic by *The Times*, complained bitterly that Sherwood offered no solution to the threat and horror of war. This lamentation seemed somewhat unreasonable and like rebuking a doctor who advocates early diagnosis of cancer but fails to come up with a cure. Jimmy Agate, in *The Sunday Times* (no relation to the daily), having praised playwright and players to the skies for "a masterpiece of light theatre," pecked away at Bob for his failure to strengthen the international munitions maker!

A playwright with a serious theme is not necessarily compelled to write a dull play. Bob wrote a side-splitting farce up to the moment when the war comes. Presumably Bob anticipated that his admonitions of 1936 would be disregarded.

I played Harry Van for six months and then left the play to rehearse for *Abe Lincoln in Illinois* in New York. Lee Tracy took over Harry Van and played him until the humiliation of Munich ended the London run of *Idiot's Delight*.

228

# 29

On September 5, 1938, the *Queen Mary* was full of Americans going home, cheered to leave the tensions of Europe behind them. That majestic progress up the harbour and round the Battery to the Cunard docks was a never-failing delight. To arrive in New York on a sunny, fall day with the job of a lifetime waiting for you was as thrilling an experience as could be imagined.

But over-confidence has never been a weakness of mine. Study of Bob's play on the voyage had disclosed some pitfalls which I would have to avoid. I would have to overcome the noble, folk-hero aspect of the character I was to play, particularly in the later scenes. I must remember that a pedestal was not a prop which accompanied Mr. Lincoln at any time, and that I must keep away from any reverence or awe of the very human being I was to interpret. That would be no easy job.

The play I was about to rehearse was to be the first production of the Playwrights Producing Company. Five top-ranking Broadway playwrights (Bob Sherwood, Elmer Rice, Sidney Howard, Maxwell Anderson and S. N. Behrman) had banded together to produce their own plays. Their reasons were "dissatisfaction with the economic conditions of the contemporary theatre" and a "desire for autonomy in production." In plainer language, the five playwrights wanted a bigger slice of the melon and full charge of all facets of production. The professional producers took a dim view of the withdrawal of plays from their market by the five most lucrative authors on Broadway. "They'll never make it!" was the malevolent wish voiced in many a manager's office.

Bob Sherwood and the Playwrights' press representative, William Fields, came out to Quarantine to meet me. As the ship moved up the harbour, Bob briefed me about cast and production matters. I wanted to know who would be the actual producer. I was afraid his duties might be carried out by the quintet of playwrights acting as a committee. I was relieved to learn that the author would be the producer and that all decisions about the cast would be in his hands. Bob smiled as he added that whatever went on between the producer-author and the other four would not be inflicted on the company. That seemed fair enough. And for our own play, we would have as capable a producer as could be found in the theatre.

Bill Fields turned the conversation to my American ancestry, my ties with the United States, my American uncles, aunts, grandmothers and other kin. I soon realized what he was getting at. I asked point-blank if there was resentment that a Canadian should play Abraham Lincoln. He admitted that some such feeling had been expressed in newspapers. My heart sank.

There was no anger in Bob's voice as he put in, "I just say we wanted the best actor we could find for the part. And we got him!"

Sure enough, next morning the *Daily News*, a widely read New York tabloid, came out with an editorial headed, "A Canadian as Abraham Lincoln?" The editorial allowed I was a fine actor and looked like Lincoln; but suggested that as a Canadian, little better than an Englishman, I would soon run into prejudice. Under my photograph was the caption, "Raymond Massey – good but not Lincoln." No one in the cast of forty I met next day seemed to agree. They went out of their way to express warmth and friendship.

Only one scene in the play had been altered since Bob finished the script a few months earlier. It was the only scene not based on documentary evidence. Bob Sherwood had found that after Lincoln broke his engagement to Mary Todd there was a lost year in his life. At the end of that year, about which virtually nothing is known, Lincoln returned to Mary Todd, begging her forgiveness, thereby accepting his destiny. Bob sensed that the missing year contained the key to the central question of his play: how did this man of doubt and indecision, this shiftless fellow, become a man of passionate conviction and decision?

The absence of documentary evidence gave the author freedom to write what must be the pivotal scene of his play. This so-called "prairie scene" was taking shape in Bob's mind as he chose presents for the chorus girls in *Idiot's Delight* one December afternoon in 1936. His account of its germination had its moments of hilarity. As he was swept along to the perfume counter at Bonwit Teller's, he had no idea what characters would be in the scene ("I want six small bottles of perfume, please"). He clearly saw a covered wagon by a campfire ("They're for six chorus girls"). Lincoln would be praying to God for the life of a sick little boy. It would be a prayer for the

230

survival of America, the turning point for this shiftless drifter who, in thirty years, would become President of the United States. The prayer would be the acceptance of responsibility.

Bob took his parcels across Fifth Avenue to a nearby Childs Restaurant and ordered butter cakes. He took a paper napkin from the dispenser and started to write.

Never, Bob said, did any speech come more smoothly. By the time he had written the two hundred-odd words, his butter cakes were cold, but the first lines of *Abe Lincoln in Illinois* were on paper.

He did no more work on the play for six months. Before he left for England that June he gathered up his notes preparatory to writing the play that summer of 1937 at Great Enton. The first thing he looked for was the prayer he had scribbled in Childs. The apartment in Sutton Place was turned upside down but the napkin could not be found. The first thing he did aboard ship was to write the speech again. He remembers being confident about the prayer but far from satisfied with the rest of the scene. The rest of the play came together with unusual ease and the script, covered with Christmas stickers, arrived at my door in Sussex on Christmas Eve of 1937, tagged "From guess who!"

Not long before his death in 1955 Bob told me of the discovery of the Childs paper napkin, neatly folded in a manuscript of his play *Acropolis*, which had been its resting-place since his return from shopping in December 1936. Comparison of the prayer, as scribbled in the restaurant and as rewritten aboard ship six months later, revealed a difference of only three words. Unaltered throughout rehearsals and try-out, the prayer survived. It took the masterminds of Hollywood to cut it from the motion picture. But more of this incredible blunder later on.

Elmer Rice, one of the five founding members of the Playwrights Producing Company, was to be the director of *Abe Lincoln in Illinois*. A prolific and successful author, he had already written some twenty plays starting with his hit *On Trial* in 1914, and including a range of style from the expressionist play *The Adding Machine* to the realism of *Street Scene* and *Counsellor-at-Law*. I had played with a very young Laurence Olivier in the London production of *The Adding Machine*, my first encounter with the fascinating avant-garde theatre of the twenties. Elmer had directed all of his own plays but Bob's was the first he would stage by another author.

I soon had complete confidence in Elmer Rice as director. His feeling for the play and for Lincoln's character was profound. He was

231

articulate but never said an unneccessary word. (The gabby director, even when his comments are sound, can ruin the performance of an over-receptive actor.) Elmer had been a law clerk as a young man. He had the clarity of a legally trained mind.

I tried to keep my Lincoln simple. I had done no research beyond reading Carl Sandburg's *The Prairie Years* and the Lincoln books that everyone reads. I relied on Bob to supply the character in his script. I have always feared over-embellishment of a character, having seen some brilliant performances of historical characters marred by excess of detail and self-conscious emphasis. For instance, I knew that Lincoln had a nasal, high-pitched voice. Dr. John F. Goucher, president of Goucher College in Baltimore and an old friend of my father, had told me so when I was a boy of thirteen. Dr. Goucher, when he was that age himself, had sneaked into a reception for Mr. Lincoln in Cleveland on the way to his first inaugural in 1861 and heard him speak. He also said that Lincoln had enormous hands.

One of my difficulties in rehearsal was deciding what to do with *my* hands. Grasping the lapels of that old frock coat was one mannerism I used. Apparently Mr. Lincoln never put his hands in his trouser pockets because they were too big. He used two long fingers to extract a coin or bill when necessary, which was not often. I frequently let my hands just hang or find a mooring place on my knees.

*Abe Lincoln in Illinois* was designed by Jo Mielziner, one of the two designers who dominated Broadway for forty years. (The other was Donald Oenslager.) Mielziner faced the difficult task of mounting twelve scenes with no more than a 32-second wait between any two. He succeeded, an achievement made possible only by meticulous calculation. The stage of the Plymouth Theatre, our Broadway destination, was notoriously shallow. This complicated Jo's task, but he was undaunted. Bill Fields used to stand out front during performances and listen to the whispered comments during the scene changes. Invariably he heard the question, "How do they do it?" Invariably the answer was, "Oh, revolving stages!" In reality, no revolving stages could have handled the large scenes.

Early in rehearsals we had been shown working models of the sets and platforms. Jo had done as perfect a job as he had for *Ethan Frome*. It seemed exactly what the play required—imaginative realism. It had been decided to set up the production at the Plymouth, which was dark, on the Wednesday of our final rehearsal week, have two run-throughs in the sets and then set up in Washington for a final dress rehearsal on Sunday. The company was in pretty good shape

232

but I was still far from settled in my own performance. What I saw on the stage of the Plymouth that Thursday morning did nothing to raise my spirits.

Mature playgoers may remember the time of the transparencies, when suddenly the lights onstage would dim and behind what had been a solid wall a scene would be revealed and acted out in a spooky half-light. This would fade out and the painted wall appear again as the lights onstage would come up. The innovation was much in vogue at the turn of the century, particularly in melodramas and mysteries, for flashbacks and short scenes. Mother is softly singing, "Where is my wandering boy tonight?" and behind "boy's" big coloured photograph on the flowered wall-papered wall, there he is hung on a bar in Singapore! And with these new-fangled dimmer spots, you could have mother lit softly while the native cops carry "boy" off to jail. The transparency was used sparingly in serious plays but I saw a flashback most effectively handled in this manner by Fred Terry in his production of *Henry of Navarre* in 1909. The use of the transparency ended with the advent of the movies, for the cameraman had much better tricks at his command.

The device was simple. A vertical area of gauze or scrim stretched tight, with light thrown on it from the side of the viewer, is quite opaque. It can be painted in any manner desirable. When the lights in front are dimmed out, and the area behind the gauze is lighted, the gauze is almost transparent. The action behind the gauze is somewhat diffused and out of focus.

As I walked on the stage I saw an enormous gauze curtain which, on closer examination, I found was tightly stretched on a huge frame. This was hung downstage of the false proscenium and just upstage of the house curtain. The house lights were out and from upstage I could see that the gauze was painted with a huge book or album and a conventional period décor. I realized at once it was a transparency. The stage was set for the opening of the play, the Mentor Graham scene being in place. All I could figure out was that this gauze was to introduce the opening of the play or perhaps each scene or maybe, God forbid, it might be used for the whole prairie scene!

Jo Mielziner came up the rehearsal steps from the front of the house.

"Jo, that's the biggest transparency ever. It isn't for our play, is it?"

"Yes, it is."

"Really? When do you use it? For act or scene curtains?"

233

"It will be there all through the play.... The whole play will be played with the transparency. Come out front and have a look. It's a fantastic effect."

At this point Bob Sherwood, who was sitting in the orchestra with Sidney Howard and Elmer Rice, called out to me to join them. I was still speechless. Jo came with me. He called out to the chief electrician to give us the opening fade-in. The house lights went up showing the big book on the huge scrim. The house lights dimmed, the stage lights faded in, and behind the scrim, which was now transparent, was the schoolmaster's cabin, artistically out of focus. Jo called to Elmer Brown, the stage manager, to have somebody sit in the Mentor Graham cabin. Somebody did and was artistically out of focus. There was silence. Jo spoke.

"Of course this isn't the lighting. We haven't started to work on that yet. But even so, I think it's beautiful, like something out of an old album!"

"What do you think, Ray?" said Bob.

I struggled for speech.

"Yes.... It's got that old album feel, like you're looking at it after four doubles.... Say, that's an idea. Is Sardi's open yet?"

"No, it's only ten."

"And I'm not hung over. But that set looks to me as if I was..."

I walked up on the stage and relieved old "somebody." As I sat in my chair in the first scene set, there was a completely opaque curtain in front of me; it might have been a blanket or wall. I could not sense the presence of anyone out front. I was not on a stage. I was in another room.

"Come up here and see for yourselves. There could be no audience out there."

They did come up onstage and they did see and they did not say to hell with it. I will never understand how four knowledgeable theatre men failed to realize the handicap which any actor was under in facing that seemingly solid wall. I didn't use any of the obvious objections to the whole idea of using the transparency–the fact that it detracted from the reality of the play, that it complicated the lighting of the scenes, that the clarity of the audience's vision would be diminished and so on. I just put my case on the fact that the absence of any rapport with the audience made my job impossible.

Elmer Rice, who had said nothing up to this point, suggested that we proceed with the run-through and decide afterwards about the gauze. I agreed and we started.

Like all first technical run-throughs, it was stop and go without much performance value but it did prove my fears to be well-grounded. The experience of delivering the debate speech against what seemed to be a blanket was the most frustrating ordeal I ever had, for the audience would be quite invisible to me. The farewell speech from the train was just as impossible to do. I gathered that the playwrights and Jo were out front and said very quietly: "The gauze has struck out. The company can't stand it and we've given it a fair try. I can't think of a single argument in favour of that monstrous contraption but I know one overpowering reason for striking it–I cannot give a good performance in front of a blanket. If it's there tomorrow, I will jump through it. Let's fly it now and get a good run-through without the cursed thing!"

We did and we went to Sardi's afterwards. Everything was in focus and nobody mentioned the gauze.

The next morning when I came to the theatre for the dress rehearsal, I looked up to the flies to see if the thing was there. It wasn't. Bob came up and whispered in my ear, "Don't worry, Ray. It's gauze with the wind."

The earlier scenes of *Abe Lincoln in Illinois*, with Mentor Graham, Judge Bowling Green, Jack Armstrong and the Clary's Grove boys, Josh Speed, Ninian Edwards, Billie Herndon, and Abe's tragic little romance with Ann Rutledge, so beautifully acted by Adele Longmire in her first Broadway role, gave me no trouble. It was the last five scenes of the play which I found difficult. Not that the performance of Muriel Kirkland as Mary Todd left anything to be desired. Muriel Kirkland, and Ruth Gordon in the motion picture, both acted that pathetic person with a grace and sensitivity that contributed much to the character. The part was underwritten as the author confesses in his comments in the published text of the play.

The Playwrights Producing Company had commissioned Norman Rockwell to do a drawing of me as the young Lincoln. This had been made from a photograph of myself and one of Mr. Lincoln. The result was a brilliant approximation of what could be done with my face to obtain a likeness. (The picture was used for promotion purposes.) I was a good deal thinner in 1938 than I am now and the hollowing of the cheeks and building of a respectable nose were my major objectives in making up each night. I am probably the only actor who ever had his make-up designed by an artist of the stature of Norman Rockwell.

Rehearsals proceeded with surprising smoothness at the Plymouth in New York. Meanwhile, Bob was writing his third version of the prairie scene. He rewrote it on the train to Washington and we played it at the Sunday dress rehearsal so that we could get it in for the Washington first-night. It was a real improvement.

I felt much the same about my performance as I had at the start of rehearsals. The character was now set and technically under control. I was not over-rehearsed nor could I have benefitted by further work. And yet I knew I could be better. Maybe the answer was the need for an audience–the traditional excuse of the bad actor: "I'll be all right on the night." I am ashamed to write it.

After the Washington dress rehearsal I asked for a run-through at the theatre–really just to pass the time. I knew my lines. I went to the theatre early, unwilling to take chances with that wretched putty nose. On my dressing-table were a bunch of telegrams, mostly from England. I do not usually open first-night wires until after the show, but on a try-out they are mostly from friends. I picked one up and opened it–and immediately wished I had not. Adrianne would not be joining me. I would not be needing the big apartment I had leased in New York.

I built the nose twice before I got it right. It was close to the five-minute call before I had it done. I checked the wart, wig join, fly buttons. When would I escape into the performance? I went onto the stage. It was dark and silent. I found my stool and sat down. Already I felt better. A tall figure sat down at the table. It was Frank Andrews who played Mentor Graham. I loved this scene. Nothing could go wrong when that old pro was with me. We sat in silence in the dark. I heard Elmer Brown whisper, "Curtain going up."

"Break a leg, Frank!" I whispered.

"Have fun," was the answer.

Then came the soft whine of the spools on the guide lines as the curtain swiftly rose. The lights faded in. Frank's line came, calm and clear: "The moods. . . . Every one of us has many moods. You yourself have more than your share, Abe."

The play was on. Nothing else mattered.

There was a party afterwards at the Hay-Adams Hotel where some of us were staying. We had received an ovation, the audience demanding fifteen curtain calls. There had been small accidents but for such a production at a first performance it had been a technical miracle. Bob and Elmer were ecstatic about play and performance. John Wharton, a lawyer, the business brains of the Playwrights, a man not given to effervescent enthusiasm, was fairly bubbling over with de-

236

light. Bill Fields predicted a triumphant press. The company was floating on clouds. The dreary fumed oak-panelled lounge of the Hay-Adams seemed almost cheerful.

I still felt I had failed to give an adequate performance. It is not unusual for an actor to be dissatisfied with his performance, and I have always had periods of frustration in bringing a big role to performance pitch. As a director, one always had to deal with actors' imaginings. I remembered Charles Laughton's lamentations about his failure to lick Harry Heegan into shape in *The Silver Tassie*. But such frustrations had to be overcome before an audience was faced. I believed that I had missed that deadline.

It was ironic to listen to the cheers and bravos on the stage of the National Theatre, to take call after call, to be acclaimed by your fellow players and producers and then, in calm earnest, ask to be replaced in that role.

That is exactly what I did. I took Bob and Elmer aside and asked that in view of my misgivings I be replaced in the part. I suggested that the play be kept on the road until the replacement was ready; I could continue to play until that time.

Bob was speechless, I think from anger. Elmer was, as always, patient and understanding. He said he had sensed my dissatisfaction but had said nothing, sure I would regain my confidence.

He continued, "I still feel the same. Actors are seldom sound judges of their own work. I believe your misgivings are due to an excess of zeal. As far as I am concerned, as director, I want to hold you to your contract. I think Bob and the others will agree."

Bob had regained his composure and agreed. He added, "I don't know what your misgivings are based on but you are acting Abe exactly as I had hoped for. I want you to continue."

"Bob, I—of course I won't withdraw unless you're anxious to make a change. If I knew what was the matter with my performance, I would ask for help and we could fix it. All I know is that my Abe is—well—he's too damned noble. I want to get him right, to my own satisfaction. It's important to me."

There was a long silence. Then Elmer asked me, "Were you satisfied with your Harry Van?"

"Yes, I was."

"Have you found it difficult to get away from Harry and into Abe?"

"No, not really. As an actor I have to adapt myself. There's a terrific gap between these two characters."

Elmer had his opening.

"Not really. The externals of the two are poles apart but the basic characteristics of Harry Van and young Abe are pretty close. It doesn't matter a damn that one was a pigmy and one was a giant. Harry was a complete failure and remained so. Abe was a failure at everything he tried until late in life; even after he married Mary Todd, he was an intellectual drifter. But Abe Lincoln and Harry Van had the same clarity of vision, both were terribly lonely and both had the point of view of the little man–the common touch."

Next day I could hardly wait to get to the theatre. Outwardly I doubt if there was any difference in my performance. The change was in my mind. That self-conscious feeling of awe, of reverence, was gone.

Two weeks later when I arrived at the Plymouth for the Broadway opening, I found an envelope in Bob Sherwood's hand. I tore it open. It read: "If Abe could see your performance tonight (and perhaps he can) it's my guess he would like it better than the Lincoln Memorial.–Bob."

# 30

To this day I do not understand the trouble I had in the development of the Lincoln of Bob's play. Whatever the reason, it ceased to be a factor in my performance after the Washington opening. My attempted withdrawal was never mentioned afterwards.

We went into Ford's Theatre in Baltimore for three nights and the story was the same as in Washington, sell-out business and a wonderful press. But successful try-outs did not guarantee a welcome to Broadway.

There are times in the theatre, most infrequent times, when audience and players are in complete harmonious accord. This state of rapport is not necessarily evidenced by applause or audible reaction. The audience can be quite undemonstrative, but after the final curtain you will hear actors exclaim, "They were with us tonight," or "They almost played it with us." I suppose psychologists would have some explanation for this phenomenon but I choose to believe that such a manifestation of accord is one of those miracles with which the theatre is sometimes blessed.

An opening performance is not a likely time for wonders of this kind. The tensions and strains aren't conducive to harmony. First nights are too often battles in which victory goes to either side of the curtain. But maybe the Lincoln legend cast a spell over the Plymouth Theatre that night of October 17, 1938. Certainly the magical unison of audience and players was realized at that Broadway opening. For me it remains the only first night in fifty-five years when it has so happened. For once I had no terrors, no sinking feeling, no strains at an opening. I enjoyed that wonderful night, every thrilling blessed minute of it.

As the curtain rose I knew, as did everyone waiting in the wings, that out front there were one thousand two hundred and more people and most of them were determined that Bob's play would be a smash hit.

There was one participant out front who was more fiercely partisan in support of the play than anyone else in the theatre. Mrs. Arthur Sherwood, the author's mother, was hard of hearing and had been given a seat in the front row. "Gaggie," as she was known in the family, was a scholarly matriarch with a thorough knowledge of American history. She also had that prevalent tendency of the deaf, to be quite unconscious of the decibel level of her own voice.

With this in mind, Bob detailed his eldest brother, Arthur, a colonel in the regular army, to sit with Gaggie and control the sound. For the first two acts this tactic worked admirably. However, as the curtain rose on the debate scene which opened the third act, I looked down and was somewhat confused to see, instead of the white shirtfront of Colonel Arthur Sherwood, U.S.A., an eager little old lady with hand cupped to ear. Gaggie was in her own seat.

My only thought was, Arthur has deserted his post! During the Douglas speech I was accustomed to make notes and look around and quite justifiably in character was able to scan the audience. Gaggie was in full cry as a commentator, though from my vantage point not quite intelligible. But in a slight pause of Albert Phillips playing Stephen Douglas, I distinctly heard her explain to her companion, "Robert knows he has not been fair to Douglas." This was the only comment which came out clearly but it was enough to alert me to what I would probably face. When my cue came and I stepped forward on the platform, I heard before I had spoken, "Robert has found this material from many sources." The comment was muffled but distinct, at least to me. But it seemed quite consistent with the scene and I thought that if I were any kind of an actor I should be able to steal the action away from Gaggie who was on my side anyway. I never played that speech better and the dear old lady herself seemed quite absorbed in it. I only heard three subsequent remarks: "This is from the Peoria speech," "This is from a letter to Horace Greeley," and "Now he's winding up for the finish."

Bob, who watched the play from an upper box which he and Madeline shared with some kleig lights, said afterwards he had a little difficulty in understanding some of his mother's narrative but was confident that she came through loud and clear to us on the stage. Bob took Gaggie's performance in the same way that I did. He did not hear it as well as I, and there was nothing he could do except enjoy her enthusiasm.

A family court of inquiry held on Sunday morning (as a means of passing part of the agonizingly long Sunday before the critics would present their verdict) exonerated Arthur of any dereliction of duty.

240

*R.M. as Abe Lincoln in Robert Sherwood's play Abe Lincoln in Illinois, as conjectured by Norman Rockwell. Working only from photographs of R.M. and his imagination, Mr. Rockwell completed this black-and-white impression of the young Abe Lincoln. It served as the basis of the make-up both in the stage and screen versions of the Sherwood play.*

241

*R.M. as Abe Lincoln and Adele Longmire as Ann Rutledge in the stage play Abe Lincoln in Illinois, at the Plymouth Theatre, New York, 1938-39.*

*Left to right: Howard da Silva, R.M., Marion Rooney, Herbert Rudley and Hubert Brown in the prairie scene in the stage play Abe Lincoln in Illinois.*

*The election scene in Abe Lincoln in Illinois. Mr. Lincoln does not share in the elation at his victory.*

*The departure at Springfield station in Abe Lincoln in Illinois.*

243

Gaggie had merely asked her son to let a friend sit by her during the last interval. When the time came to resume his seat, the two old ladies were hopelessly marooned in the centre of a long row of intense first-nighters and the house lights were dimming. After the critical score was in, it turned out that Gaggie had several non-committal press comments, such as, "The lady in the front row was not a heckler but the author's mother." Bob remarked with some admiration, "Gaggie got a mixed press." As for me, I wondered how I could get along playing the debate scene without her.

There was a party afterwards which was unique among opening-night carousals in that it was not interrupted by the arrival of the first morning papers with the inevitable disruptive reverberations of anger or ecstasy. Being Saturday, we would have to wait until Sunday midnight for the Monday morning papers. But as everybody assembled had experienced that audience reaction and assumed that we were a smash, critics were not on anybody's mind and joy was unconfined.

Bob Sherwood was not joyful. He was professionally a pessimist and in his eyrie among the lamps, he had sensed no well-wishing urge in the audience. He considered it apathetic and polite in spite of the ovation at the end of the play and the twenty-six curtain calls.

Elmer Rice shared Bob's misgivings as to the play's hold on the audience. He had watched the first two acts with Bob and also failed to feel the audience's intense sympathy with the play which had been so real to us. Afterwards Elmer had been cheered by the news that the critic George Jean Nathan had hated the play (Nathan had been heard to say so by Bill Fields) and the master carpenter had told Elmer that the twenty-six calls constituted a "record number of applause."

But for all of us, optimists and pessimists, that Sunday after the opening was an agonizingly long day. There are always some actors who profess to ignore critics, who say they don't give a damn what is written about them. If that be true, they have reached a plateau of self-esteem and security to which most of us in our insecure and vulnerable profession will never climb. The actor, like Shakespeare's Cardinal Wolsey, feels himself "naked to mine enemies," for regardless of the fact that acting is an interpretive art, that the actor is conveying the creative effort of the author to the audience, it is the actor's personal contribution, his physical presence, his voice, his expression, his movements—to sum up, his talent—which the critic makes his target for praise or abuse.

Bill Fields and I picked up the four morning papers at Times Square

244

about 11:30 P.M. With the aid of a cigarette lighter, I read Brooks Atkinson's as our taxi went east on 44th Street. It was a panegyric! The page blew back in my face and caught fire. The taxi driver just asked, "What's the matter, bud? Is it a stinker?" Bill reassured him as to the safety of the cab and added, "We're going to run forever!" We went to my apartment and read the others. Bill and I couldn't believe our eyes, and the evening ones next morning were just as good.

When more than 150 reviews were finally in print, even Bob had to admit that the press for his play had been "bloody marvellous." The praise that meant most to me, and I believe to Bob as well, was written by Wolcott Gibbs in the *New Yorker*.

It isn't easy to account for the feeling of rising excitement I had through the twelve scenes it takes to tell this. I suppose it was just the surprise and gratitude and somehow the sorrow of seeing a very great man exactly as he must have been.

Two weeks after the play opened the New York *Daily News* commented in an editorial:

Some weeks ago we were expressing doubts in this column as to whether a Canadian actor could be expected to give an adequate rendition of the role of Abraham Lincoln.... We'll say now that it's a great show; one of the greatest historical plays we've seen—and that Mr. Massey in our opinion measures up to every requirement of the Lincoln role....

It was a most thorough ingestion of crow and I heartily enjoyed it.

*All actors who have played Mr. Lincoln have found it a glutinous role, liable to stick to a player offstage. Some actors have revelled in this. I have always maintained that my efforts as an actor belong exclusively in the theatre and do not carry over into my private life. So I carried on with my pursuit of New York night life without regard to what Mr. L. would have done. My attendance at the more lively night spots did cause a few eyebrows to rise, but the box office at the Plymouth Theatre remained radiantly prosperous. Above are pictured the Committee on Admissions and some prominent members of Jack White's exclusive Club 18 in the cellar of 18 West 45th Street, New York City. Left to right: Frankie Hyers, Dorothy, Pat Harrington, Jack White, R.M., Noll Gurney and my favourite arbiter of elegance, Sir Cedric Hardwicke.*

246

# 31

In the twenties and thirties a stage actor was hardly ever chosen to repeat his role on the screen. George Arliss and the Lunts were about the only exceptions. Good plays acquired by the studios were reserved for the many stars on contract. Independent producers found it difficult to obtain a release for any picture which did not feature one or more big screen names.

I did not hold much hope that I would play Lincoln in the movie which was certain to be made of Bob's play. Offers for the movie rights started to come in the moment we were established as a hit. All the big studios were interested. In trade papers and gossip columns, about the only star who was not mentioned as a probability for the screen Abe was W. C. Fields, in spite of his identification with a stovepipe hat.

The five playwrights, however, were all seasoned screen writers. They had experienced the frustrations of writing movie scripts for the big studios. It was natural that for their first movie sale they would pick an independent producer. *Abe Lincoln in Illinois* was entrusted to Max Gordon for screen production. He paid a quarter of a million for the rights, a big price in 1939. What was a surprise to the trade and a delight to me was that I was picked to play Abe.

It all seemed too good to be true. Bob was to write the script himself; he assured me it would follow the pattern of the play. The movie was to be made the following summer (it was now mid-April), and Richard Gaines, who understudied Abe Lincoln, would take over my role in the play while I was in Hollywood for the picture. Then regardless of how the play was doing on Broadway, I would rejoin the company for a national tour. Bob wanted his play to be seen throughout the country as soon as possible, and with the original cast.

In June Bob Sherwood was already in Hollywood working on another script, and I was a little perturbed that his full attention would not be on his own play. A Hollywood script writer named Grover Jones had been brought in to work on the Abe script and eventually was given equal credit with Bob for the screenplay. This had been sent to me in New York and it read pretty well.

Of all the stage dramatists, Bob was by far the most experienced in film-writing and movie-making. For years he had been the movie critic on the old *Life* and had been a leader in bringing film criticism to maturity. I will never understand why a collaboration was needed in the writing of the screenplay of *Abe Lincoln in Illinois*. The resulting script was very good but somehow the inevitable expansion of the action, the splitting up of the tightly compact scenes of the stage play which the screen version was supposed to demand, seemed to accentuate rather than diminish the episodic nature of the play. However, the direction was to be in the experienced and talented hands of John Cromwell, originally a stage director and actor, who had a fine record of movie-making to his credit. John had directed me in *The Prisoner of Zenda* two years before.

I left the Broadway play in July 1939 to make the movie in California with the assurance that I was to go on tour with the original cast as soon as the movie was finished.

Adrianne and I were amicably divorced before I left for California. Our children Daniel and Anna remained in England with Adrianne. My elder son Geoffrey remained with me, as he had done since he was five years old. He was at preparatory school age by then, spending holidays at home with us.

Dorothy Ludington Whitney and I were married that summer. Dorothy is a Connecticut woman of the same early Puritan ancestry as myself – a graduate of Vassar College, class of 1922. Immediately upon graduation from the Yale School of Law in 1925, she went to work in the law office of the late John Wharton, a distinguished theatrical lawyer and one of the founders of the Playwrights Producing Company and our cherished long-time friend.

It was brave of John to take a chance on the untried legal ability of a 23-year-old girl fifty-three years ago, long before women's liberation found its sometimes too-strident voice. He never regretted this rash step.

On our way to California we stopped off for a week's holiday in Sun Valley, Idaho. The second day there we received a cable from Adrianne in France telling us the news of her marriage to a prominent international lawyer. We exchanged good wishes for mutual long happiness. These wishes have been fulfilled for all of us. Adrianne remains a dear and valued friend.

My desire to "kill" a salmon in one of the rugged Idaho mountain streams put a severe strain on our fledgling marriage. I immediately discovered that Dorothy was no outdoor girl. A golf course was and is the extent of her acceptance of the great outdoors—happily I confess it is mine too.

The stream we were to fish was only six miles distant from the inn, but the resident Nimrod who was to guide us neglected to tell us that the trail, which we were to follow on horseback, was largely vertical. It proved to be quite a climb. Dorothy soon declared that her horse was "mentally retarded" and also "much too wide"! The complaint was repeated with increasing emphasis as the expedition proceeded over the dizzying trail.

As a small boy I had a box of lead cavalry troopers. The rider could be detached from his mount but remained in a hopelessly bow-legged condition. When we lifted Dorothy off her mount at our destination, I was instantly reminded of my toy soldiers. Her horse had indeed been too wide!

After a turbulent night in adjacent pup tents, listening to Dorothy's complaints that "two men in fur coats were looking at her" (they proved to be bears), I decided to cut this expedition short and we headed back to the inn. The guide and the wranglers departed with the pack horses loaded with the few provisions the bears had left.

It was 8:00 A.M. I saddled our two horses and found a suitable boulder as a mounting block for Dorothy. But she had decided to walk. She would not, could not, mount that "cart horse." She allowed that she could walk anywhere a "feeble-minded horse could." And she did.

Dorothy's New England spunk made her scramble over rocks and boulders, through dust and streams, in those stout Republican tennis shoes. Meanwhile, her humiliated husband arrived back at the inn at Sun Valley in the middle of the luncheon cocktail session, dejectedly riding his charger and leading Dorothy's "wide" horse. Looking fresh and lovely, she walked behind, gaily declaring to all, "I don't own a horse. They are not for sitting on."

The happy result of this unfortunate adventure was to prove to Dorothy that I was not a hunter or a nature boy, and all was well.

In California we rented a house in Bel Air and were joined by Dorothy's two daughters and Geoffrey. Dorothy's housekeeping couple, Cleo and Prince, drove out from Connecticut to look after us. They, like Dorothy, were totally unacquainted with the goings-on out here. Our house was near that of the late W. C. Fields. It was Mr. Fields's whim, on occasion, to walk around outdoors late at night declaiming whatever he felt like declaiming. Cleo, still with her rosy Connecticut notions of the idols of Hollywood, reported to Dorothy, "My, my! That Mr. Fields! He sure works hard, long hours. I've heard him learning his part out loud, outdoors, just about every night."

Dorothy went with me to Oregon for the New Salem location shots of the movie, leaving the little girls, their fraulein and Geoffrey in the cheerful hands of Cleo and Prince, where they all splashed together in the first swimming pool any of them had ever seen.

There were plenty of salmon in the McKenzie River, which flowed past our actual location, but they were not disturbed by the film people as they swam upstream past the replica of New Salem. We were much too busy with other fauna of the Midwest such as chipmunks, deer, oxen, pigs, etc., which had been introduced into the screenplay in the best Walt Disney manner to illustrate Abe Lincoln's early Illinois background.

In the opening scene of the picture Abe was described in the script as "stretched on the floor of the cabin reading a book, a chipmunk watching him." Just what characteristic of the young Lincoln the chipmunk was supposed to reflect was not made clear. The chipmunk's role was presumably to be "ad-libbed"; but for this momentary appearance of the rodent, a "trainer" with three chipmunks, all presumably with literary tastes, travelled from Hollywood to Oregon. None of the little beasts made the histrionic grade. On being liberated on the cue of "action," the first two fled up the chimney of the cabin to a larger life in Oregon. The third bit the property master, and I declined to act with him. The attempt to get performances from the uncooperative rodents had occupied two hours at $1,500 per hour and anyway the idea of the scene was phoney as a three-dollar bill.

The deer, a local amateur, ended up on the cutting-room floor after a lacklustre performance; but the barnyard fowls, pigs, cows, ducks, oxen and dogs, as well as a hundred or so humans, all non-pro and resident Oregonians, performed in excellent fashion as inhabitants of New Salem, Illinois, circa A.D. 1830. This was particularly true of the fifty pigs which the young Lincoln managed to deposit in the McKenzie River when, by his inexpert navigation, a raft carrying the pigs careened over a waterfall.

It was a scene which could only be shot once, at least once a day, for it took some eight hours to get the raft back above the waterfall. But without any rehearsal, the pigs entered into the spirit of the scene and all gave superb performances, acting with porcine abandon. They

250

*R.M. and Dorothy on location at Eugene, Oregon, with bovine friends, Even Tenor and Dilemma, professionals from California who performed in the movie Abe Lincoln in Illinois with very deliberate precision.*

*Abe on location for the movie. The pigs played very rough.*

*The frenetic atmosphere of movie-making is sometimes unbearable.*

were all tilted into the river and showed the onlooking salmon how swimming should really be done. We got it on the first take with all the cameras. I don't consider swimming with a bunch of hogs as habit-forming. It's a spectator sport. The pigs were very rough and they didn't really know what it was all about. They had no "game plan." And the noise was like the Paris Bourse in a panic.

The three weeks on location in Oregon had produced an astonishingly small amount of finished footage, about 8 percent of the total picture. But once back in the studio we really made progress. In only one night on the RKO back lot, in a stifling temperature of 101, we shot the Lincoln-Douglas debate scene. That was about thirteen minutes of finished film. Two days had been used up on location to shoot the pig sequence which lasted one minute in the picture.

John Cromwell had cast the film production entirely with experienced stage actors. To play Mary Todd on the screen we had the incomparable Ruth Gordon. It was our first time together since *Ethan Frome.* There may have been a bit of Ethan in my Abe Lincoln (Ethan and young Abe had something in common) but there wasn't a vestige of Mattie Silver in Ruth's Mary Todd. There is practically nothing which this superb actress cannot play to perfection; and now in her eighties she is pleasuring everybody by her continuing career in

252

films. Gene Lockhart as Douglas, Minor Watson as Josh Speed, Harvey Stephens as Ninian Edwards and Alan Baxter as Billy Herndon, were part of a fine acting company, and John Cromwell's direction was steady and effective.

We saw little of Bob Sherwood and less of the producers, Max Gordon and Harry Goetz.

Film-editing can take a long time, often two or three times as long as it took to shoot. But Bob Sherwood was determined that the film be released by mid-January 1940. Incredibly the final print of the picture was ready in mid-December. I was on tour with the play. In Detroit Dorothy and I saw the movie in a projection room at the RKO office.

I am always ill-at-ease watching a film I am in. For eight reels it seemed to be a really good picture and I was not ashamed. But then a sort of time-bomb went off in my head. I realized that an entire scene had been cut, the prairie scene with the beautiful prayer for the sick boy! The fulcrum of the stage play, the germ of the play which Bob had written on a paper napkin in Childs Restaurant, the scene which explained Abe Lincoln's recognition of his destiny—that scene had been excised from the picture! Without it the story had become a documentary, a procession of episodes.

I telephoned Bob at once. He was in New York. Yes, he knew about the cut. It was too bad. He was heartbroken about it. But there were reasons, valid reasons he believed, for cutting it. I interrupted with a suggestion: "Why not cut the Harpers Ferry scene? It has about as much point in the picture as a skunk at a picnic." (This sequence, showing John Brown's raid at Harpers Ferry, had been interpolated in the picture. Although it was well produced and acted, it seemed excess baggage to me.) Bob defended the sequence. It was a painful conversation. Bob had been talked into condoning the cut. By whom?

I telephoned Max Gordon. A telephone call to Max under any conditions was a traumatic experience. In agreement, his voice was ear-splitting; in disagreement, alarming. I tried to explain my misgivings at the cut. The conversation at once became acrimonious. When gentle Max shouted, "You've been paid, mind your own business!" I hung up.

The Keith's Theatre in Washington was chosen for the premiere. We were in the middle of a Chicago run of ten weeks on the national tour. RKO Pictures, which was releasing the movie, had suggested that I arrive by train in Washington in make-up, stovepipe hat and

253

*Ruth Gordon as Mary Todd and R.M. as Abe Lincoln, in the motion picture Abe Lincoln in Illinois, Hollywood, 1939.*

shawl. Bob rejected the idea with the angry contempt it deserved.

Dorothy and I flew the last leg of our journey from Chicago in a period flying machine, in the foulest weather and in abject terror. We stayed at the Hay-Adams. Memories of that opening-night party when I tried to give up Abe returned in clear and frightening focus. It had been a scant fourteen months ago.

The movie was to be shown to the President on Sunday evening. Bob and Madeline Sherwood and Dorothy and I dined at the White House. Bob and I sat next to President Roosevelt at the screening. He was in jovial spirits and seemed to enjoy the picture. He muttered, "He wrote those speeches himself!"

It was the second time I had seen the film and the loss of the prayer seemed more damaging than ever. I looked at Bob. His head was bowed, his eyes closed.

*R.M. in the Lincoln-Douglas debate scene, in the movie Abe Lincoln in Illinois.*

254

Next morning the Keith's Theatre was heavily picketed by blacks and whites protesting the Jim Crow regulations then prevailing in Washington. When we had played our single week at the National, no blacks had been able to see *Abe Lincoln in Illinois* except in segregated areas. The same isolation would prevail in the nation's capital. Mrs. Roosevelt was to attend the opening escorted by myself. As this good lady had always scrupulously observed the sanctity of the picket line, we were sure she would not come to the world premiere. But on telephoning the White House I was told she would attend regardless of the demonstration. So I had the honour of escorting the First Lady on the only occasion when she crossed a picket line. She explained that the picketing organization was not approved by the NAACP.

Still, I knew it was hard for her to ignore the pickets. She was calm but silent as we drove to the theatre. Near the entrance we could see the signs bobbing above a big crowd. As the First Lady stepped out of the car, onlookers and even pickets cheered.

*R.M. and Mrs. Roosevelt.*

*"Good-bye, my friends and neighbours." The final scene in Abe Lincoln in Illinois.*

# 32

Following the national tour of *Abe Lincoln in Illinois* I played John Brown in a picture called *Santa Fe Trail*. At this time, in 1940, all the big studios were paying homage to the railroads by working the story of their early days into what were really big-scale Westerns. *Santa Fe Trail* was Warner Brothers' genuflection to the Atchison, Topeka and Santa Fe Railroad. How did John Brown fit into such a picture? The answer was quite simply that he didn't fit into the picture, he just took it over.

Robert Buckner, who wrote the screenplay, told me that when Jack L. Warner asked him if he had any ideas about an action story of how the railroad was put through Kansas in 1857, he replied that there wasn't much going on in Kansas at that time other than the attempt of John Brown and the Free State men to take over the state; and he went on about the massacre at Pottawatomie, the battle of Palmyra and the Harpers Ferry raid. Warner was impressed and told him, "Fine, go ahead. We'll make the son of a bitch the heavy."

Buckner took his instructions literally and, as he was a good historian as well as an excellent screen writer, the result was a thundering good story of John Brown from Palmyra to his execution in Virginia with one token scene of laying tracks in Kansas as a reminder of the original purpose of the movie.

From Abe Lincoln to John Brown is a dream transition for an actor. There was total contrast in the two characters. Historically Lincoln disliked and distrusted Brown intensely. If Brown knew of Lincoln, which he probably didn't, these feelings would have been reciprocated. I had the rare privilege of reading both the John Brown and Abraham Lincoln passages in the stage presentation of Stephen Vincent Benét's poem, "John Brown's Body." This was a fascinating acting experience. I also played John Brown in the Mirish picture, *Seven Angry Men*, some years later. Thus I had opportunities to play John Brown in three different circumstances.

*Santa Fe Trail* had, in addition to the excellent script of Bob

Buckner, the benefit of lively direction by Michael Curtiz, a Hungarian with benign eccentricities and a fanatic interest in American history. He had only recently been naturalized but his knowledge of the American past and particularly the period we were dealing with was astonishing.

Mike Curtiz was an avid reader but his inability to observe common English usage in speech was profound. To say that he had little command of the English tongue would be wrong. Mike had conquered it. He had a joyous disregard of conventional English semantics and syntax. He had contrived his own phrasing which invariably was brief and succinct. For example, on one occasion Mike wished to alter the background grouping for a long panorama shot. In conventional English it would be necessary to say, "I would like those saddled but riderless horses to face the opposite direction." But Mike just hollered through the bull-horn, "Aim the empty horses the other way."

He had a European abhorrence of waste and extravagance. On one occasion several actors, including Alan Hale, Jr. and Guinn ("Big Boy") Williams, were playing around on a camp set with big round loaves of bread using them as footballs. Mike Curtiz had a short and towering temper which came into instant action. "Stop, you rich bums," he cried. "You insult the good bread.... That is bread, Big Boy. That is bread, Alan. You are for shame, you bums!" He strode off. There was no "people are starving" or any such cant. Just that the good bread had been insulted.

Curtiz had a heartless streak in him. He was lining up a shot in the execution sequence on the process stage. John Brown was to be seated on his coffin in the cart with a parson sitting opposite him. The process background was to be projected on the big screen behind the cart. Mike, as he used to do, was framing his shot with his hands and stepping backwards to find the camera spot. Behind him was an empty concrete tank used for water shots. The little man who was to play the parson stood well behind Mike and moved backwards with him. Nobody warned him of the empty tank. Nobody saw him except Mike, who had eyes in the back of his head. The little man disappeared into the tank. Before he hit the bottom Mike muttered, "Get another parson!" A pile of folded tarpaulins broke the parson's fall and he wasn't badly hurt. Although he was paid, he didn't get to ride in the cart. Mike's request produced "another parson" who fortunately had no lines to learn.

Mike Curtiz had trouble remembering names and he would often compromise by addressing us by the names of the characters we acted. These he would frequently scramble beyond recognition. Thus I was known as "Joe Brown," an appellation singularly disconcerting to one who is about to deliver one of John Brown's thundering invectives. The thought of that amiable comedian with the panoramic grin was not conducive to the portrayal of fanaticism. The soubriquet of "Broadway," which he reserved for relaxed moments, was happily inappropriate in the light of my ferocious make-up. Errol Flynn, who played Jeb Stuart, got the red-carpet treatment of his own name, albeit in the scrambled form of "Earl Flint."

Two young actors, Van Heflin and Ronald Reagan, gave initial and impressive performances in *Santa Fe Trail*. Both these successful acting careers have ended, Van Heflin's in his untimely death a few years ago and Ronald Reagan's by his taking up a new career, to the screen's loss and the nation's gain. In this movie thirty-eight years ago, Ronnie showed signs of the energy and initiative which made him such a good Governor of California. He played a young George Custer just out of West Point and serving with the U.S. Cavalry in Kansas. Under the command of Jeb Stuart, the squadron has been assigned the job of stopping the activities of John Brown and his abolitionist raiders. I wasn't in the scene which I am about to describe but I saw the incident.

The squadron leader, Errol Flynn, is informed that John Brown's raiders are nearby and the troopers are ordered to mount and take action. The scene had been rehearsed and the camera was being readied. The action was simply that the three troops mount and move off at the trot. The officers were in the foreground. Ronnie was holding forth about the direction. "This is a scene of action. We're too apathetic. There should be a feeling of urgency. We wouldn't mount formally by the drill book. I'm going to vault into the saddle and make it look like we're in a hurry." The other officers, including Flynn, mindful of the potential discomfort of jumping into a McClellan saddle, indicated that they would do it as rehearsed.

The assistant called out, "All right, this is a take.... Just as we rehearsed.... Roll 'em.... Speed.... ACTION!" Everybody proceeded to mount "by the book" except Ronnie who sprang forward with a prodigious leap which carried him with his sabre in its sling to an ignominious landing on his behind on the other side of his horse which was being held by an astonished orderly.

*R.M. as John Brown, the abolitionist, in Santa Fe Trail.*

260

Mike shouted, "Cut! .... Acrobat bum!"

They got the scene in the next take and I remembered a line in *Macbeth* which seemed appropriate. It's supposed to be bad luck to quote *Macbeth* in the theatre, like whistling in a dressing-room. But I don't think it counts on a movie set. Anyway, I did quote *Macbeth* to Ronnie: "Vaulting ambition, which o'erleaps itself, and falls on the other."

*Santa Fe Trail* was a satisfying picture for the studio, the public and for those of us who acted in it. The scenario may have flouted history a bit in places (almost every general in the Confederate and Union armies seems to have graduated from West Point in the same class) but it gave a good account of John Brown.

# 33

Walter Huston was on the Warner lot when I was working on *Santa Fe Trail*. We sometimes lunched together and the subject of Lincoln's tenacious hold on an actor would come up. Walter and I had both been born in Toronto and he had done a Lincoln movie at Fox a few years before. I recall his words on one occasion: "I had trouble escaping from Abe and I only played him in one movie. You have sewed yourself into that shawl and nailed the high hat on with a Broadway run, a year on the road—and the movie. We'd better get Bogart over there to play Booth and finish you up while you're hot." He chuckled. "You're set for Abe from here in."

Just as we were finishing the shooting of *Santa Fe Trail*, four months after the *Abe* tour had closed, and it seemed as if nobody on Broadway would ever take a chance on me in anything that didn't wear a stovepipe hat, I got a telegram from Kit Cornell offering me the part of Colenso Ridgeon in her next production, Shaw's *The Doctor's Dilemma*. I read the telegram over and over. It was true. My good luck was holding. Kit was going to emancipate me. She had cast me in one of the best high-comedy roles I would ever play, a character which was the complete antithesis of Lincoln. She had solved for me my own dilemma as to what would follow Bob Sherwood's play.

It was a daring bit of casting on Miss Kitty's part. If the public and the critics rejected me in a comedy role after *Abe Lincoln*, and this was by no means unlikely, her production would suffer. But Kit wasn't the sort of manager to be troubled by such possibilities. She told me during rehearsals that one thing which confirmed her choice of me for Ridgeon was Shaw's description of him as wearing a high hat in the last act. She was tickled that there should be one vestigial remain of Mr. Lincoln even though I made it an Ascot grey topper.

Rehearsals of a high comedy, when it is well cast and directed, are a joy for any actor. *The Doctor's Dilemma* was particularly so for me because not only were play, cast and director all that could be hoped for but because, for the first time, I was in one of Miss Kitty's productions. In the next three years I would act in three plays under her management. Katharine Cornell's productions had a professional quality I rarely saw equalled. It used to be said that Kit was a lovely figurehead in her management, that Guthrie McClintic, her husband and her director, and Gertrude Macy and Stanley Gilkey, her business managers, were responsible for that amazing production record of twenty-five years. I think nobody who ever worked with Kit would say that. Guthrie was a very fine director—I knew that from *Ethan Frome*; and Gert and Stanley knew theatre management inside out. But in the theatre there must be a focus of authority. Somebody must be the boss and when the program read "Katharine Cornell presents," it meant just that. It meant that Miss Kitty, gentle but firm, knew everything that was going on in her theatre wherever that theatre was, be it on Broadway or the road. She was the last of the great player-producers who had led the English-speaking theatre through the nineteenth century.

I think Kit chose *The Doctor's Dilemma* as a producer in quest of a good comedy full of lively fun with Shavian wisdom tossed in, and not as a star in search of a great role. She cared not a whit that at least three of the doctors whom Shaw was lampooning provided the actors who played them with better parts than Jennifer Dubedat, the character in which Kit had cast herself. She knew that Jennifer was an abbreviated version of Candida, her favourite role, and that she had the power to generate genuine emotion. As Brooks Atkinson said in his notice, "Whenever she appears, this skittish and garrulous drama comes to attention."

Shaw takes a healthy swing at the medical profession in this play and in so doing provides a half-dozen actors with as much fine comedy as they could expect in a lifetime. A good cast was rewarded with those acting plums, or perhaps I should say prunes, which were advocated by one doctor, Sir Patrick Cullen, as a cure for all human ailments. Shaw had called this panacea "greengages" but Guthrie wisely changed the name to "prunes" for American audiences.

The realistic trend in playwriting and acting was gaining momentum in England and America by the early forties, and casting a Shaw play, or any of the literate drama of the Edwardian period, was not an easy task. The younger actors and actresses in their search for actuality ignored diction and indulged in every kind of underplaying—which ruined the dialogue of such writers as Maugham, Galsworthy, Sherwood and many of their contemporaries including G.B.S.

264

But the Cornell management had gathered some Shavian veterans for the *Dilemma* and it was certain that G.B.S.'s dialogue would be heard. Ralph Forbes, Cecil Humphreys, Whitford Kane, Clarence Derwent and Colin Keith-Johnston played the clutch of assorted medicos who were the targets of Shaw's satire. Bramwell Fletcher played the artist Louis Dubedat, Jennifer's husband. In a sort of prophetic taste of the anti-hero of today's drama, he was Shaw's wry concept of a Class-A bounder—a philanderer and a swindler. I rounded out the medical collection as Ridgeon, a fashionable consultant, the doctor with the dilemma, bedevilled by the problem of saving either the life of a brilliant but worthless artist or that of a poor but worthwhile doctor. As the *New Yorker* put it rather more accurately:

Ridgeon is faced with the undesirable embarrassment of a physician who, admiring a shapely lady, is suddenly given a chance to exterminate her husband with no foolish questions asked.

The medical profession has usually been treated with sentimental reverence in both literature and drama, and the public likes it that way. When *The Doctor's Dilemma* was first produced in London in 1906, there was an outcry against Shaw's so-called slanderous lampooning of the medicos. Subsequent productions have not provoked such a strenuous defence of the profession, and the comedy has been greeted as a "literate, amusing and rewarding evening."

But loyalty to physicians and their practice remains as strong as ever in the public heart. The popularity of the medical shows on television bears witness to this fidelity. I share in such constancy for I like and trust doctors. But there were times during my five years at Blair General Hospital when the bland virtues of old Dr. Gillespie and young Dr. Kildare became a bit oppressive. Then I hankered for the cynicism of Ridgeon and the foibles of Shavian medicine in *The Doctor's Dilemma*.

I think there is nothing in an actor's life so fascinating as the preparation of high comedy for performance, particularly in the final stages of rehearsal. The first encounter with a paying audience is indescribable, with the audience in a sense taking over the direction and unwittingly telling the players if their timing and inflections are right or wrong. There will be little doubt as to the nature of this direction. It will be fair, accurate and instantaneous and, with a good company which has been well rehearsed, it will be encouraging and informative. Most times the audience wants to help out but it will be fair.

Guthrie had given us a fine four weeks of rehearsal and we were as prepared as we could be. As often happens, the cast would see the scenery for the first time at the one dress rehearsal we would have–on a Sunday night in Detroit. We had, of course, seen the models. Donald Oenslager had given the production four spectacular scenes–painted scenery, not heavy-built sets–which perfectly presented the Edwardian atmosphere of 1906. The company was to travel to Detroit on Friday night, which would permit one more rehearsal in a hotel ballroom on Saturday and the dress rehearsal on Sunday night. It looked to be a smooth program for us.

But on arrival in Detroit on Saturday morning I was put to bed at the hotel with a high fever. A doctor whom Dorothy summoned announced that I had the current flu, which in 1941 meant three days in bed. The dress rehearsal was out for me and the opening seemed doubtful. The doctor enthusiastically dosed me with a new drug called sulpha-something and attempted to inject an antidote into Dorothy. This resulted in a chase round our room, with Dorothy remaining inviolate. I didn't make the dress rehearsal and Guthrie read my part, the understudy being unprepared. On Monday night I struggled through, getting a couple of notices the next day for "looking very ill." It was a disaster for me and not helpful to the play which was in great part an ensemble effort. Gradually through the Detroit week I got to the stage I had reached in rehearsal.

At the opening in Cincinnati the following Monday I felt in control of Ridgeon for the first time. As a company, we gave our best performance and the audience response was excellent. But on Tuesday night the horror which every actor dreads and few ever experience struck me without the slightest warning. The first of the five acts of *The Doctor's Dilemma* ends with a scene between Jennifer and Ridgeon in which she attempts to gain his help in saving the life of her artist husband who is in an advanced stage of consumption, as tuberculosis was then known. Ridgeon explains that if the artist, Dubedat, is admitted to his treatment, another patient must be removed– hence the dilemma. Jennifer persists in her plea, shows Ridgeon some large charcoal drawings, examples of her husband's genius; and obviously smitten by the lady's beauty, he agrees to alter his limited list of patients. The dilemma has been solved, at least temporarily.

It was a short scene which introduced Kit and stated the theme of the play. I loved playing this scene. Every word counted and I had to show a growing interest in the charms of Miss Cornell, which was very easy to do. We were in the middle of this scene during our second performance in Cincinnati and I was thinking it would be our best so far when just about a minute or two from the curtain my mind suddenly became blank. It was not a "dry up"—not just forgetting lines. It was total. I had no idea what I was doing. Kit was unfamiliar to me and I remember trying to think of my own name. I had no idea what play I was in but I could see that I was on the stage of a theatre. Usually when a blackout of memory comes the victim has no recollection of what happened. The astonishing thing about this episode is that I can clearly recall my frustration and terror as I looked at the lady who was sitting on a chair opposite me. She was gazing at me with a sort of puzzled look. With an actor's instinct, I suspected that a cue for me to speak had just been given. I have never forgotten my exact words at this moment. I lifted up one of the drawings to hide my face and I whispered to Kit, "I'm no use. I don't know what I'm doing. Just get the rag down as soon as you can."

Then came the most amazing example of presence of mind I have ever seen in the theatre. Katharine Cornell had played Jennifer only nine times before an audience, but without hesitation she gave a resumé of fourteen admittedly short speeches of Jennifer and Ridgeon, picked up the drawings and at the door delivered the curtain line which I should have given after her exit: "Consultation free, cure guaranteed."

I remember this incredible achievement of Kit and my helpless admiration of this lovely lady as the curtain fell and it was over.

The next thing I recall was a doctor in my dressing-room. Kit and Guthrie were there. There was no longer any confusion in my mind. I knew once again what I was doing and the doctor was doing his part, taking my pulse and the like. His questions were few, the most pertinent being: had I been taking sulpha treatment recently. To my affirmative reply he added, "That, I believe, is the cause of your memory failure. You have had an attack of sulpha amnesia. These attacks are rare and brief and you won't, I am confident, be troubled by another. Now I would like to see the rest of the play, which I am enjoying very much." The rest of the play went very well.

I wasn't troubled by another attack and it was a relief to know that there was a specific cause for this one.

Columbus and Cleveland completed a successful try-out tour. The Shubert Theatre in New York was our destination, and by acting there I would achieve my goal of playing in all four of these con-

*"That Boldini hat! It upstages my grey topper." Katharine Cornell and R.M. in The Doctor's Dilemma, at the Shubert Theatre, New York, 1940.*

tiguous theatres on 43rd and 44th Streets, which seemed to me to be the heart of Broadway: the Booth, the Plymouth, the Broadhurst and the Shubert. *The Doctor's Dilemma* had been a joy to play on the try-out in spite of the misfortunes in Detroit and Cincinnati. I could hardly wait to work in Donald Oenslager's delightful scenery again; to hear Cecil Humphreys' "lose the thread of his remarks"; to see beauteous Kit in mesmerizing Boldini hat; to play in that comedy death scene which Shaw had written on a dare by the critic, William Archer. At last, after four dress rehearsals, we opened with a dandy performance to a rapturous audience.

It was a Friday night with a matinée the following day so there was no party. Eleanor Caskey, Dorothy and I went to Hamburger Heaven on Madison Avenue for a quick supper before early bed. As we were eating our medium rares and gloating over the evening's result, I felt a hand on my shoulder. Standing behind me was a smartly dressed man with a large Doberman on a leash. The man bent over and muttered, "I don't like the company you keep!" I told him to buzz off and resumed my supper. But the fellow was persistent and three times he returned and repeated his mystifying comment. The last time I advised him to go to hell, paid my bill and left the place with Dorothy and Ellie. I took the precaution of going out first on the chance the charming stranger might be waiting for me. He was. Leaving the dog who seemed to be a passive neutral in a seemingly menacing situation, the fellow started towards me, this time proclaiming very loudly that he still disliked the company I kept. I positioned him on his back in the slush (it was a stormy March night) and turned to the girls. As I did so, Ellie shouted, "Look out!" I half turned as a short jab caught me in the area of my right eye and I went down. From my prostrate position I could see the Marines, in the person of Dorothy, land and secure the situation. She was wearing an enormous topaze ring which was a perfect knuckle-duster and with two short steps she delivered a beautiful right hook which left my adversary as prone as I had been.

"Taxi!" she cried, and the last thing I saw was the pacifist Doberman administering first aid to his master.

Victory in this Mack Sennett brawl clearly belonged to Dorothy. Ellie Caskey, a former classmate of Dorothy at the Yale Law School (at which I must assume pugilism was a required course), was ecstatic about her performance, and so was I. But when we reached home the awesome consequences of the fracas became apparent. My right eye had begun to close and it was obvious that by the morning I would have a king-size shiner, most inappropriate for the immaculate Harley Street physician whom I had to portray in a few hours at the first matinée on Broadway.

Fortunately Dorothy was not only a good boxer and a fine lawyer but as a physician's daughter she was also a handy paramedic. A hunk of steak in the refrigerator was immediately tied on to my eye and in the morning there was just enough swelling to prevent me using a monocle, a most important prop. An impressive chromatic design had developed around my eye, however, which certainly would defy concealment.

I was in trouble. In a few hours I had to face an audience, looking as if I had just been caught in a barroom brawl, which was in a way what had happened. Worst of all, I would have to face Katharine Cornell, whose eyes, usually so soft, could on occasion really glower. This would be one of those occasions. To see her leading man with a "mouse," which could only have been acquired by impact with a fist, could not have happened to her often.

On the way to the theatre I stopped at my make-up shop and found out that quite a bit of the bruising could be hidden, at least as far as an audience view was concerned, and they patched me up there. Thus fortified, I went straight to Kit's dressing-room. Her dresser inspected me in the little sitting-room outside, giggling, "My, my, somebody touched you up real good, but Arthur" – Arthur Drysdale, my dresser and her husband – "can help you look just elegant. You go in and show Miss Cornell!"

I did and merely said, "I'm sorry, Kit."

Miss Kitty's eyes didn't glower one little bit. They remained soft as usual as she said, "Don't worry, Ray dear. But do remember not ever to have anything to do with drunken fans."

Everything went well at the matinée with the nearly concealed mouse of Sir Colenso Ridgeon.

I could not complete the New York run of *The Doctor's Dilemma* owing to a movie commitment. This was, I think, one of the most happy engagements I ever had. I left the play with a heavy heart, and for its last two weeks on Broadway and a subsequent tour, Ridgeon was most successfully played by a promising young actor named Gregory Peck.

# 34

Before Dorothy and I were married, John Wharton told me that in six months she would know more about my professional business than I did. He was right. I have never had or needed a press agent, secretary or business manager.

The operative word was "business" which I did not realize at the time. But for forty years I have been heartily grateful for Dorothy's business sense. She is still trying to understand actors in general. Me, she has long since figured out, but other members of my profession defeat her. An unnatural shyness takes over. She is scared of them.

It seems that her theatrical law office job was to help John in his efforts to straighten out the untidy business affairs of his clients in my disorganized profession, not to meet the customers. So I am the first actor she ever met and that was socially at a party at John and Carly Wharton's home.

Dorothy had no idea of the change her life would take when she joined up with me in my erratic profession, so unlike the quiet, tidy offices of her own legal profession. Luckily for me, the change continues to delight her in spite of her diffidence when confronted with an actor, actress or director. She has long since given up active law practice, but she happily holds a firm "watching brief" on my contracts and general business, with a keen eye for the potholes along the road. Her wit and humour have smoothed out many difficulties which go with the territory I have staked out. We are a good team and it's still fun.

Dorothy has always been the complete opposite of the actor's wife who haunts dressing-rooms and movie sets, the bane of directors, producers and the acting company. On the few occasions when she has reluctantly been out front in stage productions – only at the request of directors – she has suffered from stage fright so severely that she has usually ended the ordeal by a fast retreat to her bed at home or in our hotel room, and a reach for the Dramamine bottle of seasick pills. Film studios bore her with the eternal waiting around between shots. On her rare visits to share my lunch hour, she was invariably armed with a book. I enjoyed the horsing around between takes, but Dorothy was uncontrollably impatient for us to get on with the job at hand and go home to our private life.

In the summer of 1940 when I was hesitating whether to sign a contract with Warner Brothers for a series of pictures, Dorothy had the perception to give sound advice.

"Don't sign this contract," she said. "Don't put yourself in the situation of being told what to do. The big studios are going to break up. You'll be used in any junk they produce. You are riding high now. Trust your luck. Remember, the theatre is your base."

Dorothy was right on every point. Within a few years the big studios that seemed immortal in 1940 were struggling for existence, reduced to a few productions a year, renting studio space to the independent producers and relying on television productions to pull them through. The stables of contract players had been emptied. The movie industry had entered the doldrums that still persist. The energy and imagination that built up the Hollywood of the 1920s and 1930s was now spread abroad.

For the first and only time, I ignored Dorothy's advice. I signed a two-picture-a-year contract with Warner Brothers. With extensions, options and a year in the Canadian Army, this deal lasted fifteen years. I did eighteen pictures under it.

I have forgotten most of those Warner pictures. My press books awake no memories. I have a blurred impression of acting one heavy after another, a procession of tedious villainy.

Six or seven of these movies were straight Westerns in which I enjoyed the companionship of a nimble cow-pony named Kentucky who carried me with spirit through all the gulches of the Warner ranch and the weather-beaten façades of the Western streets. She could find her marks at a canter and she would shake her head and fidget if some misguided cameraman questioned my accuracy in stopping on a designated stick or stone. It was as if Kentucky would snort: *I* find the marks. He has to remember *his* lousy dialogue. And while I've got your attention, why don't you give him a decent part to play like we had in *Santa Fe Trail*?

She was a smart mare and she knew the answer just as Dorothy did when she warned me that I would not get good movie parts as a contract player. I was being fairly treated, for these anonymous pictures were part of the product which the studio had to make. If I was used in a dreary script, I was well paid for my work and that was what I had settled for.

# 35

In the summer of 1941 I was working in my first picture under the Warner contract. I was miscast, the script was dreary, the war news was awful. That Dorothy was with me was my sole relief in the general gloom. She never once said, "I told you so." Only the eloquence of her silence flashed it like a neon sign.

One evening I received a cable from my brother, who was Canadian High Commissioner in London: "Michael Powell will call you. Please cooperate.—Vincent." I was reading it in the hotel lobby when a voice behind me said, "I am Michael Powell."

That is how Mickey entered my life. He has played an important part professionally and as a friend for more than thirty-five years. I have acted in three of his films, he has directed and produced the only play I ever wrote and even now he is trying to persuade me to ignore my arthritis and act in another of his films. He can be extremely persuasive. By eleven o'clock that night in Hollywood I had agreed to act a small part in a propaganda film to be made in Canada for the British government. The budget would not have covered a week's shooting in a Hollywood B. But the script was a fast-moving, hard-hitting war thriller. Mickey had already signed Leslie Howard and Larry Olivier for two other small parts.

Mickey left with a characteristic understatement: "There may be difficulties but it should be an effective film. See you in about five weeks' time at Niagara Falls."

The movie—eventually released in the U.S. as *The Invaders*—told the story of a foray across Canada by a Nazi landing party stranded when its submarine was sunk in Hudson Bay. How Canada dealt with the six Nazis was told in a series of episodes in which the Nazis were confronted by various Canadians—a French-Canadian trapper, a Scottish factor, a religious cultist, a Mountie, a scholarly aesthete and, finally, a soldier. Each Canadian is murdered in cold blood while the invading party dwindles in numbers by death or capture until at last its leader is alone with the soldier, in a baggage car on the Inter-

*Eric Portman as the Nazi leader and R.M. as a Canadian soldier in Michael Powell's film, The Invaders. This sequence shot in Canada, 1941.*

national Bridge at Niagara Falls. The Nazi is trying to cross into the U.S., which was then neutral. Naturally he does not succeed.

I played the soldier, a honey of a part, a slap-happy private who is A.W.O.L. and in civilian clothes. Emeric Pressburger wrote the sequence the night before we started shooting. That my part had a lot of comedy was a tremendous help. It actually increased the tension.

The difficulties of production were colossal. Filming had to be done in Canada, which had virtually no film industry and no professional theatre. All the bit parts, Mounties, military police, customs men, and the hundred-odd extras had to be played by local amateurs or the few available radio actors. There were no sound stages in Canada. For the baggage car the real thing was used.

Everything was on location and the greatest exterior camera artist in the world – Osmond Borradaile, who had shot the exteriors for *Things to Come* – was brought over from England.

The biggest obstacle was lack of money. There was a prodigious amount of improvisation and scrounging (an army euphemism for outright thievery).

Larry, Leslie and I had effective roles and we made the most of them. But the performance that held the film together was the ruthless Nazi lieutenant of Eric Portman. It was a superb film characterization, particularly gratifying to his friends in England as he had just completed four years of a Warner contract without being given a thing to do.

Just how effective a propaganda weapon *The Invaders* would have been was never tested. The attack on Pearl Harbor had already in-

274

volved the United States in the war by the time the picture was released. But Mickey had produced a thriller which certainly pleased the box office.

I worked with him in two other pictures, *Stairway to Heaven* and *The Queen's Guards*. Both bore the stamp of his originality. But my brightest memory of filming with Michael Powell will remain the five days I spent as Private Andy Brock in *The Invaders*.

*As Jonathan Brewster in the Warner Brothers movie Arsenic and Old Lace, 1942.*

# 36

It was in late March of 1942 that I got a telephone call from Kit Cornell asking if I would play Morell to her Candida in four special matinées of the Shaw play with what she hoped would be an all-star cast.

She went on to say that the project was to focus attention on the American Theatre Wing Service and that all proceeds would be turned over to Army and Navy Relief organizations. There would only be one week of rehearsals and she said the cast she was aiming for had all played their respective parts before–"except you, Ray, and you played Marchbanks once so that means that you know the play. I'm trying to get Dudley Digges for Burgess, Millie Natwick for Prossie, Stanley Bell for Lexie, the curate, and I've already got Burgess Meredith for Marchbanks. He's at some camp in California, I think. He has just been called up and the army is going to give him leave of absence for two weeks and, Ray, I think it's sweet–he'll be the only one of the six of us to get paid, for Burgess will draw $21 a month, his army pay, while he's rehearsing and doing the matinées. Now, dear Ray, please say yes and the rehearsal week starts April 19."

Of course I said yes.

In America the special matinée, or benefit, is to this day not widely used as a means of raising funds for charitable purposes. But in England, where I had worked for eighteen years, such theatrical performances had always been and still are the mainstay of stage charities and many other benevolent funds. As such they were usually successful, but artistically the benefits were suspect. The "all-star" performances were usually great fun to do but these scratch productions, often miscast and under-rehearsed, were all too frequently far below professional standards.

But as Miss Kitty outlined her plans for the four matinées, I had a feeling that the phrase "Katharine Cornell presents" would bring the same professional quality to this project as to her previous productions. And indeed it was so.

I forget the name of the movie I was making when Kit had called me but I remember that I only had two more days' work in it and what a joy it was to learn the lines of Morell as an antidote to the dialogue I had to deliver in the picture!

I was word perfect in Morell when I came to the first rehearsal at the Shubert Theatre. Kit said I reminded her of her own early days when she was so frightened of being fired that she learned her few sides ahead of time. The six Shaw veterans she had told me she was hoping to get were all there, including the affluent Private Meredith. As everybody, as well as the director, Guthrie McClintic, knew the play thoroughly and, with the exception of myself, were rehearsing roles which they had acted before, it did seem that we would be off to a good start. That we certainly needed. I never knew why we only had that paltry single week for rehearsals. But even with the usual month, it would be hard enough to bring to *Candida* the freshness and invention which any revival needs. As we began the first of the seven rehearsal days it did look as if Kit's third production of Shaw's play could at best only be a carbon copy of her previous success. By the end of that day my thoughts had changed drastically.

In its forty-six years (*Candida* and I share the birth year of 1896) Shaw's most human of plays had by 1942 justly acquired the status of a modern classic. That is something that directors and players just don't mess around with. G.B.S., the bearded old devil with his curled horns, was a compulsive satirist. Whenever he wrote scenes of tenderness or emotional insight, he felt compelled to compensate with some intellectual irony. Subtlety never deserted him and his raillery was usually controllable by the interpretation given by the performer. For instance, the ending of *Pygmalion* can be romantic or ironic depending on the performances of Eliza and Higgins, even with faithful observance of the sanctity of the Irishman's script.

Shaw knew this. He respected the actor's power of varying interpretation without changing a word of the text. Accordingly, the prefaces and stage directions of all Shaw's plays were explicit. He ran a tight ship for the voyages of all his varied craft. In broad terms, he leaves no doubt as to the characters of his plays and how he wished them to be played. Morell in *Candida* is a "vigorous, genial, popular man...robust and good-looking...hearty, considerate manners... with the clean athletic articulation of a practised orator." In short, a rather pompous stuffed shirt. Marchbanks is "a strange, shy youth...

278

with a delicate childish voice...slight, effeminate...miserably irresolute." Both these descriptions are at variance and even in conflict with the personalities indicated in the dialogue Shaw wrote, and fail to express qualities so evident to the reader with imagination.

At rehearsal it was immediately clear that Guthrie was not going to be content with a rehash of the 1937 production of *Candida*. He urged Buzz Meredith and me not to feel bound by Shaw's performance instructions but to follow the lead of his basic characterizations in the play itself.

"You are playing genuine human beings, not satirized freaks, as G.B.S. would have you believe." He went on in confidential tones. "Don't worry about the comedy and the humour—all that will look after itself. There will be bigger and better laughs if you show Morell and Marchbanks to be real, credible people than if Morell is acted as a comic stuffed shirt and Marchbanks as an irresolute, shy genius. Remember this is still a play about a woman who must choose between two men and so selects the weaker because he needs her more. Now let's get on with it and try to make Candida's choice a difficult one."

The seven rehearsal days passed rapidly and smoothly, and we were untroubled by any feeling of haste. For myself, I faced the April 28 matinée opening with a greater than usual sense of readiness.

The reception of *Candida* by the opening audience was rapturous and heartwarming. The critics gave cast and production outright raves. I quote here, without embarrassment, the opening sentence of the *New York Times* review by Brooks Atkinson, who expressed the concordant approval of his colleagues:

> Although Bernard Shaw's *Candida* has been put on the stage many times, no one ever saw it until yesterday afternoon when it was really acted at the Shubert Theatre.... Certainly it is the best thing that the theatre has accomplished for a long time.

It was indeed, as Brooks Atkinson said, a theatrical irony that the old play revived for four matinées should prove such a sensation. There was an immediate, furious demand for an extension of the run; and in the end we played nearly fifty performances, including a week at the National in Washington.

This was a regular eight-performance week and we stood them up to wonderful business. It was most notable for a hilarious and dramatic incident backstage after the final performance in Washington. I was in Kit's dressing-room just after the curtain when General Marshall was announced. The great soldier was very interested in the

*Katharine Cornell and R.M. as Candida and Morell in the revival of Shaw's play for Army and Navy Relief.*

theatre. I think his wife was a former actress, and he had been delighted by the play and its new interpretation. Suddenly he asked Kit if he could see Burgess Meredith. Kit said, "Why, certainly. Ray, please fetch him here." I was on my way when the General asked me to take him to Buzz's room. I was about to knock on the door when the General motioned me aside with a wink. Tapping the door himself, the Chief of the General Staff of the U.S. Army inquired, "Is Private Meredith in there?"

"Who is it?" came a gruff answer.

"I am General Marshall."

"Oh my God!"

The C.G.S. entered the room to discover a very lowly and embarrassed soldier clad only in baggy long johns, desperately searching for the proper military procedure on such an occasion. Like all raw recruits (Buzz had only been in boot camp for two weeks) he decided to follow the instinctive routine–when in doubt, salute! The rapid assumption of rigid attention plus the vigour of the salute caused the drawers to slip. The left hand grabbed them. The resultant posture was too much for General Marshall. "At ease, Private Meredith!" he gasped as he added, "Congratulations on a superb performance." The extremities in rank of the U.S. Army shook hands mirthfully.

This production of *Candida* netted $84,000 for service funds. This seems a paltry sum today but when it is multiplied by three and a half to compensate for inflation, the resulting $300,000 does not look so small. The only expenses, besides some theatre rentals which were incurred, were the 15 percent royalties Shaw insisted on receiving and which caused widespread resentment. Shaw had indeed given up his sacred 15 percent for the first five performances, but that was the limit of his largess.

The *Oakland Tribune* and many other papers across the country ran editorials on Shaw's demands for his royalties on these service relief benefit shows. The *New York Times*, whose own Brooks Atkinson had led the critical corps in their eulogies of the revival, ordered its London representative to get the straight facts from Shaw himself. This intrepid journalist got the aged playwright on the telephone at midnight and insisted that his questions be answered. Instead of receiving a blast of Shavian rancour, the *Times* correspondent was told by the sleepy old man (he was eighty-five in 1942) that it made very little difference whether he collected his royalties or not, but that they were due him, and the famished British Exchequer would get nineteen shillings on every pound that he was paid anyway. Then he returned to his bed at Ayot St. Lawrence.

I was inclined to agree with Shaw. My gratitude to him went back to 1926 when I was one of the management of the struggling little Everyman Theatre and he had gladly let us do six of his plays at 5 percent straight. We were certainly not more deserving than the relief funds of the American Army and Navy. I think he was just older.

But the real contribution of the Katharine Cornell special production of *Candida* wasn't only the money that came to the relief funds. It was the evidence of the willingness and the eagerness of the theatrical profession—actors, producers, directors, writers, the whole blessed lot of us—to step in and do our job for whatever cause that needed us.

Katharine Cornell, with the *Candida* revival, had rallied our whole profession to the needs of those hundreds of benefits, hospital visits, war-zone tours and all the other endeavours in which the stage helped the war effort.

# 37

One of my Warner films has remained in clear focus, perhaps because it was the first time I worked with Humphrey Bogart and Jerry Wald. The picture was *Action in the North Atlantic*, one of those synthetic projects which started with Jack L. Warner saying, "Let's make a picture about—" Nudged by the government, Warner had set a film in production to boost the Merchant Marine. It was just after Pearl Harbor and the U-boats were taking a frightening toll of our ships, especially on the Murmansk run.

Jerry Wald was the producer. Like some other movie producers, he was an ex-newspaperman. He remained a newspaperman at heart even when he became one of the most successful (and certainly the most cheerful) producers in Hollywood. Jerry had, in some ways, been the pattern of Randall, the editor in *Late Night Final*, one of my favourite roles, and Jerry and I talked often of his days on the staff of the old New York *Daily Graphic*. The three pictures I did with him were a relief from the dreariness of the Warner routine. Jerry Wald's untimely death in the late fifties was a loss to the movie business and to everybody who knew that delightful man. Constance Wald, Jerry's widow, remains our very dear friend in Beverly Hills.

Jerry had this film in production just five weeks after he had been told of the project. Two ships, the old freighter which is sunk in the first part of the film and the new *Victory* ship which gets through to Murmansk, were both built on Warner stages before John Howard Lawson's script was completed.

Outright war propaganda, the movie was an excellent example of a made-to-order job, perfectly executed in every department. It showed Hollywood at its technical best.

Everything was shot in the studio. There was no location work. The old freighter burned fiercely for several days and finally sank in a moderate sea, all on the huge Stage Nine. The *Victory* ship in convoy on the Murmansk run was twice attacked by U-boats and from the air–on Stage Five. There were cases of seasickness (in our audiences!) when our lifeboat drifted on a heavy swell in the special effects tank.

In this maelstrom of action there was some pretty good acting by a typical Warner Brothers cast. From Bogart, as always, there was the matchless performance. In a picture like *Action* you were lucky if the character you played was sufficiently defined to be recognizable. Bogie did not have much to go on in this respect. But he knew enough to trust his own understated style to get him through. Most actors, especially those with a stage background, are inclined to over-stress a thin role. Not Bogie. He understood the why and the wherefore of underplaying better than most screen actors of his time. William Powell knew it too, but after fifteen years of talking movies it was amazing how few screen players were aware that the camera was timid of over-acting.

Bogie's style often reminded me of Gerald du Maurier in England. As men they were wildly dissimilar but as actors both had the same restraint and economy of style and both used the studied techniques that made it all look so easy. The strange thing is that Gerald never tried screen acting because he was afraid his style was too low-keyed for the camera.

I acted with Bogie in only two pictures, the second being a story of the airplane industry in which he was a test pilot and I a thinly disguised Howard Hughes. All movies, good or bad, entail an excessive amount of boredom in the making. But there never was any ennui when Bogie was around. He loved to laugh. As Rafael Sabatini says of his hero, Scaramouche, "He was born with the gift of laughter and a sense that the world was mad."

One day during the shooting of the burning tanker sequence Bogie and I were told at the lunch break that we were finished for the day. A long shot of us in the lifeboat would be shot with our doubles. It would take all afternoon to shoot. So off we went to Lakeside Golf Club, right by the Warner lot, for lunch and maybe some golf later on.

The special effects at Warners' was astonishingly good. The burning tanker was really terrifying, to actors as well as audiences. The effect was achieved by dozens of gas jets controlled at a set of valves which looked like an organ console. This was operated by the so-called "smoke bum" who could play his valves with such skill that the actors seemed to walk through the flames.

Sitting at the bar we extolled the smoke bum and speculated about the relative intrepidity of our doubles. Each of these heroes was a battle-scarred stunt-man.

After the fourth martini Bogie faced me with that "Play it, Sam" look and said, "Come to think of it, I guess I'm braver than you."

I said, "Maybe so. Are we going to let two men risk their lives to make us look good?"

"Are we men or mice?"

We grabbed a sandwich and returned to the set. Our request to do it ourselves was cordially received by Lloyd Bacon, the director.

The shot had already been rehearsed with the stunt-men. The smoke bum, a big handsome guy, demonstrated for our benefit. He made the flames dance from the bridge down to the boat deck.

We rehearsed the action without the fire. Lloyd did not want a rehearsal with the flames. He said he would go for a take. "Smoke bum won't make a mistake—if either of you gets fried it'll be your fault and we'll have to alter the script."

Action! We could not see well. There was a lot of smoke on the deck as well as flames. Each of us had to follow a coloured line from the bridge down a companionway to the boat deck by the davits. The flames parted like the Red Sea as we staggered on. It was damned hot.

The camera on the big crane followed us pretty closely. There was no sound being recorded so we could shout whatever we wanted. Bogie got to the taffrail first and as he climbed over to grab a line his pants caught on a cleat. As he slid down the falls to the boat, one leg of his pants was torn off.

"All right, Bacon," he barked. "You can fix my pants in the script!"

I slid down unscathed and shouted, "Lower away." Alan Hale started paying out the stern lines. But the rope slipped. Before he could hold it, the boat was forty-five degrees down by the stern. J. M. (Joe) Kerrigan, playing the cook in his dirty whites, was thrown at my feet. This former member of the Abbey Theatre in Dublin inquired philosophically, "Do you think, now, that all this realism is going to ultimately affect the legitimate theatre?"

"Don't split infinitives, you Hibernian savage!" yelled Bogie from the bows.

We hit the studio sea.

Lloyd Bacon shouted, "Cut! Perfect! Print it! You're not actors— you're all bums. I love you!"

Among the famous talent in that boat there was one name that would never be heard of again. It was Bernard Zanville, and it be-

*Left to right: Humphrey Bogart, R.M., and "José O'Toole" on the bridge of the new Victory ship, in Action in the North Atlantic.*

*The torpedoed crew of the old freighter adrift on the vast wastes of Warner Brothers' process stage, in the movie Action in the North Atlantic, 1942.*

longed to an excellent young actor whom Warners had just put under contract. Bernie had been told by his new employers that his own name was not suitable and he should think up another. Credulous and combative, Bernie made the grievous mistake of seeking advice from Mr. Bogart. Bogie immediately came up with what he described as an ethnic gem in nomenclature. He suggested "José O'Toole." Bernie turned away in a huff.

Two days later Bogie got a note from Jack Warner: "Don't start christening young actors and get this one off my back. His new name is Dane Clark. J.L.W."

I knew Bogie best away from the studio. Before the war we had done some pub-crawling around Hollywood. Bogie and I had once ended up at what was then a new *boite* called the Cock 'n' Bull on Sunset Strip. It was late for Hollywood and, as both of us had early calls, the check had been called for. Suddenly I felt a hand on my shoulder and heard a well-known voice: "I want to talk to you about a mutual friend–that damned Dane!" I looked around. It was Jack Barrymore.

I had been in front at a matinée of *Hamlet* at the Haymarket in London about fifteen years before. In that performance Jack, maddened by a persistent cougher in the stalls, had obliterated the pest. Without breaking rhythmic stride he had interpolated in the "Rogue-and-peasant-slave" soliloquy his own line, "Bark! Bark! Bark on! Thou phlegm-beclotted cur!" It was a heroic moment that rocked London.

But now I was ill-at-ease. This was not the John Barrymore of *Hamlet* glory. I knew Jack was hardly able to read "idiot cards." As the Irish say, "He had drink taken." Jack turned to Bogie. "This man is the first Hamlet to have mouthed the lines of the goddamnedest bore in literature, that pompous ass the Ghost."

Then back to me. "You were much sinned against, my friend! Master Will assumed that role himself for no one else would take it! Sustenance, bartender! Grain distilled from Scotland for my friends and for myself."

Bogie agreed that escape was impossible. We would have to learn tomorrow's dialogue in make-up chairs in just a few hours' time.

It was well that we stayed. For the next hour or two Bogie and I heard one of the greatest Hamlets of all time recall his greatness. For a short time the flame was relit, the memory became alive and we heard that magical performance once more.

About two weeks later we were in Chasen's when Bogie looked up

286

and exclaimed, "Angels and ministers of grace defend us!" It was John Carradine. Unable to refuse a cue he responded with the entire lines of the Ghost, followed by all the principal soliloquies in the best manner of Mantell and E. H. Sothern, which is still mighty good to my way of thinking.

John was rightly pleased. He had given a good performance and as a true classical actor knows, the size of the audience does not matter. When two or three are gathered together, as St. Chrysostom says, that is enough.

Bogie looked at me with that smile of his. "No, you don't," he said. "Twice is enough. Besides, you're not enough of a ham to remember the lines."

In 1957 Bogie died of cancer. He and the twentieth century were the same age. His last weeks were very painful. I saw him several times. These visits were distressing to Bogie and his friends. In the past we had always played for laughs but now it hurt him like hell to laugh and I think it may have been worse for him when he tried not to.

Betty—that is, Lauren Bacall, the wonderful wife of his last ten years—had to ration visits and keep them as passive as possible.

Just before I was to fly back home I visited Bogie for what I knew would be the last time. He was very weak but in good spirits. I carried on a desultory conversation and Bogie seemed to be egging me on to be louder and funnier. Betty came in and listened objectively. After a long pause Bogie bluntly demanded what he called "The Hardwicke Story."

Cedric Hardwicke used to tell an old theatre yarn which convulsed any actor who heard it and invariably laid an egg with laymen. A long-unemployed actor has somehow raised the funds to revive a musical called *Nights in Old Vienna*. It is the morning of the opening night of a third-rate tour of the production in a Lancashire town called Wombspit. The theatre manager is on a ladder putting up the letters of the canopy sign. The actor-impresario approaches.

"Good morning. It is a fine morning. Is there any movement in the box office?"

From the top of the ladder in the broadest Lancashire: "Movement in t' box office? Well, ah'll tell thee, there's just abaht as mooch mouvement in t' box office as if we was in Vienna and we were playing *Nights in Old Wombspit*!"

I looked at Betty. She nodded. I told Cedric's story as well as I could. I hope that Bogie's laugh was worth the agony it caused him.

# 38

Pearl Harbor stunned me as well as the rest of the world. I felt I must take part in this war in some way, but I didn't know what I could do. At forty-five I was probably too old for active service.

Although I was still a Canadian citizen, my wife was American, home was New York, and my professional future seemed to lie in the United States. I decided that whatever service I might be able to contribute should be under American auspices.

Many of us oldsters from the Kaiser's war were trying to get into the scrap. A friend at Twentieth-Century-Fox told me that a Colonel Jerome in the air branch of the U.S. Marine Corps was taking on some older men for military intelligence work. I set out for Washington to find out about it.

Humphrey Bogart, at Warner Brothers, had voiced his disapproval: "Are you out of your mind? At your age you'd be just a publicity stooge for the Marines! People of our vintage aren't worth a plugged nickel in any army or navy in this war no matter what service we have had in the last one. Get the ants out of your pants and pay your taxes, that's all you can do in this one."

Bogie had a point. Still, I found the Colonel an affable but forceful officer, obviously clear-sighted and honest. When I had told him about my service in the First World War he thought me qualified for combat intelligence work – briefing pilots for operations. "Actors can think on their feet and this work needs that ability."

I went back to the Hay-Adams Hotel to talk it over with Dorothy, much inclined to follow up Colonel Jerome's idea.

I found a telegram waiting for me at the hotel. It read: "LIVES THERE A MAN WITH SOUL SO DEAD WHO NEVER TO HIMSELF HATH SAID THIS IS MY OWN MY NATIVE LAND STOP PLEASE PHONE ME." It was from Colonel Ralston, Minister of Defence in Mackenzie King's government in Canada. How he tracked me down in Washington I never found out.

I telephoned him at once. The minister said, "The papers have it that you are joining the American Marines."

"I'm expecting to do so, Colonel Ralston."

"Well, look here, Massey, if you're going back into service, you must do it with us. We'll welcome you gladly. I assure you there is plenty for you to do."

"I don't know, sir. I'm almost committed to the Marines—"

"Nonsense. Your duty is here. You can be in your old regiment again. Can you come to Ottawa right away?"

It was no use resisting.

"Yes, Colonel."

I telephoned Colonel Jerome the next morning. I read him Ralston's telegram, expecting some acid comment, but he just said, "Of course, you have no alternative."

In Ottawa I left Dorothy at the Château Laurier while I went to the minister's office. He seemed in jovial spirits, as if my extrication from the U.S. Marines were a matter for jubilation. I was introduced to Lieutenant-General Stuart, Chief of the General Staff of the Canadian Army. After describing the varied employment I would be given, Colonel Ralston declared, "We have great plans for you!" The very words Junior Laemmle had used at Universal just ten years ago.

I was to be commissioned in the Royal Canadian Artillery as a major and would be attached to the Special Services section under the Adjutant-General.

Luncheon with General Stuart at the Rideau Club was pleasant. We had quite a few mutual friends to talk about. He told me about the new army. It was all a mystery to me.

"Can you tell me, sir," I asked, "where I can get a soldier suit?"

As soon as the general finished laughing, he directed me to a military tailor.

When I arrived at the Adjutant-General's office, I was correctly dressed. Major-General Letson was a genial fellow, about the only senior officer I would meet who had a sense of humour.

"What the hell are we going to do with you?" he said.

This dash of cold water cooled my patriotism a bit. There was suddenly no doubt in my mind that I was an embarrassment to two ranking general officers of the staff of National Defence Headquarters. As it turned out, I was militarily useless in Canada.

Assigned to Brigadier James Mess who ran a section of the Adjutant-General's branch which dealt with "recreation, entertainment and athletics," I was never once invited to take any part whatsoever in my own field of entertainment. This was not Jim Mess's fault, I think. The whole entertainment activity of his section was deemed to

*A coffee break from Ottawa. R.M. and Dorothy, 1943.*

be functioning efficiently without any help from Major Massey. I saw only one of their productions the whole time I was incarcerated in Ottawa, and it was pretty fair. I shuffled, mislaid and generally fouled up papers in Jim Mess's office, made a few hands-across-the-border rousing speeches in the United States, toured all the training centres from Halifax to Vancouver, met a few old First World War comrades who seemed incredibly aged, and was utterly miserable. The only bright spots of my useless life were the sympathetic and merry co-shufflers in the office and the hospitality of the great Billy Bishop and his wife Margaret.

A little over a year later my futile service in the Canadian Army ended. I had learned a bitter lesson – that a man of forty-seven, who is not a professional soldier and completely inept at paperwork, is utterly useless in any capacity in any army. Wretched Brigadier Mess was a good friend. He succeeded in getting me returned to civilian life in order, he confided to me, to protect his own mental health and mine.

The return of the desk warrior from the paper wars is a humiliating occasion; and although my spirits rose as I greeted Dorothy on the doorstep of 132 East 80th Street, I was still somewhat crestfallen as Dorothy led me into the living-room.

"Cheer up, Major, you are Mr. M. once more," she said, pointing to a play script lying on the table. "Kit Cornell has bailed you out again. That script arrived last night and I read it. It's no great play but it's not so bad either. It is a woman's play and it will make a lot of money."

"How did Kit know I was out of the army?"

"I don't know but she did. Gert Macy telephoned yesterday to find out when you would be home. All the vital statistics are right, co-star billing and the works, rehearsals and try-outs through October and November and a Broadway opening November 29 at the Plymouth. Those are the production details and you will make the decision yourself."

I reached for the script but Dorothy stopped me. "No, you get out of that soldier costume first. Oh, in the first scene, a sort of prologue, you're a young British officer in the First World War who meets Kit in Regent's Park on a blind date. You could wear that old First World War jacket with the shrapnel tears and you'll look very young and handsome all over again."

I read the play, first of all glancing at the curtains. These were all right. I would share the act curtains with Kit. Dorothy was quite right. *Lovers and Friends* was a "woman's play" and it would certainly make money. A woman's play is a professional term for any theatrical piece in which the leading woman behaves with intelligence, wit, humour and cunning while the leading man is a consummate ass and conducts himself accordingly. Such plays are usually about triangles with a second woman in the cast but in *Lovers and Friends* the formula involved a rhomboid, if my schoolboy recollections of geometry are correct, a second man being added to make a romantic quartette.

Dodie Smith, an English writer, had "scripted" (I use the movie term on purpose) *Lovers and Friends*. Her previous Broadway plays had included *Autumn Crocus, Call It a Day* and *Dear Octopus*: none of them in the category of women's plays and all of them a good deal better than *Lovers and Friends*.

Usually my first reading of a play gives me some indication of whether I'll do it. The odds are heavy that I will, of course, because I hardly ever refuse a stage role. Jobs are not so frequently offered that many are turned down, at least as far as I'm concerned. But this time I really was in a quandary. I certainly needed the job. I needed a theatre job and here was one with knobs on, a lead opposite the first lady of the American stage. What was holding me? Just that it was a thankless, silly role. But I knew that I wouldn't be held responsible for that if I acted the character well.

I went back to Dorothy in the living-room. She looked at me. "You hate the part but you want to tell Kit that you'll play it, and you can't make up your mind. You can play that part well if you don't hate the character so much that you can't act it. Come on, Mr. M. It's Kit and Guthrie and the stage again. Not a single paper to shuffle."

I called Kit at once and said yes, firmly, happily and gratefully. Both Miss Kitty and I knew that I would do my best.

My last play had been *Candida* and I felt, perhaps not without some reason, that I was forgotten on Broadway. In *Lovers and Friends* Katharine Cornell was to play the leading role and I was to co-star with her as Rodney Boswell. Guthrie McClintic would direct and my old friend Jack Wilson was to co-produce with Kit. The angelic management even advanced me three months' salary on a handshake as, following two years of army pay, my finances were in sore need of repair. I was, of course, to refund it if the play were a flop. But the thing that really made it all worthwhile was that I would have the chance to act with Kit again. The idolatrous admiration which I had felt towards her when she was playing Meg in *Little Women* in London twenty years before was just as strong as ever.

However, rehearsals revealed that all would not be fair weather. The play was described by a critic as a four-angled triangle which was told in a prologue in the First World War and three acts and an epilogue in the Second. The interval between the wars and the playing time of *Lovers and Friends* seemed about the same in length. It was written in British tea-talk and was rather twittery.

The plot was commendably simple. Stella and Rodney meet in 1918 and, in a lengthy prologue, fall out of love with two other people in order to fall in love with each other. We find them in 1930 happily married until Rodney is bewitched by a priggish young lady who doesn't wish to mess around with him unless the clergy are involved. So he wants a divorce. By the time he discovers his innamorata is a fraud, Stella has found solace (righteously short of the bed-chamber) with a pompous theatrical producer. Whatever will they do? Well, the third act curtain is a regular teaser. So we have an epilogue dated 1942 and Stella and Rodney are still at the same address. Rodney presumably is too antiquated after a plethora of twittering to be in any way capable of any more dirty business.

It seemed the longest play I ever acted in. The dialogue was neat but self-conscious, as Wolcott Gibbs said in the *New Yorker*, "written

292

*Katharine Cornell and R.M. The blind
date meeting in 1917.*

*Katharine Cornell as Stella, R.M. as
Rodney, and Carol Goodner in
Lovers and Friends, New York, 1944.*

with that peculiar bird-like lilt that makes British clichés so much
more irritating than our own." There was endless talk of sex which
was approached with what Louis Kronenberger described as "antiquated up-to-datedness."

Carol Goodner, the tear-stained heroine of *The Black Ace*, played
an amorous voice of experience and shared most of the comedy with
Henry Daniell, who was Stella's solace. Carol had one Homeric line
which used to stop rehearsals whenever we came to it. It was, "Do
you ever take your youth out and play with it?" Guthrie had an
impish streak in him that would not be downed and refused to cut it.
But it had to go eventually as Carol couldn't stop the tears caused by
repressed giggling. The excision was regretfully made on a train call
between Detroit and Cleveland. So Broadway missed a great moment
in the theatre.

I faced Rodney Boswell for some two hundred performances and
found him a constant and deadly bore, as did the audiences. Only the
presence of beloved Kit made the performances bearable to me.

Dorothy always maintained that I did not understand Rodney. But
as he was about as subtly drawn as Peter Rabbit and the inhabitants of
Mr. McGregor's garden, I feel the accusation is unwarranted.

The play itself was either panned or gently rejected by the critics,
but Kit scored a triumph as Stella. The rest of us did pretty well or
were acquitted of professional malfeasance on the grounds that "it
wasn't our fault." By nightfall following the opening the ticket rack in

293

the Plymouth box office was clean, a sign that for the first six performances we were sold out. *Lovers and Friends* was indeed a woman's play, as Dorothy had said. Jack Wilson in my dressing-room afterwards said to both of us, "Cash the cheque and tear up the handshake, dears!"

A very important event in my life took place while I was playing in *Lovers and Friends*. On March 21, 1944, I became a naturalized citizen of the United States. My home was here in the United States. My future lay here. This country had been good to me and I wished as a matter of principle to assume the obligations as well as the privileges of citizenship.

*Lovers and Friends* was the third and last play in which I acted with Katharine Cornell. I am forever grateful to my dear friend for those three opportunities to play opposite her. The word "star" has been used indiscriminately in the past few decades and it has therefore been cheapened. Kit Cornell was a veritable star in the traditional theatre sense—the brightest stage star of her time. I think she has no successor. Of all her contemporaries, Kit alone served her beloved theatre to the exclusion of its mechanized offshoots. This was not because she scorned the movies, radio or television. The stage demanded and received all her strength, her talents and her devotion. Kit was a little larger than life, like the theatre she loved.

# 39

In December 1944 I asked the American Theatre Wing to put me on their list of stage players for overseas work. The Theatre Wing was a civilian committee of knowledgeable theatre people. At no public expense they handed over fully rehearsed productions to the United Services Organization at the docks, the U.S.O. being the military equivalent of the Shuberts in presenting entertainment overseas.

I told them I would hold myself available for rehearsals at two weeks' notice and I made no stipulation as to what I would do or where I would do it. I did suggest that *Our Town*, Thornton Wilder's play, would be my choice if I had it to make.

In 1944 *Our Town* had not yet achieved the enshrinement in the hearts of people which it now enjoys. I anticipated some objections to the play itself. When I went to the Theatre Wing offices I found the committee opposed to touring *Our Town* in the European combat zone on the astonishing grounds that it would induce homesickness in the troops.

"Do you think they're not homesick now?" I asked. "These men are homesick, every mother's son of them, and the plays we bring over to them aren't going to be any relief to them in that quarter whatever they are. One reason I suggested *Our Town* is that it will be a good dose of what's eating them, a kind of life and home most of them are longing to come back to. It will be that catharsis that psychologists are always bleating about, a kind of release. It won't cure the homesickness but it will help explain it."

I didn't make a sale right away. There was a deal of talk about my doing *Abe Lincoln in Illinois*, to which I pointed out that the movie of Bob's play in which I had appeared had long since been released to the U.S.O. and in any event the play would be a very difficult production to tour. After further discussion during which I became determined to take *Our Town* overseas, the matter was left to the U.S.O. to decide.

In a few days I was informed that the army had agreed to *Our Town* and the tour was to be in the European sector. Apparently the U.S.O. people were not worried about the nostalgic propensities.

Rehearsals did not start until late March. That was nearly three months later than the U.S.O. had originally planned. I think the army had deliberately and very wisely delayed our production and that of several other plays. During the final months of the fighting in March, April and May, it would have been impossible, and indeed folly, to attempt to introduce any entertainment to the troops. The action had become completely fluid and every one of the fifty or sixty U.S. Army divisions in Europe was actively engaged. While the frenzied, all-out combat with its sweeping movement was reaching its climax and the German surrender came nearer and nearer, we were working away in a rehearsal hall in New York preparing the U.S.O. production of Thornton's play about life in Grover's Corners.

I think that anyone who has appeared in that fascinating combination of Greek chorus and narrator whom Thornton called the Stage Manager will agree with me that there is a special relationship between him and the audience which is not suggested by such terms as actor, player or performer.

Frank Craven, who created the role, told me he never really knew if he were part of the audience or part of the company. Thornton Wilder so loved the part of the Stage Manager that he went on for Frank Craven for several performances in 1938 when Frank was ill. Many times he guided audiences through the mysteries of Grover's Corners in stock productions. Thornton really loved to act. "The Stage Manager belongs to both the audience and the company, I think," he told me long afterwards.

Thornton was, of course, much pleased about the U.S.O. tour. He never saw our production because by 1945 he was a lieutenant-colonel in the U.S. Air Force, Intelligence. But Isabel, his sister, who also served as his business manager, attended many rehearsals and was most helpful. The script of *Our Town* was the most comprehensive direction guide I've ever seen and rehearsals were smooth and productive. The play was well cast. *Our Town* always seems to inspire its interpreters, for I have seen a number of productions, I've worked in three different ones, and I have never found an indifferent performance in any of them.

Hostilities ceased on May 11, 1945, and a few days later we sailed on a virtually empty troopship for Le Havre. There were upwards of fifty people in our company. There was no scenery and the only props we brought were twenty-five or thirty kitchen chairs and two stepladders. In war-ravaged territory they would be difficult to find. Lighting equipment and a generator would be picked up in France, as would a false proscenium, a draw curtain and a cyclorama, in case we needed them.

On disembarking at Le Havre we were met by a U.S.O. lieutenant-colonel who welcomed us and briefed us on the tour. We met a captain and his non-commissioned staff who were to be with us all the way on the road. The fighting had ended less than two weeks before. In Western Europe more than one million U.S. troops had been relocated in those final days, and five U.S. armies had advanced from fifty to two hundred miles. Despite the devastation and disorder, the colonel handed us a scheduled tour of some seventy performances mostly in the areas of the Seventh and Third armies. The schedule included billeting provisions, descriptions of the auditoriums, theatres, outdoor platforms or other methods of presentation, and indicated the expected size of the audiences. There were one or two days off for travel and there were quite a few double-headers. Transportation was to be by bus. Many of the dates were in places captured only a short time ago from the Germans.

I could not believe my eyes as I looked at the schedule, which covered three months. It was nothing short of a miracle that such a list could have been arranged in the face of such incredible disorder. What is even more wonderful is that everything went smoothly, with only one hitch. At one Rhenish town the regiment of infantry from which we were to draw our audience moved out the morning before our matinée performance. It didn't matter—we were switched over to a neighbouring town and played in a huge hangar to an Air Force wing.

I do not remember the names of the places we played on our tour. I have lost the schedule. But I have some vivid and precious memories of that wonderful experience with the U.S.O.

As I've said before, I'm am objective actor. I believe most actors are. I cannot imagine a theatre where the players have not disciplined themselves to control their emotions, where a performance is not under constant objective scrutiny. My characterization is a second person and I am outside looking in. Only in the U.S.O. production of *Our Town* have I faulted that technique.

When we arrived in France the letdown from the frantic tension of the last days of conflict had come. The realization that the fighting was over had brought the depressing question, "How long are we going to be kept here?" I wondered how our play would fare in that atmosphere. I'd been pretty voluble about it to the Wing people but I was going by the feelings of my generation a quarter of a century before. Also I wondered what audiences we would have. Would most of them have had some experience of live theatre? Would they understand a play that had puzzled some critics? Would they walk out or would they be bored? We soon found out.

The first performance was somewhere in eastern France, in a big town hall. We played on a platform with our false proscenium. There must have been at least twelve or thirteen hundred in the audience. The hall was full and they were standing at the back and the sides. There was no electricity in that town and the house lights were six naked bulbs powered by our own generator. As these were dimmed and the stage lighting came up, I started placing the chairs to mark Dr. Gibbs's house and Editor Webb's.

There was absolute stillness as I read the credits and described Grover's Corners, the location of the five churches, the railroad station, Morgan's drug store (as the Stage Manager I double Mr. Morgan), the public school, the high school, and, of course, the Gibbs and Webb houses which occupy the downstage area. Main Street runs across the stage back of the chairs I have just set.

It's early morning in Grover's Corners and the day is May 7, 1901. It is in New Hampshire, just across the Massachusetts line. Mrs. Gibbs goes through the motions of lighting a fire in the kitchen and Mrs. Webb duplicates the breakfast preparations next door, each lady exhorting her respective children to hurry down or be late for school. Presently George and Rebecca Gibbs and Emily and Wally Webb appear severally and simulate (there are no props in this play) the hurried ingestion of breakfast in silence and depart. Howie Newsome, the milkman, makes his deliveries with gossip, and Joe Crowell brings editor Webb's *Sentinel* to the Gibbs house.

I announce Dr. Gibbs's approach on Main Street. He has just officiated at the birthing of twins in Polish Town. Mrs. Gibbs serves him his breakfast and informs him that their son has once again neglected to fill the woodbin in the kitchen.

The description of the town goes on and there is still utter silence from the audience. You could just hear the faint chug-chug of our generator a block away, and the low chuckles at Thornton's wit coming through. This audience is not demonstrative, I said to myself.

I carry on a further discussion of Grover's Corners. Editor Webb and Professor Willard of the neighbouring university aid me in giving a comprehensive political and social report on the town. Questions

298

about the behaviour and customs of the inhabitants were posed by "members" of the audience. The dissection of Grover's Corners was Thornton Wilder at his wittiest, most humorous and his kindliest, and to play it to an audience at last was a joy. But it was a very quiet audience.

The Stage Manager has been the centre of the action for quite some time. Now the Gibbses and Webbs take over and I lean against the proscenium, light my pipe and watch the audience.

What I saw made me choke. There was a spill from the stage lighting which allowed me to see the faces of many men quite clearly. I will never forget those faces—the tense, rapt, even desperate looks. Some were wiping the tears from their eyes. We were telling them of a day in a little New England town at the turn of the century. And the whims and the truths that were revealed in that story had touched them. Wherever these men were from, Grover's Corners meant home to them that night, and it was home that was still far, far away.

It is now evening in Grover's Corners. At the Congregational Church the choir is practising "Blessed Be the Tie that Binds." From the rear of the stage two tall stepladders are pushed out in Gibbs and Webb territory. When Emily Webb and George Gibbs have mounted them they represent the second storeys of their respective homes. Emily can't work because the moon is so bright; George can't work because he can't get the algebra problem. Emily helps him with it and then George's father calls him. It's an intimate talk Dr. Gibbs has with his son.

Dr. Gibbs is neither a permissive parent nor a stern one. He believes that wit and irony in moderate dosage are effective cures for adolescent thoughtlessness. He tells George that in his office he had heard an all-too-familiar sound—George's mother chopping wood. He supposed that she had got tired of asking her son to do it for her...and anyway, baseball was a more important occupation. He goes on with his indictment of George's delinquency when suddenly he stops and hands him a handkerchief with the propitiatory comment that he knew he only had to mention it to him.

The act draws to a close with George back at his window up the ladder, where he has been joined by his sister. There is a short scene of youthful though cosmic content.

The lights fade. There was polite applause. I had watched the audience throughout as closely as I could; the men were still held as in a vice. There were more eyes being rubbed. Most of them sat on their benches or chairs all through the interval. I spent those ten minutes telling myself to be a professional and to remember that the slightest quaver in my voice would wreck the play. If I failed to maintain the quiet detachment for one second, I could give up being an actor and look for another kind of job. The difficult scenes were all to come. And I couldn't get those faces out of my mind.

In the second act, Love and Marriage, I was more involved in the action than I had been in the first (called The Daily Life), and I didn't have to look at the audience so much. I played the minister at the wedding of George Gibbs and Emily Webb. There was a good deal of humour in this act, which I thought brought more laughter than in the first. But in the moments when I viewed the audience there was the same eager tenseness as before. I thought I played this act satisfactorily. It ends with the marriage ceremony acted in pantomime under the minister's comments.

The bride and groom come happily down the aisle and I tell the audience there will be a ten-minute intermission.

Now the third act comes. I take my place by the proscenium down right and talk to the audience. It is nine years later, the summer of 1913. I tell of the changes in Grover's Corners and describe the cemetery—on a wind-blown hill—and the view that can be seen from it. I tell of the old stones over in the far corner—1670, 1680—and of the Civil War veterans.

There are now a number of chairs on the right side of the stage, lined up in rows. These are the graves of the Grover's Corners dead. The dead are sitting upright in them—Mrs. Gibbs, Simon Stimson, Mrs. Soames, Wally Webb and others. I tell of this new part and the people who have been brought here and something of their illnesses.

A lot of thoughts come up here, night and day, but there's no post office... Now I'm going to tell you some things you know already... Everybody knows in their bones that something is eternal and that something has to do with human beings... There's something way down deep that's eternal about every human being... the dead don't stay interested in the living people for very long. Gradually, gradually, they let hold of the earth... and the ambitions they had... and the pleasures they had... and the things they suffered... and the people they loved. They get weaned away from the earth... weaned away... They're waiting for something that they feel is coming... Aren't they waiting for the eternal part of them to come out clear?...

How will Thornton's metaphysics fit in with the soldiers' fatalism?

300

Death has been almost a comrade of these men for years. As I had spoken these lines I watched the faces I could see intently. Thornton's thoughts were not rejected. These men knew they were at a play which was far more than the nostalgic dream it had started out to be. What they thought only they themselves knew but they did think and they hung on to every word.

Emily's funeral takes place. She has died in childbirth. In the group of mourners upstage holding umbrellas Emily appears. She is wearing a white dress. Her hair is down her back tied by a white ribbon, like a little girl. She walks slowly, wonderingly, toward the dead. They greet her with cheerful hellos. She sits down next to Mrs. Gibbs.

"It seems thousands and thousands of years since I—" Emily is saying when her attention is attracted by the mourners. "How stupid they all look here—they don't have to look like that!"

"Don't look at them now, dear. They'll be gone soon."

"Oh, I wish I'd been here a long time. I don't like being new here."

The mourners are now leaving the stage. The funeral is over. Dr. Gibbs has taken some of the flowers from Emily's grave and is bringing them to Mrs. Gibbs. Emily notices the grief in his face.

"Oh, Mother Gibbs, I never realized before how troubled—how in the dark live persons are. From morning till night that's all they are—troubled . . ."

Emily is trying to adjust herself to the new conditions. Mrs. Gibbs tells Emily that she can go back to earth and relive one day but warns her against it. The Stage Manager agrees but Emily is persistent. She chooses her twelfth birthday. The town is the same as it was then. It is lovely. Everybody is young and beautiful. It is her birthday but just another day for her mother and everyone else. Life is too fast. She cannot bear it. She asks the Stage Manager to take her back to her grave. As they reach the cemetery she asks him this pitiful question:

"Do any human beings ever realize life while they live it—every, every minute?"

"No," says the Stage Manager, "the saints and the poets, maybe—they do some."

And now someone is coming into the cemetery. It is George Gibbs. He has come to Emily and his mother and stands before them for a moment. Now he has flung himself prostrate at Emily's feet.

The dead murmur their disapproval. Emily looks down wonderingly at George.

"Mother Gibbs?" she murmurs.
"Yes, Emily?"
"They don't understand much, do they?"
"No, dear, not very much."

The Stage Manager starts across the stage pulling the curtain with him. The clock can be heard softly striking the hour.

"Most everybody's asleep in Grover's Corners," says the Stage Manager. "There are the stars—scholars haven't settled the matter yet; they seem to think there are no living creatures up there, just chalk...or fire. Only this one is straining away, straining to make something of itself. The strain's so bad that every sixteen hours everybody lies down and gets a rest. Huh...eleven o'clock in Grover's Corners...you get a good rest too. Good-night."

As I left the town hall I was perplexed and a bit troubled. If the play had been in the conventional dimensions of the theatre, I would have had to admit that our first performance had been a failure. As at the end of acts 1 and 2 the final curtain had brought but moderate applause. But in the performance of my role in *Our Town*, I was at times part of the audience and I had felt the tension and seen the tears and the faces of those men. I knew that Thornton's play had not failed at its army opening.

There were about thirty trucks lined up outside the hall and most of our audience were climbing into them. A group of men stood by the door. A young sergeant a little separated from them addressed me as I passed.

"Sir, that is a very great play...and we are very lucky to have seen it."

"Thank you, Sergeant. This has been our first performance to an audience. I would like to talk to you and your friends about the play."

"I'm sorry, sir, but we have to go back to our hutments. There's a sort of curfew still on around here. We're all from an armoured regiment that's on its way to embarkation for home. Some of us in this unit have been overseas since the Kasserine Pass in Africa. Don't worry about the applause being quiet, sir. These men here"—he

*Dorothy Whitney, my stepdaughter, as Emily Webb and R.M. as the Stage Manager in Our Town, at a dress rehearsal at the Marblehead Playhouse, 1950.*

302

pointed to the group behind him—"are about the only ones in the whole regiment who have been in a legitimate theatre before. Movies you don't applaud. Mr. Wilder's play is great. Thank you, sir."

"All right, get aboard the trucks, men." There were cries of thanks and good luck as the trucks began to roar off. I felt better.

The pattern of the tour had been set. Practically all of the seventy performances were similar in response but some audiences were more demonstrative. None appreciated *Our Town* more than those tank men who were soon to go home.

I played in *Our Town* twice more. Once in summer stock for a short tour, which was memorable to me because of a touching and beautiful performance of Emily Webb by Dorothy Whitney, my younger stepdaughter, in her stage debut at age sixteen.

The third time I acted the Stage Manager was in the first television showing of *Our Town* in the "Theatre Guild on the Air" in 1948. This TV production was well done by the Guild, faithful to Thornton's text but, I think, unfair to the play itself. Thornton's play stubbornly resists film and television presentation. Most of the charm and simplicity of the stage play are lost in the embellishments of the screen and the box. There is no audience to help the players.

In my memory, Thornton's play will always conjure up the rapt faces of those battle-worn young Americans for whom we played *Our Town* in France and Germany in 1945.

# 40

Following the U.S.O. tour and Michael Powell's *Stairway to Heaven*, which had been shot in England, I returned to the U.S. aboard the *Aquitania*, which was carrying what seemed like an entire division of troops. They had to sleep in relays, but they wouldn't have cared if they never slept at all. They were "going home!"

About this time Geoffrey, who had gone overseas with a Canadian paratroop battalion, came home. I hadn't seen him for nearly two years. Airborne service is never a joy ride in any army but Geoff is one of the few who is ready to admit that if you get through alive you are a better man than you were before you were a paratrooper. He doesn't cite his flunks at school followed by war service and then honours at Harvard as proof of the academic efficacy of parachute jumping but that's the record.

The season of 1945-46 was a freak year for me. By playing in a weekly radio series, acting in a Broadway play, doing a major movie in Hollywood and appearing in two CBS shows in the infant television medium, I read in my old press books that I established a record by appearing in "all four branches of the thespian art." I was quite unconscious of this achievement at the time and can only remember my distaste for the strange antics which we were called upon to perform in front of those huge packing cases on tripods which concealed the early TV camera, and my gratitude for the generous amount of employment which had come my way in that year.

I started the "Harvest of Stars" radio series in early October. This was essentially a musical show with weekly guests, usually opera singers. We had a seventy-piece symphony orchestra and I was the host or narrator of the show. I did a ten-minute dramatic sketch on each show on some American historical character or incident and also an "institutional" for the sponsor which was the International Harvester Corporation. An "institutional" is a trade term for a high-hat commercial that isn't hard sell but is a spiel which sets out to repeat each week the basic truths about the sponsor and which usually ends

305

up with some startling phrase, like "lasting benefit to the American people." Actors at that time fought shy of personal salesmanship but they were quite shameless in their willingness to deliver the most pharisaical sermons on the sanctity of commerce. There was never any mention of the bitter rivalry between the agricultural machinery companies in the 1860s and 1870s which I had heard about. I think my father, if he had heard of my "institutionals," would have laughed his head off.

The "Harvest of Stars" aired on Sunday afternoons at one. There was a rehearsal on Friday which lasted three or four hours and a run-through before the airing on Sunday, and that was all. It was in truth the golden age of radio. When I got back from Europe all I had to do was sign the contract which Dorothy had nursed through its negotiation stages and we were off and running in early October. It was a good program and I was glad to be in it. The sponsors were perfectly willing to let me do a play in the theatre or in films if something came my way.

About two weeks later an offer as welcome as anything I could wish for came from Beatrice Straight and Richard Aldrich. Dick came to my place on 80th Street and there ensued the shortest casting and production conference in my experience.

"We've formed a production company. It's called Theatre Incorporated and Bernard Shaw is going to let us start it with *Pygmalion*. Gertrude Lawrence is going to play Eliza." Dick had married Gertie not long before. "We'd like you to direct, or play Higgins. What would you rather do–act or direct it? Shaw would rather have you direct."

I thought of that postcard I got from G.B.S. after he had seen my direction of *The Silver Tassie*. It had started: "Yes, but I have a considerable grudge against you for letting me slave over *Saint Joan* when you could have produced"–that is, directed–"it as well as I or better...." Nevertheless, Actor Massey, without hesitation, replied to Dick, "I'd rather play Higgins."

"You'll be co-starred with Gertie. Have you any suggestions about a director?"

"Cedric Hardwicke is the ideal director of any of Shaw's plays," I said.

"Shall we see if he's free?"

I called the Château Marmont in Hollywood and got Cedric at once. "Cedric?... It's Ray here...Ray Massey... Are you busy? ... Good..." [He says he's in the middle of rereading a Trollope

306

but he's open to offers.] "Beatrice Straight and Richard Aldrich are producing *Pygmalion* here in New York. With Gertie Lawrence and me... Would you direct?... Good. Oh, fine." [He says yes, of course, he'll direct it and that George (Melville Cooper) is there with him and he'd like to play Doolittle.]

Dick Aldrich eagerly assented. Then Cedric said that Cecil Humphreys was free in New York and would be ideal for Pickering. "All right—look, I'm going to put Dick on," I said, and handed the receiver to Richard Aldrich.

I assured Dick that my radio series was no complication. "It's just three hours on Fridays and three hours on Sundays. I have long since found out that there is no easier way of earning a living than in radio."

Beatrice Straight had cabled Shaw asking him to relent on his customary fee of 15 percent straight, pleading at length that Theatre Incorporated was "a young organization of young actors and actresses and dedicated to the non-profit production of new plays by young playwrights." As it turned out, the first production was his vintage play and the combined current ages of the author, the director and four principal players came to a total of 351 years.

Some seven weeks later, after the production costs had been recouped and we were a solid hit, one of those postcards with the picture of a fierce G.B.S. on the back arrived addressed to Theatre Incorporated. It read: "Dear Theatre Inc.—Grow up. G. Bernard Shaw."

At that time the youngest member of Theatre Incorporated was a man named Robert Fryer who was the office boy and general factotum. It was his first theatre job. In 1976 I worked for Fryer in his revival of *The Night of the Iguana* at the Ahmanson Theatre in Los Angeles. He had become a distinguished theatre and motion picture producer.

It was now near the end of October. There would be plenty of time for this production. I had seen *Pygmalion* with Beerbohm Tree and Mrs. Patrick Campbell in its first production at His Majesty's Theatre in 1914. To me it was and still is the perfect romance. In spite of G.B.S.'s persistent and wilful attempt to defame his enchanting play by labelling it a "farcical comedy," and a didactic comedy at that, I believe that my first impression in 1914 was right. Now I had the chance to play this fantasy as I believed it to be.

I knew that Cedric Hardwicke would agree with me, for we had many times talked about Shaw and his constant efforts to conceal and defeat his inveterate romanticism. Cedric was a romantic himself. Gertie was, too, and I was already imagining how she would employ her feminine artifices, with which she was so lavishly supplied, to bring about the happy ending which G.B.S. had scorned.

I had known Gertie for years. I had done a number of charity shows with her in England but never had I acted with her in a play. She was perfect for Eliza Doolittle. I'd always thought of Eliza, the Covent Garden flower girl, as being in search of a character. Gertie, in real life, I think, wondered each morning what she would be that day. It could turn out to be any one of a dozen persons. Noel Coward used to ask her, "What is it to be this morning, dear? Duchess day, gamine day or just plain-Jane-and-no-nonsense day?" Noel treated these moods lightly. They were a volatile accompaniment of a vivid imagination and were not evidence of temperament. Noel was of untold value to Gertie. He taught her a great deal about acting and she was an eager pupil. He was smart enough to realize that Gertie–who shared the nickname "Gee" with Gladys Cooper–was one of the few actresses who could not capture her performance and keep it in control. She had to have a bit of leeway. Her spontaneity had to be of a genuine variety. This led to some funny moments but to no real trouble.

On one occasion Gertie and I were helping at a charity affair called the Jewel Ball at a hotel in London. The feature of the occasion was the attendance of some fifteen or twenty Indian princes in costume and wearing their jewels or watching their respective Ranees bearing the pleasant burden of "karats unlimited." Gertie was to sing a couple of numbers and I was to act as master of ceremonies. There were several unusual and valuable *objets d'art* to go under the hammer and a much-publicized Pekinese puppy was to be auctioned by Gertie as the finale of the affair.

Tables in the big ballroom of the hotel had been sold for as much as five hundred pounds each. It was soon evident that the Maharajahs, Nizams, Khans and Begums considered the purchase of their tables to be the extent of their contribution. The fat cats from the subcontinent snapped their purses shut as the auctioneer dealt with the modest bids from indigenous wealth.

Gertie had spent the day preparing her act, and her performance was excellent. She was an auctioneer with a heart, she wanted the charity to do well (I don't think she knew what it was), she wanted the puppy to have a good home whether it be in Bikaner, Oudh,

Kapurthala or Kashmir, and above all she wanted to be a good auctioneer.

The puppy was passed around the ballroom in his basket to a chorus of ohs and oohs and ahs. The very young of any species are always appealing. I myself am a push-over for infant wart-hogs. But this puppy was irresistible. Gertie could see it scampering around, say, the palace of Hyderabad with a string of turbaned attendants to gratify each canine whim.

Gertie's preamble was perfect. The initial bids were promising, rising rapidly in five-pound amounts. At about seventy-five pounds the contest had narrowed to two Maharajahs. I'll call them Kunwar and Gokral. The bidding climbed grudgingly by single pounds to eighty-eight. Thereupon Gokral ostentatiously retired, leaving Kunwar in undisputed possession of the puppy.

Gertie had set her sights much higher. She resorted to that old dodge of the auctioneer—"I have eighty-eight—who'll give me ninety?"—which was always the cue for a stooge to keep it alive. I looked down at the professional auctioneer who was sitting at a table nearby. I was no stooge but he nodded at me. Just at that moment Gertie in her search caught my eye. "Who'll give me ninety?" she asked for the third time. I could not resist. I nodded to her and she turned to Kunwar. "I have ninety pounds!" she said in triumphant tones. But Kunwar wasn't listening. His Ranee had lost interest in the puppy. "Do you hear me? I've got ninety pounds. . . . Oh no, you can't!"

The tears were now flowing. She picked up the hammer or gavel or whatever it's called and I thought she would hit either His Excellency, the pro auctioneer or maybe the puppy. Instead she banged the block of wood on the table, crying, "Sold—to you, Ray. And I didn't mean it that way, darling!" It had been a fine performance with a denouement not in the script, nor had it been in the mind of Gertie Lawrence until the kindliness of that lady prompted it. The puppy I gave to Marie Tempest, affording him or her a future much preferable to roaming around some Taj Mahal in India.

In suggesting that Cedric Hardwicke should stage *Pygmalion* I had said that he was the ideal director for any of Shaw's plays. I was quite honest in my belief and, as subsequent events proved, quite accurate. I could not recall at that time if Cedric had ever had any experience in directing plays nor did I ever find out. But I knew that he had acted in almost all of G.B.S.'s plays, and that he had the wit, urbanity, humour, intellect and imagination to put *Pygmalion* on the stage. He also had the respect and friendship of Shaw.

Just why Cedric had not done more directing in England I do not know. He was low-keyed in his style, one of those directors who was silent whenever possible, sparing in his encouragement and in his criticism. He had the ability to make a player feel that any constructive notions had come from his or her own inspiration. There was no flattery involved. Rather the reverse, for Cedric was a master of the devil's advocate approach in which he would deliberately build up a weak case for some idea to which he was opposed. The innocent actor would preen himself on his perspicacity.

There wasn't much need of these subterfuges in the staging of *Pygmalion*. Cedric saw the play as a romantic comedy in which the story itself would surmount any complications of motive and character. As he saw it, there was only one way to play *Pygmalion* – as it was written. Cedric had no time for G.B.S.'s derogation of his play. Shaw had described it as a "pot-boiler which had been done to rags." In an epilogue to the printed version he had written a tongue-in-cheek account of what had happened after the famous final curtain. Eliza married Freddy Eynsford Hill and they lived in "reduced circumstances" of five hundred pounds a year in Earl's Court, eking things out with subsidies from Higgins and Pickering who still lived in the comfort and style of Wimpole Street. Higgins remained a mamma's boy. What nonsense! What really happened was this, as already indicated in countless different ways: Eliza came back and she and Henry Higgins were married, had lots of fights and lived happily ever afterwards.

*Pygmalion* was a delight for me and I believe for Gertie as well as for everybody else connected with the production. It was a perfect company that Theatre Incorporated assembled to act that lovely play: Melville Cooper, Cecil Humphreys, Katherine Emmet, young John Cromwell and all the others.

Rehearsals were the smoothest and most professional that could be hoped for. Cedric was a wonderful director. We broke the house records for non-musical productions. The play ran for 179 performances at the Ethel Barrymore.

*Gertrude Lawrence as Eliza Doolittle and R.M. as Henry Higgins in the revival of Pygmalion by Bernard Shaw, at the Ethel Barrymore Theatre, New York, 1945. Shaw denied a romantic interpretation of his comedy, but who could possibly resist being romantic about Gertie Lawrence?*

310

From the outset it was certain that we were to have the perfect Eliza in this revival. I had seen four productions of the play and there was never a moment of doubt in my mind from the first reading to the final performance six months later that Gertie was the definitive flower girl. There was a resilience, a spontaneity, which I rarely saw in any other actor or actress. She had a firm control of Eliza's character but within the bounds she had set, there was incredible variety. She never pressed or exaggerated, and this was a role which could easily provoke such treatment. Her "fine lady" was lightly borne and, though played with comic intent, was quite moving.

The better Eliza is acted the easier it is to play Higgins. In this well-balanced production Higgins became so insufferably irritating that the audience was exasperated almost to the point of retaliatory measures.

To relieve the audience's aggravation, at one point Shaw indicates that Eliza snatch up one after the other of Higgins' slippers and fling them at him. But Shaw's stage direction misfired. For the first two or three weeks of the run on Broadway, Gertrude displayed a feminine inability to hit the mark and the audience would sigh disappointedly.

In his biography, *Gertrude Lawrence as Mrs. A*, Dick Aldrich quotes from a letter I wrote to him:

"I knew Gertrude actually had the accuracy of a big-league catcher throwing to second base," I said, recalling those days. "I pleaded with her to use her powers. The audience wanted her to hit me. Or at least to come gaspingly close to it. But it was no use. She was really afraid that my powers to dodge were inadequate. But after a week or so the tomboy in her—and that was considerable, God love her—or perhaps the role itself, overcame her caution and kindness.

"One night, when I had given up expecting anything, a whizzing slipper caught me on the nose. Gertie was as startled as I. 'Oh!' she exclaimed. 'I've hit you ...' She dropped the other slipper in horror.

"Then she caught my gratified laughter and the delighted hilarity of the audience. She picked up the slipper and let me have it. For a season afterwards I had to duck pinpoint pitching."

In the jubilation which attended our success on the try-out and on Broadway, it was easy to brush off the shocking technical ineptitude which marred our Boston opening. Nearly thirty-five years later I still

*... especially in that yellow dress.*

shudder at the thought of it. Within one minute of the close of a well-nigh perfect performance the curtain was lowered three times prematurely! The first time its fall was almost to the stage when it was rapidly pulled up again. The second false drop a few seconds later was only halfway and followed by a hesitant re-ascent and a momentary reappearance. The final correct cue was then missed, and left alone on the stage I waited for what is called a bumped curtain, used to steal unearned curtain calls. The closing moments of the play had been ruined and Gertie's exit lost as the curtain took over with its yo-yo routine.

The Boston first-night crowd was angelic. The reception of the play was rapturous; but if they had not liked the performance, this sorry mishap could well have turned the evening into a disaster.

What happened? I never found out. I was a hired hand in this show, paid to act, and the causes of this snafu were none of my business. Cedric and Dick, of course, sifted through the facts and they couldn't make head or tail of it.

The curtain was counter-weighted and operated by a stagehand standing by the stage manager in the prompt corner. There could have been no communication difficulty. The cues for the curtain were normally given by hand signals. What happened I think was an initial misreading of the signal that resulted in panic on the part of the man on the curtain. In any event, it shouldn't have happened in high school theatricals but in a professional theatre it was a painful embarrassment. It is typical of the fairness of theatrical critics that no mention was made of this incident in any notice in Boston.

After we opened at the Barrymore in New York, Cedric stayed on. There were some experimental television shows in which he was interested. TV got its start in the East and Cedric and I did a couple of dramatic programs. We appeared in one together. At that time the shows were live, and what the camera saw and the sound people heard went out over the air. If you dried up, you couldn't take a prompt. You couldn't read a script. There was no help for you.

In this particular show Cedric was playing a scene with an actor and I was in another little set waiting to play the next scene. From where I sat I could see Cedric plainly. Suddenly he stopped speaking. His lips continued to move but there was no sound. It seemed to be a very long speech which I didn't remember in the script. I realized that he was simulating speech and the reason must be that he'd forgotten his lines and was trying to remember them. The other actor was speechless and looked terrified. Suddenly Cedric got his lines back and

314

everything was in order again. When Cedric started the dumb show, the director in the soundproof booth shouted "Audio's gone!" and they went digging into the sound equipment. They nearly "found" the trouble when Cedric started to speak once more. If he hadn't, it is probable that the audio machine would have been ruined.

Nobody but Cedric would instantly have thought of that way of gaining time to find his wandering lines. He was the only completely unflappable man I ever knew in the theatre.

In early June I had to report at Warner Brothers for a picture with Joan Crawford, and *Pygmalion* closed its Broadway run about that time. Gertrude was going on a national tour with Dennis King as Higgins. I hated to give up the part but Jerry Wald, my old friend, was producing *Possessed*, the Crawford picture I was going to be in, so there were compensations.

I now had to do my Harvester radio show from the Coast, my contributions being practically telephoned from a studio in Hollywood. I arrived in California in time to do the rehearsal on Friday and then, forgetting about the Sunday morning airing at nine, I went to bed at the Beverly Hills Hotel on Saturday night without leaving a call and looking forward to a blissful sleep-in. I was awakened at eight and reminded by a frightened assistant at CBS that I would be on the air in half an hour's time. I did the broadcast in my pajamas, arriving at the studio with five minutes to spare.

The next week *Possessed* started shooting, and so within the theatrical year of 1945-46 I had worked in all four branches of entertainment – theatre, radio, television and the movies. It had been a busy and rewarding year for me but the most wonderful part of it was acting with Gertie Lawrence in *Pygmalion*.

*The Theatrical Garden Party, 1948. Noel Coward admits that beneath his summery Ascot attire he is wearing long johns and a sweater against the chilly blasts of that English June.*

This "costume" was for real. My second honorary degree, as LL.D., was conferred at a special convocation of Queens University at Kingston, Ontario, 1949. My brother, the Right Honourable Vincent Massey, joined me in incredulity at this sequel to my Oxford flop.

# 41

In 1949 I acted the title role in Strindberg's *The Father* on Broadway. I also directed the play. This venture produced a "haunt" who is a most unpleasant fellow and a persistent visitor. In my professional memory he's the only ghost I actively dislike.

Although *The Father* only had a brief appearance on Broadway in 1931 when Robert Loraine, the English actor, played the lead, and a more recent off-Broadway run of some length in 1948, the play had the aura of a classic and had acquired the usual small quota of critical devotees with fixed ideas as to its interpretation. That was a constant hazard when taking on a play of classical status.

In the case of *The Father*, unlike plays with a more complex thesis, it is perfectly fair to describe it in one sentence. A Swedish captain of cavalry is driven to madness and eventual death by his iron-willed wife who, in order to control the upbringing of their daughter, gradually and with consummate cruelty insinuates in his mind the belief that their daughter is not his own. That's all there is in the play; no variation of theme, no sub-plot, and absolutely not one tiny spark of wit or humour. Moreover, it is underwritten in a sort of abridged telegraphese, as if the author were in a hurry. In a way I suppose he was, for the play is a misogynic diatribe by a woman-hater in the desperate throes of his third marriage.

Again the question arises: Why did I do it? The answer is: I don't quite know. I do know that Dorothy pleaded with me to turn down the offer. Not one to mince matters, she went straight to the jugular: "It's a damned silly play!" In this, she anticipated the audiences and two-thirds of the critics. But I remembered Robert Loraine's performance in London and I wanted to have a crack at that part. I reread the notices of the New York production in 1931. I had been playing *Hamlet* there at the time but I had missed seeing *The Father* as it only ran twenty performances. The critics thought highly of Loraine's acting but most of them were not very kind to the play. Percy Hammond of the *Herald Tribune* wrote that "owing to the sturdy Strindberg histrionics of Mr. Loraine, you may be blinded to the fact that *The*

*Father* is just another superstition—a bad play with a good reputation." When I played *The Father* nearly twenty years after this production, the critical consensus seemed to be that it was a bad play with a bad reputation.

Two young theatre men, Robert Joseph and Dick Krakeur, gave the play a first-rate production and cast. I was co-starred with Mady Christians in the pivotal part of the wife. No other actress could have equalled her frightening, pitiless performance. As Brooks Atkinson said, "She is defiant and powerful—a terrible force let loose on the stage." This after her unforgettable *I Remember Mama*. What an acting range Mady had! It's ironic that this bitter performance should have preceded her untimely death in 1951 which certainly was hastened by the persecution she herself suffered so undeservedly for her alleged political beliefs. Mady was a dear friend of Dorothy and me. We knew what that kind, gentle woman endured in the last years of her life.

The whole play was about the control of the daughter, and it was essential that this part be well played. I auditioned twenty-four girls. The third one was named Grace Kelly, but I had to see the remaining twenty-one before I gave Grace her first Broadway job. She was just about the most beautiful youngster I ever saw and she gave a lovely, sensitive performance as the bewildered and broken-hearted child. We lost a very fine actress when Grace Kelly became Her Serene Highness, Princess Grace of Monaco, a designation never so aptly bestowed.

At the Boston try-out we realized that a clinical report of the aberrations and extravagancies of insanity were no longer of dramatic interest. Both in Boston and on Broadway the press was very good for the performance but found the play to be a bore, as did the audiences. Elliot Norton, a devotee of the play, attacked me for failing to convey the fact that the captain was quite sane at the beginning of *The Father* and is driven mad by jealousy as the play progresses. We had lunch together after the opening and he made a persuasive case for his criticism. But as the play was written by a paranoid, I found it impossible to avoid the psychotic emphasis which seemed to me to be present throughout it. George Jean Nathan, then nearing the close of his long and gentle contemplation of the American theatre scene, proclaimed my performance as the worst of my career. As he had welcomed each of my previous appearances on Broadway with similar derogatory superlatives, I was well satisfied with his recognition of my progress. It is bad to stand still.

319

*Grace Kelly, the future Princess Grace of Monaco, makes her New York stage debut in a revival of The Father, at the Morosco Theatre, New York, 1949.*

Due to an advance in the till of over $150,000, much of this in benefits for charity, the play had its longest run on Broadway of seventy-nine performances. It was a slow and agonizing death. Benefits are almost always difficult to play to, even in successes. In the case of failures, they are ghastly ordeals. Tickets, which have cost whopping sums, albeit tax deductible, are constantly in the minds of the customers who, as the show progresses, acquire a growing resentment of the wretched players. The escapees at the act intervals are viewed with envy by those doomed to sweat it out by sadistic hostesses determined to have their husbands' money's worth. The hatred, which passes across the footlights (how I wish they still existed!) in two-way traffic, fills the theatre with venom. Inevitably a bad time is had by all. For ten weeks we endured this with *The Father*.

I had to play the last scene in a straitjacket which had a frightening claustrophobic effect on me. I dreaded the moment when I was inveigled into putting it on by Mary Morris who played the nurse, and I knew that my genuine fear did no good to my performance. It was just at the height of the "Method-acting" vogue, a fad I had no use

320

for, and I remember chiding myself for living my part. I still have the damned thing and it makes me sweat when I look at it! This is the only physical "haunt" I ever had.

In 1947 at the Hudson Theatre on Broadway I played a part which recalls exasperating memories. The play was called *How I Wonder* and as in all my major mistakes, the omens of the offer were propitious. The author was Donald Ogden Stewart. Between the wars he had written some successful plays, *Rebound* and *Fine and Dandy* among them. The brief but unforgettable stage career of Hope Williams had its origin in *Rebound*. A merry soul, Don had also written a number of good screen scripts and humorous books.

*How I Wonder* was to be the first managerial effort of beloved Ruth Gordon and her husband, Garson Kanin. I read the play aloud to Dorothy and we were at once intrigued and baffled. The script was described as a comedy by the author but although there were patches of Don Stewart's own brand of featherweight wit, most of the play consisted of unbaked considerations of life, political thought, astronomy and the atom bomb. I was invited to play the role of Professor Lem Stevenson, a scientist involved in astronomy and a disturbed, truth-seeking man. There is little comedy in the cosmos and there was plenty of cosmos in the play. To compound the confusion, the author had the whimsical idea of introducing "an unusual character"–namely, the Mind of the professor with whom the hapless fellow had several long debates in which the professor was inevitably the loser. The message of the play, and the message was spelled out in various explicit terms, was that unless the selfish war-makers, who were apparently exclusively of the western free world, were halted in their wicked work, the earth would become just another flaming star for another astronomer on another planet to discover.

As I put down the script of *How I Wonder*, Thornton Wilder's play *The Skin of Our Teeth* came to mind. I wasn't comparing them, Heaven forbid, but it did occur to me that Don Stewart's play was a sort of *Skin of Our Teeth* in reverse. Thornton's theme had been the will of mankind to survive. In *How I Wonder* the human race seemed bent on self-destruction.

If anything could be done to bring the real play to the surface of the muddle of irrelevancies in which it was buried, Garson and Ruth could and would do it. Gar was to direct, Don Oenslager design and my old friends Bill Fields and Vic Samrock from the Playwrights Company would be associated with the management. I was assured that surgery and the best of therapeutic skills would be brought to bear on the ailing script. Confidence in my long-time friends prompted me to say yes.

A few days later it was arranged that Ruth, Gar, Don Stewart and his wife would come to our house for a story conference. For some reason, Mrs. Stewart, who was known as Ella Winter, was to be given VIP treatment. Ruth explained on the telephone that Miss Winter had formerly been married to someone called Lincoln Steffens and Ruthie added, "Now, you behave yourself, Dorothy Massey, and keep a civil tongue in that New England mouth of yours! You serve tea and no drinks!"

The conference revealed the dismal probability that we would play *How I Wonder* pretty much as it had come to us. It also disclosed Ruth Gordon as a succinct commentator. She was ensconced in a big Victorian armchair, her feet dangling demurely a few inches from the floor. Miss Winter, a large and voluble woman looking the stereotype of an awesome intellectual, opened the proceedings with a lengthly eulogy of the play, which was followed by some timorous reservations from Gar and myself. Don Stewart, with a fixed smile, said nothing. Miss Winter then took over again, brushing our comments aside and renewing her praise of the existing script. She wound up, "... and of course, as we all say, the play's the thing, is it not?"

"Oh, shit!" said Miss Gordon.

Rehearsals proceeded with an ominous stability as far as the script was concerned. Some minor surgery took place but precious little therapy. Miss Winter continued in her active capacity as author's agent, collaborator and manager.

In this, the third of my disasters, Carol Goodner was again in the company playing my wife. She had no tear-shedding dialogue this time. Lest it be thought that dear Carol was my albatross in the matter of defeats, let me make it clear that we were together in *Late Night Final* in London in 1931. It was one of the best plays I ever did in England, a big hit, and Carol was splendid in it.

The dual business of the professor and his "Mind" proved from the outset to be a headache. If the author carries out this whimsy sincerely, the professor bereft of his Mind becomes, in the words of Archie Bunker, a meathead. If the professor retains some intellectual capacity, which he must to maintain any discourse, he becomes "a man of two minds." What happens when his Mind is absent as it frequently was in the play? The answer is that the device just produces another character.

322

In our play my Mind was played by Everett Sloane, a crisp and beautifully accurate actor. Everett was a friend of many radio shows and movies. He died tragically a few years ago. Dorothy and I always called him Sir Everett because of an uproarious impersonation of an Englishman he used to do at parties. I can still hear him describe his family: "There were my brother Evelyn, my brother Vivian and my sister Jon." As rehearsals moved along, Ev got to hate his part passionately. This made him more effective in it.

We were told to go and get our wardrobe. As we were supposed to look alike as far as clothes went, we were asked to go together on this mission. I foresaw trouble. These were the days before professors wore headbands and bell-bottomed trousers and I thought Brooks Brothers would be best for the conservative shirts and other attire required. As we approached the shirt and tie department, the manager greeted me with, "Ah, Mr. Massey, delighted to see you again."

I replied that I would like to look at some shirts and ties. Everett cut in with, "*We*'d like to look at some shirts and ties," adding, with a sidelong glance at me, "He wants me to dress like him!"

The man produced some shirts in a distinctly cooler manner.

"We're in a play, you see," said I.

"That's what *he* says!" added Everett with a giggle.

We completed the purchase of identical coats, slacks, socks and ties in my mounting embarrassment. We were nearly thrown out of a shoe store. Several years later I ordered some shirts from Brooks Brothers—by mail. I have never been in the store since.

Inexorably the days rolled by. Perhaps nothing could be done to salvage what there was of the play, but Ruthie and Gar didn't even try, so far as I could see. A dismal opening in New Haven was followed by a catastrophic one in Boston and a horror in New York. Among the hundreds of telegrams at the Hudson in New York was one which I treasure more than any other. It merely said, "All work and no play. Love you. Mrs. M."

There is nothing more dismal than working off the weeks of an advance ticket sale when a play is a resounding flop. You go to the stage-door, which should be the most exciting entrance outside of the pearly gates, and it's like the iron gate at Newgate. You feel like a leper. Nobody comes backstage after the show, not even the management. We never saw Ruth and Gar after we opened at the Hudson. I don't blame them. Nobody wanted to look at anybody. I like to think that, unknown to me, they had done their best to get through a stone wall. I love them and as long as they think I did my best, all's well.

When we see them, we do not mention this production.

There's a tiny epilogue to this tale. After the ghastly opening at New Haven we all retired to our room at the Taft. Present were Dorothy, Ruth, Gar, Bill Fields, Vic Samrock, Don Stewart, and Ella Winter who took charge of the gathering. From her great handbag she took a big handful of notes and laid them out carefully on the floor, as one sets out a patience deck. Then she went through each note in a monologue. When she was finished she gathered her papers, a lengthy job, and she and Don left the room.

There was a long silence. Then Bill Fields spoke: "When we were down on the border with Pershing in 1916, there was a sergeant in my outfit bragging how he could screw a watermelon."

He paused.

"Yes, Bill," said Ruthie gently.

"So the next morning at six o'clock there were about eight hundred fellows down by the Rio Grande to see him do that thing. But, you know, he couldn't!"

I'm not haunted by Professor Lem Stevenson but by the watermelon!

# 42

Dorothy was a thoroughly urbanized New Yorker. Whenever I murmured something like, "Snow is so enchanting in the country but it's just slush in the city," "The dogwood must be so beautiful now in Connecticut," or "We're missing the chromatic charms of the turning leaves," I was made aware that such rural delights did not figure in her scheme of living.

"I will not live in any place where there are no sidewalks," she would say.

Actually my hankering for the country had no basis in my heritage. I was just as citified as Dorothy and I liked New York as it was in the 1940s just as much as she did.

One hundred and thirty-two East 80th Street was a lovely little house that we lived in for nearly ten years with much pleasure.

But in 1948 a house near Wilton, Connecticut, came to my notice through a broker. It was half a mile up Honey Hill Road, west of the Danbury Road, and we first saw it in the spring when the blossoms were at their peak. There were 420 apple trees. The original house had been built in 1712. A kitchen wing and a guest wing had been added. Quite recently the old barn had been attached to the house, making a huge living-room which the owner, Lawrence Tibbett, the Metropolitan Opera star, used for concerts. There were farm buildings, a big garage and caretaker's living quarters. Most of the apple trees lay on twenty acres across Honey Hill Road. Thirty acres were on the north side where the house was. Lawrence Tibbett was not in residence, and we were shown around by a sour Yankee who obviously regarded us as foreigners. It was a lovely place and, with those apple blossoms, quite unforgettable. Even Dorothy was impressed. I thought it best to dream about it for a while and I went to the Coast to do a movie.

In the fall of that same year we looked at Honey Hill again. This time the turning leaves were simply magic. The owner was our guide and he showed us the inside workings of the house – the kitchen and, to my slight shock, the five furnaces required to heat the place. Heating oil was expensive and in short supply even twenty-nine years ago. However, most everything about the house seemed in good order.

The Merritt Parkway, which was fairly new at that time, was and still is the most beautifully landscaped expressway in the country. And that fall it was fabulous. No trucks disturbed you and the drive was a delight. As we left the Merritt I said to Dorothy, "I could do that drive twice a day and like it."

"How about doing it in the dark in winter?" she asked.

But I could see that her resistance to the idea of country living had weakened a bit.

As we threaded our way through the Bronx she said, "I'm going to find out what it's like to live in the country, in Wilton. What's more, I think that in a very few months property is going to be about double the value it is now within sixty miles of New York. About a million people have the same idea that we have. They'll be coming in covered wagons to settle outside the city. It will be the biggest people shift in a hundred years. And all those covered station wagons will be full of children.... You watch the property taxes go up when the new schools have to be built!"

Next day at dinner Dorothy said, "Well, I've made some inquiries. You know, Honey Hill would be minimum security for me. There's a train from Wilton to Grand Central at 9:00 A.M.. and one back at 5:30 all year round. It's just one hour on the New York, New Haven and Hartford Railroad."

I grabbed my opportunity for a deal.

"Mrs. M., it'd be an experiment. We can leave '132' furnished as it is for a year, and if you don't like Honey Hill, back we'll come. We've got enough furniture in storage to do with at Wilton. I promise you'll be eligible for parole the day you arrive at Honey Hill. I'll have a driver for you! And I'll get a hotel room for nights before the matinées."

"I'll make an offer for Honey Hill tomorrow, before the covered station wagons start arriving."

So the rustic adventure started with our covered station wagon in the vanguard of the ex-urban invasion, with "132" on lease to Leland Hayward and held in reserve as a base for retreat.

Our two alley cats, Hammacher and Schlemmer, never took kindly to Honey Hill. They were used to the concrete and gravel of New York backyards and now there was all this green stuff called grass. In all the time they were in Connecticut I never saw either of them step

326

*Dorothy gives in about Honey Hill. "There are no sidewalks but let's give it a try."*

on the grass. For a while these city slickers used to follow me up Honey Hill Road high-stepping on the macadam, not even looking at the smart little striped-coated field mice who watched from the tall grass. Dorothy described these processions as "the Squire walking his cats."

I was well informed of the woes which attend husbandry in New England, and Connecticut in particular. Having played in *Ethan Frome* and *Beyond the Horizon*, I had reason to distrust the stone, the soil and the elements which had caused Ethan and Rob Mayo such adversity. My own ancestors had chosen to leave New England two hundred years before for the greener pastures of New York and Canada.

But I wanted to make some attempt to farm this little parcel of land. To that end I decided to revive the orchard which had, according to Clancy who was staying on as resident pessimist, produced very bad crops for the last five or six seasons. "Them trees wasn't worth a cuss when they wuz planted twenty years ago. They's the wrong kind of apple for hereabouts."

Nevertheless, a new spraying machine was purchased and a spray-

327

ing program initiated. I was on the Coast but I was back in time for the harvest. I don't know how thorough the spraying was but all the spray had been used up. There seemed to be a plenteous crop but on cutting open a couple of dozen apples a large cozy worm was found in the core of each. On the basis of a TV rating survey, this could be taken as conclusive evidence that 100 percent of the Honey Hill apples were wormy.

But the merry peasants from Norwalk came out to pick the harvest. The resulting injuries were not serious but cost me about $150, for I was not insured. I was unable to sell any of the apples to the market and a barrel sent to the hospital in Norwalk was rejected with thanks, as was another sent to my club in New York.

On each of the trees were at least two tent caterpillar habitats, cocoons the size of footballs and bigger. The caterpillars were still in residence. Connecticut caterpillars don't turn into moths or butterflies. They just remain caterpillars. Clancy said, "You gotta burn them bastards. Prune the branches that's got 'em on ... and the chain saw's clean wore out. We gotta get rid of 160 barrels of rotten apples and that's always tough."

In six weeks' time all 420 apple trees had been cut down with a new chain saw, the wood stacked in a huge pile to dry (this would take two years) and the stumps removed by a bulldozer. I was $2,600 poorer but it's impossible to assess the value of experience. We had a good supply of firewood for the last eight years of our stay at Honey Hill. There were still fifty apple trees on the north side of the road near the house. In spite of spraying and nursing they refused to change their habits. The bounties of Pomona were plentiful and quite inedible but the trees did look lovely at blossom time.

About a year after we moved to Honey Hill a new member of the family—with four enormous paws, a big head with floppy ears and nothing much else—arrived from California. The newcomer, a gift from Greta and Gregory Peck, was a white Alsatian puppy about nine weeks old. When I picked him up at the airport he had just spent twenty-four hours in a small crate. Frightened, tired and hungry, he continued to cry all the way to Wilton where he had his dinner without regaining his composure.

That weekend we had a few friends staying with us—Dr. Sara Jordan, the great internist, and her husband Penfield Mower, Tom Logan and his wife who was Sara's daughter, and Bob and Mary Montgomery. They were all old Boston friends of ours. My two step-

*Dorothy Whitney and Bunga, who has just arrived from California. He is nine weeks old and it is cosy to be in the arms of this nice dog person after twenty-four hours in a crate in an airplane, and these silly ears will look a lot better in a few weeks.*

daughters, Margaret and Dorothy Whitney, were home from boarding school.

When I joined them on the terrace with the new puppy, there was much laughter from our guests. The puppy was still stiff from being cramped in his crate and at his age he was very awkward anyway. For all his life (he was with us fifteen years) he was embarrassed at being laughed at. This time he was also scared. He just put his head on my lap, piddled on the flagstones of the terrace and went to sleep at my feet, all four of his own in the air.

There was general hilarity and Tom Logan told a time-worn, lengthy, scatological but funny story while the puppy slept. The pay-off word was "Bunga" and when Tom got to it there was a shout of laughter which awakened the puppy who put his big paws on my knees. He felt better after his little nap. His ridiculous ears bent every which way, all eyes were upon him.

"Puppy," I said, "you've got a name." The scrawny rat-tail wagged. "You are Bunga."

Within a few days Bunga had become the deciding factor: the move to Wilton was no longer experimental. Dorothy announced one morning that she was going to sell "132."

"Bunga and I can get along here at Honey Hill very well," she said.

Bunga's timidity soon vanished. His father, Perry, was an imaginative dog who had taught the Peck children to retrieve sticks which he

329

had thrown in the swimming pool with his teeth, thus reversing the usual procedure. Bunga had inherited this inventive faculty. As an adolescent he learned to open the kitchen veranda door with his paw and was seen by Josephine, our cook, investigating the refrigerator with obvious nefarious intent. Dorothy persuaded him that anything to do with the icebox was a no-no to him.

When I was on the Coast doing a Warner movie soon afterwards, Dorothy phoned me one night. It was midnight her time.

"I haven't told you before but Bunga has been missing since yesterday morning. This afternoon he came back on three legs. He barked at the kitchen door because he couldn't open it. The paw he uses is badly hurt. I took him to Dr. Guthrie who said he had been caught in a muskrat trap. He said he can't understand how Bunga got out of the trap. He must have opened it with his teeth and the other paw. Dr. Guthrie put twenty-two stitches in the hurt paw. He said Bunga will be all right, and he says it's a miracle because Bungie is only nine months old."

Bunga himself removed the stitches that night and neatly piled them on the floor, I found out afterwards. The tongue is a great healer and Dorothy didn't take Bunga back to Dr. Guthrie.

Our neighbours were the Ferros, Matt and Ted, who lived almost opposite us on Honey Hill Road. They were writers and became our close friends. Doug and Maida Findlay, whose house was a bit down the road, were weekenders in winter but full-time in the summer. At the top of Honey Hill was Mrs. Casserly, who lived in a large house practically hidden from view in a grove of trees; and a little further up were Elsie and Bob French and the Belknaps, Chauncey and Dorothy, summer residents, or no-heaters as Clancy would describe them. South of us where the apple trees had been was the Howell property. Janet Howell had a lovely house there, with enchanting walks which she was delighted to have her friends use. All these people were more or less affected by Bunga's sketchy ideas of Meum and Tuum.

Bunga had become an active hunter who used to bring home his trophies of the chase—hedgehogs, rabbits and smaller fauna—and bury them somewhere in back of the barn unknown to me.

Mrs. Casserly, to whom Dorothy and I were but nodding acquaintances, was the principal victim of Bunga's acquisitive impulses. A half-carved turkey was deposited inside the veranda door of our kitchen and sometime later the remainder of a three-rib roast also

330

*"This door is nothing.... I can get out of a muskrat trap."*

*"What big bone are you talking about, boss?"*

*The Script Reader. "I'm halfway through it, boss, don't touch it. It's a dog."*

found its way to the same destination. I had good reason to believe that Master B. was the culprit and that he had purloined this sizable booty from Mrs. Casserly's premises. Just why the turkey and the roast should be placed on our kitchen veranda no one could figure out. Perhaps he had done it for Dorothy, a sort of canine knight errantry. Anyway there was nothing to be done about it. You cannot reason with a dog on the moral aspects of his transfer of property. I could have sent an anonymous letter to Mrs. Casserly suggesting that she abandon the old New England custom of cooling food in an outside larder. In truth, I think that is exactly what was done, for there were no more instances of meat or poultry theft.

But a series of milk bottles began to disappear from all the neighbours. A cache of almost empty glass milk bottles was discovered near a stone wall by our garage. Each bottle had a tell-tale hole pierced through the cardboard stopper, a hole just the size of one of those big canine teeth we knew so well. Soon after this revelation, Chuck Belknap found Bunga lying on the slope in front of our house with a milk bottle draining into his mouth, as if in blatant admission of his guilt. Rocking with laughter he came in and told me of his find, adding, "I did not realize that Bunga was still being bottle-fed."

When we went out the bottle had joined the rest down by the garage. Bunga was nowhere to be found. He hated to be laughed at and Chuck may have cured him of his desire for dairy products. The neighbours were not troubled any more on the milk bottle score.

331

*Dorothy and Bunga.*
*Homage is rendered to*
*the Interpreter.*

Dorothy raised Bunga by herself. I failed lamentably in my efforts to train this willing but independent creature. I was away from Honey Hill a great deal. There were three stage plays, TV, the movies–ten of them–and two or three long tours in *John Brown's Body* and *The Rivalry*, and my play in England.

Bunga was very fond of me. I was the boss, but I was rather dumb and difficult to communicate with. He would always go to Dorothy when he wanted anything from me. She was the interpreter. For instance, when Bunga wished to be let out of the house he would put his paw on her knee and she would say, "Bunga would like to go for a . . . " Before she could say "walk" he would let out a squawk and go into a dance of delight.

Bunga was now about a year and a half old and he had developed a bad habit of following the car or station wagon when it left Honey Hill for New York or Wilton. I determined to cure him of this dangerous practice with the old water treatment. It was fall and already chilly, an ideal day for such training. Accordingly, Dawson, our new chauffeur who had succeeded Clancy, put a bucket of water on the floor of the front seat. I was city dressed for New York. He started off and Bunga galloped beside the front wheel, as usual. I shouted "bad dog" and opened the door. As Bungie drew level with us I swung the bucket back to hurl it in his face. But it caught on the gear lever and all the icy water covered me from head to foot. Dawson pulled to a stop and Bunga got in beside me on the seat quite dry and grateful for the lift. By lunch time in New York I was almost dry too and convinced that the training of a boisterous Alsatian weighing 120 pounds was not my métier.

332

*East side of Honey Hill. Wilton, Connecticut, 1950.*

*North side of Honey Hill. Bunga and R.M.*

Just after the end of the first tour of *John Brown's Body* my little flock of Dorset horned sheep had arrived at Honey Hill. There were four ewes, four lambs and Big Daddy, the ram, and I thought they looked most pastoral and impressive. In this breed the girls have horns just like the boys and even the lambs were sprouting little bumps. I had decided on this animal husbandry adventure against Dorothy's strong resistance.

It was now mid-May and unusually warm. My first night at home I heard barking out by the barns near the apple trees which were in a big meadow. I told Dorothy I was going to see what was going on. Bunga was sound asleep in the next room. I wore just a nightshirt as it was quite warm, and I took a torch.

Nothing seemed amiss, so I started back to the house. All of a sudden I remembered that the sheep were in this field and at the same moment I heard the pounding feet of what could only be the ram behind me. I didn't stop to think. I ran for the fence as fast as I could. Big Daddy was right at my heels. He got me just below my bottom and with my own momentum and his speed he lifted me onto the top of the rail fence, my nightshirt caught on the post and one foot on each side of the top rail. Then I toppled over, with the nightshirt torn off my back, naked as a jay. I guess the torch was back on Big Daddy's side of the fence. I wouldn't have gone back for it if it had been a diamond necklace.

The door of the big room had slammed shut and I had no key. I threw some stones at our window until Dorothy opened it. She pointed her torch at me.

"Oh," she said, "the informal type. In Fairfield County we dress when we go calling."

When she let me in, she had brought a towel with her and I covered my nakedness. She just asked, "Mr. M., when are you going to give up trying to be a farmer?"

Greta and Greg Peck were spending a weekend at Honey Hill when Bunga was two years old. It was impossible that he could remember the Pecks but they were soon the targets of his exuberant attention, particularly Greta. She had bottle-fed him, there being no room for all his twelve siblings at his mother's lunch arrangement. Bunga now weighed 120 pounds, quite a few more than Greta, and I was a bit worried that he might be somewhat rough for her to play around with. Greta was tiny. I said to Greg:

"I hope Greta doesn't ask Bunga to dance."

I didn't think that he would hear me–"Dance" was one of his

334

*Greg Peck had a much more handsome nose than Bunga but he couldn't do Bunga's trick. Honey Hill, Wilton, Connecticut, 1953.*

words. But he did. He used to "dance" on his hind legs with Dorothy, a sight to behold.

When we picked up Greta she wasn't hurt and Bunga was the most solicitous of us all. Greta said, "Bungie, you're the tallest of all the puppies that Perry and Flip have had. I think you're as tall as Greg."

We were in the big room after dinner when Bunga entered carrying in his mouth a small bag which he deposited at Dorothy's feet. He sat gazing intently at her. Dorothy took a small biscuit from the bag and placed it on the tip of his nose saying, "Bunga would like to show you a trick he has invented himself demonstrating the magician's claim that there are things quicker than the eye."

Bunga was motionless, still gazing at Dorothy.

"Would somebody please snap their fingers?"

Greg did so. There was only a snap of jaws—no biscuit and no movement.

Three times the magician was baited, took his cue from various sources and ate his biscuit. Nobody could follow the lightning passage of the bait.

There was a contest in which Greg tried to emulate Bunga's invisible transfer of the biscuit from the nose to palate, unsuccessful on Greg's part. Greg said he had decided to abandon any further attempts to duplicate Bunga's trick.

"The juxtaposition of nose and jaws gives him an insurmountable advantage over me," he declared sadly. "I must talk to his father, Perry, about it."

335

# 43

On a July afternoon in 1952 Dorothy and I arrived at Batterwood House, my brother Vincent's home near Port Hope, Ontario. We were there at Vincent's invitation to travel with him to Ottawa in the vice-regal train, with his two sons, Lionel and Hart, and their wives, for his installation as Governor General and Commander-in-Chief of Canada. Since I had stood up as his best man when Vincent married Alice Parkin in Kingston in 1915, I had not been present at any of the conspicuous occasions of his notable career. He and I had rarely been in the same country at the same time, but this event would be the most memorable of all.

I happened to be visiting my brother a few weeks earlier when the appointment had just been made. Vincent had had some doubts about accepting the office. His beloved wife Alice had died in 1950. She had shared his life for thirty-five years and the thought of carrying out the duties attendant on representing the Sovereign in Canada alone seemed more than he could bear. In the event, it was his daughter-in-law, Lilias, who took over the hostess duties most ably throughout his tenure. Vincent would be the first Canadian-born Governor General and the first without a title to accept the office. Just how these two innovations would be received by Canadians was, of course, unknown.

For nearly one hundred years a distinguished list of dukes, marquises, earls, viscounts and their consorts had graced Rideau Hall, the vice-regal house in Rockcliffe Park, an Ottawa suburb. Only once had a commoner been appointed Governor General of Canada – John Buchan, the author and statesman – but he was promptly raised to the peerage as the Earl of Tweedsmuir.

My brother told me that the Queen had wished that the Order of the Garter be conferred on him in recognition of his service as Canadian High Commissioner in London throughout the war. The Order of the Garter carries with it a knighthood which is not hereditary. It is the most coveted order of chivalry in the world. It had only recently been bestowed on commoners as recognition of service, Sir Winston Churchill being a notable example. So the time-worn remark of an aged peer, "I like the Garter–there's no damn merit about it," is quite out-of-date. But the Canadian government refused to make any exception to its policy of ending the granting of all titles. The gracious offer of Her Majesty had to be refused.

This was known only to a very few and was told to me in confidence. But over the years it has become widely known. My brother died twelve years ago. I am certain that the honour which Her Majesty wished to bestow on Vincent was as valued by him as if he had been allowed to accept it.

My brother knew that technically the Governor General was appointed by the Sovereign on the advice of the Canadian Prime Minister and therefore that the appointment was theoretically a Royal Command. His misgivings were soon swept aside and Vincent accepted the office fully confident that he could fulfil his duties to the satisfaction of the Queen, the Canadian government, his fellow Canadians and himself.

Dorothy and I arrived at Batterwood House in time for the ritual of tea. Vincent's sons, Lionel and Hart, were there with their wives, Lilias and Melodie. Lionel explained that his father was upstairs in his bedroom preparing for what is known in the theatre as a "dress parade." He said, "Lady Tweedsmuir–that's John Buchan's widow– has given Father his uniform and all the trimmings, sword and whatnot. He was pretty much the same build and the coat and trousers needed hardly any alteration. This is the first time he'll have tried the whole outfit on."

"Is this the uniform the Prince Consort designed for colonial governors?" I asked.

"Yes, it's substantially the dress kit of an admiral as far as the coat goes except the buttons and trimmings are silver instead of gold."

"I think the nether garment is the old overalls, half wellingtons and box spur set-up, isn't it?"

This gibberish will be unintelligible to most readers and I hasten to explain that it refers to the mid-nineteenth-century style of formal dress for both military and civilian attire–long, tight, uncreased trousers fitting closely over calf-high boots known as half wellingtons, into the heels of which are fitted detachable spurs of varying size. In the case of the governors, these were enormous "goosenecks." Lionel admitted that this was the case and also that Vincent had never before attempted to adorn himself in the Prince's design.

I realized that at last I might have the opportunity of doing something for Vincent, that after fifty-six years the "kid brother" might perform a miracle. For I had guessed what the trouble was upstairs and I knew from long experience with costumes how to deal with it.

We burbled on about trivia and irrelevancies, about the responsibilities which Lilias must assume as hostess for her father-in-law at Rideau Hall, about the welter of duties which Lionel would face as his father's secretary, but not a word about the grim struggle which must be going on above. I nursed the thought and indeed the hope that soon my great moment would arrive and I would show the Governor General of Canada how to get into his pants.

"Things seem to be going rather slowly," murmured Lionel. "Don't anybody go up, Mircha will steer him through any difficulty."

"Mircha" was Miroslav Stojanovich, Vincent's valet and general factotum. He was formerly an officer in the Yugoslav army. But I was sure that Mircha would not anticipate my solution of the predicament they had encountered. The days of Balkan military splendour, of tasselled boots and epaulettes, were long since gone. Mircha had been a fighting officer of the Second World War and had never heard of box spurs or sword slings. Mircha entered the big living-room in haste.

"Mr. Massey wants to see Mr. Raymond if he has arrived."

I found Vincent in a state of nervous exhaustion, trying with no success to roll his overalls with a broad silvered braided stripe up over his calves. The boots lay on the floor, the spurs nearby.

"We got these blasted trousers and boots on in an hour and a half, but the second time it's much harder. I can't devote a day to putting on this confounded costume! Do you know anything about it?"

Concealing my overweening sense of triumph was not easy. "Mircha, pull off His Excellency's overalls.... Let me have the half wellingtons.... Thank you.... Now slip the overalls over each of the boots and button the straps under them.... Slip the spurs into the spring catches in the heels.... Now roll the overalls down over the boots.... Will you please step into the boots, sir, and pull those trousers up.... It's quite easy, isn't it?"

Vincent was speechless with relief and gratitude. In his undershirt above but completely garbed as to his lower extremities, he paraded around the bedroom.

I warned him, "Please remember that you are wearing two of the largest goose-neck spurs I have ever seen. They can throw you for a loop if you're not careful."

"How did you learn these tricks?"

"Oh, I was in a Hussar regiment in *Zenda* for several months. I was in the German cavalry for six weeks. There's nothing like the theatre and the movies to teach you about uniforms and clothes. Put the rest of your outfit on and come down and give the girls a treat. And be careful of those stairs!"

The dress parade was most successful, the only problem being the feathers on the cocked hat. These floated up and down as H. E. walked, reminding us of those propeller hats the kids wore at that time. Anchored with Scotch tape by the three ladies, the feathers behaved with suitable restraint on the terrace at Batterwood and at the Parliament Buildings in Ottawa three days later.

Vincent had a fine sense of ceremonial custom and tradition. He loved pageantry and so it seemed did his fellow Canadians. He restored to use two means of transportation which had been abandoned: one for reasons of austerity during the war and the other due to the passing of the horse.

The two blue-and-white cars which constituted the "Governor General's train" were restored to active duty and carried the new incumbent and his party to Ottawa, receiving as warm a welcome as my brother did, according to the press.

In a previous visit to Rideau Hall my brother had discovered in the stables a fine state landau in excellent condition. This vehicle, when used in pre-mechanized days, had been drawn by horses and drivers supplied by the Royal Canadian Horse Artillery at Kingston, a permanent force unit now defunct. But Vincent was not to be deterred. He got full cooperation from the RCMP training establishment which maintained a mounted squadron. From this unit a four-horse team with two postillions in proper liveries was provided.

The police also detailed a mounted escort carrying lances as the army no longer carried a single horse on its strength.

Vincent used to tell a tale of the drive from Rideau Hall to the Parliament Hill which I am sure the victim won't mind my repeating.

Vincent sat on the right of the rear seat, Lionel on his left. Opposite sat the G.G.'s equerry, the Lieutenant-Colonel commanding the First Battalion Canadian Grenadier Guards, a much-decorated officer in full dress uniform, and Captain Nicholas Eden, Anthony Eden's son, the duty aide-de-camp. The little cavalcade proceeded at a trot through Rockcliffe Park, little knots of people waving flags as it went by.

Vincent noticed that the Colonel was wiping his eyes intermittently with a handkerchief which he carried up his sleeve.

*The cavalcade leaving Rideau Hall for the Parliament Buildings when my brother Vincent was installed as Governor General in 1952.*

"It's fairly warm, isn't it?" said Vincent.

"Oh, it's not bad, sir," said the Colonel, removing a tear from his cheek.

They clattered along as Vincent, between waving and scattered small talk, noticed the lachrymation increasing. He wondered if the occasion had not awakened some sad memories. The handkerchief must be dripping wet.

"It really is very warm," said Vincent.

Just another wipe by the Colonel, but a big one.

"I say, are you feeling badly, Colonel?" Vincent was really serious now and they were nearly there.

"Sir, I am allergic to horses!"

# 44

Dorothy has always been an avid albeit discriminating reader of thrillers, cliff-hangers and whodunits, and when I got home to Wilton after the show one night in 1949–I was acting in *The Father* in New York–she handed me a novel called *The Hanging Judge.*

"I have just finished it," she said, "and I think it would make a play. I read it through this evening. You go to bed after your sandwich and read it tomorrow morning. It's by a writer who lives in Barbados, Bruce Hamilton, and he can write."

By mid-afternoon the next day my agent Katharine Brown had secured for me a year's option on the dramatic rights to *The Hanging Judge.* Like Dorothy, I had been fascinated by a well-told melodramatic tale which seemed to have the makings of a stage play.

The novel turned on a striking reversal of fortune. A merciless High Court judge is made to stand in the dock and watch the law, which he has always held to be infallible, condemn him by fair trial for a murder he had not committed.

The judge appears at the outset as self-satisfied and unimaginative. He makes no allowance for human panic. His refusal to believe that people behave irrationally in a sudden crisis has probably sent innocent men to the gallows; and that is his reputation. His manners are forbidding, proper, cold.

For some years this seemingly upright judge has led a secret life. His illegitimate and deranged son, the legacy of an affair of thirty years ago, confronts the judge at his cottage in the country where he lives under an assumed name. The son has worked out a diabolically cunning way of revenging his dead mother's past miseries. He stages his own suicide in such a way that the only witness to the event will be accused of murdering him, and the witness is the judge. He panics. He not only tries to dispose of the dead man, but back in London he tells impulsive, foolish lies. From this point to the condemned cell, after what the judge admits to have been a fair trial, strictly according to law, was the sweep of the novel with all the intrigues and the deceits, the rancours, in and out of the courtroom.

The novel held suspense and interest for the reader by concentrating on the High Court judge himself, on the duplicity of his private life, on his genuine faith in the infallibility of law and its procedure, and on his final breakup in the face of the law's failure. It was a fascinating psychological study, but psychological studies rarely run beyond the first Saturday after an opening in the theatre. This play must be primarily one of action and not introspection.

The puzzle of working out a play occupied my mind off and on for nearly the whole year of the option. I finally convinced myself that I'd seen, read, acted in and directed an awful lot of plays–and why not have a crack at writing one?

My experience in directing had given me some know-how in play construction. I had days free from the theatre and other work and it might be fun. It was the only thing in the theatre I had not done. So I went to work.

I have always been agonizingly slow as a writer. I still am. I could spend a morning in the composition of a letter of condolence. Nevertheless, this time I was my own boss and I could crack the whip on my own ineptitude.

By the time I started work on the play some important decisions had to be made. The story which had gripped both Dorothy and me had been a thriller, dependent upon the narrative, atmosphere, pace and movement. The play which was to come out of it must be written in the terms of melodrama. Hardly any legal point or wildly exciting incident in the tale is plausible. While improbability is a hated intruder in the theatre of reality, it is a welcome guest when we revert to theatre which is a little larger than actuality, and melodrama takes over. The novel's inherent weaknesses–such as the revenge suicide of the unhinged bastard son of the judge and the latter's inexplicable behaviour–are acceptable in the atmosphere of melodrama.

The style of the play determined the treatment of the principal action. Where was this to be carried out? Was *The Hanging Judge* to be a courtroom drama? Was it to have the fluid movement of the novel? Or was some other focal point to be found for the playing of the principal action?

Having decided on a melodramatic treatment, I abandoned the courtroom idea. It was essential to get comedy and lots of it into the play, and the courtroom is not given to comedy.

The novel's numerous locales seemed unsuitable for stage treat-

342

ment, and so I got the idea of making a London club the centre of the action.

Structurally the play seemed to fall into order almost automatically. The principal action would take place in this club called the Adelphi where five major scenes would be played. There would be a scene in the house of the judge, Sir Francis Britten, and six short highlights at the trial in Norwich. But the bulk of the story would happen in the Adelphi Club. It was most satisfying to have settled on a structural design for the play but the story was no nearer being told.

In the novel there was no villain. Britten faced a sort of built-in adversary in the panic he was unable to resist. But this melodrama needed a "heavy." So I made up my own latter-day villain—Sir George Sidney, M.C., M.P., a resilient manipulator with a sense of humour, politician, company director and jack of all deals. He would be the pivot of the faction which detested the "hanging judge." As the play grew, Sidney became, next to Britten, the most potent character. In the end he saves Britten from the gallows.

In accordance with the melodramatic treatment, I deliberately "aged" the dialogue a decade or so, using slang and colloquialisms which were not quite current. Melodrama needs a veneer of the recent past to make it convincing.

In spite of two movies, a play on Broadway and a spate of radio and TV productions, I made clear progress in the script in late 1950 and early 1951. I will remember to my earthly end what Dorothy did for the play, particularly at this stage of its progress. She had practised law for years, and the legal aspects of the novel fascinated her, as they did me. But Dorothy's influence had not been in the legal department but the reverse. She kept reminding me that I was writing a thriller. "Britten's faith that the law could do no wrong and the improbable legal points that come up may be of some interest to a few lawyers," she would say. "But the meat in this play is the chase. Will he hang or won't he? Forget about the law. It's a thriller and a good one. Always remember that."

The play had to be done in England first, whatever happened afterwards. I told Michael Powell of my intention to write the play as a melodrama, to put the action in a London club and to subordinate the legal aspects to the action of the play. This old and dear friend's answer to my letter was: "WHEN CAN I HAVE A SCRIPT STOP I WANT TO DIRECT STOP LOVE MICKEY." This was about July 1951.

In the late spring of the following year I sent Mickey my final draft. He was as good as his word for he cabled back in four days: "SCRIPT

SWELL LIKE PRODUCE AS WELL AS DIRECT STOP WE OPEN SEPTEMBER TWENTY-THIRD NEW THEATRE STOP MY PARTNER WILL BE WALTER P. CHRYSLER JUNIOR STOP HAVE GOT GODFREY TEARLE FOR BRITTEN STOP COME AS SOON AS YOU CAN MICKEY.''

It was just like Mickey. In three days he had read the script, got his backing, engaged the best choice in the English-speaking theatre for the title role and booked the New Theatre, just about the best house he could have picked.

I tried out the script on several friends, with somewhat disappointing results. Bob Sherwood wrote me: "Because I have such real affection and respect for you, allow me to pay you the compliment of candour. In its present form the play seems pretty poor to me. The story–fabricated. The theme–muddy. The characters–uninteresting. The stagecraft–cumbersome. The whole–lifeless.... I feel sure you could write a better play if you wrote your own and threw off the shackles of adaptation...." It must have been a brutally difficult letter for Bob to write and I appreciated his honesty.

Samuel Taylor, author of *The Pleasure of His Company*, was more hopeful: "I like a good story and this is a good one, for my money," he wrote. "The thing is all of a piece and you've done a hell of a good job...." He then made some invaluable suggestions for improvements, which I followed immediately. The generosity of other authors is one of the most gratifying things about writing in the theatre.

Dorothy and I arrived in London about the first of August. I had been delayed by a movie, and rehearsals started immediately. I never had the slightest qualm about having a director who had had no theatre experience. In England the stage and the screen are much more closely associated than in America. There wasn't a play that Michael Powell couldn't direct perfectly anyway, for he had stage sense, something you don't learn or acquire, you just have it.

The first rehearsal I went to was like a family reunion. Almost everybody in the cast had worked with me before. I'll never forget the thrill of hearing my lines read by good actors. Mickey had picked an ideal company.

First there was Sir Godfrey Tearle, the "noblest Roman of them all," perhaps the best-loved actor in England. A short time before, Godfrey had announced his retirement, and it was wonderful that he wanted to play the judge.

I did not know John Robinson, who was cast in the role of Sir George Sidney, but he looked perfect for the part and he read the lines beautifully. Henry Caine, the veteran of all those Sunday shows

344

*Aboard the R.M.S. Mauretania on the way to London for rehearsals of*
*The Hanging Judge.*

with me; Harry with that constant look of astonishment, those up-swept eyebrows, was my idea of the rotating Home Secretary, Major West. I hadn't seen Julian Summers before but he looked as if he were born to play the part of Ronald Pond, the crafty solicitor. And there were the old Green Room Club friends – Jack Melford, the dry politico-barrister who prosecutes, and Peter Williams, the emotional advocate who defends Sir Francis Britten. There was another friend, James Raglan, who would be the Chief of the Norfolk Constabulary and Britten's pursuer. Bartlett Mullins, a roly-poly little man with twinkling eyes, would be wonderful as the judge who tries Britten. Then there was John Byron, who was frighteningly good as the half mad, illegitimate son of Britten.

Experience had taught me to disregard first readings as any indica-tion of future performance. But this time there was enthusiasm and unison not often felt at a first reading. The players really put out for me. I thought my euphoria could not last but it did.

Mickey started to put the play on its feet that afternoon. It was a

345

simple production. The large club scene occupied the whole width of the stage, with two reveals on each side in which the smaller scenes could be played. The London rehearsals came together rapidly. Some cuts and alterations were made but Mickey wanted to get audience reaction before we made any serious cuts. I wanted to get twenty minutes out of the play. We were over three hours in playing time, counting intervals, and that is dangerous.

Mickey was in complete agreement as to the melodramatic treatment of the production and he got great vitality out of the company right from the start. As is usual with such a cast, they were ready for the customers a week before they met them.

We were to open in Manchester, my favourite provincial date. I love the audiences in Lancashire. They're boisterous and fun-loving. Lancashire has developed a humour all its own, vehement and hardhitting. I can never step on the platform of a Lancashire railway station without thinking of the lady who accosted a porter who was pushing a luggage trolley at Wigan Junction. "Hi, porter, where do I get train to Blackpool?"

"It's t'other side for Blackpool."

"You mean, it's t'other side for Blackpool?"

"Aye, lady, it's t'other side for Blackpool."

"Tha means t'cross t'bridge?"

"It's t'other side for Blackpool!"

"But, porter, I've got a tin trunk."

"A' don't mind whether tha's got brass boobs ... it's t'other side for Blackpool!"

The opening at the Opera House was true to my record of good luck in Manchester. As one critic put it, "Out they came from the Opera House, Manchester, buzzing with the excitement, which indicates that the audience had been well and truly entertained."

I watched them all through the play, and they really were having a good, tense and happy time. As I went backstage I picked up my telegrams and put them in my pocket to read later at the hotel. One dropped on the floor and I opened it. I'm glad I did. It was from Charles Morgan, my long-time friend from Oxford, and it said: "I HOPE THAT WITH GODFREY YOU SHARE MY BEGINNER'S LUCK." Charles Morgan had been the dramatic critic on the *London Times* most of the years between the wars. We'd been up at Oxford at the same time and had acted in the O.U.D.S. in 1920. He had left the *Times* in 1938 and written his first play, *The Flashing Stream*, which Godfrey Tearle had produced and acted in. It had run six months at the Vaudeville.

The Manchester press was excellent: "A real meaty, gripping drama which will give the London audiences many a thrill when it reaches the West End"; "The audience loved every minute of it"; "Moving, modern melodrama on an intelligent level"; and several more to that effect. This was the tone of the notices at all of our four provincial dates: Manchester, Liverpool, Newcastle and Leeds.

At the big Opera House we sold out on Wednesday night. At the end of the first interval I found one empty space among the standees in the balcony. Just as the house lights were dimming I felt a tap on my shoulder. Tap is not the right word. It was a bump. I turned and faced an irate gentleman.

"In Manchester ya don't steal standin' space in t'interval. This is my place, next to t'post 'ere and I'll have it, if ya please. I'm interested in t'play."

I apologized in delighted embarrassment for my trespass.

I did a lot of revisions, rewriting entire scenes on the strength of audience reaction. I think in Manchester I worked most nights in order to meet rehearsal hours the next day. One scene had troubled me, the one in which Sidney reverses his stand of vindictive animosity towards Britten and becomes his defender. Two industrious and sleepless nights produced a version which displayed a crisper and far more characteristic Sidney and which contained, I believed, some good comedy. About 4:00 A.M. I fell asleep in our Mansard garret of a room at the Midland Hotel, confident that I had licked my problem.

At 11:00 A.M. I walked onto the stage at the Opera House with six copies of the two pages I'd written. Mickey, John Robinson, Julian Summers and Jack Melford were there. All read the two pages. Mickey stared at the ceiling while the others contemplated their navels in silence. Finally John Robinson rose and gently placed his little script on Mickey's table.

"Sorry, old chap, it just won't play." He walked towards the prompt corner.

I spoke. "All right. I'll have another go at it. I won't promise it here but I'll try for the Liverpool opening. I'm sorry that I—"

John whisked around, bursting with laughter. "I can't go on with it," he said. "Look, old fellow, these low lifes are having you on. This is perfect. It's just what was needed and you know you've done the hat trick. You've got three laughs on consecutive lines! You can go back to your attic at the Midland and tie one on!" We rehearsed it

*Sir Godfrey Tearle, James Raglan and John Robinson in The Hanging Judge.*

*Sir Godfrey Tearle as Mr. Justice Britten in The Hanging Judge, New Theatre, London, 1952.*

then and there and it went in that night even though the Lord Chamberlain hadn't seen it. John Robinson was dead right. We got three laughs on three consecutive lines.

It was a stirring first night at the New Theatre in London. The audience seemed to know instinctively that this was not to be an evening of realism. They wanted to be entertained and they responded to the entertainment that we gave them. They saw a fine, taut performance of a thriller and they were willingly gripped by the story for every second. When the curtain finally fell there was wild applause and cheers.

It was an emotional occasion, for Godfrey had announced that this would be his final role, and he was a much-loved actor. The audience was very kind to me. I made a stuttering sort of speech. I don't think the tears showed.

Dorothy and I were booked on the *Queen Elizabeth* to sail home the following day, the boat train leaving Waterloo at twelve noon. By that time we had the nine or ten daily papers, and Mickey and Dorothy and I read them over at the station. All the critics agreed that the play was good entertainment: "The piece comes through as thumping, full-scale drama"; "Superbly, overflowingly, un-selfconsciously

348

theatrical"; and "Altogether a most luscious evening's entertainment."

But the new realism had pervaded the theatre and the bogies of improbability and implausibility were brought up in most of the notices. Quite a few of the critics admitted that they had enjoyed themselves and were gripped by the drama but they were also reluctant and embarrassed to admit it. This had not been the case in provincial papers.

Harold Conway, who wrote for the *London Evening Standard*, is a case in point:

There was scarcely one credible character and certainly not one credible incident during the entire three hours of *The Hanging Judge* at the New Theatre last night. That a roistering time was enjoyed by all, including me, indicates how the London stage has been starved of plays with plots. Especially deep melodrama plots.

From the *Queen Elizabeth* that afternoon I wrote this letter:

Dear Mr. Conway:

I've read your review of my play with much interest and a measure of agreement! I wrote *The Hanging Judge* as unabashed melodrama. I tried to develop characters who were slightly larger than actuality to tell an interesting tale without too meticulous a regard for plausibility and to dispense an amalgam of comedy and suspense with a view to entertainment. *I* wanted the play to be billed as *modern melodrama* (a field of theatre for which I have the highest respect), and in this desire I had the complete agreement of Michael Powell, the director and producer. Unfortunately our intentions or desires were denied. The play was presented to the public in London as a *modern play* and therefore subjected to distortion and inevitable ridicule. Believe me I did not intend my play to be, as you suggest, a "profound psychological study"!

Sincerely
R. M.

I received the following reply from Conway:

Many thanks for your nice–and interesting–letter. I'm sure you had the right idea in wanting the play to be billed straightforwardly as a melodrama; I apologise contritely for having been misled into thinking that you (and Michael Powell) might possibly have harboured loftier ideas about it.

At any rate I do hope I expressed myself clearly enough in my notice for you to have realized that I thoroughly enjoyed myself. I am pleased to hear that the box office response is good; and I hope it continues that way.

Do come back soon and let us see you act again too. Even if it is only for 182 days!

Best wishes and regards.
Yours sincerely,
Harold Conway.

The weeklies and glossies were better but most of them were just a little shamefaced about their support.

I want to quote from one of J. C. Trewin's notices. Thank heavens he wrote and still writes for a number of weeklies. Mr. Trewin is a stage historian and scholar who believes there can be a lively theatre which is not dominated by Shaw, Ibsen and Chekhov.

... this is a right down, regular, royal melodrama, a spanking affair that on its first night kept the house in anxious silence. At the end cheering burst like the breaking of a dam.

I claim nothing for this play except one thing: the dramatist can tell a tale that, nonsense or not, keeps us rooted until the end.

There was one whose professional knowledge and know-how, wisdom and friendship made it possible for me to finish the script of *The Hanging Judge* and get it produced in England. She was Katharine Brown, the best dramatists' agent in the business. Kay saw me through all three years of struggle. Her criticism, patience and encouragement were priceless. Kay gave up her annual holiday to see me through the rehearsals and the first two weeks of the try-out in England before she had to return to New York.

When Dorothy and I left London after the opening, we didn't know what was going to happen to the play. The first night had been sensational but the press had been only fair. It was fitting that when we got home to Wilton on Sunday morning it was Kay who telephoned to tell us: "Mickey has just phoned me that business has jumped to standing room only and you have a hit!"

The play ran on merrily until late November when the following announcement appeared in the press:

Mr. Michael Powell, who presented and produced Mr. Raymond Massey's play *The Hanging Judge*, in which Sir Godfrey Tearle is at present appearing at the New Theatre, has announced that the run of this play would end on December the thirteenth.

The decision to withdraw *The Hanging Judge*, stated Mr. Powell, "has been forced upon us by Sir Godfrey Tearle's doctor, who has ordered him a complete rest."

The play was produced on September 23 and by the time it is withdrawn it will have played 94 performances.

Godfrey's heart condition, of which we all had been aware, had worsened. In spite of his courage and determination he had to withdraw from the play. Godfrey's superb performance had carried *The Hanging Judge* to success, and the only replacement who could have succeeded him, Clive Brook, was unable to accept Mickey's offer.

Godfrey may even have shortened his life by the strain of acting in my play. He died on June 8, 1953. I treasure the letter he wrote just before the opening at New Theatre: ".... I pray devoutly for success tonight. I hope you will believe that this is not a selfish wish. We have a new dramatist and I am proud to be with him at the launch. My love always, Godfrey."

351

*The Hanging Judge* had some electronic afterglow. A BBC radio version, with the title role performed by Boris Karloff, was produced in 1953. I never heard it. The next year a television play was made in England. I played Sir George Sidney and had to take over from the director when he became ill. In 1954 another TV version was produced on the "Climax" series in the United States. I acted Britten in this one, Sir Cedric Hardwicke was Sidney, and it was directed by John Frankenheimer who insisted on having a billiard table in the main lounge of the Adelphi Club. The show got good ratings, but unfortunately the video portion of the West Coast showing went sour and all that the California audience could get was sound. Fritz Lang sent me a telegram saying he was fascinated by the revival of good old radio.

My play was never tried on Broadway. Possibly Al Woods would have attempted it but Al had died in 1951.

I wrote what I thought was a good movie version, with all the pomp and pageantry of an English assize opening, the ever-impressive full courtroom and, I think, several improvements in the story. Mickey liked it very much and plans were made for a film company of our own to produce it, but somehow we never got around to it.

My first and only play now remains a very pleasant memory. Four loyal people are in the foreground–Godfrey, Mickey and Kay Brown, and most prominent among them is Dorothy.

# 45

In the nineteenth century it was the fashion for authors to give readings of their works. These "lectures" became a distinct form of theatre. Many Victorian writers were colourful personalities and modern acting, in reproducing some of the readings, has shown what first-rate entertainment was provided. Emlyn Williams in his Charles Dickens performance and Hal Holbrook in *Mark Twain Tonight* have proved that the "lecture" can still be good theatre.

By 1950 a dozen or so stage stars were regularly engaged on the book-reading circuit. Of these Charles Laughton was unquestionably the most prominent and successful.

Charles was ideally suited to this one-man type of show. Although his formal education had ended with high school he was one of the best-read men I ever knew. Armed with a pile of books he would make his entrance, spill the books on a table, and give his audience a full evening of varied and fascinating theatre.

Paul Gregory, who had booked Charles on these reading tours, was a rarity in the theatre, an agent and producer with imagination and intelligence. In partnership with Laughton he produced Bernard Shaw's *Don Juan in Hell* and the third act, normally considered unplayable, of *Man and Superman*. Charles Boyer, Agnes Moorehead, Cedric Hardwicke and Laughton himself played it successfully in 1951.

In the late spring of 1952 it was announced that the second offering of the Gregory-Laughton management would be an arrangement of "John Brown's Body," Stephen Vincent Benét's epic poem about the Civil War.

This left me bewildered. My immediate reaction was fear that my friend Steve's magical verse would not survive the perils of recitation. But I knew that if the attempt were made to bring his words to the stage, I would have to be a part of it.

Dorothy said, "I think Paul and Charles will have a great hit.

Steve's poem will be perfect on the stage. You had better say yes when Paul calls."

He called as predicted and I said yes. I asked for details.

Nothing had been settled. There was only the intention to do the show, set the cast and the opening date. Charles, who was to direct, had not started to adapt the poem. Dame Judith Anderson, Tyrone Power and myself would make up the cast of three. From that sketchy beginning Paul had started to book a tour. It was scheduled to open in only five months, on November 1, 1952, at Santa Barbara.

Charles Laughton came on the phone.

"Next week I propose to descend on your Connecticut abode and spend a day and a night in the discussion of Benét's poem," he said. "This meeting should be considered private and the public should not be admitted by ticket or invitation. Dorothy, of course, must be present."

In due course he descended and the three of us talked "John Brown's Body" for nearly twenty-four hours. Charles knew the poem with a depth I had not anticipated. He loved it with the appreciation of a scholar, with the patriotic fervour of newly acquired citizenship and with the admiration of a theatre man for a great play.

Charles appreciated, as we all did, Steve Benét's use of varied metre in the structure of the poem. The continual stress of one metrical cadence, such as Longfellow, Tennyson and other classical poets employed, can become monotonous to the ear, if not the eye. But Steve had such a bag of different metres that neither reader nor listener ever had to fear lack of variety.

Charles had identified a clear narrative line, which both Dorothy and I readily appreciated. There was much discussion of the descriptive flesh to be attached to these narrative bones. But by the time I drove Charles to Wilton station to go to New York, I knew and agreed with the structure of the playing version.

Charles quite rightly would not discuss the assignment of material between the three players until the final acting version was settled. But I did want to do the Lee bit and had great difficulty keeping my big mouth shut.

Dorothy and I decided to make our own cut and see how it compared with Charles's. The final acting script had to be about one-quarter the length of the complete poem. When the acting version arrived about a month later there was a variance of only five percent between Charles's script and ours.

Of the three of us who were to act *John Brown's Body* (Charles

354

would blow his top when the word "read" was heard!) Judith Anderson and I had had lengthy stage careers. Judith had proved herself a great tragedienne. But Tyrone Power's professional experience had been almost entirely in movies, and the cardboard characters in which he had been cast had given him little chance to show his acting talent. He was proud of his family connection with the theatre. His father and his great-grandfather had been fine classical actors. As a schoolboy I had seen Ty's father's Brutus, and he had been a boyhood idol of mine. So it was no surprise to me when Tyrone Power III was startlingly good at his first rehearsal. He had studied acting with his father as a boy but after his father's death in 1931 Ty had abandoned all thoughts of the stage and drifted to Hollywood. His striking good looks and fine voice landed him a dazzling movie career. He had done nearly fifteen years of movie work interrupted by three war years as a Marine pilot.

His performance in Steve's poem was to be in expiation of his desertion of the theatre and a tribute to his father. I have seldom seen such determination to succeed.

The staging of *John Brown's Body* was complex and venturesome. There were no precedents. The production had to be geared for every kind of meeting place, small and large proscenium theatres, auditoriums, huge convention halls, gymnasiums, field houses. Sound and lighting equipment would have to be trouped and obtrusive microphones would be necessary.

Charles staged the poem in a sombre style. As in the *Don Juan* reading the actors were in evening clothes. But for this one there was a section of balustrade with a red bench-top which we could each use as a base and a group of red upholstered chairs where the chorus could sit in the shadows.

The bleakness was relieved by our moving around informally. When Judith had a long speech Ty would go offstage and I would relax in one of our chairs. Our performance was informal, Charles even allowing us to step out of character for a moment or so.

The arrangement avoided identifying any of us with a particular character or function. Tyrone and I divided the two Robert E. Lee passages. Judith took the descriptive portion of the Harpers Ferry raid and the trial. I played the John Brown soliloquy and the Lincoln sequence, and all three of us shared the narrative. But we did not play parts, we played the poem.

Written for the printer rather than the actor, the text lacks dramatic force. This Charles supplied by deepening the intensity of the performance and raising the pitch in the second act. He conducted us like a maestro, bringing the performance to dramatic climaxes and modulating us to the moments of horror, pity and doom.

Cohesion and continuity were achieved by a chorus of twenty, including two soloists who were placed in the shadows at one side of the stage in the formal Greek manner. This chorus provided a varied and successful accompaniment.

We met the chorus for the first time at a run-through about a week after rehearsals began. Any misgivings I had about the chances of our show vanished when I heard these twenty young men and women chant in unison, sing the old-time songs, mimic the sound of marching feet and the din of battle, the plucking of a banjo, the chilling rebel yells, the echo of violins at a Georgia plantation ball, bird calls in a Tennessee swamp, the scream of the rivetting hammer in the finale, and a hundred other American sounds.

The man who had written the incidental music and developed the sound effects was Walter Schumann, an accomplished composer who described himself as a "commercial musician." He was in fact a musical magician.

*John Brown's Body* opened at the Santa Barbara's Lobero Theatre, a small, old-fashioned house, but we used our sound amplification anyway. As usual, my spirits had sunk. I was thankful that the trip back to L.A. was only eighty miles. As we waited behind the curtain, roly-poly Charles bounced onstage and in his most affectionate tones addressed the three of us: "Well, my dears, you have done exactly what I asked of you. I think I have ruined my career and yours! Yours too, Walter!" Then in the continental manner he added, "Break a leg! May all your children be acrobats!" He vanished through the pass-door, giggling.

The show went beautifully but at the final curtain instead of the usual applause we heard a thunderous stamping of feet. None of us had ever heard this kind of response to a show. The stage manager hesitated about taking a call. Then Paul Gregory burst through the pass-door shouting, "They love it–they love it–take it up!" We took about fifteen calls.

It seemed that the stamping of feet as a sign of approval had been the custom in Victorian times and the Lobero was the only theatre

*Tyrone Power, Dame Judith Anderson and R.M. when the three played the two bus and truck tours of John Brown's Body by Stephen Vincent Benét, 1953-54.*

where the tradition survived. Since that night I have read of it in several books, notably Kipling's *Soldiers Three*.

We made two tours in successive years. They were bone-crushers. The first was more than eighty dates, mostly one-night stands, the average travel being three hundred miles by chartered bus. All sense of place was lost in a blur of hotels, motels and guest houses.

The two tours presented an unforeseen hazard. Musical people seek relaxation in music: our miraculous chorus spent the six or eight hours of daily travel in constant harmonic research, melodic reminiscence or just plain rehearsal. The energy of these young people was incredible and, in the confines of a Greyhound bus, deafening. Being in the forward seats, we three actors and the patient driver bore the full impact.

Early travel calls were the rule. Ty had charming memories of his colleagues at these morning bus departures. Judith muttering in a voice of doom, "Don't you dare say good morning to me!" Charles Laughton, having closed a Hartmann suitcase with his jovial bulk, cutting off a protruding silk shirt-tail with a knife. Myself on the sidewalk, bleary-eyed, a cigarette hanging from my lips with a half-inch of ash about to drop into a bag which I was trying to close. Ty said I looked like a monkey trying to f—— a football! So I was "Monk" from then on.

Early on the first tour Tyrone announced to Dorothy and me (occasionally she joined us for a day or two) that his motto as a Marine had been IGMFU. It had been painted on the fusilage of his plane. I think even the most innocent reader will be able to decipher this cryptogram. Ty said it signified "self-reliance"! This declaration had come when on a stranded train at a whistle-stop in a blizzard in northern Michigan. After we had found some doughnuts and coffee Dorothy suggested we take something back to Judith, asleep in the train. "Igumfoo!" was his answer. From then on Ty was Iggy. The soubriquet was perhaps not quite appropriate, for I had noticed a steaming carton of coffee secreted under his overcoat. But it stuck.

On the stage after a performance in the enormous Municipal Auditorium in Oklahoma City, Iggy, Dorothy and I were talking. It was a few days after Ty earned his title. A large, stout woman strode past us and faced Tyrone.

"I am Hazel Underwood," she announced. "I'm the president of the Bracegirdle Drama Society. You were *good*!" The last three words were delivered in a tone of amazement.

"Thank you," said Tyrone.

358

Mrs. Underwood was not finished. She had a limited vocabulary but a limitless power of inflection. She slowly inspected Ty as if he were on the auction block, repeating, "You were good," with a varying emphasis of astonishment which I still remember. With the sixth and final delivery on a suitable ruminative note, she departed shaking her head as if in disbelief. Iggy turned to Dorothy.

"How am I doing?" he asked.

"You were *very* good," was her reply.

"Thank you, Hazel," said Iggy. The trio was complete, "Iggy, Monk and Hazel" joined "Athos, Aramis and Porthos," "Shadrach, Meshach and Abednego" and other triple companionships of fact and fable.

# 46

About ten days before the close of the first tour of *John Brown's Body*
I started to run a low fever every afternoon and spent the night dripping in sweat. I knew that it was virus pneumonia (I had had it before) and that there was nothing to be done except go to bed for a
week. But that was impossible, for I had no understudy. So I did
nothing and I don't think my performances suffered much except
that I had to sort of swim through them. Dorothy, of course, knew
nothing about the trouble and was back home in Connecticut preparing for my little holiday break before the Broadway opening.

Finally, and unknown to me, Curly Thomas, our manager, telephoned Paul Gregory in Los Angeles and told him he had a sick actor
without an understudy. The result of this call was that on our arrival
at a Phoenix hotel, where we were to play our final performance,
Paul, Charles and a doctor greeted us. It was noon. We had had a
short ride from Tucson.

The doctor gave me a look-over and said that if I didn't go to bed
and stay there I would have the real bug kind of pneumonia and
recommended that I go to a hospital in Phoenix. Charles took over.
"I hate hospitals," he said. "You can rest up in my house much
better. We'll fly you to L.A. in a chartered plane and Elsa will nurse
you." Elsa was both Elsa Lanchester and Mrs. Charles Laughton, a
fascinating success in both capacities. "You are a pig-headed old bastard and completely unmindful of my interests," Charles went on.
"You must know that I have an insatiable desire to play your part in
this production which I shall gratify tonight by replacing you. I shall
telephone Dorothy at once and tell her of your selfish behaviour. Oh,
will you catch it when you get back East!"

So within a few hours I was bedded down in a large, sumptuous
room in the Laughton house in Hollywood with August Renoir's
"Judgment of Paris" hanging on the opposite wall beyond my large
feet. I still remember those three bouncy, undraped goddesses who
danced in my fever. The nurse looked very like Elsa Lanchester, a

girl I had worked with years before at the Cave of Harmony, a cabaret in Soho. I kept singing the lyrics of a number Elsa had sung there.

*I never told him, not up to now,*
*And if I 'ad very likely there'd 'ave been an awful row.*
*I really don't consider it woulda done any good,*
*But the truth of the matter is that one of my legs is made o' wood.*

The nurse kept joining in. She seemed to know the lyrics.

The next day I was much better. My own doctor had loaded me with pills and the fever was nearly gone. Tyrone visited me in the afternoon to tell me of Charles's impressive performance of my part at Phoenix. He gleefully recounted how with only a director's familiarity with the part, Charles made it seem as if his was the only way in which it should be acted.

At that point Charles and Elsa entered and Ty gave them his prognosis. "I think I have restored the patient's will to live but if he's permitted to lie here watching that bunch of nudes (Charles winced!) for any length of time, I doubt if the old bastard ever works again."

Accordingly, a few days later I parted company with Renoir's three goddesses and was shipped back east by air to Dorothy, who had never been painted by Renoir but far outclassed any of the three candidates in his version of that ancient beauty contest.

I was still a bit wobbly for the Broadway opening. Although we had played about eighty dates to great audiences and had had an almost unanimously good press, the New York run was still an unknown quantity. Up to now we had been playing the "culture belt," mostly one-night stands on a subscription tour, and the approximate score of each game was known beforehand. But nobody had any idea of what we would do in the regular commercial traffic of Broadway. In the Century, a big theatre usually housing musicals, it was certainly not going to be just another in-and-outer. But would we be there long enough to send out the laundry?

We knew right away, as the cheers and bravos came with innumerable curtain calls, that our laundry problems were solved. For eight weeks we stayed at the Century. Right away it was certain that Steve's words had made it on the Main Stem, that we were a hit on Broadway as well as on the culture circuit.

The notices confirmed Steve Benét's success. The reviews on the road had been as good as could be but it was a delight to read what the "pros" thought. The New York notices were almost all raves. As nearly always happened, the best critic of all, Brooks Atkinson, epitomized the lot. "*John Brown's Body* is a work of art not only in print but on the stage," he wrote. "It refreshes the whole conception of theatre."

The second tour went out the next fall. Without touching any place we had played on the first trip, again there were about eighty dates. This time we hit the Deep South and there were some spots we played where Lincoln had not yet been canonized and fiery crosses on the lawn were not unknown. Nevertheless, the show always went over beautifully.

Judith Anderson did not come with us on the second tour. Her part was played by Anne Baxter. Comparisons would be quite impossible and also fatuous. Both these ladies are actresses of great accomplishment and of high though differing talents. Charles's direction accommodated each performance to its greatest effectiveness.

Charles was one of the finest stage directors I ever worked with. He lived and breathed theatre; he was resourceful, sensitive and inventive. He was adaptable; he could be firm and also gentle, expressive and taciturn. Above all, Charles was honest and never devious. "Trust me, Ray," he said once in rehearsal. "I trusted you in Sean O'Casey's play." He made me do about the most difficult acting job I ever faced. Charles will always be remembered as an actor of matchless talent but, though he had directed very few plays, he was the tops as a director. Few people realize what a loss the theatre suffered when Charles Laughton died at sixty-three.

Walter Schumann was a composer and a musical innovator who was touched with genius. His music and effects for *John Brown's Body* were an outstanding embellishment of Charles's production, and the only musical composing he ever did for the living theatre. He died just a few years later at forty-four.

I don't know how Paul Gregory came to offer Tyrone Power an acting opportunity which might have baffled a player with ten times Ty's experience. But nor do I know how Paul put the whole of *John Brown's Body* together. It can only be because Paul is a fine impresario. Anyway, Ty grabbed his chance and delivered himself of a performance that required post-graduate acting. I don't detract from Ty's achievement when I add that Charles Laughton was his director. It was the only such chance Ty ever had. He never complained. He had proved to himself that in the theatre he could be as great as his father and as his father had hoped he would be. He remained a dear

362

and close friend of Dorothy's and mine for the rest of his short and merry life. He crammed an awful lot into it.

But I think what counted most with him was *John Brown's Body*. "I've paid my dues to the theatre," Ty would say. He had a great capacity for having fun, a capacity distressingly rare these days, and he would laugh as he talked of himself as "the aging boy." This, Dorothy claimed, described all actors. "Iggy," as we still think of Ty, died of a completely unexpected heart attack on a movie set in Madrid in 1958. He was just forty-five.

When the second tour ended we had travelled about 30,000 miles, mostly by bus, played some 160 dates, most of them one-night stands, all of them in enormous halls, and we had touched forty out of the forty-eight mainland states. We missed one of the Dakotas, but we made up for it by hitting three Canadian provinces. It had been bone-crushing, fascinating, nightmarish and, in retrospect, a satisfying experience.

I believe there were two reasons for the phenomenal "hold" which our play exerted on the people. One was the power of Steve's words to stir the imaginations of the audiences; and the other was his ability to make his listeners belong as individuals to the story he was telling, to make that story belong to them.

Steve opened the imaginative powers of his audiences. No two people out front at our reading or recital ever saw the same show. The folks we were playing to weren't sitting on theatre seats – they were riding on Steve Benét's magic carpet.

Five years after *John Brown's Body* I had my other experience in the bus-and-truck theatre. Paul Gregory offered me the Lincoln part in a Norman Corwin play which he proposed to send on tour prior to a Broadway run. This was in 1957. It was almost twenty years since I had acted Abe Lincoln in Bob Sherwood's play.

I accepted the part with my eyes open. It is a basic instinct of most animals to protect their territory. I did not want any other actor to play Lincoln. I was not very smart.

The play, called *The Rivalry*, consisted of excerpts from the six debates between Abraham Lincoln and Stephen A. Douglas in their campaign for a U.S. Senate seat in 1857. There were several short fictional scenes connecting the oratory. The characters were Lincoln, Douglas and Mrs. Douglas. When I first read the script it was a flat documentary without development and progression.

Norman Corwin, a competent and prolific radio writer, was also directing the production. It is my experience that authors are rarely effective in staging their own plays. Corwin had a reverence for the authentic text of the debates, which blinded him to the fact that most of the thirty hours which the two candidates spent discussing the rights of man were just politics and, as such, a bore in the theatre.

The cast which opened on the road was composed of Agnes Moorehead, Martin Gabel and myself. Aggie was an old hand at bus-and-truck. She had done her own one-woman show called *The Fabulous Redhead* for Paul on several tours and had been a member of the great Drama Quartette who had acted *Don Juan in Hell.* Aggie was a fabulous actress – incisive, witty and intriguing.

Martin Gabel was new to the platform theatre. He considered Chicago as an Australian thinks of the Outback. His idea of touring was a try-out in Boston or Philadelphia, where he was born. Essentially a patrician, he regarded the Republican Party as upstart, much as Douglas himself did in 1857. Marty is an actor of precision, authority and grace. He was superb as Douglas and utterly miserable facing the rigours of the tour. Once Marty and I were dressing in a locker room recently vacated by a basketball team. The make-up tables were ill-lit, and on Marty's was a pair of dirty shorts. He opened his make-up box, removed the shorts with a pair of tweezers, and stared dejectedly at a mirror which was ominously cracked. He muttered, "I engaged in this venture solely out of deep respect for your professional standards, Ray. I never knew how low those standards were!"

We visited some really savage outposts of Academe where Marty could not even get a good dry martini after the show.

We tried a faculty party at one date. A tipsy lady asked me if I would oblige the gathering with the "Lincolnsburg" address. Marty gravely informed her that Mr. Lincoln had changed his address after the battle of "Gettysville," and anyway that was after he had grown a beard.

The lady said, "Oh, yes, that's right, isn't it?" and departed.

By the time we approached the close of the tour not one word of the debate material had been changed or any of the direction altered. The play seemed lifeless and the polite and kind reception which we were accustomed to was worse than outright disapproval. I told Paul I did not want to open on Broadway with *The Rivalry* in its present form.

It was fifteen years since *Abe Lincoln in Illinois* had opened on Broadway and one or two critics denigrated Bob Sherwood's play because they said so much of it had been derived from Lincoln's own speeches and letters. I never heard any complaints of this sort from the public. The truth is that Bob didn't use any authentic material in the debate scene or other historic moments in the play. He used dramatic material from sources other than the actual debates. However, Corwin's *Rivalry* suffered from "authenticitis."

# 47

One blessing the theatre bestows upon her servants is the solace they receive in failure. No matter how abrupt or severe the defeat of a play may be, how painful the disappointment for those involved in the venture, there is consolation for them in the memories of the preparation and performance of the job.

But there is one theatre venture which recalls not one single moment of professional satisfaction for me and in which I wish I had not engaged. This was my next-to-last theatre engagement in the East and I did it with my eyes open and fully aware of the difficulties and hazards involved. The auguries attending this misadventure were baleful. And yet I accepted the offer.

About 1951 with the Shakespearean theatre in Stratford-upon-Avon in England playing flourishing summer seasons and Stratford in Ontario about to begin its annual festivals, Lawrence Langner had the splendid dream that an American Shakespeare Festival Theatre in Stratford, Connecticut, would complete the triangle.

A most successful patent lawyer, though best known as the business leader of the Theatre Guild, the Welsh-born Lawrence set his sights on the realization of this dream. And by the beginning of 1955 a lofty octagonal building, reminiscent of those contemporary drawings of the Elizabethan Globe Theatre, had appeared on a meadow by the Housatonic and reportedly was to open its doors early in the following summer.

In February Lawrence and Armina Langner came to lunch at Honey Hill and we had a long talk about the new Festival Theatre. The Langners had a country house over in Westport and we were all just about ten miles from Stratford. Lawrence wanted me to play Brutus and Prospero in *Julius Caesar* and *The Tempest*, which were to be the two plays in the opening season. I was delighted to be asked to join the venture but very much in the dark about its organization. I'd heard rumours of conflict as to leadership, policy and the like. I had ample confidence in Lawrence himself. Although I had never acted in a stage production of the Theatre Guild, I had worked in many of their radio and television shows and I knew Lawrence Langner to be a straightforward and honest theatre man.

I wasted no time. "I would like very much indeed to be a part of your project, Lawrence. But I would like to know first who is boss and who will be boss of this adventure. Will it be you, please?"

After a few moments of silence, Lawrence said, "The Stratford project is not a commercial stage venture.... I don't think any one person can be what you call 'boss.' I've had to raise more than a million and a half for this scheme and in doing so I've obtained contributions from some people who are not prepared to sit back and watch things happening but who would like to have some say in the development and operation of the project. To your question, my answer is no–I am not in sole control and there will be, must be, some committee action, I expect, at all times."

"The theatre doesn't like committees, Lawrence," I replied. "It thrives under autocracy, dictatorship, if you must have it."

"What about the Theatre Guild? We've worked under a committee for thirty years and more and we haven't done so badly."

"I must point out to you, Lawrence, that the Guild Board, or whatever you call it, is composed of active theatre people, and from what I hear of the Festival trust or committee there isn't a full-time professional theatre man among them. Remember what the architects say–'A camel is a horse designed by a committee.'"

We aired our views until my inevitable acceptance of Lawrence's offer. Dorothy had always told me that I was incapable of a final no to any theatre proposal. But in this case there was a very private reason for me to say yes, one that only Dorothy knew about. For many years I had harboured a secret notion of acting King Lear. I won't dignify this whim by calling it an ambition, and the possibility of my ever playing this supreme role was so remote that I would frequently put the matter out of mind as far as I could. However, I confess that I had long since learned the big speeches, and whenever the opportunity came in the great outdoors I would deliver them fortissimo to whatever audiences of birds and beasts would listen. Nobody knew about this quixotic fancy of mine but as I listened to Lawrence Langner tell of his dream of an American Shakespeare Theatre and his determination to make it a reality, I thought of my own whim and that maybe Lear might fit into the future plans of this Stratford scheme if I were able to deliver in my first assignment.

I joined up to do Brutus and Prospero. Movie commitments were postponed until the fall to enable me to play the eight-week season at Stratford.

Successful Shakespearean or classical theatres anywhere have usually been formed on a repertory basis, the result of a single director-producer's efforts, a director who has built up a well-balanced, homogeneous company. Developing a company takes time and patience, but many theatre groups have grown to maturity in just such a way. They flourish in the shade of academic or municipal patronage and they often wither under the glare of metropolitan bright lights.

The Stratford Festival Board had chosen Denis Carey as director of the two plays which were to compose the initial season. He had a wide experience in the repertory theatre in England and Ireland, had proved himself to be a very good repertory director in England, and had considerable acting experience gained in Dublin at the Gate and the Abbey theatres. He had just completed six successful years as director-producer at the Bristol Old Vic where he directed thirty-one Shakespearean plays, and the board felt that Carey was a perfect choice to lead the Festival Theatre in its opening season.

But the American Shakespeare Festival Theatre in Connecticut was not really a repertory theatre. The undertaking was a big-time commercial venture, with all that means in showmanship. Top-notch productions that would meet Broadway standards were needed to make the sixty-mile trip down the Merritt Parkway worthwhile.

Denis Carey arrived in New York in May and I took him to lunch at the Century Club. I knew full well that he must be pretty anxious to talk to somebody who knew the English theatre. Carey was a charming, rather shy, scholarly man of about forty-five, and I thought he seemed perplexed by what he had undertaken in Stratford. The first few days after his arrival he interviewed the twenty-five or so players whom the casting people at the Theatre Guild had chosen for his approval. His comment to me was sombre.

"How could I tell what these good people were like when I was looking at them for the first time? In rep when a director chooses anyone for his company he has known their work and what they can or can't do, and they know all about him as well. But here I was a rubber-stamp of approval for the lot of them."

He had what seemed to be a slight Irish lilt in his speech and I asked if he were Irish.

"No," he replied. "I'm English but four years at T.C.D."–Trinity College, Dublin–"and a good few more acting at the Abbey and the Gate can't be discarded entirely, now can they?"

368

He had the casting list in his pocket and he handed it to me.

"Here's what I have to work with. Can you tell me anything about them?"

It was my first look at the casting and I must admit that I was impressed. I knew most of them, at least by reputation. But the collection lacked the homogeneity the new repertory people were always bleating about.

"You'll have a dandy Mark Antony and a perfect Ferdinand in *The Tempest*. Unlike most of the young people, Christopher Plummer can play the classics. He has a remarkable talent. A few years ago my wife and I saw a play that Katharine Cornell brought to Broadway for a short run. Ty Power was her leading man. It was called *The Dark Is Light Enough*. I remember nothing about it, except a young actor who played a Cossack in one scene with Kit and Ty. He had only a few lines, no movement, but he could listen. During the scene neither of us could take our eyes off him in spite of the competition of two of the most expert eye-catchers in the business. In my book such a stage presence means a star. Of course, the young actor was Christopher Plummer. He's a Canadian. I went to school with his father. He's played about 125 parts in rep in Ottawa, Canada, and in Bermuda of all places.

"Roddy McDowell you'll probably remember as a child star at Twentieth-Century-Fox but there's nothing child-like about Roddy now and he'll make a scintillating Ariel, which is I think a brute of a part to cast.

"This fellow Fritz Weaver, who's down for Casca and Antonio, I have worked with and I'm certain he will be fine. The women are all well chosen and there are two comics, Jerry Stiller and Rex Everhart, who will be just what you want. Oh, Hurd Hadfield is a fine choice for Caesar. I think you've got some good people."

Carey reached across the table for the cast list and gazed at it, unconvinced by my optimism.

"What about this Jack Palance?" Carey asked. "He's been given two key parts and I've never heard of him. Without a good Cassius and an outstanding Caliban your two roles Brutus and Prospero mean very little."

There had been rumours of this casting and now I knew they were true. I admitted that I knew nothing about Palance's work, which I gathered had been almost entirely in films.

"I hope he's had some stage experience," I said. "A screen actor is a soloist and the movie actor knows nothing of the team effort which

369

is the heart and core of our work in the theatre. But you bring up one of my favourite subjects, namely myself. I'm going to need a lot of help from you, Carey, for my Shakespeare experience has been limited. Fabian in *Twelfth Night* at the Everyman in Hampstead way back in 1922 and Hamlet in Norman Bel Geddes's production in 1931 in New York – that's all there is, there isn't any more. That Hamlet was a controversial production and my performance provoked a pro-and-con battle among the critics that I think you may have heard of in England.''

I told Carey some of the highlights of the Geddes adventure and he was much amused but I think a little frightened. I managed to reassure him about the cast here which he had been given, at least I thought I had.

The next night I flew to London where my daughter Anna was to make her stage debut in *The Reluctant Debutante*, acting with her mother. The flight was delayed and I just made the opening, driving straight to the Cambridge Theatre from Heathrow. Loud was my applause and great was my pride for her impeccable performance. She was just eighteen. It was a joy to see beloved Nanny Burbidge, who had the care of Dan and Anna since their births, functioning equally well as Anna's dresser. This she continued to do in Anna's subsequent stage appearances. Nanny was the mainstay of the household while Dan and Anna were growing up and moved over to perform her invaluable functions for Anna when her David Huggins was born. Our family devotion to comfortable, kind, wise Nanny was total. Her death left a hole in our hearts.

The next time I saw Carey was about a fortnight later, the end of May, not long before we were to start rehearsals. He had telephoned me at Wilton, saying he wanted to see me, that it was urgent. I was doing a TV show in New York and I decided to stay in town that night. Again we met at the Century. Carey had just been hit with the theatre building at Stratford, the design for the scenery and the sketches for the costumes. He was in what is known as "a state." It was between agitation and despair.

"I've just seen that barn at Stratford.... Can I have another drink? It's a proscenium stage, the biggest I have ever seen or heard of. The proscenium opening is fifty-five feet wide and it's sixty feet deep – they have scenery, painted scenery for *Caesar*. The fellow has designed the Forum with a huge perspective backdrop and a lot of steps dead centred, and built scenery each side of the stage. They don't need a director for this job, they need a bloody shepherd. The stage is fifteen feet wider than Drury Lane."

The man was pacing up and down now and the several would-be diners in the club were fascinated by the intensity of "these theatre people."

It's the sort of scenery that Beerbohm Tree would have considered too elaborate. You'd have to have a hundred extras to fill it."

I interrupted. "Surely there's an apron for Mark Antony's speech. It'll all be in the foreground."

"Yes, but the whole idea of realistic scenery is preposterous. I have no idea how to use the acres of space I've got. I'm used to English stages that are half the size of this damn football field! You must be too – you've directed plenty of plays in England."

I tried to calm him by changing the subject.

"What about the costumes?" I asked. But this only touched another nerve, a nerve that seemed even more tender.

"The costumes! You would have thought that of all of Shakespeare's plays the costuming of *Julius Caesar* would be safest from trickery, innovation and substitution. This production is not to be a stunt like the modern-dress affairs we've seen. It's an historic play and it must be dressed in a proper, authentic manner. Yet I've been handed sketches in the style of Renaissance Venice for the Forum part and seventeenth-century neo-classic in the battle scenes. I can't understand it."

Carey was much calmer now. I asked him what he had said about these horrendous plans for the production.

"What could I say? It's too late to do another decor plan or redesign the costumes or build another smaller stage! We start rehearsing in ten days."

"How about *The Tempest*? Have you seen those designs yet?"

"Not the costumes. I'll get them tomorrow. The setting is a huge rock piece and it will look like a pimple on that big stage, but it's a lot better than the *Caesar* scenery. There's a rather good impression of the shipwreck at the start. Maybe we can pull off a miracle with *The Tempest*."

Rehearsals for *Julius Caesar* revealed pretty much what I had told Denis Carey. Chris Plummer, Roddy McDowell and Fritz Weaver showed up the rest of the men even after a few days, not so much by their reading of the verse but by their vitality and spirit. When there is uncertainty in a Shakespearean performance a sort of leaden reverence takes over, at least it did with me. I could feel it, and try as hard as I could I was unable to do anything about it. I bored myself.

371

The "Method-acting" vogue was at its height in 1955. Almost all screen actors practised the "Method" either consciously or unconsciously. Jack Palance seemed to be no exception. In the movies it is impossible to attain any objectivity in a performance. A screen actor is tempted or rather forced to rely on his own emotions in interpreting a character which has been handed to him in bits and pieces. He seldom has the chance to look at his part as a whole from the outside as the stage actor has. It was natural for Jack to bring the Method into practice in putting his Cassius and Caliban together. But in so doing he was working under a set of rules that had no place in the theatre. His performances in both roles were solos, or close-ups, and they were not linked up with the rest of us.

At that time Carey had not done much work in TV or the screen. He did not realize Jack's problem any more than Jack did. Jack's unevenness was not his fault. He's a good actor but he could not find his place on the team at Stratford. His performances in both his roles at the opening and immediately afterwards were undisciplined and rough. But a sense of discipline is infectious in the theatre and Jack caught the idea. For most of the run his technical control in these two contrasted characters was impeccable.

We moved to Stratford just a week before the opening of *Julius Caesar* and a week later than planned, after rehearsing both plays in New York for nearly a month. The theatre was still far from ready, particularly the backstage portion of the building. With the installation of the lighting equipment, the rigging, and the dressing-rooms far from completion, the condition of the stage was utter chaos. Final rehearsals were constantly accompanied by the sound of saws and hammers. The first dress rehearsal was actually interrupted so that the act drop could be tried out for the first time.

On the evening of the first dress rehearsal a heat wave was in progress with night-time lows in the nineties. Those cursed costumes were unbearable–a sort of gabardine, topped by a surcoat of velvet, headdresses with ear muffs, each outfit weighing eighty-six pounds. Nor were the costumes comforting for Carey as director. From the front, he said, the conspirators all looked like members of some occult religious group, without any visible identity.

When called upon to run the assassination scene through a second time, I discarded my fifty-pound surcoat with this apposite comment, "It's too damned hot and if Caesar's wearing one of these overcoats he's safe as houses, for nobody could stick a knife through this plush." So we all pulled off our topcoats and sweated away without

372

them. But the revolution was unsuccessful—the board liked the clothes and we had to suffer for the sake of "art."

The heat wave reached its peak of 101 on the first night, and the rainfall during the day resulted in eight inches of water in the lower dressing-rooms, which remained there for several days due to faulty drainage.

Among the many messages which came to the Festival Theatre in Connecticut on its opening night was one from Sir Winston Churchill in which he described the project as "an outward evidence of the cultural links that bind together in harmony the English-speaking world." In that same high-minded spirit we acted *Julius Caesar* before a most distinguished international audience with a deferential, awe-struck performance that, with the exception of the three actors I have mentioned, lacked the excitement which this play has always evoked.

The press was quite properly destructive, though as kind as possible. At the first performance every conceivable accident that could happen to me did. At the assassination of Caesar, as if to confirm Jack Palance's augury, my knife got entangled with Hurd Hadfield's voluminous robes and I thought I would never extricate it. Hurd's line should have been, "Et tu, Brute. You're wasting your time."

In a play called *The Solid Gold Cadillac*, Josephine Hull had what has become an immortal line: "Shakespeare is so tiring, only the kings get to sit down!" I wasn't playing a king but in the tent scene at a particularly emotional moment I did get to sit down. It was on one of those folding canvas stools with three legs. As I sat, one of the legs broke with a loud report and I was deposited (I may add, very painfully) on my back on the stage. Incredibly there was not a sound of a laugh, but a low-life of a local critic wrote that "Brutus fell off his chair."

Two weeks later *The Tempest* opened and went into the repertoire. The production was much better than that of *Julius Caesar*. The scenery simulated a rocky setting of caves and promontories. It was not enchanting but it was eerie. The costumes were imaginative and quite in the spirit of the play, with the exception of Jack's Caliban outfit, which was sinister instead of being intriguing. Roddy's Ariel costume lit up the stage with assorted sequins.

The notices for *The Tempest* were better than the *Caesar* ones. But the verdict was now in –"Guilty on the count of failure to rise to the occasion." There is no doubt that *The Tempest* was better acted than *Julius Caesar*. The audience enjoyed this poetic delight with all its

373

mystery and enchantment. But Brooks Atkinson said: "The perform-ance as a whole does not match the sweet lyricism and forgiving gentleness of the text."

Carey was showing signs of wear and tear. He was now enduring interference both in his *Caesar* production and in *The Tempest*. This interference came from various quarters, notably from a Festival Board member, an amateur who had the gall to approach the *Julius Caesar* cast with suggestions as to performance. Later on he had the effrontery to call rehearsals of some of the cast of both plays without Carey's knowledge or, I believe, that of Lawrence Langner.

This is the final insult to a director–to have an outsider attempt to tamper with his production behind his back. It was more than the kindly, gentle Carey could take and he ceased any efforts to improve the performances. There was nothing to be done at this stage, with only a few more weeks to play. Dorothy and I brought him over to Honey Hill for an overnight respite from the scene of battle. He seemed almost in a state of shock when we got home but a good rest and a walk with Bunga did wonders for his spirit. Soon after this Carey returned to England and resumed his directing and acting ca-reer most successfully.

Of course the Stratford Festival was not a complete failure. Three fine performances came out of the wreckage. Roddy McDowell's Ariel, Fritz Weaver's Casca and, above all, Christopher Plummer's Mark Antony.

For myself I choose to remember the misadventure at Stratford as the beginning of an enduring friendship with Chris Plummer. He has become a world-famous movie star and has done some notable tele-vision plays. But these activities have not prevented Chris from keep-ing faith with the theatre. He still looks on the stage as his base and his prodigious talent has allowed him to excel in every phase of the-atre endeavour from musicals to Shakespeare. His industry is aston-ishing and it exhausts this old man even to write about it.

Dorothy and I don't see Chris and Elaine very often lately. His work carries him all over the world. But whenever we meet we com-pare our recall of those eight inches of water in the dressing-rooms on the opening night, those Torquemada-designed costumes in *Caesar*, and all the other strange vicissitudes we encountered in Connecticut in 1955.

The towering octagonal building stands by the lazy Housatonic River, the theatre quite often dark and still waiting for the fulfilment of Lawrence Langner's dream.

# *48*

In 1954, two years after the Warner contract had come to an end, I returned to the Burbank lot to act one of the best parts I ever had in the movies. It was the role of Adam Trask in the Warner Brothers film of John Steinbeck's novel *East of Eden*. It was one of the few three-dimensional characters I ever played in the movies.

The screenplay had been written by Paul Osborn, a successful playwright with an equally good record in film-writing. He had tried six times without success to compress Steinbeck's huge novel into a two-hour film. In his seventh script he stuck to the last quarter of the book. The result was a well-integrated and moving drama. It received the production and direction it deserved from Elia Kazan.

Kazan, known to our profession as "Gadge," had already made a name for himself as an actor and director on the New York stage. He had been a leading figure with the Group Theatre and was the acknowledged "high priest" of the Actors Studio, the American home of the Stanislavsky "Method."

There was nothing particularly novel about Stanislavsky's ideas. What Kazan had gleaned from the Russian director's verbose and often ambiguous notions was a fervent belief in the naturalistic style of acting.

Yet Kazan was sensible enough to recognize that no style or theory fits all occasions in the theatre. When necessary, the Method could be put on ice.

*East of Eden* needed naturalistic acting. Kazan picked his cast from the theatre, four of his chosen players being products of the Actors Studio: Julie Harris as Abra, Richard Davalos playing Aron, James Dean as Cal, and Jo Van Fleet as the mother. The three older characters were acted by Burl Ives as a kindly sheriff; Albert Decker, who had staged the duelling in the 1931 *Hamlet*, as a friend of the Trask family; and myself as Adam Trask, the father. Naturalistic acting was not an exclusive property of the Method School and we were apparently what the director wanted.

Gadge Kazan is a director of wide abilities. With remarkable skill, he can keep a sense of the whole and mind the details. He knew exactly what he wanted and how to get it. He devised a vital production and achieved near perfection from the cast he had so carefully chosen.

The character of Cal, the "bad" son, was an early example of the anti-hero. Gadge had wanted Marlon Brando for this role and when he proved unavailable, had chosen a young actor, James Dean. Regardless of his inexperience, James Dean was a good choice. In every respect he was the Cal of Steinbeck's novel. He was to become a sort of cult with the young.

Jimmy had only to act himself. But that is a difficult role even for an experienced actor to play. A rebel at heart, he approached everything with a chip on his shoulder. The Method had encouraged this truculent spirit. Jimmy never knew his lines before he walked on the set, rarely had command of them when the camera rolled and even if he had was often inaudible. Simple technicalities, such as moving on cue and finding his marks, were beneath his consideration.

Equally annoying was his insistence on going away alone once a scene was rehearsed and everything ready for a take. He would disappear and leave the rest of us to cool off in our chairs while he communed with himself somewhere out of sight. When he was ready we would hear the whistle Gadge Kazan had given him and he would reappear. We would assemble to our appointed spots and the camera would roll.

Gadge did nothing to dissuade Dean from these antics. Most directors would not have tolerated such conduct, myself included; but Gadge knew his boy and he must have figured that his only course was to pamper him and winnow the grain from the chaff as we went along. After all, he had drawn great performances from Marlon Brando, and Dean was of the same breed.

So Gadge endured the slouchings, the eye-poppings, the mutterings and all the wilful eccentricities. He said to me one morning as I waited near my camera marks for that damn whistle to blow, "Bear with me, Ray. I'm getting solid gold!"

I remember a scene at a big ice-house which had been built on the Warner back lot. The key moment of the scene was Jimmy in a rage pushing the huge blocks of ice from the cool storage loft down a long chute to melt quickly in the sweltering California sun. This was Cal's senseless attempt to destroy the refrigeration experiment. The action was simple. Jimmy just had to push the blocks down the chute as Burl

376

Ives and I looked up at him. It was a set-up favouring us in the foreground, Jimmy being up on a platform and not in clear focus.

Everything was ready for the take. But nothing happened. Jimmy just continued to pace up and down glaring at the blocks of ice.

"What the hell goes on?" I said.

Burl Ives looked at his watch. "Jimmy's got to get to hate the ice," he muttered. "It takes time."

It was nearly five minutes before Dean signalled his readiness to perform. When his close-up was shot a half-hour later he was much quicker. It seems his hatred of the ice had lasted although the ice hadn't.

There was only one time when I lost my cool and, as always, I much regretted it. There was a big scene between Cal and his father in which the boy is rebuked for his misdeeds and is made to read a passage from the Bible as an admonition. The reading is not to the father's satisfaction and he demands that Cal read it again with proper reverence.

It was a long scene and Gadge had covered it lavishly from every angle. He finally got to my close-up when Jimmy read the passage off screen for my reaction. I was astounded to hear the Bible being read, revised by Jimmy, with profanity and obscenity injected. I did not wait. I shouted "Cut!"–an insult to a director on his own set–and walked over to Gadge, saying, "I'll be in my dressing-room when this young man is ready to apologize."

I sat in my portable for a few minutes repenting my action when there was a knock on the door. I opened it and there were about fifteen or twenty of the crew standing there. The head grip was in the centre. "Ray," he said, "we just wanted to thank you for what you just did." There was a murmur of assent and as they turned to go, Kazan came through the group. We went into my dressing-room together. He shut the door and we sat down.

Not a word was spoken until Kazan said, "I put Jimmy up to that. I thought it would get the reaction from you that I wanted."

There was a pause.

"Gadge, you're too smart a director to think that a kid's trick like Jimmy pulled could get anything from me that you could print. It just shamed me into a burst of temper which I regret. You know and we all know that Jimmy's got it. He's good. But there are rules to go by in our profession and he'd better abide by them. One is to stick to the script."

Within five minutes Jimmy had made a gracious apology, not for any breach of good taste, though I think that was implied, but for spoiling a take of my close-up! He was quite professional and I reciprocated by expressing my regrets at my own behaviour.

Gadge shot the picture almost in continuity. After the Bible scene we were in the final sequences in which Cal seeks a reconciliation with his father. In this phase of the story Jimmy revealed a sensitivity and a tenderness which was quite unexpected to us all. The whistle was no longer heard or needed, for the solitary "conferences" had been abandoned.

Jimmy was openly antagonistic in our early scenes, as called for by the script. All indicated a lack of understanding between father and son. At the end of shooting a sequence in which a reconciliation had been initiated, as Jimmy and I left the set he linked his arm in mine and said with a chuckle, "You know, we were just lousy with rapport in that one."

"Lousy" had, in Jimmy's personal lexicon, no derogatory or entomological connotation. You might say it meant "suffused." The remark impressed me as it seemed to indicate a sense of surprise and satisfaction in Jimmy at what he, or rather we, had accomplished in the scene just played. I had a notion that he didn't know or care whether it was Cal or himself he had just talked about. All along, I think, Jimmy had been following the Method theory of the actor identifying himself with the character he is portraying.

Of Jimmy Dean's performance in the final edited film, a critic later wrote, "Dean tries so hard to find the part in himself that he often forgets to put himself in the part."

From a welter of emotional extravagance, Kazan had contrived a performance which seemed so expert that it persuaded the same critic to write that "the four major players play together like a fine string quartette, not as though they were creating the beauty but as though it were passing through them. Julie Harris is the viola...Raymond Massey the cello, and Richard Davalos, as Aron, plays a strong second to the soloist, James Dean ... who is the biggest news Hollywood has made in 1955."

This comment was a tribute to the direction of Kazan. One of the most difficult problems to solve in direction, either in the theatre or in films, is the coordination or integration of acting styles. In this aspect of direction Kazan was supremely effective. I found him equally so in stage direction when I acted in *J.B.* some four years later in New York.

*East of Eden* was both an artistic and a box-office success although

378

*R.M. and Julie Harris in the movie East of Eden, Hollywood, 1957.*

*James Dean and R.M. in East of Eden.*

the movie had many detractors in the press and among the public. It has gained in popularity since it was first released, largely due to TV showings. Being shot for the wide screen there are many scenes which show only the noses of actors at the side but that doesn't seem to matter. The picture has now reached the stature of a classic. It is a fitting memorial to Jimmy Dean, whose career ended so tragically in the wreckage of his new sports car just about a year later.

# 49

The last play I acted in on Broadway was *J.B.*, the poet Archibald MacLeish's retelling of the story of Job. Alfred de Liagre's production, directed by Elia Kazan, opened at the ANTA Theatre on December 11, 1958. In 196 performances I played the part of Mr. Zuss, the old actor who represents God. I had to leave on June 12, 1959, to fulfil a movie commitment, and Basil Rathbone took over.

Over the years my memories of this play have not faded. Its glamour, its passion, its thunder, above all the beauty of its verse, are still with me. It was a rich experience to play Mr. Zuss to the brilliant, diabolic Nickles of Christopher Plummer. The intricate, discerning direction of Gadge Kazan is beyond forgetting. And I remember, too, how the power of the awesome story defied the simplification of the author's resolution. I think everybody who saw *J.B.* wrote in their hearts and minds their own ending. Perhaps there is no ending to the story of Job.

I first learned of the play in England, where I was rehearsing in the TV production of *The Hanging Judge*. Dorothy and I read about it in a *New York Times* review by Brooks Atkinson. He described a Yale Drama School production of the published version, and there were no bounds to his enthusiasm. I knew I wanted a part in it and I asked for it. I soon tracked down Alfred de Liagre, who had acquired the performance rights. Delly was an old friend. With the approval of Gadge Kazan I was cast as Mr. Zuss.

Gadge was described by Kenneth Tynan as "the best man alive to direct plays that rumble with passion, blaze with violence and flower in a climate of frenzy." *J.B.* was certainly such a play.

An article published in the May 1959 issue of *Esquire* records the changes the text underwent in rehearsal and the development of Gadge's ideas about it. "The Staging of a Play," consisting of an exchange of letters between Kazan and MacLeish, gives a fascinating account of what was in the minds of author and director.

In his view of the conflict between Mr. Zuss and Nickles—or between God and the Devil–Kazan recalled my conflict with Jimmy Dean in *East of Eden*. "This old actor," he says of Mr. Zuss, "rather than be on TV and be made a fool of, prefers to cover his face and sell balloons."

He says clearly what he wants from me in the part.

"Ray Massey must have a very, very strong characterization and go the whole hog. But–though it is beneath his dignity to play or argue with this third-rate Jimmy Dean–meaning Nickles–he, as much as Nickles, wants to play this play and affect its outcome."

Pat Hingle was to play the latter-day Job, J.B., a prosperous businessman happy with his family. But God afflicts him with a series of cruel disasters–the loss of his children, his wealth and health, and the desertion of his wife. Not the least of his afflictions are the "comforters" who pester him with advice–preacher, psychoanalyst and communist.

Gadge showed us Boris Aronson's original drawing of the set.

"Will I be treed up in that pulpit all the time, Gadge?" I asked.

"I'm afraid so. The devil has much clearer access to man than God. At least, in this play he has."

In the two months following this meeting, I underwent surgery in Boston, grew a beard and enjoyed more than two weeks' rest at Honey Hill.

The new script arrived about the end of August.

The first call for the cast came late in October. We were a big company, twenty-one in all, and I knew only about half of the players. Several were members of the Actors Studio. Nan Martin as Sarah, J.B.'s wife, was a strikingly handsome girl, making her third Broadway appearance. And there were Ford Rainey, Clifton James, James Olsen and several others I had worked with before.

Gadge began by expounding his views on verse. He considered it important to the play, so important that he had invited the author to read it to us.

"I've never done this before," he said. "In fact, at one time I used to tell authors to attend rehearsals at fixed intervals, well-spaced fixed intervals. But now I've asked Archie to read his play to you. I want you to feel, as I believe you will as you listen to him, that this verse of his is not a burden. It is an asset. Not only will the audience enjoy the language but you actors will find it a pleasure to work with, a help and a support.

"Good poetry is not an affectation. It is a necessity–the only way the author can say clearly and directly what he wants to say. I say a necessity because one feels the author is being forced to find a way to say things that are ordinarily so difficult to say that they remain inarticulated.

"This play is not a thesis play. It doesn't prove a point about God or Man. What it does is illuminate an inner experience of living today."

Archie MacLeish read his play simply and eloquently, as if to reassure suspicious players that they were not being initiated into some mysterious cult.

From the start Gadge had the acting of J.B. under his benevolent control. He paid meticulous attention to individual performances. The Jimmy Dean concept of Nickles fascinated him, and Chris rewarded him with a snarling and dazzling Satan. I think Mr. Zuss bored Gadge slightly. I would pester him for suggestions to improve my performance, and he would answer, "You're doing everything I have asked you to do and more. Don't worry."

This individual attention did not preclude Gadge's orchestration of the whole production. He devoted at least half of every day to runthroughs of sections and scenes and entire acts. This allowed him to set a tempo and tone early in rehearsals.

Gadge's concern was less with performance than with the script. There were a great many alterations, cuts, restorations and new bits during the first three weeks of rehearsal.

We opened in Washington to a mixed press—a phrase George Kaufman used to translate as "good and rotten." Everybody thought we were in trouble. We were terribly depressed.

Gadge later recalled his own experiences in Washington. He felt we had lost our audience in act 2: "On Wednesday morning I woke up early and I knew at last where the trouble was. We had left out Aristotle's 'recognition scene.' The very turning point in the history of our protagonist had been undramatized."

He put the difficulty to Archie.

"It took him that day and the next morning to write it. But then we had it."

We finally opened at the ANTA Theatre in New York on December 11. The play seemed to be airborne from the opening lines which Chris and I had at the back of the orchestra seats. Looking back on that first night of *J.B.* I cannot help thinking of the Broadway opening of *Abe Lincoln in Illinois* and that miraculous audience we played to in 1938. Both plays had trouble on their try-outs in Washington (at least as Abe I had trouble) and both companies had faced their New York

openings with apprehension. Both had been welcomed to Broadway with overwhelming enthusiasm and both plays won the Pulitzer Prize.

Unanimous and exultant reviews from the eight daily critics were not seen by the public. A newspaper strike had begun the day before the opening. Word of mouth again proved to be the best promotion. Despite the strike, those beautiful lines began to form next morning at the box office. By noon we knew we were a smash hit. All of us went to work to spread the good word—Chris, Pat, Gadge and myself went on all the TV and radio talk shows and read the critical panegyrics "with feeling." I doubt if they made much difference but they were fun to read.

Brooks Atkinson, who had discovered the play in New Haven, was steadfast in his admiration. The tributes from other critics were no less enthusiastic. But there was less agreement about the meaning of Archie MacLeish's play.

John McLain in the *Journal-American*: "But the human maintains his faith, even repelling the 'comforters' who bring him balm. He will not settle for pragmatism, philosophy or cant. Even his soul is adamant."

Dick Watts in the *Post*: "Mr. MacLeish is clearly on the side of God, but the Devil makes an extremely convincing case. The fact is that no doubt due to something perverse in human nature, the theatre can dramatize the sadness, bitterness and desperation of mankind far more tellingly than it can explain the inscrutability of providence, and J.B. cannot escape it."

Frank Aston in the *World-Telegram*: "Mr. MacLeish takes his man to the very depths of despair, then raises him to renewed hope with the understanding that 'your sin is being born a man' and that 'the end is the acceptance of the end.'" (I have no idea what Mr. Aston meant by this.)

John Chapman in the *Daily News* brought God into the resolution: "God triumphs over evil as J.B. is restored, in mind and body, by love—not by theoretical or theological love, but by the present love he feels when he sees his wife walking toward him once again."

Brooks Atkinson in the *Times*: "The glory of Mr. MacLeish's play is that, as in the book of Job, J.B. does not curse God. When he is

*Christopher Plummer as Nickles and R.M. as Mr. Zuss in Archibald MacLeish's play J.B., at the ANTA Theatre, New York, 1958-59.*

385

reunited with his wife, two humbled but valiant people accept the universe, agree to begin that life all over again, expecting no justice but unswerving in their devotion to God.''

But Walter Kerr in the *Herald Tribune* had a different impression of the resolution: ''In the end, after every effort to find the meaning to so much pain has failed, Job gets to his feet, flexes his good right arm, and concludes 'we are'–and that is all our answer. We are–and what we are can suffer.''

Again, as in *Our Town*, I found it difficult to maintain, in the nearly two hundred performances, that sense of detachment and objectivity which I believe to be basic to the actor's art. I do not mean that I had a tendency to identify myself with my part. In the role of God, that would have been presumptuous. As a man, and a man of religious feeling, I was inwardly in conflict with the humanism which seemed to be the ''resolution.'' To me the theme was too immense and awesome to permit such simplification. It always seemed inappropriately cosy.

We had passed our hundredth performance when an accident nearly killed Pat Hingle. On the morning of February 20, in a fall of over thirty feet down the elevator shaft of his apartment building, Pat was seriously injured. Ford Rainey stepped into the role.

It was three days before Chris and I were allowed to see Pat, and then only for a few minutes. He never rejoined the company, although in time he made a full recovery.

Three weeks later James Daly took over the role of J.B. and played it for the remainder of the Broadway run of 364 performances.

After my last performance Dorothy and Chris threw a riotous party in a rehearsal room under the stage. It was a family affair–just the cast, crew, box-office people and Andy, the stage doorman.

One guest who did not belong to *J.B.* was present, being entitled to inclusion in any stage gathering of any nature, any time, anywhere, just because she was Radie Harris. A columnist who loves theatre, she has been the loyal friend of all of us, including Dorothy and me. Cedric Hardwicke was the only other ''outsider.''

The proceedings were boisterous. The main event was the removal of my beard, with the entire company participating. I had not foreseen what preparations ''Belial'' Plummer would devise for me. I was sheared ceremoniously while strapped into a barber's chair. Irving Pasternak, the master prop man, produced scissors, and a queue was formed so that everybody could have a snip. Cast and crew came to some forty souls; on the principle of one soul, one snip, the risk of losing considerable areas of my epidermis increased as the beard disappeared. With only four more snips to go, Nan Martin approached, scissors poised, but at the last moment she gave them to Andy and kissed me. Andy made to follow Nan's example.

"No, Andy. I prefer you to use the scissors!"

Chris read an unprintable and unsolemn requiem in verse on my Mr. Zuss in a devastating parody of my mannerisms. This convulsed the assembly, including me, and also set me about eliminating some of my quirks.

The saddest yet happiest incident of the evening was the brief appearance of Pat Hingle in a wheelchair. It was his first time out of his home and he looked very weak. Most of us had seen him in the hospital and at home. We knew the chances of his complete recovery were good. Now Pat was able to tell us the doctors had at last assured him that he would be fit by the end of the year. Indeed he was, and today he is one of our most able actors.

I arrived in Hollywood looking like a German student covered with duelling scars.

# 50

In the early fall of 1959 we moved to a house in Beverly Hills, California. It had a swimming pool, a lemon tree and a magnolia tree in the back; and in front there were palm trees and, unlike our Wilton house, a sidewalk. We looked native in a conventional Beverly Hills way, but only on the outside. When Dorothy had finished with the move, installing books and our antique English furniture, the inside had become that lovely kind of home she had always made for us back East.

The television work, one reason for our move, soon started.

Nearly all dramatic shows which had been produced in New York had either closed down or moved to the Coast. Jobs were plentiful. My homesickness for the theatre, though, could not at that time be satisfied in Los Angeles. There was plenty of the experimental, off-Broadway kind of theatre, but the big legitimate houses played only the national roadshows. There was almost no stage production at a Broadway level.

I wanted to act with my children Dan and Anna, for I had been much impressed with their work. But my hopes of acting on the stage with either of them were never fulfilled. I did act in a picture called *The Queen's Guards* in which Dan had played my son. Daniel had made his film debut at the age of six with his godfather, Noel Coward, in a movie called *In Which We Serve*. In 1968 he was one of the nominees for the Oscar supporting actor award for his performance of Noel Coward in the movie *Star*. Noel was delighted by Dan's interpretation of his godparent, a rare occurrence when an actor plays the part of a living person.

Geoffrey, my elder son, is now a prominent architect in Vancouver, British Columbia. He and his wife, Ruth, have given me three stalwart grandsons—Raymond, Vincent and Nathaniel—and a lovely granddaughter, Eliza Ann.

In mid-fall of 1959 I did a dramatic show in the Alfred Hitchcock series at Universal. It was called "Roadhog." I don't remember

*Dorothy.*

much about it except for the acting of the young man who played my son. I thought him remarkable. His name was Richard Chamberlain. He had just left the army after a two-year stretch in Korea and did not have much acting experience, yet he was the first young player I had seen in a long time with good diction and capable of realistic acting.

Television series in various forms was the principal mode of broadcasting at this time. I had mixed feelings about doing a series even if an acceptable offer were made. I was aware of the exposure which such work gave an actor. Many times the total number of people who had seen me in all the stage plays I had ever done would watch me in any single episode of a TV series. Yet at sixty-five I was less impressed by that fact than I should have been. I was still gun-shy of long-term agreements. I had not forgotten the Warner contract. I knew the servitude a series inflicted on its principals. Even a long run in the theatre could become boring.

Still, by the following January I had committed myself. At a meeting with Norman Felton, the TV producer, I agreed verbally to play the role of Dr. Gillespie in a television series entitled "Dr. Kildare," based on the MGM movies, the title part to be acted by that almost unknown young man, Richard Chamberlain.

One factor in my decision was the motive Norman Felton expressed for producing the "Dr. Kildare" series. Norman is a forthright, intelligent and articulate man. Even more, he is a man of ideals and ideas. Believing that medicine is an honourable profession, he thought he could express that belief by producing a series dealing with the daily round of a great general hospital: its staff, its patients, its practice of modern medicine and surgery. The two principals were to be the Chief Medical Officer of Blair General Hospital, Dr. Gillespie, and a young intern, Dr. Kildare.

The names of the doctors were all Norman was taking from the MGM movies. His concept of Gillespie and Kildare would have nothing to do with their namesakes in films. His notion of the elder doctor was somewhere between the impersonal specialist and the old-fashioned family doctor. Gillespie was to be in line with the old-time consultant – highly trained and modern in method but with a heart as well as a mind.

The younger doctor was not to be a precocious genius, nor was he to be obsequious to his superior. The relationship between the two could be summed up as one of mutual respect, both personal and professional.

When Felton announced that he was going to give the role of the young intern to Richard Chamberlain, I was delighted. I told him about the Hitchcock show "Roadhog." Felton had seen it and admired Chamberlain's performance. MGM had also spotted his talent; he had been signed by the studio at once on a seven-year contract to do almost anything. Felton's decision to use Richard in the series had saved him from any Hollywood fate like mine.

Felton agreed that my age entitled me to a clause stipulating a six o'clock quitting time. Alas, it did not specify a starting time. That turned out to be when the first bird woke up.

I knew almost nothing about the legal problems involved in bringing "Dr. Kildare" to the airwaves. Three parties were interested—Norman Felton's Arena Productions, which owned the property; MGM, which had originally produced the Kildare movies; and NBC, the network which was to broadcast the series.

After more than four months of bargaining, production of the series started in June 1960. I signed no contract. When we wound up operations after five years and when the residuals had all been paid a few years later, I still had signed no formal contract. The integrity of Norman Felton had been enough.

The series was to be filmed, not live. Before we started shooting, Norman gave Richard and me copies of *The Book of Health*, a large medical encyclopedia by two doctors, Randolph Clark and Russell Cumley, both of the University of Texas. It was an informative compromise between the chatty journalistic medical columns and the straight textbooks. Norman thought the information we gleaned would make us sound more professional. He was probably right, but that was not the only effect it had.

Richard and I pored over the book, each of us acquiring a considerable amount of medical information. By nature an earnest hypochondriac, I diagnosed myself as an incipient victim of most of the diseases as they came to Blair General Hospital. Greeting the new guest star of the week I sometimes felt like saying: Let's go to my office and compare symptoms. I'm sure I've got it much worse than you.

One disorder I had diagnosed in myself in our first season was a myasthenia gravis, a dread ailment characterized by progressive muscular weakness. The patient was supposed to be a resident in the hospital and the dialogue was thick with medical jargon. After we had rehearsed the diagnosis scene, the director, Elliot Silverstein, said, "I'm going to get David Victor to look at this. I can't tell which of you has the disease."

391

Richard pulled me aside. "I've read further in the book than you have. Listen, you can't get myasthenia gravis, you're too old!"

The show attracted the best in writing, directing and guest stars. One of the rewards of being a running character on "Dr. Kildare" was that every eight days I would be co-host with Richard to one or more guest stars. In that way we acted with about two hundred of the best-known players of the day.

The routine of series television was more burdensome in the early sixties than it is today. We did thirty-nine shows each season as compared with the twenty-six or thirteen required of most current dramatic series. The average accomplished in a ten-hour day would be not less than ten pages. That's quite a lot to memorize each day.

My routine was to get up at 5:30, an hour's walk at 6:00 with my script and Bunga. Breakfast at 7:00 and a half-hour's drive to MGM in Culver City. In make-up at 7:45 and dressed at 8:30.

Bunga was now seventy years old in dog years and comparatively older than I. By the second year of the series he was completely urbanized, his boisterous country behaviour abandoned and a decorous leash-tolerated manner adopted in its place. Like me, he already suffered from the warning twinges of the arthritic ailments which would eventually fell both of us; but in 1961 these were not yet severe. The geriatric disorders of dogs are very similar to the human indignities of aging.

Bunga liked his life in Beverly Hills. The area he had to patrol was much smaller than the fifty acres he supervised in the East. There were now very few invaders and predators to deal with–just a few squirrels and two cowardly cats compared with the hordes of hedgehogs, rabbits, foxes and other wild fauna which had made Honey Hill a dog's paradise. The series-induced weariness which descended on Dorothy and me had not extended to Bunga. Early-morning walks with me and a script were nice and regular. He knew where his boss was and I didn't disappear for months as I had done at Honey Hill. In winter these walks took place in darkness and I would have an electric torch to read by. Sometimes I read out loud but never that yelling of "Blow, winds, and crack your cheeks!" to which I had given vent at Honey Hill. Bunga and I knew every street and alley in Beverly Hills.

It is almost inevitable in any series that the plays will become a little soapy. I have to emphasize that this is in no way a disparagement. In my book, "soapy" means melodramatic. Melodrama is like fancy icing on a realistic cake, as Al Woods once told me.

During the last season of filming "Dr. Kildare" Bunga aged alarmingly. He was now nearly fifteen years old – a canine centenarian – and his arthritis had progressed until his hind legs were almost useless. At the magic word "walk" he would bang his tail on the floor but he could no longer come with me. We had to carry him out to the garden where he would lie by the hour in the sun, his only remaining pleasure. He also suffered from severe kidney trouble. Like the gentleman he was, he would struggle to go outside without help but it was impossible. Dr. Sheldon Rosenfeld had given Bunga as much relief as possible but he had to admit that the old dog was in constant pain. In addition to his private practice, Dr. Rosenfeld was in charge of keeping alive the experimental animals at Cedars-Sinai Medical Center. He is one of the kindest men I ever knew.

Finally Dorothy and I made the decision which all dog lovers dread. One Saturday morning when I didn't have to go to the studio, Dr. Rosenfeld was to call and give him rest. Bunga lay on some blankets near the door of the living-room. A bowl of small biscuits lay on the table. He hadn't done his favourite trick for weeks but I thought I would let him try it once more – the trick Greg Peck couldn't do, nor anyone else. Bunga looked interested as I put the biscuit on the tip of his nose. For a moment he balanced the biscuit and I snapped my fingers. Then he shook his head and the biscuit dropped off. Bunga didn't look at it. He just rolled over, licked my hand and closed his eyes. He was awfully tired.

The doorbell rang. It was Dr. Rosenfeld.

Bunga is not forgotten. His name is the licence plate of my car, and his picture is on a table by our bed.


After the first season of "Kildare," foreign releases had been sold, and when letters started coming in from all over the world – from palaces and slums, from apartments, farmhouses, cabins and hotels – that warm, personal touch of the theatre almost seemed to be with us.

It was a pleasure to be greeted by a London bus conductor with, "And 'ow is Dr. Gillespie this rainy mornin'?" The doorman at our hotel in New York said, "I had a stretch in a hospital up in the Bronx last year. . . . It wasn't Blair General but I saw you and Dr. Kildare on TV twice while I was there. It was kinda nice to know you were both around."

The series was a great venture and I am grateful to Norman Felton and proud that I was part of it. I did my best to keep Gillespie close to

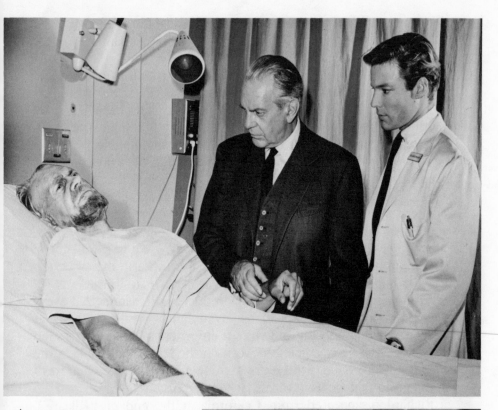

▲ *A vaguely familiar patient gets Dr. Gillespie's attention. I don't know how they managed these double-exposure shots. The patient seemed healthy enough to me.*

*One of our five "Kildare" birthdays. Richard, Dorothy and R.M.* ▶

◀ *R.M. as Dr. Gillespie and Richard Chamberlain as Dr. Kildare in the television series "Dr. Kildare." MGM Studios, Culver City, 1960-66.*

the character I had played the first two seasons. But in the last years he sometimes appeared in the scripts as a rather petulant copy of his former self. Maybe I was just getting older.

In the end the feeling of servitude, of being cut off from the stage, became severe. As the series crawled to a close this weariness alarmed me. It was the first time in my life I had been bored by anything to do with work. I fought to hide it and I think I succeeded. For an actor to display lassitude on the set is contemptible.

Working with Richard through the long pull of production had been pleasant, completely without the petty frictions that sometimes come from working closely for a long time with another player.

There was a speculation on the lot about Richard's plans after we shut down. One forecast seemed to voice the general impression, "Why, Dick will do another series right away. He'd be a fool not to cash in on 'Kildare' while he's as hot as a firecracker!" I knew better. Richard had a determination as strong as my own at his age.

All through our fifty months of production Richard seized every opportunity–evenings, weekends, even lunch breaks–to work at singing, dancing, fencing and voice training. He told me that as soon as he was free he was going to work on the stage, if possible in the classical field. I believe this extra training did a lot to keep him fresh in the grind that we went through. I envied his energy.

Richard disappeared from California at the end of "Kildare." When I heard from him six months later he had just played Hamlet with the Birmingham Repertory Theatre Company. I believe he was the first American player to have been given the role on the English stage since John Barrymore's performance at the Haymarket in 1925. It took great courage for Richard to tackle Hamlet in England on the famous Birmingham Rep stage. The hours and hours of hard training during the series paid off and Richard scored an unqualified success with his first essay at the Dane. Dorothy and I saw his TV perform- ance in the role shortly afterwards, produced by our mutual friend George Le Maire. It was superb.

Not long ago Richard took Dorothy and me to lunch at the Polo Lounge in Beverly Hills. He makes movies and TV specials all over the world and acts in so many plays in England, New York and Cali- fornia that we do not see him as often as we would like. Inevitably the series crops up in our conversation.

"Did you ever get bored with the series, Richard?"

"Are you kidding? Didn't you?"

396

# 51

After the "Dr. Kildare" series closed production I was able to enjoy a certain amount of sloth–indeed a whole lot of sloth, if travel and my debased form of golf can be so described. My mobility was now restricted by arthritis and I had to use a cane. My golf consisted of a wide variety of chip shots, for I was unable to take a full swing. But Dorothy and I were still as keen as ever, and at last I was almost as straight as she was and sometimes chipped as long a ball.

Television guest spots came sporadically and usually with a cheery, "You can sit down most of the time, Ray," or "The old fellow that you will have to play is old enough to need two canes..."

During these years I did several movies without much difficulty, the parts having little physical action. But the last one in 1968 was a "super-colossal Western" called *Mackenna's Gold*. It had one of those all-star casts headed by Greg Peck. The theme was strikingly original, that "nothin' good could come out of that thar gold." I was supposed to ride in this one, and without trying to see if I could get on a horse (I had not ridden for at least ten years), I told Carl Foreman, the producer, that I could. On location in Kanab, Utah, I found I could not even mount a horse. I had to suffer the humiliation of being lifted onto the saddle. As I was unable to spread my legs sufficiently to straddle the horse, I had to make a compromise in the manner of a woman's old-time side saddle with my right knee up against the horn. I could only be photographed from the near side. The director thought this would be okay, and that's the way we worked for six days. It was not exactly a comfortable time.

In the next six months I had two x-ray examinations–one in Los Angeles and one in Germany–which disclosed a degenerative arthritic condition (how reassuring medical nomenclature can be!) in the right hip and an inflammatory state in the left leg. Both doctors made the same ominous prognosis–I would get worse steadily; but neither would make a guess on the probable progress of degeneration. One suggested surgery and one demurred with vigour. I agreed with the latter, as did Dorothy, and found myself a second cane.

*The movie Mackenna's Gold on location at Kanab, Utah, 1968. My last shot in my last movie.*

*Across the mountains in Las Vegas we celebrate. Left to right: Burgess Meredith, Dorothy, Mrs. Meredith and R.M.*

My recent experiences before the movie and television cameras had not been inspiring for me. I hankered after the theatre. The stage had been my first love and I longed to act just once more in a theatre. It had been ten years since I set foot on a Broadway stage and thirty-two years since my last London play in 1938. Love affairs don't often survive an interruption as long as that. The theatre is a notoriously capricious lady and the return of an elderly suitor might well be greeted with an icy stare. Discretion told me to forget the theatre dreams and come back to reality. But on a morning early in February 1970 it was lucky for me that I was sitting down at my desk when Dorothy entered with a cable in her hand.

"Brace yourself, Mr. M. Someone called Marvin Liebman wants you to play the father in Robert Anderson's *I Never Sang for My Father* in London. That, in case you don't know, is a very good play. I read some of the Broadway notices when they did it last season."

She handed me the cable which was from my London agent. My hands were shaking so I could hardly read it.

"I can't believe it. I suppose they don't know about my being lame."

"Rubbish! The part they want you for is the father. He's supposed to be eighty. You'd have to learn to limp if you didn't know how to already."

I got two copies of the play from French's and we read it by mid-afternoon. We both thought it was first-rate, and I knew it was a honey of an acting part.

The play posed two questions. What do adult children owe their parents? How much of their own lives must they sacrifice?

The play dealt with old age, that subject most people would like to ignore – the aged and how they feel about it, the younger generation and their responsibility for the older.

My role of Tom Garrison, the father, was that of a self-made and self-absorbed businessman. His whole life has been conditioned and embittered by the hard time he had as a boy and by his hatred of his own father. He is an anecdotal bore, a tyrant, mean and arrogant, approaching senility and ever anxious to relate the poor-boy-makes-good story of his life. In spite of this repellent but accurate description of Tom Garrison, I knew I could make the old man worth caring for. I loved to have to fight the prejudice of the audience for a fair judgement of the man I was playing. Randall of *Late Night Final* and Joe Cobb of *Spread Eagle* were roles like that.

400

The impetus of the play is the effect old Tom has on a middle-aged son who has only a distant respect for him, a daughter who is indifferent towards him, and a wife who stoically tolerates him. Conversely, we feel their effect on him.

Not a cheerful play perhaps, but a great acting chance for me. It struck me at once that the part of Gene Garrison, the son, would be perfect casting for Daniel, my own boy, which would mean that we would be together on the stage for the first time. It is a matter of continuing sadness to me that Dan felt that Gene in *I Never Sang for My Father* was not suited to him. Perhaps he was right but it would have been a lasting pleasure to me to have acted on the stage with my son.

Within a week I had everything I wanted in my contract, with an opening date of April 24 for a try-out in Brighton and a London opening date which allowed for a week of previews.

We arrived at the Dorchester Hotel on a dismal rainy day in mid-March, having barely survived the ordeal of passing through that hell-hole of porterless confusion known as Heathrow. Nobody ever tries to meet anybody at Heathrow. It would be a Stanley and Livingston chance at best so the arriving party is left to his own devices to get through. Possibly prayed for but no more. Marvin Liebman met us at the hotel and we had what was for me a badly needed drink. My spirits were subdued when I learned from Marvin that as of this date he had no London theatre. Any experienced manager knows that securing a West End theatre should be his prime consideration. But Marvin and his associates had reversed the order and done everything but get a London theatre.

Marvin had no experience as a producer. He had formerly been in the advertising business in New York. He was an agreeable fellow and it was a pity that he had to be in this predicament, for the theatre can always do with eager managers with production money.

So we started rehearsals a few days later in a rehearsal hall. I intensely dislike such places with the inevitable upright piano, a ballet rail on the inside wall, an empty half-acre of bare polished hardwood flooring. But there was no chance of getting on a stage when you haven't even a nodding acquaintance with a theatre. The company seemed good to me. George Baker was a particularly happy choice for Gene Garrison, the son, a key part, and Catherine Lacey in the mother's role was perfect casting. George Baker I knew by reputation as a director and a manager as well as an actor, and Catherine Lacey went back to my London days with a long record of beautiful performances. I didn't know the rest of the cast but they all read their American parts very well.

My first reading was, as it always has been, unsatisfactory to me, but I still believed I could get at the understandable and rather pathetic human being who was hidden in the ogre I was playing. It might take a deal of finding but it was there.

Vivian Matalon, the director, showed us a model of the setting in which we would do the play. Structurally the model seemed to be a clever arrangement of revolving panels which could be rapidly adjusted to suggest the scenes indicated in the script. Unfortunately the decor in the model, I thought, reflected various dismal aspects of Heathrow Airport rather than the comfortable middle-class atmosphere of the Garrison home. I couldn't really tell from the model what the scenery would convey on a stage, and anyway, there was nothing I could do about it.

I wasn't directing this one, for which I was thankful. In his stage directions the author had indicated a blending of realism and abstraction. For instance, in most of the scenes he implied the use of properties, a loaded luggage truck at the railroad station, table fittings in a restaurant, various hand props all through the play. In the mortuary scene, on the other hand, the half-dozen caskets from which Tom Garrison was to make his choice for his deceased wife were imaginary. But both the coffins and the mentality of old Tom seemed to be on display as the scene unfolded and the consistency of the production seemed undisturbed.

As we neared our opening date of the Brighton try-out there was still no sign of a London theatre for us. But when the author arrived on a cloud to straighten out some rehearsal kinks it was a joy to receive his encouragement and his appreciation of what I was trying for. On the last day of London rehearsals Bob Anderson said he thought I was "extricating" the long-forgotten phases of gentleness which Tom Garrison must have had, which he, the author, intended him to have.

To those of us who knew the theatre the Brighton opening seemed more like a wake than a first night. Mickey and Frankie Powell came down from London "to hear you roar like a lion again," as Mickey put it. The lack of a London theatre, now that our West End opening was only three weeks away, was desperate. Peter Fox, the company manager, said that Marvin Liebman had no prospects of a theatre and had made no arrangements for an extension of the try-out. This meant that, at best, we would have to fold up the play for at least a fortnight, or, at worst, Marvin might call it quits and the notice would go up for Saturday night. Both of these dire possibilities would cost him heavily but that was the outlook. I was pretty sure he would make a good fight for it, but long ago I had experienced two provincial closings for lack of a London theatre and the thought of burying a live production was horrible.

"Muff" Brackett, our dearest friend in California and the widow of Charles Brackett, the movie producer, had flown over to see *I Never Sang* because, as she said, "I want to see Ray really angry again." I had two rousing scenes with my middle-aged son in the play and Dorothy had told Muff about it.

The three of us were in Brighton at a little east-end hotel. It was Sunday and raining torrents and blowing a gale; and when it does that in Brighton, it doesn't mess around. I had a dress rehearsal that night. It would be the only one as the previous dress rehearsal had been cancelled in favour of a long technical run-through. Dorothy, as usual, refused to come to the dress rehearsal or let Muff come.

"It's not fair to you to have anybody there tonight. It'll be tough enough to get through without having us on your mind."

She was right. It was a ghastly rehearsal, with almost everything in the way of scenery and lighting going wrong. Everyone was depressed except Marvin who confided to me that he had two leads to London theatres which he was following. Robert Anderson was very down in the mouth. And a rather dismal time was had by all.

The opening performance itself was a complete reversal. Everything went perfectly. The scene changes were as smooth as silk, the lighting was fine and individual performances were first-rate. For the first time I got old Tom Garrison into high gear to my satisfaction, and without softening the old bastard in any way I managed to get moments of gentleness and decency to come through. Bob Anderson was in much better spirits after the play. Dorothy and Muff were delighted. I don't know whether it was our performance or being thawed out in a warm theatre that had put both the ladies in such convivial spirits at supper. I suspect the thermal process was the governing factor.

The audience responded well for a try-out and the local press was good for play and players.

The rain stopped the next day but it was still blowing and cold as Greenland's icy mountains. We didn't rehearse and I took Muff and

Dorothy to see the Brighton pavilion. The Prince Regent's palace always reminds me of my Aunt Lillie's Moorish room in Toronto except that the pavilion is larger and very much draftier. Muff and Dorothy seemed to ignore the icy blasts which ripped through the arches and delicate columns of the Prince's folly; but after an extensive tour of the assembly room and kitchens I caught a man-sized chill. After a week of sneezing and coughing, during which I played old Tom Garrison, it settled into a cursed pneumonitis which was still with me when I reached home three months later. It was *John Brown's Body* all over again.

The Brighton week ended with our London fate still undecided. We began a period of waiting, the company resembling a big airplane circling an airport and waiting for permission to land. Only in our case we also waited to know where to land. I spent the first week in bed at the Dorchester, and at the end of that time I felt almost human. The nights are the bad time for this virus. You sweat, with the lousy feeling that comes with a low-grade infection. Dear Muff didn't feel she could wait for an opening that might never happen, and she flew home.

About the end of the week Marvin Liebman rang me up with the joyful news that he had got the Duke of York's Theatre and we would have a week of paid previews before opening on May 27.

My doctor attacked the virus with some antibiotics which put me in pretty good shape for the opening night but I knew that they really hadn't quite done the trick.

I dislike previews and the first one showed that we had not benefitted by the two-week layoff. The audience seemed cold and apathetic, and I think our performance was limp, as were the subsequent previews.

Bob Anderson, unable to wait for the Duke of York opening, had gone home. The director, Vivian Matalon, after seeing one preview, decided to proceed with his planned holiday in Jamaica. So in our remaining preparatory performances, which were running uniformly flat, we were without the director's scrutiny. However, George Baker, who was experienced as a director and manager, gave us his unofficial and inestimable help during that dismal preview week.

After the first night, we received a charming letter from our vacationing director in which he told us of the pleasure of basking in the Caribbean sun and congratulated us on our success. It was the only time I ever knew a director to remove himself from his own opening.

The first-night performance, as in Brighton, reversed the torpid

*I Never Sang for My Father at the Duke of York's Theatre, London, 1970. My last stage appearance in England. Old Tom Garrison tries the revival of an old joke. Left to right: George Baker, Catherine Lacey, Valerie Colgan and R.M.*

pattern of rehearsals. The company came to life with the best perform-ance so far.

For me it was an emotional experience unlike anything I had ever encountered in the theatre. There was a personal feeling out front and on my part as well which was entirely outside of professional consideration. I think my acting at times was not as precise and defined as I would have had it. I dried up in the undertaker's scene, and the stage manager, against my previous instructions, threw me a prompt. But on the whole I believe I maintained the character of old Tom pretty well through an emotionally supercharged evening.

It was not only a performance but an actor's return to his base that those people out front were there to see. The reception at the final curtain was overwhelming to me. I was being welcomed home.

405

Because I shared his apprehension about my return to the London stage perhaps in even greater measure, I am going to quote from Felix Barker of the *Evening News*:

All too often we have seen the return, after lotus years in Hollywood, of the once-famous stage actor.

Now a film star and soft round the edges, he takes his expected applause without really earning it in a well-tailored undemanding role. For this reason, I was a bit apprehensive about the comeback of Raymond Massey. That gaunt, ravaged face, that steely voice and angular grace have haunted me from the time London last saw him in *Idiot's Delight* in 1938. Further back, I remember his ruthless editor in *Late Night Final* and the adulterous schoolmaster with burning eyes in *The Rats of Norway*. Would he have been spoiled by too much Dr. Gillespie-ing? The wonderful answer is not at all. At seventy-three, Mr. Massey is still a dynamo able to generate tremendous dramatic power. He can summon up sudden terrible rages, and make us share his moments of intense anguish....

The critics were wonderful to me. Their notices were sprinkled with phrases such as "in towering form," "roaring like a lion," "in complete command of the stage," making me, seldom a reticent actor, wonder if I hadn't gone just a little too far. Perhaps J. C. Trewin, writing in the *Illustrated London News*, pleased me most: "Thanks to Raymond Massey ... the father has a fine hearing; the man is maddening and touching." That is what I tried to do.

But the majority of the press was definitely hostile to Bob Anderson's play. When a performance is acclaimed and the play dismissed as a bore and worse, I have always been puzzled. I believe that it is unfair to an author to say that a performance of a certain character is excellent and then to destroy the play in which the performance is being given. The author, who has after all created the character, deserves some credit for the actor's success. The actor has only interpreted what the author has written.

This critical inconsistency was the occasion for the only ghostly manifestation in my experience, that is if ghosts recognize an "occasion."

In the critical acclaim which Bob Sherwood's play *Abe Lincoln in Illinois* received, the only dissenter was John Mason Brown of the *Post* who slammed the play on the grounds of its derivative nature although he praised the acting and production.

406

Nearly twenty-five years after *Abe* had been produced, John Mason Brown's biography of Robert Sherwood was published, a sympathetic, honest and fascinating story of Bob. Brown had been troubled by his own critical treatment of *Abe Lincoln in Illinois*. In this book he withdrew much of his adverse criticism, although he still contended there was some validity in his comments. It seemed as if he wished he hadn't made them. At this time, I must add, I had not read the Sherwood biography.

*I Never Sang for My Father* had been running for three or four weeks at the Duke of York's when after an evening performance I was talking to some people, a man and two women, who had come backstage to my dressing-room. I was standing facing my guests, having just prepared drinks for them, and I had a glass in my hand. My dresser had closed the door of the dressing-room after showing the guests in, remaining as usual in the corridor outside as the room was on the small side. The door was on my left. One of my guests, the man, was attacking the London critics who, he thought, had been unfair to Robert Anderson.

As he talked on I became conscious that someone was standing close to me on my left. I turned and there was a figure between me and the door. I knew the face at once and then, as so often happened to me all my life, I could not remember his name. Before I could stammer out my predicament he spoke. "*This* was an admirable play," he said. "I would have given *this* a good notice." In both sentences there was emphasis on the word "this." I turned back to my other guests with the intent of bluffing out some kind of introduction which would be difficult as I didn't know their names either. The man was still droning out his indictment of London critics, the ladies sitting in mute boredom. I realized to my horror that the man and his female companions were not aware of the fourth visitor's presence, and at the same moment I knew he was John Mason Brown. Brown had died the previous year. I turned back towards the apparition with the ultimate in banality, "Would you like a drink?" The vision disappeared. My proferred hospitality was refused by the lecturer who departed with his ladies forthwith. I think he gathered that I was not quite "with" them, tired perhaps!

When the dressing-room door was opened for the guests to leave, there was my dresser, Bob Webb, standing by. On casual interrogation he said that there had been no importunate autograph hunters or suchlike wandering backstage that night. I sent him home and took my make-up off in solitude. I secretly willed the friendly ghost to return but without success. This is a true account of a strange visitation, which even I do not believe.

I played *I Never Sang for My Father* for seven weeks to attentive, appreciative audiences. The play had failed to draw and the management had to quit, but London had given me the warmest of welcomes. It was grand to walk or limp the London boards again. As I left the theatre that night it was still before pub closing time. The patrons of the pub opposite the Duke of York's in St. Martin's Lane all came out on the pavement, mugs and glasses in hand, and drank my health. It was my farewell to the theatre, at least I thought it was.

# 52

By 1975 even golf had become a memory for me except when I watched the tournaments on TV. It is surprising how your game improves in retrospect after watching these miraculous young people play. Travel is out for the aged save in dire necessity. Nothing must interfere with geriatric routine. I am finally tied to home. Our joint families increase and flourish but we only see those who can come to us.

At last count, Dorothy has five grandchildren and two and a half great-grandchildren, while I have six grandchildren. They are all scattered about Canada, England, Massachusetts, California and New Hampshire. It's a lot of birthdays to remember. We feel guilty when we forget one, but we generally hover benignly in the genetic background.

*Left to right: Daniel, Geoffrey, R.M. and Anna on the only occasion all four have been in the same place at the same time. London, 1964.*

The theatre has always been reluctant to accept stage leave-takings at face value. They have the taint of the traditional "annual farewell." And anyway, in 1970 I had not really said good-bye out loud. When Robert Fryer beckoned me back to the stage with a suggestion that I play Nonno, the old poet, in his forthcoming production of Tennessee Williams' *The Night of the Iguana* at the Ahmanson Theatre in Los Angeles, I was surprised. I was seventy-nine years old and it had been five years since my 1970 London sort-of-farewell. I was much fitter physically than I had been then, but I was now a one-cane-in-public, two-canes-at-home arthritic victim. I was almost immobile, and so I demurred, as the lawyers say. Bob Fryer, calling from London where he was producing a movie, pointed out to my agent, Arthur Park, that Nonno in Tennessee Williams' play was ninety-three years old and that such an age should be well within my competence as an actor. I accepted the offer with the old excitement of another show.

I was to be co-starred with Richard Chamberlain, Dorothy McGuire and Eleanor Parker, and directed by Joseph Hardy.

Robert Fryer was managing director of the Ahmanson Theatre, the big drama house of the Centre Theatre Group, and he had made his annual four-production seasons a national theatre feature.

Theatres should reflect people. Most of the new theatre construction is concrete – cold and forbidding. The Ahmanson tries hard to be human and I think in the main it succeeds. But being a public building it comes under the security system used in all such property, at least in the Los Angeles area. The result is a gaggle of pistol-packing guards stalking around backstage, the man or woman at the stage-door being armed to the teeth. This constant surveillance was not only annoying but the guards and the stage-door custodian are changed every day. The result is the irksome routine of continued identification. The stage-door man has traditionally been a friendly sort of fellow in most Broadway and West End theatres, and that's not consistent with toting a gun. Several times friends of mine and other players were refused admission to the dressing-rooms, apparently at the whim of the guard. This rudeness certainly was not anything to do with Bob Fryer's department. His staff had no more need of the guards than the actors did.

Although seeing *A Streetcar Named Desire* on its try-out in Chicago in 1947 was one of the greatest experiences I ever had in the theatre, and *Cat on a Hot Tin Roof* and *Suddenly Last Summer* had fascinated me, I had never acted in a play by Tennessee Williams. Now I had

410

been given the chance to do so in a most intriguing role in one of his best plays.

I was delighted that I was going to act with my friend Richard Chamberlain again after an interval of ten years. Dorothy and I had seen Richard in most of his stage and film successes in the interval since "Kildare" and he had been in front at the opening of *I Never Sang for My Father* in London, but I had almost given up hope that we would ever be together on the stage. Now I was indeed in luck.

As in *A Streetcar Named Desire*, the theme of *Night of the Iguana* is loneliness. An inner sense of isolation, of separation, engulfs the principal characters of the play.

The Reverend T. Lawrence Shannon is a renegade defrocked clergyman, a neurotic lecher, an unstable weakling, who is about to desert his present post of conductor of a seedy bus tour in Mexico because his admitted seduction of a teenage member of the party has been uncovered. He seeks at least momentary asylum at the Costa Verde Hotel in Puerto Barrio on the west coast of Mexico. Shannon is the anti-hero of the new theatre. Only an actor of Richard's courage and talent could master this role.

The portrayal of Maxine Faulk, the amorous and lovely propri-etress of the Costa Verde, was in charge of Eleanor Parker. Maxine is an old friend of Shannon's and he is welcomed to whatever refuge he may require; but the arrival of the youthful seducee at the Costa Verde, and her avenging chaperone played by Allyn Ann McLerie, is a serious complication.

Shortly after this contretemps a strange pair arrive on the scene: Jonathan Coffin (Nonno), a 93-year-old poet, and his granddaughter and amanuensis, Hannah Jelkes. Nonno is in a wheelchair pushed by Hannah. He is one of the minor New England poets who flourished briefly in the nineteenth century. He has spent half of his life trav-elling the world eking out a living by readings of his poetry. The last twenty years Hannah has been in attendance, supplementing the "take" by selling her sketches.

Hannah is one of Tennessee Williams' most fascinating char-acters—the gentle hustler, wise-innocent, fragile but strong as Her-cules, tender but iron-willed. Dorothy McGuire played her with matchless understanding.

From day to day I watched the progress of Richard's performance of Shannon. It must have been a fearsome role to attack from scratch—to read this repellent, contemptible character in the raw and

411

try to figure out how to humanize him without in any way softening the hard and scruffy portrait the author had drawn. In a way Richard had an acting problem similar to mine when I played Tom Garrison in *I Never Sang for My Father*. Richard approached the job cautiously, it seemed to me, and there were some scenes which he never played all out until very near the previews. The result was an utterly brilliant interpretation of that mixed-up, complicated neurotic.

In rehearsals for *Iguana* I became increasingly conscious that some very fine acting was going on around me.

My role of old Nonno, although not a long one in the matter of study, proved to be most exacting physically. I was onstage through almost all of the play, my offstage periods being in a small cabin in which I was partially visible at times and during which I was constantly heard putting the finishing touches to the poem I had been working on for twenty years.

Nonno was supposed to be hard of hearing and many of my lines were purposely non-sequiturs and irrelevant. As I was a bit deaf myself the picking up of cues remained a problem during the run. The wheelchair in my first scene was, of course, indicated in the script and had nothing to do with my infirmity. But such a prop, when it is necessary as my audience might assume in my case, is liable to kill any comedy I had. So at the first preview I put in a visual resentment of the contrivance as I managed to leave it, and a joyful acceptance of its security when I was forced to return to it. Both of these resulting laughs remained throughout the run as hearty acknowledgement that the audience knew the prop was not for real.

Most of Nonno's scenes were played with Hannah, but the old fellow took a shine to Maxine. Eleanor Parker was quite approachable as Maxine, and the supper scene when she brought me the Manhattan with the two cherries was a delight to play, even though the script called for me to have a nap. One hazard I had to avoid was a too-sincere observance of Nonno's dozing-off moments which occurred frequently through the play. Sometimes in the second act when I was sitting in the dark in the cabin during two or three of Richard's big scenes, I had about twelve cues to remember. They were mostly lines of my poem which I was repeating, and had no connection with the dialogue outside. Nonno had no impulse to doze off at this time but sometimes I had. I couldn't hear the dialogue very clearly and I took the precaution of having a warning light operated from the prompt corner fixed up in my cabin. It wasn't much of a help really for it only told of a cue. I had a list of twelve cues and I ticked them off as they came. If I missed one, that was too bad. I never did but I could not afford to doze.

After sitting there in the dark, ticking off cues for nearly an hour with flashlight in my hand, the final moments of the play came swiftly.

Towards the end, after the scene with Shannon and Hannah with its revelation of mutual loneliness, Shannon goes to free an iguana which has been tied up in a bag awaiting its destined appearance on the table of the Costa Verde. Hannah sits back in her chair. Suddenly Nonno stumbles out from the cabin with a shout that he has finished his poem at last. He tells Hannah to get paper and pencil and take it down—"Quick, before I forget it." Nonno finds his chair and sits. There is a pause. He then recites his poem, six short verses. It is the dream of twenty years and it is finished. It is a beautiful poem.

> *How calmly does the orange branch*
> *Observe the sky begin to blanch*
> *Without a cry, without a prayer,*
> *With no betrayal of despair.*
>
> *Sometime while night obscures the tree*
> *The zenith of its life will be*
> *Gone past forever, and from thence*
> *A second history will commence.*
>
> *A chronicle no longer gold,*
> *A bargaining with mist and mould,*
> *And finally the broken stem*
> *The plummeting to earth; and then*
>
> *An intercourse not well designed*
> *For beings of a golden kind*
> *Whose native green must arch above*
> *The earth's obscene, corrupting love.*
>
> *And still the ripe fruit and the branch*
> *Observe the sky begin to blanch*
> *Without a cry, without a prayer,*
> *With no betrayal of despair.*
>
> *O Courage, could you not as well*
> *Select a second place to dwell.*
> *Not only in that golden tree*
> *But in the frightened heart of me?*

*Left to right: Eleanor Parker, Dorothy McGuire, R.M. and Richard Chamberlain in* The Night of the Iguana, *at the Ahmanson Theatre, Los Angeles, 1975-76.*

*Dorothy McGuire as Hannah Jelkes and R.M. as Nonno in* The Night of the ▶
*Iguana.*

"Have you got it?" Nonno asks.

"Yes."

"It is *finished*?"

"Yes."

"Oh! God! Finally finished?"

"Yes!"

"After waiting so long!... And it's good? It is *good*?"

"Sleep now, Grandfather. You've finished your loveliest poem."

Nonno sits quite motionless. Hannah watches him. Maxine appears round the corner of the veranda. "Shannon!" she calls. He rises from the shadows. "Shannon, let's go down and swim in that liquid moonlight.... I want you to stay with me."

Hannah strikes a match for her cigarette. Shannon turns to look at her. "I want to remember that face. I won't see it again, Miss Jelkes. I cut loose the iguana."

"Thank you. Thank you, Larry."

"Now another one of God's creatures is going down to swim in the liquid moonlight."

"Good-bye, Mr. Shannon." Maxine and Shannon have disappeared.

Hannah puts her shawl about Nonno.

"Oh, God, can't we stop now? Finally? Please let us. It's so quiet here, now."

At the same moment Nonno's hand, which has been extended, drops to his side and his head sags. He is not breathing. Hannah bends and presses her head to the crown of Nonno's as the curtain descends.

I will never forget the drama and pathos of that ending of *Night of the Iguana*. But I wish I could forget the disaster which fell on me at the second preview. On that evening every moment of the performance had been acted to perfection by a wonderful company and even the preview audience had responded well. I got to the end of the first verse of the poem, "With no betrayal of despair."

And then there was nothing. My mind was a vacuum. This wasn't a dry-up when a cue thrown could be caught, when you could gather your thoughts and find a line. This was a void, a blank, when the mind just does not function. There was nothing from the prompt corner. I had told the stage manager to do nothing unless I asked for a line, and God bless him, Bill O'Brien took me at my word. I was beyond help at that moment. It was the beginning of the run and Dorothy McGuire had no idea what the line was. She was such an angel. She just threw her arms around me and I can still hear her saying, "It's all right. It's all right, don't worry." Then suddenly I remembered the last verse and out I came with it:

*O Courage, could you not as well*
*Select a second place to dwell.*
*Not only in the golden tree*
*But in the frightened heart of me?*

We got the rag down. We took our five curtain calls. Richard looked over at me as the fifth fell. There was an agonized expression on his face. When the curtain rose again Richard stepped down to the setting line and held up his hand for silence.

"Ladies and gentlemen, I am very pleased to announce that for this performance of *Night of the Iguana* the author, Mr. Tennessee Williams, has been in front and I see him now in the wings. Please come on stage, Mr. Williams."

I stood there as straight as I could and I wondered what would happen. Mr. Williams was said to be tough on actors in defence of his plays. He certainly had reason to be tough on me that night. I had ruined that beautiful curtain scene of his play before his eyes.

Suddenly, as the last curtain descended on the last call, Mr. Williams threw his arms around me and said, "That's not a bad ending. Thank you for a beautiful performance." Stunned with horror, I murmured my apologies and hobbled to my dressing-room. Pretty soon Mr. Williams came in. I have seldom received such wonderful and genuine appreciation of my work. Mr. Williams is a very kind and compassionate man.

My doctor assured me that the frightening occurrence was not traceable to the migraine headaches which had plagued me many years before but had probably been due only to nervous strain. "Rest as much as possible," said he.

When I got home I faced it. I said to myself, "Massey, you old fool, 'nervous strain' is a euphemism for 'you've had it.' You are not singled out to be immune to the indignities of advanced years. In your line of work, incidents of this severity spell 'curtain' to your best efforts."

I knew I had reached a time when I no longer had the stamina to sustain eight performances a week in the theatre. Few laymen realize the concentration essential to keep any acting effort alive and seemingly spontaneous.

There was no recurrence of my blackout throughout the run. Dorothy McGuire took out some insurance anyway by writing out the whole poem in her notebook.

The revival was a success at the box office and audiences loved it. Three of the principals went East to do it in New York and I was grateful for the offer to repeat my part. But I said no. New York loved them, as had Los Angeles.

Oliver Wendell Holmes, Sr. once wrote: "The riders in a race do not stop when they reach the goal. There is a little finishing canter before coming to a standstill. There is time to hear the kind voices of friends and say to one's self, 'The work is done.'"

I had had my little finishing canter. I had the sense to know that my working years in the theatre were over.

*R.M. and Dorothy. The working years were over.*

# Index

# Index

## A

# B

# C

# D

Cornell, Katharine, 16, 17, 19, 96, 117, 156, 199, 263, 264, 265, 266, 267, 268, 269, 270, 277, 278, 279, 280, 281, 291, 292, 293, 294, 369

Cort Theatre, New York, 116, 119

Corwin, Norman, 363, 364, 365

Cosden, Joshua, 142

Cosden, Nell, 142, 146

*Counsellor-at-Law*, 231

*Country Wife, The*, 56, 57, 101

Courtneidge, Cicely, 137

Cowan, Jerome, 213, 214

Coward, Sir Noel, 73, 74, 75, 76, 77, 78, 79, 85, 119, 120, 121, 122, 123, 169, 170, 171, 172, 173, 180, 181, 186, 308, 316, 388

Craven, Frank, 296

Crawford, Joan, 315

Crews, Laura Hope, 171

Cromer, Lord (Second Earl of Cromer), 57, 98, 100, 101, 102, 104, 105, 224

Cromwell, John, 208, 248, 252, 253, 310

*Crooked Billet, The*, 66

Cumley, Russell, 391

Cunningham, Robert, 40

Curtiz, Michael, 259, 262

*Cynara*, 149

*Daily Express, The*, London, 77

*Daily Graphic*, New York, 131, 282

*Daily News*, New York, 230, 245, 385

Daly, James, 386

Daly's, 226

*Dancers, The*, 69

Daniell, Henry, 293

Dare, Zena, 73, 74

*Dark Is Light Enough, The*, 369

da Silva, Howard, 242

Davalos, Richard, 375, 378

Davies, Marion, 154

Davis, Donald, 196, 200, 205

Davis, Owen, 196, 200, 202, 205

Davises, the, 196, 197, 198, 199, 200, 202, 203

Dawson (chauffeur), 332

Dean, Basil, 72, 73, 74, 76, 77, 78, 79, 81

Dean, James, 375, 376, 377, 378, 379, 380, 382, 383

*Dear Brutus*, 179

Dearmer, Mabel, 31

*Dear Octopus*, 291

Decker, Albert, 375

de Liagre, Alfred, 381

Delysia, Alice, 107, 108, 109, 111

De Mille, Cecil B., 207

Denham, Reginald, 108

Derwent, Clarence, 265

*Desire under the Elms*, 49, 202

Diaghilev's ballet company, 224

Dickens, Charles, 353

di Frasso, Countess, 155, 156

Digges, Dudley, 277

Disney, Walt, 191, 250

Doble, Frances, 73, 78

Dobson, Frank, 89

*Doctor's Dilemma, The*, 263, 264, 265, 266, 268, 270

# E

# F

# G

# H

# I

# J

# K

# L

# Mc

# M

# N

Moorehead, Agnes, 353, 364
Morgan, Charles, 26, 111, 175, 228, 346
Morgan, Sidney, 85
Morosco Theatre, New York, 149, 320
Morris, Mary, 320
Mortimer, Charles, 131
Morton, Charlton, 181
*Mourning Becomes Electra*, 49
*Movie-of-You*, 119, 121, 122
Mower, Penfield, 328
*Mozart*, 117
*Mr. Pepys*, 47, 48, 49, 56, 85
Mullins, Bartlett, 345
Municipal Auditorium, Oklahoma City, 358
Munro, C.K., 32, 33
Murphy, George, 172
Murphy, John Daly, 141
Music Committee of the Metropolitan Methodist Church, Toronto, 43
*Mutiny on the Bounty*, 213

NAACP, 257
Nanny (see Burbidge)
NASA, 192
Nathan, George Jean, 244, 319
National Broadcasting Corporation (NBC), 391
National Defence Headquarters, Ottawa, 289
National Theatre Company, London, 171
National Theatre, London, 163
National Theatre, New York, 199, 201, 202, 237
National Theatre, Washington, 257, 279
Natwick, Millie, 277
Nesbitt, Cathleen, 78
*Never Come Back*, 157, 158, 222
New Theatre, London, 19, 36, 39, 42, 45, 77, 104, 106, 109, 110, 344, 348, 349, 351
*New Yorker*, 147, 205, 245, 265, 292
New York Producing Association, The, 141
*New York Times*, 94, 168, 202, 279, 281, 381, 385
Ney, Marie, 48
*Ngana*, 152
Nichols, Dudley, 217
*Night of the Iguana, The*, 307, 410, 411, 412, 414, 415, 416, 417
*Nights in Old Vienna*, 287
Niven, David, 208, 209, 210
"No-body," 18
Nordhoff, Charles, 213
Norton, Elliot, 319
Novello, Ivor, 82, 87

# O

# P

# Q

# R

# S

# T

# U

# V

# W

# Y

Yale University Reserve Officers'
 Training Corps, 17
Yarde, Margaret, 26, 27
Yeats, W. B., 34, 35, 82, 86
Yorke, Oswald, 16
Young, Harold, 187, 188
Young, Roland, 171

# Z

Zanville, Bernard, 284, 285, 286
Ziegfeld's Follies, 141, 153

# Photo Credits

The photographs in this book are from the author's private collection.
Credit is given where indicated.

# About the Author

Raymond Massey is among the first Canadian-born actors to attain international stardom. Born in Toronto in 1896, he was educated at public and private schools in Canada and at Oxford University in England. He served for four years with the Canadian army in the First World War and worked for a time in the Massey farm machinery business, which he left to embark on a career in the theatre. That career involved acting and directing in every kind of play throughout England and North America, appearing in over seventy movies and starring in countless television shows, most notably as Dr. Gillespie in the popular "Dr. Kildare" series. Among many other plays in the theatre he has starred in *Abe Lincoln in Illinois, Ethan Frome, J.B., John Brown's Body, Pygmalion, Idiot's Delight* and *The Doctor's Dilemma*. His most popular movies include *The Scarlet Pimpernel, Abe Lincoln in Illinois, Arsenic and Old Lace, Things to Come* and *East of Eden*.

During his long and distinguished career, Mr. Massey has received seven honorary doctorates from universities in Canada and the United States. He remained active in the theatre until 1976, when arthritis forced his retirement, and then began his memoirs, the first volume of which, *When I Was Young*, appeared shortly after.